"Paul Tripp's *Everyday Gospel* is a wonder. It's brilliantly written, clear, concise, Christ-exalting, true to God's word, enriching to the mind, encouraging to the heart, and overflowing with gospel grace. Every paragraph has the ring of truth. If you want a daily dose of God's life-giving wisdom and kindness, this book is for you."

Randy Alcorn, author, *Heaven; If God Is Good*; and *The Treasure Principle*

"This deeply nourishing devotional reader gives us what we have all come to expect and gratefully receive from Paul Tripp: wise bridge-building from the depths of Scripture before us to the depths of our hearts within us, always flavored with the hope of the gospel. This will be a heartening and life-giving journey for any who receive Tripp's guidance through the Scripture each day."

Dane Ortlund, Senior Pastor, Naperville Presbyterian Church, Naperville, Illinois; author, *Gentle and Lowly: The Heart of Christ for Sinners and Sufferers*

EVERYDAY GOSPEL

Books by Paul David Tripp

40 Days of Faith

40 Days of Grace

40 Days of Hope

40 Days of Love

A Quest for More: Living for Something Bigger Than You

A Shelter in the Time of Storm: Meditations on God and Trouble

Age of Opportunity: A Biblical Guide for Parenting Teens

Awe: Why It Matters for Everything We Think, Say, and Do

Broken-Down House: Living Productively in a World Gone Bad

Come, Let Us Adore Him: A Daily Advent Devotional

Dangerous Calling: Confronting the Unique Challenges of Pastoral Ministry

Do You Believe: 12 Historic Doctrines to Change Your Everyday Life

Forever: Why You Can't Live without It

How People Change (with Timothy S. Lane)

Instruments in the Redeemer's Hands: People in Need of Change Helping People in Need of Change

Journey to the Cross: A 40-Day Lenten Devotional

Lead: 12 Gospel Principles for Leadership in the Church

Lost in the Middle: Midlife and the Grace of God

Marriage: 6 Gospel Commitments Every Couple Needs to Make

My Heart Cries Out: Gospel Meditations for Everyday Life

New Morning Mercies: A Daily Gospel Devotional

New Morning Mercies for Teens: A Daily Gospel Devotional

Parenting: 14 Gospel Principles That Can Radically Change Your Family

Reactivity: How the Gospel Transforms Our Actions and Reactions

Redeeming Money: How God Reveals and Reorients Our Hearts

Relationships: A Mess Worth Making (with Timothy S. Lane)

Sex in a Broken World: How Christ Redeems What Sin Distorts

Suffering: Gospel Hope When Life Doesn't Make Sense

Sunday Matters: 52 Devotionals to Prepare Your Heart for Church

War of Words: Getting to the Heart of Your Communication Struggles

Whiter Than Snow: Meditations on Sin and Mercy

EVERYDAY GOSPEL

A Daily Devotional Connecting Scripture to All of Life

PAUL DAVID TRIPP

WHEATON, ILLINOIS

Everyday Gospel: A Daily Devotional Connecting Scripture to All of Life

© 2024 by Paul David Tripp

Published by Crossway
      1300 Crescent Street
      Wheaton, Illinois 60187

Cover design: Jordan Singer

First printing 2024

Printed in China

ISBN: 978-1-4335-9348-2
ePub ISBN: 978-1-4335-9350-5
PDF ISBN: 978-1-4335-9349-9

Library of Congress Cataloging-in-Publication Data
Names: Tripp, Paul David, 1950– author.
Title: Everyday gospel : a daily devotional connecting scripture to all of life / Paul David Tripp.
Description: Wheaton, Illinois : Crossway, [2024] | Includes index.
Identifiers: LCCN 2023045783 (print) | LCCN 2023045784 (ebook) | ISBN 9781433593482 | ISBN 9781433593499 (pdf) | ISBN 9781433593505 (epub)
Subjects: LCSH: Devotional calendars. | Bible. Gospels—Meditations.
Classification: LCC BV4811 .T758 2024 (print) | LCC BV4811 (ebook) | DDC 242/.2—dc23/ eng/20231228
LC record available at https://lccn.loc.gov/2023045783
LC ebook record available at https://lccn.loc.gov/2023045784

Crossway is a publishing ministry of Good News Publishers.

RRD				33	32	31	30	29	28	27	26	25	24
15	14	13	12	11	10	9	8	7	6	5	4	3	2	1

JANUARY 1

*God doesn't wait long to reveal the biblical narrative. The whole
story is in compressed form in the first three chapters of Genesis.*

Genesis begins with the most brilliant, mind-bending, and heart-engaging
introduction to a book ever written. God knows how much we need the creation-
to-destiny themes of the biblical narrative in order to make sense of our lives, so
he lovingly gives us those dominant themes right up front. The beginning of the
Bible is wonderful, awe-inspiring, heartbreaking, cautionary, and hope-instilling
all at once. Since God created us to be meaning-makers, he immediately presents
us with the wonderful and awful realties that we need to understand in order to
make proper sense of who we are and what life is really all about.

The opening chapters of Genesis have three foundational themes.

1. In the center of all that is, there is a God of incalculable glory. The first four
words of Genesis say it all: "In the beginning, God." Here is the ultimate fact
through which every other fact of life is properly understood. There is a God.
He is the Creator of everything that exists. He is glorious in power, authority,
wisdom, sovereignty, and love. Since we are his creatures, knowing him, loving him, worshiping him, and obeying him define our identity, meaning, and
purpose as human beings.

2. Sin is the ultimate human tragedy. Its legacy is destruction and death. Genesis 3 is the most horrible, saddest chapter ever written. In an act of outrageous
rebellion, Adam and Eve stepped over God's wise and holy boundaries, ushering
in a horrible plague of iniquity that would infect every human heart. Because
sin is a matter of the heart, we are confronted in this narrative with the fact that
our greatest problem in life is us, and because it is, we have no power to escape
it on our own.

*3. A Savior will come, crush the power of evil, and provide redemption for his peo-
ple.* The first three chapters of the Bible end with glorious hope. We are encouraged
to understand that sin is not ultimate—God is. And he had already set a plan in
motion to do for us, through the Son to come, what we could not do for ourselves.
A second Adam would come, defeat temptation, crush the evil one, and restore
us to God. As soon as sin rears its ugly face, redemption is promised. What grace!

It really is true that three themes course through God's amazing word: *creation, fall,* and *redemption.* They form the lens through which we can look at and
understand everything in our lives. What a sweet grace it is that immediately
in his word God makes himself known, alerts us to the tragedy of sin, and welcomes us into the hope of the saving grace to be found in the seed of the woman,

his Son, the Lord Jesus. We are left with the riches of a single truth that is the core of everything the Bible has to say: because God is a God of grace, mercy really will triumph over judgment.

For further study and encouragement: Revelation 21:1–8

———

JANUARY 2

GENESIS 4–7

Redemption is where God's anger with sin and
his grace toward the sinner embrace.

It is so easy for us to minimize our sin. It's so easy for us to be more concerned about or irritated by the sin of others than we are our own. It is so easy to argue for our own righteousness while being judgmental and condemning toward the sin of others. But if you minimize your sin, then you will no longer value, seek, or celebrate the forgiving, reconciling, transforming, and delivering grace of God. If you defend yourself in the face of conviction, you are defending yourself from the best gift that has ever or will ever be given: redeeming grace.

One particular passage powerfully depicts the sinfulness of sin. These are the words of a Creator who is grieved by what sin has done to his world and to the people he made in his own image.

> The LORD saw that the wickedness of man was great in the earth, and that every intention of the thoughts of his heart was only evil continually. And the LORD regretted that he had made man on the earth, and it grieved him to his heart. So the LORD said, "I will blot out man whom I have created from the face of the land, man and animals and creeping things and birds of the heavens, for I am sorry that I have made them." (Gen. 6:5–7)

What a devastating explanation of the horrible nature of sin: "Every intention of the thoughts of his heart was only evil continually." Since the heart is the control center of one's personhood, for every intention of the heart to be constantly evil meant that the control of sin over people's lives was both total and inescapable. How bad is sin? It is an inescapable evil that lives in the heart of every person who has ever taken a breath. Stop now and permit yourself to mourn. Let yourself shudder at the power of the anger of God with sin, an anger so deep that he decides to wipe out humanity from the face of the earth. Today, remember how sinful sin is in the eyes of the one perfectly holy person—Jesus—who has ever existed.

It would be terribly sad if the biblical story ended here. The very first word that follows Genesis 6:7 is *but*. Judgment would not be the end of the story. God would not minimize sin. He would not turn his back on iniquity. Through Noah he would extend his mercy and gather a covenant people, and through them he would raise up a Redeemer.

In the story of Noah, the anger of God with sin and the mercy of God toward sinners embrace. Here we get a hint of the cross that is to come. It is the anger of God with sin that drives Jesus to the cross. It is the grace of God toward sinners that leads Jesus to the cross. On the cross of Jesus Christ God's anger with sin and his grace toward sinners embrace, and still today that is the best of news.

For further study and encouragement: Luke 18:9–14

JANUARY 3

GENESIS 8–11

The idol of idols is the idol of self. Human pride always
stands in opposition to the glory and plan of God.

The Tower of Babel is both one of the strangest and one of the best-known biblical stories. "Then they said, 'Come, let us build ourselves a city and a tower with its top in the heavens, and let us make a name for ourselves, lest we be dispersed over the face of the whole earth'" (Gen. 11:4). Most people will tell you they've heard of the Tower of Babel. But few really understand the significance of this moment in the biblical story and its importance for every one of us today.

The will of the Creator was that the people he made in his image would live in humble, obedient, and dependent community with him and be fruitful and multiply and fill the earth. The problem is that sin causes human beings to hunger for independence and self-sufficiency, to quest more for their own glory than the glory of God, and to live according to their own will rather than for the plan and purposes of God. It is these three things that initiated and motivated the building of a tower to the heavens. It was built as a monument to human glory, as a declaration of independence from God, and as a replacement plan for God's "be fruitful and multiply and fill the earth." Human pride is an enemy of the glory and plan of God. God therefore acted to confuse the languages of these people so they could not communicate with one another but would scatter. This is the Lord of lords saying, "I am the Lord. I alone reign and my will will be done."

Upon reading this story, here is what you and I should confess: we still build towers to our glory and our independent wisdom, righteousness, and strength. "How?" you may ask. Any time we take credit for what only God could have done or produced, we have built a tower to our glory. Any time we step over one of God's moral boundaries, telling ourselves we're smarter than God, we've built a tower to our glory. Any time we act like grace-graduates, no longer in need of God's rescuing, forgiving, and transforming grace, we've built a tower to our glory. Any time we act as if our life, our gifts, and our resources belong to us to use as we wish, we've built a tower to our own glory. Could it be that there are ways in which we are more like the people in Genesis 11 than unlike them?

The story of Babel is one of rescuing grace. The pride that erected this tower is the same pride that necessitated the erection of the cross on which Jesus died. Sinners need to be rescued from themselves and transformed by grace from those who crave their own glory to those who humbly and joyfully live for the glory of God. This rescue is still needed by each of us as much as it was in that dark moment in Genesis 11.

For further study and encouragement: Psalm 53:1–6

JANUARY 4

GENESIS 12–15

Hope in this life and the one to come is found not in your pursuit of God, but in the grace of his choosing to make a covenant with you.

"Now the LORD said to Abram, 'Go from your country and your kindred and your father's house to the land that I will show you. And I will make of you a great nation, and I will bless you and make your name great, so that you will be a blessing. I will bless those who bless you, and him who dishonors you I will curse, and in you all the families of the earth shall be blessed'" (Gen. 12:1–3).

Read these verses again. There may be no more important passage in the Old Testament than this one. The apostle Paul knew the thunderous, redemptive significance of this moment when he wrote:

> Know then that it is those of faith who are the sons of Abraham. And the Scripture, foreseeing that God would justify the Gentiles by faith, preached the gospel beforehand to Abraham, saying, "In you shall all the nations be blessed." So then, those who are of faith are blessed along with Abraham, the man of faith. . . . And if you are Christ's, then you are Abraham's offspring, heirs according to promise. (Gal. 3:7–9, 29)

God's covenant with Abram was vastly more than him shining favor on one ancient man and his family. Embedded in God's promise to Abram was blessing that would extend to the whole earth. This groaning, sin-scarred world, with all of its inescapable sin and suffering, finds its hope in the blessings of grace that were poured down upon Abram and his descendants. How do we know this? Paul's words make it clear when he connects Abraham to Christ; the promises made to Abraham belong to all who are united to Christ by grace through faith.

Today, your hope as a mom or dad, a husband or wife, a young or elderly person, a man or woman, a child or teenager, a worker or boss, a friend or neighbor is not to be found in your position, prominence, money, accomplishments, family, or talents. It is not to be found in your wisdom, strength, or track record of obedience. It is found in one thing and one thing alone: as an act of undeserved and sovereign grace, God chose to include you in the eternal blessings of his covenant promises. You could never have achieved, deserved, or earned your place of glory and grace at God's everlasting covenant table.

No matter how biblically literate you are, no matter how long you have known the Lord, no matter how theologically astute you are, and no matter how spiritually mature you have become, you have hope now and forever not because of any of these things, but because God chose to include you in the covenant promises he made to Abraham. Celebrate this amazing grace today and all the days that follow.

For further study and encouragement: 1 Peter 2:1–10

JANUARY 5

We are often tempted to try by human effort to
accomplish what only God can do.

When you yell at your children, thinking strong language and increased volume will change their hearts, you are trying to do by human effort what only God can do.

When you have been hurt by your spouse and you punish with the silent treatment, you are trying to do by human effort what only God can do.

When you deal with your sin by programs of self-reformation instead of crying out for rescue and empowering grace, you are trying to do by human effort what only God can do.

When you force open doors of ministry instead of trusting the guidance of your Lord, you are trying to do by human effort what only God can do.

When you impatiently pound people with the gospel instead of letting the Holy Spirit work in their hearts, you are trying by human effort to do what only God can do.

This was Abram's struggle. God had promised that he would give Abram and Sarai a son. This was not just a son, but the son through whom the promise God made to Abram would pass down to the generations that would follow. Sarai and Abram waited year after year after year, but the child did not come. Now Sarai was getting too old to conceive (Gen. 16–18).

When we are in a situation where we are banking on a promise of God and the promise does not seem to come, it's hard to wait. First we are a bit concerned, but that concern turns into fear, and fear morphs into panic. In our panic we begin to think about how we could do for ourselves what we have been waiting on God to do. Ask yourself how many of the things you do are formed more by fear of the "what ifs" than by faith in God.

So, Sarai gives Abram the servant girl, taking the situation into her own hands to fulfill God's promise. Abram should have said no, but he doesn't. Hagar conceives, Sarai becomes jealous, and she begins to mistreat Hagar. Hagar flees out of the home to escape the horrible situation that has developed. The house of Abram is forever divided because Abram and Sarai tried to do by human effort what only God can do.

But God is a God of grace. Not only does he not suspend his covenant promise to Abram, but he provides the promised son and blesses Hagar as well. God will not turn from his promises even when we are unwilling to wait but instead try by our own wisdom and power to do what only he can do.

Today will you be tempted to try to do by human effort what only God can do? Will you be willing to wait? Will you trust in your Lord's presence, power, and faithfulness? Will you find peace in the fact that his timing is always right? Will you rest in the surety of the promises of the Lord?

For further study and encouragement: Mark 4:26–32

———

JANUARY 6

GENESIS 19–21

So much of our fear, discouragement, anxiety, and worry is the result of underestimating what God is willing and able to do.

Rest and patience of heart are not found in figuring out what is going on or conjuring up in our minds how in the world God is going to do what he's promised us that he would do. Rest and patience of heart are found in trusting the one who has it all figured out and knows exactly how he will accomplish what he has promised he will do. We are limited human beings. We all carry spiritual, mental, emotional, and physical limits with us wherever we go. We are all limited in righteousness, wisdom, and strength. Unless we are resting in the presence and power of the Lord, we will evaluate situations from the perspective of our many limits. This means that what appears to us to be completely impossible is quite possible with our Lord. His strength, his understanding, his compassion, and his grace are infinite.

Sometimes we make good-hearted promises that later we realize we are unable to keep. We know things need to get done, but we do not have the power or the wisdom to do them. There is nothing that God has promised to do or that we need him to do that he is unable to do. Nothing. We have every blessing that we have because he has the power to control the forces of nature, the events of history, and the unfolding of situations. Not only has he created everything, but everything he has created does his bidding. He is magnificent, almighty in power and wisdom. He can and will do what he has promised to do.

So God was not limited at all by Abraham or Sarah's age, any more than any other human limit would inhibit his ability to do what he has promised he would do. Genesis 21:1–7 records the birth of the promised son, Isaac. It also records that Abraham was one hundred. That's right: one hundred years old. The God who is the Lord of heaven and earth is also Lord of the womb of an old woman, and he can do through it what he has promised to do. He is the Lord. He is not limited by our weaknesses.

When I read the story of Abraham and Sarah's long wait for a promised son, I think of another Son that was promised. The hope of the world rested on the shoulders of this promised Son, but as century followed century, it seemed as though this Son would never come. But one night in a stable in Bethlehem, to a lowly carpenter and his wife the promised Messiah came. Nothing in all of those centuries that had passed was able to stop the promise of God. Jesus, Son of Man, Son of God, the Lamb, the Savior was born at just the right time to provide justification, reconciliation, forgiveness, and new life to all who believe. God's promises are not limited by human weakness or the passage of time. Don't give way to fear; God will do what he has promised to do.

For further study and encouragement: Isaiah 55:1–13

———

JANUARY 7

GENESIS 22–24

When life seems to make no sense, we are not without
hope or help because we are the children of God.

I was facing my sixth surgery in two years. For me, it was a moment of irrationality. Life didn't make sense anymore. This surgery was going to be much harder and more painful than the others, and it would require a much longer recovery. If you have a surgery every four months, your body doesn't have the time it needs to recover before the next surgery. My body was weak and worn down. I wasn't able to sleep well and had little energy to face the day. I had the most wonderful ministry opportunities I had ever had. I had more gospel influence than I thought I would ever have. I looked around and saw so many places that needed gospel explanation and application. But I simply had no strength. It made no sense that I would be in the moment of my greatest ministry influence and yet physically unable to do what I had been called and gifted to do. Where was God? What was he doing? What had he given me for this moment?

Such was the life of Abraham. The miracle son, Isaac, had been born. God had been faithful to his promise. But now, in a shocking turn of the story, God asked Abraham to sacrifice the promised son (Gen. 22). It seemed like the cruelest trick ever: build hope and destroy it in a moment. Here is life seeming to make no sense at all. In recounting the story, Hebrews tells us that God was testing Abraham (Heb. 11:17–19). This was not a test where Abraham would get a pass or a fail. This was like the tempering of metal, heating it to a high temperature to make it stronger. In asking Abraham to sacrifice Isaac, God was not doing something *to* him but doing something wonderful *for* him. God was building the faith of Abraham by proving his willingness to obey God no matter what and by giving Abraham the opportunity to experience the faithfulness of God's provision in moments of dire need.

You see, from the perspective of Abraham's covenant-making and covenant-keeping Lord, this seemingly senseless moment was a very sensible part of his plan for Abraham and all who would be blessed through him. And it needs to be noted that in this difficult moment Abraham was not without hope or help. Because he was a covenant son, Abraham possessed powerful, life-changing treasures. What did he have? He had the clear command of God, he had the clear promise of God, he had the blessing of the presence of God, and he was blessed to be the object of the infinite power of God. Abraham was not without help or hope because he was not alone.

The story of the near sacrifice of Isaac points us to the sacrifice of another promised Son, Jesus. This Son died so that we too would be blessed in moments of need with God's presence, power, commands, and promises, always having the help and hope we need, even when life doesn't seem to make sense.

For further study and encouragement: Luke 4:1–15

———

JANUARY 8

GENESIS 25–26

Our covenant-keeping God is a God who speaks to us. In his words we find comfort, assurance, and direction.

In my seminary days, I would bound up the stairs to our third-floor apartment in Philadelphia to share with my wife, Luella, everything I was learning. I was so full of the glories to be found in the pages of the Bible that I felt like I could burst. I told Luella that I wasn't just learning to think biblically, but was learning how to think, period. I now look back on those days from the vantage point of fifty years of ministry. For fifty years, day after day, I have lived in, studied, preached, and taught out of the endless warehouse of spiritual treasures that are found in God's word. God, in condescending love, has spoken to us. I cannot imagine what my life would be without his words.

Every bit of wisdom I have comes from the words of his book. I found my identity in the words of his book. I was drawn to put my trust in him because of the words of his book. I have meaning and purpose right here, right now because of the words of his book. I have found peace during times of trial because of the words of his book. I have future hope because of the words of his book. My life has been rescued, empowered, and defined by the words of his book.

So it is not a little thing that God comes to Isaac and communicates, in words that Isaac can understand, that Abraham's blessing is now being passed down to him. God speaks his covenant blessing in human words. Transcendent and eternal blessing is communicated by the King of kings in common human words that finite human beings are able to understand, believe, and build life upon. God's words to us are a miracle of divine grace. To every generation he makes his presence, his love, his grace, and his plan clear.

To Isaac he says:

Sojourn in this land, and I will be with you and will bless you, for to you and to your offspring I will give all these lands, and I will establish the oath that I swore to Abraham your father. I will multiply your offspring as the stars of heaven and will give to your offspring all these lands. And in your offspring all the nations of the earth shall be blessed. (Gen. 26:3–4)

Here God communicates his blessing, one that could never be earned, achieved, or deserved. In words he promises his presence. In words he promises to Isaac a place for him and his descendants. In words he promises that through Isaac blessing will spread throughout the earth. God speaks, and because he does Isaac knows who he is, what his life is about, and what God intends to do through him.

Today, God is still speaking to us through his word. Salvation, identity, purpose, and hope are ours because God has spoken to us. Amazing grace is communicated in just two words: *God speaks.*

For further study and encouragement: 2 Timothy 3:16–17

JANUARY 9

*Even though God's plans will sometimes surprise and confuse us, all
of his ways are right and true all of the time and in every situation.*

God created us as rational beings. We have been blessed with the ability to
think. We never stop interpreting our lives, seeking to make sense out of what
is happening to us or around us. But God never meant for our reason to be our
ultimate guide. The prophet Isaiah writes:

> My thoughts are not your thoughts,
>   neither are your ways my ways, declares the LORD.
> For as the heavens are higher than the earth,
>   so are my ways higher than your ways
>   and my thoughts than your thoughts. (Isa. 55:8–9)

In Genesis 25–26, we are confronted with the difference between what seems
right and logical to us and what is best in the eyes of God. It is logical to expect
that the covenant promises, with all of their global and eternal blessings, would
be passed down from Isaac to his oldest son Esau, but that is not what God had
planned. For us this is a shocking turn in the redemptive story. When we study
the story carefully, it is clear that we can't attribute the blessing's going to the
younger brother, Jacob, just to human manipulation. Before the boys were born,
God told their mother, Rebekah, "the older shall serve the younger" (Gen. 25:23).

It is right to use your mind. It is good to think about life. It is a blessing that
we have meaning-making abilities. But, as with every other ability we have been
given, we must use these abilities with humble admission of our limits and a willing submission to the greater plan and purposes of God. By faith we are all called
to live as if we really do believe that God is holy in every way, all of the time, and
in every circumstance. It is therefore impossible for him to do anything that is
not right and good or to ask us to do anything that is not the best thing for us.

Because God's way is not our way, there will be times when what God is
doing won't make sense to us and what he asks us to do will be different than
what seems best to us. These are fault-line moments, when either we will let our
logic be our guide or we will submit our reason to the infinitely holy wisdom
of our Lord. In this confusing Jacob and Esau story, God is not abandoning
his covenant promises or doing what is evil. No, God is doing what he knows
is best to secure his blessing to that generation and all the generations of his
people that will follow.

Sometimes God will surprise, confuse, or even confound us, but he will never do what is evil. He is unshakably holy and incapable of wrong. So, even when he confuses us, he is worthy of our trust. We experience ultimate safety when we surrender all of our mental capacities and gifts to his lordship. He is good and, because he is, even in our confusion we can know peace.

For further study and encouragement: Romans 8:28–30

JANUARY 10

GENESIS 30–31

God's covenant promises do not mean that our lives will be predictable, comfortable, easy, or trouble free.

I have jokingly said many times that if God's ultimate plan is to unleash his power to deliver comfortable lives to us, he is a massive failure. God's ultimate plan is to unleash his wisdom, power, and grace for our final and eternal redemption. I don't know about you, but I like comfortable things. I love those seasons when life just seems to work without interruption or difficulty. I don't really enjoy having to struggle or being asked to wait. But I have been confronted again and again with the reality that the God who loves me and who gave up his Son for my redemption will lead me through difficulty.

Such was the life of Jacob. The blessings of Abraham, by God's wise plan, had been passed down to him, but his life was surely not without difficulty. In Genesis 30–31, Jacob is in conflict with his father-in-law, Laban, over payment and possessions. God had prospered Jacob, and Laban had benefited greatly from Jacob's prosperity, but he did not want to give Jacob what Jacob thought was rightfully his. This story of extended family drama is all too familiar to us. We are well aware of family conflict. We have all had moments when we wished life with family were easier and more comfortable. Many of us have at times disagreed with family members about what is rightfully ours. Many of us have been hurt and felt wronged by those close to us. In these moments, it doesn't seem like we are the objects of the blessing of the King of kings and Lord of lords.

In these hard moments, when life just doesn't seem to be working as it should and when God may seem distant and unattached, we are being called to hold on to God by faith and to persevere. The biblical call to persevere is in God's word because between the "already" and the "not yet" we will all face seasons and situations of hardship. These times of hardship are not to be understood as a failure of the promises of God or as evidence that he has abandoned us. In these times, God is working out his plan and deepening our trust in him and our willingness to live as he calls his children to live. Perseverance is deeper than working to make a situation better. It is about refusing to let hardships convince us that God is not good or that his promises are not trustworthy. Perseverance is holding on to faith in God when it seems he is not near or what he is leading us through is too hard. In these moments of unexpected conflict and trial, God meets us with his grace, empowering us to hold on to him as he holds on to us. God was not done testing Jacob, and this moment of family conflict would not stop the march of his covenant plan.

For further study and encouragement: James 1:2–4

———

JANUARY 11

GENESIS 32–34

God will interrupt moments in our lives to recapture our hearts, to strengthen our faith, to bless us with his grace, and to instill in us, once again, our identity as his children.

Genesis 32 gives us the strangest wrestling match that has ever taken place. At first it just seems weird and bizarre, but the more you examine the story, the more you realize what a gift and blessing the struggle was, and what a perfect picture it is for us today of how God meets us by his grace. Jacob is on his way home to Canaan after a twenty-year stay in Paddan-aram. But rather than being glad to be going home, he is terrified of the anger of his brother, Esau, who is on his way to meet him with four hundred men. Jacob is convinced this is not a celebratory greeting party, but the army of an angry man who wants vengeance.

As fear would cause, Jacob is having a restless and sleepless night when a strange man shows up and begins to wrestle with him. At some point during the match, Jacob realizes he is wrestling with God and says he will not let go until God blesses him. God not only blesses him, but leaves him with a new identity, *Israel* ("strives with God"). This is more than a name; it is a foreshadowing of the huge role Jacob will have in the plan of God.

It's important that we pay attention to how God meets, blesses, and strengthens Jacob. It is a picture of how God's grace often operates in our lives. In times of trouble, we think grace will come to us as a cool drink, a soft pillow, a reassuring hug. We don't expect God to interrupt times of trouble with more trouble because he loves us. But as Jacob is now wrestling with God, he is no longer thinking fearfully about Esau, his heart turns toward the Lord rather than escape from Esau, and what he longs for is blessing from his Lord.

God will use whatever he thinks is best to draw our hearts and minds to him, to cause us to cry out for the blessings of his grace, and to deepen in us a sense of what it means to be his children. In love, God will come to us and trouble our trouble, because that interruption is exactly what we need so we don't lose our sense of who we are and what we have been blessed with as his children.

God's grace comes to us in many different forms. God's grace is not always comfortable. Sometimes the last thing we think we need is, in God's hands, exactly what we need. God will wrestle with you, not to weaken and defeat you, but to leave you blessed, renewed, and strengthened, even if you limp away. No interruption is more important than divine interruptions. They are tools of the grace we need, delivered by a God who always knows the right time and always chooses the best way.

For further study and encouragement: Hebrews 12:3–11

———

JANUARY 12

GENESIS 35–37

It is important for us to frequently and humbly examine our hearts, to purge them of the idols that have gripped us, and to recommit ourselves to worship and serve God alone.

God said to Jacob, "Arise, go up to Bethel and dwell there. Make an altar there to the God who appeared to you when you fled from your brother Esau." So Jacob said to his household and to all who were with him, "Put away the foreign gods that are among you and purify yourselves and change your garments. Then let us arise and go up to Bethel, so that I may make there an altar to the God who answers me in the day of my distress and has been with me wherever I have gone." (Gen. 35:1–3)

We've come to another significant moment in Jacob's life with his Lord. It is a beautiful thing that it has been recorded and preserved for our example, for our instruction, and for the reclamation of our hearts. God calls Jacob to build an altar to "the God who appeared to you when you fled from your brother Esau." He is reminding Jacob of who the one true God is, the one who meets his chosen children at just the right time and blesses them in just the right way. Jacob knows that if he is going to build an altar for the worship of God, there is something else he must do. While he was dwelling in a foreign land with his extended family, they opened themselves up to the idols of the people around them. Jacob knows that if he and his family are going to offer acceptable worship to the one true God, these foreign gods have to go. So, he tells his family to rid themselves of these idols and to purify themselves in preparation for building an altar to the one who answered Jacob in distress and has been present with him wherever he has gone.

This moment of purification is not just about getting rid of physical idols. The presence of the physical idols in Jacob's family is a picture of what had happened to their hearts. While away from Canaan, the hearts of Jacob's people had wandered away from worship and service of the one true God.

Scripture reminds us that these accounts have been preserved for us because these people were just like us. It is possible for us, like Jacob, to name ourselves as God-fearers but to have collected idols along the way. An idol is anything that for a moment, a season, or a lifetime exercises the rule or control over your heart that only the Lord should have. Whatever controls your heart controls your thoughts and shapes your desires and, because it does, it controls your choices and actions. As long as sin still lives inside of us, we will struggle with idols of the heart. God meets us not with condemnation but with convicting and empowering grace, so that he may purify us again to serve him and him alone.

For further study and encouragement: Colossians 3:5–10

JANUARY 13

GENESIS 38–40

*Do we love our Lord so much that we are always willing
to run from the temptation to do what is wrong in his
eyes, no matter what the consequences may be?*

The story of Joseph would make the best dramatic and engaging Netflix series ever: a proud favorite son of his very important father is deceived and sold into slavery by his brothers, bought by an officer of Pharaoh, and given success by God and is now an overseer. What an incredible story! But the plot is about to thicken. The Egyptian officer's wife takes a liking to Joseph. He is a handsome, brilliant, and successful man. She is so bold as to ask Joseph to have sex with her. Now, it is clear that this situation is going to go nowhere good. If she's after Joseph, she will continue to tempt him, and if he continues to resist, she has the power in her anger to do him harm. One day she grabs Joseph by his robe to force him to be with her, and he resists and runs, leaving his robe behind. She uses the robe as evidence that Joseph was trying to seduce her, and as a result Joseph ends up in prison (Gen. 39).

What a picture of life in a fallen world. Even when your heart is in the right place, you will be greeted with temptation. Even when you are experiencing God's blessing on your life and work, the seductive voice of temptation will try to woo you into crossing God's holy boundaries. We will be free from temptation only when we are on the other side, residents of the new heavens and new earth where peace and righteousness rule forever and ever.

Joseph explains to Potiphar's wife why he could never think of having a physical relationship with her. His words move and convict me: "How then can I do this great wickedness and sin against God?" (Gen. 39:9). What empowered Joseph to say no was not just his relationship to Potiphar, not just his thankfulness for what Potiphar had done for him, and not just his sense of responsibility as overseer of this officer's house. No, Joseph had a deeper and more powerful motivation: the depth of his fear of God. I don't mean terror of God's judgment, but rather a life-shaping awe of and loyalty to God. Joseph was able to say no because he couldn't conceive of doing such a wicked thing against the God who was with him and had blessed him so abundantly.

There is a connection between the depth of our fear of God and the strength of our resistance against temptation. When fear (life-shaping awe) of the Lord rules our hearts, we will resist temptation no matter what the consequences of our resistance may be. May we cry out for grace to fear the Lord more than we fear man. May we pray for help so that we would love our Lord more than we love a comfortable life. And may we believe that hardships that come because we have said no to sin are never the end of the story. They surely weren't for Joseph.

For further study and encouragement: Proverbs 16:6

———

JANUARY 14

GENESIS 41–42

*In this broken world it is important to remember
that hardship is not ultimate—God is.*

If you're not dealing with hardship now, you will someday. And if you're not dealing with it now, you are near someone who is. The Bible is very honest about the condition of the world we live in. The apostle Paul says that our world is groaning, waiting for redemption (Rom. 8:22). Peter writes that we should not be surprised when we face trials (1 Pet. 4:12). The blood and dirt of this fallen world and the theme of suffering splash across the pages of your Bible from Genesis 3 until the end of Revelation. Because this broken world is not functioning the way God originally intended and because it is populated by flawed people, hardship is the environment in which we live. From our irritation with little things that just don't seem to go right to tragic, life-altering moments of suffering, we all have to deal with the unexpected and the unwanted.

It's easy to get disheartened with how hard life is. It's easy to become cynical and negative. It's easy to allow yourself to question the goodness of God or the reliability of his promises. It is here that the story of the troubled life of Joseph can help us. In Joseph's story we are confronted with the fact that suffering isn't ultimate—God is. Hardship doesn't rule—God does. We are never the victim of negative forces that act under the control of no one. It can be a bit discouraging to read Joseph's story. He's sold by his brothers, bought by someone in a foreign country, and then thrown in prison for refusing to give way to the lust of that man's wife. At this point you may begin to wonder where God is in all of this and what in the world he is doing to this fine young man.

But it becomes very clear that none of these hardships are failures of God's plan, nor are they in the way of God's plan. In situations where it looks like he is absent, God, in faithfulness to his covenant promises, is working for Joseph's good. In situations where it seems evil is winning, God is actually working out his wise plan. Prison was never going to be Joseph's final destination, because

God was at work. Because of his time in prison and the power God had given him to interpret dreams, Joseph goes from an overseer in an Egyptian officer's house to second-in-command of all of Egypt (Gen. 41–42). Prison was a necessary step in the plan that God was working, not a failure of that plan.

As the children of God, we are ruled not by our circumstances but by the one who controls every circumstance for his ultimate glory and our ultimate good. It may seem like hardship is winning, but whatever hard thing you are going through is not your final destination. God is preparing us for our final destination, where suffering will die and hardship will be no more, forever. The story of Joseph reminds us that God rules, a reminder we need again and again.

For further study and encouragement: 1 Peter 5:6–11

———

JANUARY 15

GENESIS 43–45

The promises of God are true and trustworthy because the one who made those promises is perfectly faithful all of the time and in every way.

"And Pharaoh said to Joseph, 'Say to your brothers . . . go back to the land of Canaan, and take your father and your households, and come to me, and I will give you the best of the land of Egypt, and you shall eat the fat of the land'" (Gen. 45:17–18). These words from Scripture should blow your mind. How could this kid, who had been sold to strangers by his brothers, ascend to such a place of power? And why would an Egyptian ruler care at all about an old man and his boys? This story goes places you wouldn't expect.

Joseph is now second-in-command in Egypt and has overseen the storage of so much food and grain that the amount can no longer be measured. A famine has set in throughout all of what we now call the Middle East but, because of Joseph's work, Egypt is rich with food. When Pharaoh hears that Joseph's brothers are in Egypt, he tells Joseph to tell them to go home and bring back their father and their households. Pharaoh will provide them with everything they might need.

What is going on here? This is way more than a story about evil brothers and Joseph's successful ascension to power in Egypt. This is a story about the power of God and his unshakable zeal to be faithful to his covenant promises. God will never let anything get in the way of what he has promised to do. He will never turn from what he has promised to do. But the way that he chooses to fulfill his great and precious promises will often confuse and surprise us. No one would have thought that selling Joseph into slavery would be the first step in God's sovereign plan to preserve his covenant people. Without Joseph's place in Egypt, Israel and his sons would probably have died in poverty and starvation in Canaan, and the line of Abraham would be no more. There would be no descendants great in number, like the stars of the sky. There would be no nation of Israel. There would be no King David. There would be no Messiah born in Bethlehem. There would be no Jesus, resisting temptations and living a perfectly righteous life. There would be no perfect Lamb for a sacrifice on the cross. There would be no victorious resurrection. There would be no forgiving grace, no adopting grace, no transforming grace, no church, and no sin-free eternity.

Although at first read it might not look like it, God was writing the story of Joseph's troubled life because he knew how much we need Jesus and his saving work on our behalf. He was being perfectly faithful to his covenant promises, preserving the line of Abraham, so he could give us the seed of Abraham, Jesus, who would come and save us from our sins. We'll never make sense of our stories until we start with the power, presence, faithfulness, and grace of God.

For further study and encouragement: Numbers 23:18–24

_____

JANUARY 16

GENESIS 46–47

True security is found not in people, places, and things, but in the faithful, loving, protecting, and providing presence of the Lord.

Moving my family was a scary prospect. There were days when the decision haunted me. Maybe this would be the most unwise choice for me and my family that I had ever made. Would I live to regret it? We had eleven wonderful ministry years in our little church in Scranton, Pennsylvania. We loved the people there. They weren't a congregation; they were family. What we had been through together and what we had built with one another was precious. The bulk of this wonderful group of people lived within walking distance of our home. We really did share life together. But now we sensed God was leading us to a different place in ministry and a different kind of ministry. I was about to leave pastoral ministry and begin working at the Christian Counseling & Educational Foundation and Westminster Theological Seminary. We were moving from a small, close-knit community to a very big city that we didn't really know.

It felt like we were leaving something warm and precious and moving to something unknown and impersonal. We had been warned about the difficulties and dangers of the big city. Questions loomed in my mind. Fear began to grow in my heart. What comforted my heart again and again as the fear came were these words: "I will never leave you nor forsake you" (Heb. 13:5). We were leaving a comfortable place, but we were not leaving the one in whom our security was found.

Such was Jacob's experience. God called him to leave Canaan and move to Egypt. For any Canaanite, that would have been a scary thing to do. Jacob's mind would have been flooded with a thousand questions for himself and his family. He would have had many fears and concerns. So, in an act of covenant love, God came to Jacob and reminded him that his hope and security had never been in his situation or location. God had been Jacob's security all along, no matter where he has been. God reminded Jacob of who he was and what he had been given as a child of God. "I am God, the God of your father. Do not be afraid to go down to Egypt, for there I will make you into a great nation. I myself will go down with you to Egypt, and I will also bring you up again, and Joseph's hand shall close your eyes" (Gen. 46:3–4).

I love the emphatic and specific nature of God's reassuring promise to Jacob: "I *myself* will go *down* with you to *Egypt*." This is not a general, impersonal religious platitude. This is the Lord of lords making it clear that he himself will go with Jacob to Egypt, and with him will come his wisdom, love, provision, protection, and grace.

No matter where you are today, no matter what you're facing, and no matter where God is calling you to go, if you are his child, he makes the same emphatic and specific promise to you. In his words *I will go with you*, you will find true hope and security.

For further study and encouragement: Isaiah 41:10–13

———

JANUARY 17

GENESIS 48–50

If you are God's child, nothing in your life is more constant and important than the shepherding care of your Savior.

I love how God, in his word, invites us to look into and eavesdrop on some of the most intimate, precious, and holy moments in people's lives. God does this to remind us of our weaknesses, limits, and neediness and of the blessings of his presence, power, and love unleashed on our behalf. We find one of these incidents at the end of Jacob's life. He is old, blind, and weak, literally at death's door. But by God's plan and grace Jacob has not only been reunited with his long-lost son Joseph, the son he thought he would never see again, but he has met grandsons he didn't know he had. I can't imagine that there was a dry eye in the room. This was more than a family reunion; this was a moment of divine blessings (Gen. 48).

This poignant family moment quickly became a time of worship, prayer, and the passing down of blessing. For Jacob there was only one summary of his amazing, blessed, and trouble-filled life, in which he had experienced the deepest of griefs and the highest of joys. Here is his final "says it all" statement: "God . . . has been my shepherd all my life long to this day" (Gen. 48:15).

It was not, "Look how wise and successful I have been. Look at the wealth I have acquired. Look at the great family I have raised." No, in his final frail moments on earth, Jacob's mind went to the things that had been his rock of surety and hope his entire life: the shepherding care of his Lord. In all of the times of fear and grief and in all of the lofty moments of hope and joy, this is the thing that had been the constant. The Lord was Jacob's Shepherd, and in him Jacob had found everything he would ever need.

In all of her weaknesses, neediness, pains, and joys, my mom found her hope in the Lord. So, as she was passing into eternity, in and out of a coma, she asked us to sing hymns to her. She loved the great hymns of the faith. We stood around her bed and sang hymn after hymn. Sometimes we didn't know if she was cognizant enough to hear and be comforted, but then we would look more closely and notice she was mouthing the words with her lips. She faced her final days as Jacob did, reminding herself of the shepherding care of her Lord.

Our lives are mixed with sorrow and joy, courage and fear, but at the end of our journey we will look back at all the mountains and valleys and we will see one thing that was always there: the shepherding care of our Lord and Savior. And we will rest, knowing we didn't have everything we wanted, but that our Shepherd had constantly supplied everything we needed.

For further study and encouragement: Psalm 23:1–6

JANUARY 18

EXODUS 1–3

*Nothing is more comforting than knowing that God
watches over his people and hears their cries.*

The Israelites in Egypt are experiencing horrible oppression. They are experiencing not just harsh treatment as slaves, but also the horror of the extermination of every infant son born to a Hebrew mother. It's hard to imagine the scene of newborn boy after newborn boy torn from the hands of a pleading mother and thrown in the Nile to drown (Ex. 1:15–22). Here is a picture of life in this fallen, sin-stained world as black as it gets. Imagine the inescapable grief in house after house. Imagine the feeling of utter powerlessness. Could there be a more dehumanizing condition you could live in?

It is important to recognize how honest the Bible is about life in this broken world. The Bible doesn't paint over the dark inhumanity, the deep grief, and the cries for help that are the result of sin living in people's hearts. The darkness of sin makes the intervening grace of God shine even more brightly. When you read passages like Exodus 1–3, you think to yourself that there simply is no hope unless God acts in mercy to crush evil. The deaths of all these innocent baby boys cry out for another death, this one on a cross outside the city. The early chapters of Exodus preach powerfully to us of the need for a Savior who would once and for all defeat sin and death.

In this dark hour, when there seems to be no hope for the children of God, a beacon of hope does shine. The light of God's presence shines on his Israelite children. Of course they wonder where God is. Of course they wonder if he hears their cries, if he remembers his promises, and if he cares enough to do something. But he is not absent. He has not ignored them. He has not forgotten his promises. He is not uncaring. He is not powerless. The words of Exodus 2:24–25 ring with as much hope for us today as they did in this dark moment thousands of years ago. He is the same God. He is for us what he was for them. Their security in trouble is our security in trouble. Their only hope in this broken world is our only hope in this broken world: "And God heard their groaning, and God remembered his covenant with Abraham, with Isaac, and with Jacob. God saw the people of Israel—and God knew" (Ex. 2:24–25).

God's people were not alone in this trauma. They had not been forsaken. God heard. God remembered. God saw. God knew. And God would act in mighty rescuing power. Remind yourself today, as you deal with the consequences of life in a fallen world, that God hears, God remembers, God sees, and God knows.

Hope knows, in your deepest, darkest most alone moment, that you are not alone. God's ears are always attentive to your cries, and he watches over you with eyes of mercy.

For further study and encouragement: 1 John 5:14

JANUARY 19

EXODUS 4–6

God calls us to represent him in this fallen world
not because we are able but because he is.

Moses is living as a fugitive in the wilderness because he had killed an Egyptian taskmaster. But God has plans for Moses. God has chosen Moses to be his tool of redeeming power. He is calling Moses back to Egypt to stand before Pharaoh and demand the release of all the Israelite slaves (Ex. 3). Put yourself in Moses's shoes. Would you be excited about going back to Egypt? Would you feel confident to stand before the most powerful ruler of the world and demand that he free a group of people that was a major element in his nation's economic engine?

In this moment, Moses does what we often do when God calls us. We compare our natural gifts and abilities to the size of the task, to gauge whether we are capable of doing what God has called us to do. God doesn't call us because we have, in ourselves, everything we need to accomplish what he's calling us to do. No, he calls weak and broken people to do huge and important things because is able. He is with us, and he empowers us to do what he wills for us to do. Every one of God's commands is accompanied by his empowering grace. Exodus 4 records how God demonstrates his power to fearful Moses to assure him that he will go down to Egypt and stand before Pharaoh not in his own power, but in the awesome power of the King of kings and the Lord of lords.

But Moses isn't easy to convince. God says, "I can even turn the waters of the Nile into blood as a demonstration of my power before Pharaoh" (see Ex. 4:9). Moses responds, "I am not eloquent . . . I am slow of speech and of tongue" (4:10). God says, "Moses, I created your mouth. I am the Lord, and I will go with you and teach you what to say" (see Ex. 4:11–12). I love this picture of the patience of the Lord, working to take Moses's eyes off himself and onto the majestic power of his God. Sadly, Moses responds, "Oh, my Lord, please send someone else" (4:13).

God calls husbands, wives, parents, workers, neighbors, friends, university students, the young, and the old to represent him in this dark world. He calls average people to do things that are anything but average. Is there a place in your life where you are responding, "Oh, Lord, please send someone else"?

Another person was later called to provide redemption from slavery, this time the slavery to sin. His name was Jesus. His call was not just to speak but to die, so that we could know freedom as the children of God. It is in the power of his redeeming grace that we are able to say yes to the call of God, because we know Jesus's death and resurrection guarantee just the grace we need to do what God has called us to do at just the time we need it. In him weak and fearful people are made able, and that's very good news.

For further study and encouragement: 2 Corinthians 3:4–6

———

JANUARY 20

EXODUS 7–9

No story is more humbling, more beautiful, and more hope-instilling than the biblical story of redemption.

If someone were to ask you what the Bible is about, what would you say? How would you describe the content of God's word? What would you tell people to convince them that the Bible is the most important book ever written? The Bible is more than a history book, a theology book, a book of practical everyday wisdom, or a book of hope for troubled times. The Bible is essentially a grand origin-to-destiny narrative. It's God's story, accompanied by his explanatory and applicatory notes. One big theme holds together all the different parts of the Bible and all its different genres of literature. That theme is the theme of redemption. The Bible is the story of God's unleashing his power in order to provide the one thing that everyone needs: redemption. We need to be redeemed not just from the trials of life or our inadequacies or our weaknesses. No, we need to be redeemed from our sin. The main target of God's redeeming grace and power is not something outside of us, but something dark and destructive that lives inside of us.

The biblical story is marked by moments when God unleashes his redeeming power, so that his plan marches on until sin is finally and completely defeated and peace and righteousness reign on earth forever and ever.

The liberation of Israel from Egypt is one of those redemptive moments. The children of Israel cannot be exterminated in Egypt because the Messiah must come out of Egypt to provide final redemption for the chosen children of God (see Hos. 11:1). God demonstrates his lordship over every aspect of creation by unleashing his power in ten mind-blowing plagues. He is a covenant-keeping King, and he will do whatever is necessary, in his incalculable might, to deliver his children. This demonstration of his almighty power makes it clear that he will not abandon his promises. His will will be done (Ex. 12:33–42).

You have to stand as a witness to this incredible physical display of the enormity of the power and rule of the Lord and ask, "Who is a God like our God? Who loves his children like our God? Who is faithful like our God?" As you stand in awe of this picture of the power of God's redeeming mercy, it is vital to remember that in this moment God is not just moving to redeem Israel from its slavery in Egypt, but he is also moving to redeem us from our slavery to sin. If there had been no redemption from Egypt and no delivery to the promised land, there would have been no Messiah born in Bethlehem to live a perfectly righteous life, die a substitutionary death, and rise victorious over sin and death. All the redemptive moments in the Old Testament are not just for the people at the time, but they are for us too. In each moment God is fulfilling the promise he made in Genesis 3 that he would send a Redeemer to crush the head of the serpent, defeating sin and death. The story of the plagues is your story. The redeeming grace is not just for then but for you right here, right now.

For further study and encouragement: Titus 3:3–7

———

JANUARY 21

EXODUS 10–12

The radical, unexpected nature of the biblical story is that the hope for the Israelites in Egypt and our hope today rest on the shoulders of a Lamb.

It is a major understatement when the Bible says that God's ways aren't like our ways and his thoughts aren't like our thoughts (Isa. 55:8). No human being, no matter how brilliant, insightful, or experienced, would have been able to write the grand biblical story. The way God chooses to work and the instruments he chooses to use surprise us again and again. The apostle Paul expresses it this way: "God chose what is foolish in the world to shame the wise; God chose what is weak in the world to shame the strong; God chose what is low and despised in the world, even things that are not, to bring to nothing things that are, so that no human being might boast in the presence of God" (1 Cor. 1:27–29). God intentionally does things in a way that defies human understanding, explanation, and credit-taking. He works in ways that cause us to step back and say, "Only God could have done this," and in saying this, humbly run to him for the help that he alone is able to give.

Such is the story of the final emancipation of God's chosen children from Egypt. Despite Pharaoh's resistance in the face of the terror of the plagues, God would not grow weary, and he would not turn his back on those who were the object of his covenant promises. He would deliver. No one would stand in the way of the divine and holy will of the King of kings and Lord of lords, not even the most powerful ruler on earth. But the way the people would be freed could never have been anticipated by any Israelite. By God's wise and holy plan, the Israelites would be saved from slaughter and emancipated from their bondage by the blood of a lamb. That blood, sprinkled on the doorpost of an Israelite house, meant that God would pass over that house. God chose a lowly but spotless lamb to provide both salvation from death and liberation to a new life for his covenant children (Ex. 12:3–7).

Our hope, too, rests on the shoulders of a Lamb. Jesus didn't come as a conquering general, to throw down the kingdoms of men. No, he came to be a sacrificial Lamb. He, too, was a Lamb without blemish, who would be sacrificed for the salvation and liberation of all who believe in him. By the power of his shed blood, we are delivered from our bondage to sin and death and liberated to a new life of freedom as the children of God. We never could have written this story. We never would have anticipated that death would be the portal to life, that God would send a Lamb to do what kings, queens, and generals could never do. Now, that's a radical story, but it's very, very good news.

For further study and encouragement: Revelation 5:6–14

JANUARY 22

*Embedded in things that are unexpected and hard are
the wisdom and grace of our sovereign Savior.*

I have to admit that I entered ministry quite full of myself. I had done well in seminary, graduating with honors and winning several academic prizes. I was ready to take on the world for the gospel. What I thought was confidence in God's word and the power of the gospel was really pride and self-reliance. Luella and I left seminary, connected with a good church, and began to work with a ministry that provided housing and a place to investigate Christianity. This was our first place of ministry. As a young married couple, we had several young men living with us. Some were fresh out of prison, others were with us simply because they had lost their way. This was not the congregation I thought I would have after all my training. None of our guys were interested in asking the questions that I felt so totally prepared to answer.

One evening one man, who had no education beyond fifth grade, said to me, "Paul, if you don't quit talking the lawyer talk to me, I'm gonna quit talking to you." *Lawyer talk* meant using big, esoteric words. That evening I sat on the edge of my bed and said to my Lord, "Why would you put me here to minister to these guys? I have no idea how to get through to them. I don't understand them, and I don't know how to help them see what they truly need." I didn't understand that God had put me in this place with these particular people not just for them, but for me. He was bringing me to the end of myself. He was working to replace my pride and fear and discouragement with trust in him. I was where I was because of God's wisdom and grace.

This is why God chose to plant Israel between the Red Sea and the approaching Egyptian army (Ex. 14). The children of Israel were on a short route to the land of the Philistines, but God in wisdom and grace knew that his children were not ready for the battles they would encounter there. God knew they might panic and run back to the bondage of Egypt. So, God led them to the shores of the Red Sea. Contrary to how it might have appeared to them (and to us), God was not punishing or abandoning his people, but he was acting with the grace of a wise and loving Father. He would demonstrate his power and glory by parting those sea waters, providing both deliverance for Israel and defeat of Egypt. His plan for his people was to defeat both pride and fear and instill in them an unshakable confidence in their Redeemer God. No hard thing for the people of God is outside of his wise and gracious rule.

God takes us to hard places not to do things *to* us, but to do things for and in us. Today, be thankful that these hard moments, in his hands, are tools of rescuing and renewing grace.

For further study and encouragement: John 15:1–11

———

JANUARY 23

EXODUS 16–18

The physical food that God provides for us is a visual picture and reminder of how he feeds us spiritually with the nutrients of his grace.

I love to cook. I love how God has not ordained to sustain us with a daily green pill but delights in blessing us with the pleasure of an almost endless variety of fruits, vegetables, and meats. I love the variety of tastes, textures, and smells. I love the world of spices, each adding another interesting layer of taste to whatever food they are applied to. I love taking what God has provided and building a delicious meal and then displaying it in a beautiful way on the plate. Food represents God's generosity and love. It reminds us that God wants us to thrive and to enjoy and, because we do, to worship the one who has lavished such goodness on us.

We live across from a food market with about one hundred and twenty vendors. As I walk through the market, I am often blown away by what I see and smell. It almost melts my brain that all of these wonderful things came out of the mind of God. It reminds me that he is glorious in creative power and gloriously generous in love. He still feeds me with good food, even in my spiritual amnesia moments.

Exodus 16 gives us an example of the extent of God's commitment to supply his children with the physical food that they need and of the awesome power he has to provide it. The people of Israel, now in the wilderness, are in a state of panic. They are wondering where they are going to get food to eat, and they are grumbling to Moses that it would have been better for them to die in Egypt because at least there they had enjoyed plenty of good food. God hears their grumbling and responds: "Behold, I am about to rain bread from heaven for you, and the people shall go out and gather a day's portion every day, that I may test them, whether they will walk in my law or not. On the sixth day, when they prepare what they bring in, it will be twice as much as they gather daily" (Ex. 16:4–5).

Imagine the magnificence of this provision. Imagine bread appearing on the ground every day like dew. What an incredible picture of providing grace, even for people who are faithless and discontented. Here are people who keep wishing they could go back to their slavery, when they have been set free by God's liberating grace and are being provided for by his generous love. They are enjoying this bounty not because they have earned it or deserve it, but because they are his chosen children.

This moment is a finger pointing to God's ultimate provision of bread. Jesus is the bread sent down from heaven (John 6:32–35). In him alone our spiritual hunger is satisfied. He alone can give life and strength to our souls. With gratitude we remember that in him we are fed, not because we've earned it but because we are the chosen objects of his faithful and generous grace.

For further study and encouragement: John 6:32–35

———

JANUARY 24

EXODUS 19–21

*God's commandments are not a means of earning his favor but
a gift of grace to those upon whom his favor already rests.*

It is vitally important to understand that God's law is wonderful and important, and that you and I cannot obey our way into relationship with God. If you and I had both the desire and the ability to perfectly keep God's law, then the entire redemptive narrative and its core message of grace would not have been necessary. Or if the law of God had the power to rescue and transform our hearts and breathe new life into us, then the life, death, and resurrection of Jesus would not have been necessary. The righteousness that God requires is impossible for us to achieve by our determination to keep his commands. God's law does a wonderful job of exposing our sin and is a beautiful guide for our daily living, but it is powerless to save us from ourselves and make us acceptable to our Creator.

Exodus 19 is an example of how God's gift of careful recorded biblical history is so helpful for us. Think with me for a moment about when God's law was originally given. Think about that moment when God led his recently freed children to the base of Mount Sinai. They were there to receive God's magnificently wise law because he had already set his love on them and had already redeemed them from slavery. God now gave them his law, not so that through it they would become his, but because they already *were* his. His law was a gift of grace to them.

Does that last sentence confuse you? God knew that the children of his love had no idea how to live, so in his law he gave them a structure for their daily living. In submission to his law they would thrive in peace and harmony. God also knew that they would be exposed to all kinds of temptations as they lived among the pagan nations of Palestine, so his law would provide protective boundaries to them. But there is more. God knew that his children were designed by him to be worshipers, that they would either worship him or surrender their hearts to idols. So at the foundation and core of his law is a call to worship him and him alone. In his law is guidance and protection, given so they might live at peace with him and with one another.

God's law was given to Israel not so they could somehow earn his love, but because he already loved them and had moved to redeem them from slavery by unleashing his sovereign power.

It's humbling to admit that we, like the children of Israel, have no power or ability whatsoever to earn our way into eternal communion with God. It is humbling to know that our most righteous moments fall woefully short of his holy standard. It is humbling to confess that we have no hope apart from his grace. But it is wonderful to remember that Jesus perfectly kept the law as our substitute and that, by grace, in him we stand before God righteous and accepted by him forever. What we could not earn, Jesus earned for us. Now that's grace!

For further study and encouragement: James 1:22–25

———

JANUARY 25

EXODUS 22–24

We worship and serve a God who knows our limits and,
because he does, he has called us to a Sabbath of rest.

The institution of the Sabbath is not so much a duty to be obeyed but rather a gracious provision from a God who made us and knows us. God created us with limits. If you remember back to the account of creation, the only being in that account that is without limits of any kind is the Creator. We have limits of time, energy, gifts, and wisdom. Think with me about the limits of time, which, by God's plan, structure your life. You will never get thirty hours in a day. You will never be given ten days in a week. You will never experience a forty-day month. And you will never be blessed with a 450-day year. In his infinite wisdom, God has established boundaries of time for us. There is nothing beyond those boundaries. There is no more time to be had. This side of eternity, we all live within the time boundaries that the Creator has set for us.

We also have significant physical limits. You and I are simply not in possession of unlimited physical, mental, emotional, or spiritual energy. Getting tired is a universal human experience. We all know what it's like to feel physically exhausted. We all know what it's like to be mentally and emotionally spent. We all have had moments when we would like to keep going, but we just don't have the strength. So God, in the glory of his wisdom and love, ordained the Sabbath. "Six days you shall do your work, but on the seventh day you shall rest; that your ox and your donkey may have rest, and the son of your servant woman, and the alien, may be refreshed" (Ex. 23:12).

The call to Sabbath is meant to humble us by reminding us of our limits. The call to Sabbath is a gift to us, reminding us that our Lord understands us and does not call us to live beyond the limits he has set for us. The Sabbath is a freedom, reminding us that rest is different from the sin of laziness. But the call to Sabbath is deeper and more profound than physical rest. It is a call to spiritual rest. Sabbath reminds us that we were not created to be independent. We were designed to be dependent on our Creator. We were made to find our strength and completion in him. The Sabbath was given by God not just so that we would rest, but so that we would rest in him. Human independence and self-sufficiency is a delusion. It is never a pathway to life. It is rather a road to destruction and death.

Admitting your need, owning your limits, and running to the one who is an endless fountain of new life and renewed strength is where life is to be found. Sabbath is God's gift to us. It welcomes us to step away from our labors and remember who we are and who he is, so that in submission and rest we may once again find life and strength in him.

For further study and encouragement: Mark 2:23–28

JANUARY 26

True and lasting hope is found in these words:
"I will dwell in the midst of my people."

There are a myriad of websites and media series dedicated to home decorating. Whether we are conscious of it or not, we are all very particular about how we want our home to look. Some of us take the look of our houses seriously and invest time and money to get them to look like our dreams. Others are more casual about our surroundings. Some of us place a high value on neat and clean; others find a bit of a mess more comfortable. But all of us somehow, someway express our personalities and our values by the way we design and keep our surroundings. That's why, when you are in someone else's home, it doesn't quite feel like home to you.

In Exodus 25 and the chapters following, we find directions for construct-ing and decorating a most important house: the house of the Lord. Read these amazing words carefully: "Let them make me a sanctuary, that I may dwell in their midst. Exactly as I show you concerning the pattern of the tabernacle, and of all its furniture, so you shall make it" (Ex. 25:8–9). You should be filled with wonder as you read these words. How could it be that the great Creator, the Sovereign King, the Holy One of Israel would ever desire to dwell among these sinful, complaining, and often rebellious people? Here again we are confronted with a major theme in the biblical story. God pours out his love on his people not because of what is in them, but because of what is in him. Nothing argues more strongly for the amazing and undeserved nature of God's grace than God's commanding his people to make a tabernacle so that he could dwell with his people. The hope of Israel was to be found in one place and one place alone: the Lord of glory and grace who lived among them.

But there is more. I don't know if you noticed it or not, but God not only said he would dwell among his people, but he also communicated that he was quite particular about how his house would be built, furnished, and deco-rated. He wanted his house to communicate who he was and what he valued. God wanted his tabernacle to communicate two things: his unapproachable holiness and the mercy of his forgiveness. This means the tabernacle is itself a prophecy.

There would be another place where God's unapproachable holiness and his forgiving mercy would meet: the cross of Jesus Christ. Here in God's mercy plan, the perfectly holy Lamb would die, so that we would become the children of God and so that he would come and dwell with us. A holy God, dwelling among his not-yet perfectly holy children, is our hope today too. What amazing mercy that by grace we have become the house of the Lord.

For further study and encouragement: Jeremiah 31:31–39

———

JANUARY 27

EXODUS 28–29

In this life there are many important things to know, but nothing is more important and life-changing than the knowledge of God.

I remember the wonder in his voice and in his eyes as he told me about his days spent at camp. He had spent a week at a Christian camp where he was encouraged to see God's created world in new and engaging ways. He had just looked through a microscope at the tiny little creatures that live in a pond. These little creatures were invisible to the eye as he simply stood and looked over the pond. He was amazed that there was a whole world underwater that most of us never even realize exists. That microscope revealed a universe of wonderful and amazing things that you could spend the rest of your life studying and seeking to understand.

Such it is with God's world. Everywhere you look is another little "universe" of sights, sounds, and beings. The study of each of these little universes could leave you with volumes of knowledge. It can be a bit overwhelming to think that in God's world there is no end to knowing. You and I will never know enough; we will never be able to say, "I know everything." This is why we must understand what is important to know and what is not. You and I have a limited amount of time and limited mental capacity, so what we commit ourselves to know is significant and life-shaping.

This is why it is important to pay careful attention to the words of Exodus 29:45–46: "I will dwell among the people of Israel and will be their God. And they shall know that I am the LORD their God, who brought them out of the land of Egypt that I might dwell among them. I am the LORD their God." Not only do these words capture the amazing grace of God's choosing to dwell among his people, a stunning reality they could never earn or deserve, but they reveal why he chose to do this. When reading these verses, you and I should pause for a moment and consider the significance of the words "And they shall know that I am the LORD their God." God says, "I am going to dwell with my people so that they will know me."

If God is the Creator of everything that exists, if he is the Lord and Ruler of all that happens, and if he holds his created world together by his powerful hand, then there is nothing more important than to know him. There is no proper knowledge of anything in this world that does not begin with knowing God. But there is more in these verses. God says, "I don't just want you to know me; I want you to know what I have done for you. I am your Redeemer. I placed my love on you, I redeemed you from slavery, I provided for you, and I have given you my law."

God has now made us the temple where he dwells, so that we would remember his redeeming grace and follow him with joy.

For further study and encouragement: Romans 12:1–2

———

JANUARY 28

EXODUS 30–32

*God created artists, poets, composers, and preachers
and endowed them with incredible gifts, so that his glory
would be seen and our lives would be changed.*

Besides being a pastor and an author, I am a painter. I have a studio a few blocks down from where we live that is one of my favorite places on earth. Consequently, the following passage is one of my favorite Old Testament gems:

The LORD said to Moses, "See, I have called by name Bezalel the son of Uri, son of Hur, of the tribe of Judah, and I have filled him with the Spirit of God, with ability and intelligence, with knowledge and all craftsmanship, to devise artistic designs, to work in gold, silver, and bronze, in cutting stones for setting, and in carving wood, to work in every craft. And behold, I have appointed with him Oholiab, the son of Ahisamach, of the tribe of Dan. And I have given to all able men ability, that they may make all that I have commanded you: the tent of meeting, and the ark of the testimony, and the mercy seat that is on it, and all the furnishings of the tent, the table and its utensils, and the pure lampstand with all its utensils, and the altar of incense, and the altar of burnt offering with all its utensils, and the basin and its stand, and the finely worked garments, the holy garments for Aaron the priest and the garments of his sons, for their service as priests, and the anointing oil and the fragrant incense for the Holy Place. According to all that I have commanded you, they shall do." (Ex. 31:1–11)

God gave specific people specific artistic gifts so that his tabernacle would reflect his glory, that is, the glory of his holiness and the wonder of his mercy. God did this because he knew that he had created people with a glory orientation. Human beings love glorious things. So our lives will be captured and controlled by his glorious glory or the glory of some created thing. God loves us enough to give people the ability to create things that reflect his glory, so that we would be drawn to love, worship, and serve him above anything else.

But God's giving of artistic gifts is not limited to his tabernacle. All forms of artistic and communicative creativity have been given by God, not just for our pleasure but for a higher purpose. Since God is a spirit and cannot be seen with our physical eyes, he gives people the ability to display his glory in what they create, so that we would "see" him and surrender the awe of our hearts to him. His purpose is not just that we would enjoy the pleasure of artistic expression or respect the artist, but also that we would be given eyes to see the great artist and would give ourselves to him. God, the author of beauty, gives people the ability to create what is beautiful so that we would be drawn to gaze upon his beauty and, as we do, be rescued by his grace. So, enjoy the art around you, but as you do, may your heart run to the artist behind the art.

For further study and encouragement: Genesis 1:1–31

———

JANUARY 29

EXODUS 33–35

The present and future hope and security of the people of God is found in one thing: the presence of the Lord.

Moses had the theology of his identity and security right. There was much that Moses didn't know that we now know as the children of God because we have access to the complete Scriptures. Yet, in the following conversation with his Lord, Moses reveals that he knows something of profound and life-shaping significance:

And he said, "My presence will go with you, and I will give you rest." And he said to him, 'If your presence will not go with me, do not bring us up from here. For how shall it be known that I have found favor in your sight, I and your people? Is it not in your going with us, so that we are distinct, I and your people, from every other people on the face of the earth?" (Ex. 33:14–16).

Before I unpack Moses's insight, let me ask you a few questions.

Where in life do you look for identity?

Where do you look for hope and rest of heart?

What makes you feel secure?

What makes you feel distinctly known or cared for?

Moses understands that there is no hope for Israel and no reason for Israel to travel further if God doesn't go with them. And he also understands that what makes Israel distinct is not their national or ethnic identity, but the fact that they are the people with whom God has chosen to dwell. As a nation, the single thing that makes Israel distinct from every nation on earth is the presence of the Lord. It is the Lord who picked Israel out from the mass of human nations, set his love on them, blessed them with his covenant promises, protected them from extinction, delivered them from slavery, provided for their physical needs, dwelt with them in his tabernacle, blessed them with the promised land, and from them would provide the long-awaited Messiah. The people of Israel could not have done one of these things for themselves.

So it is with each one of us. Our security is not found in the size of our house, how much we are respected by others, the power of our position, the amount of money we have, our family history, our human leaders, the number of our personal gifts, or our strength, wisdom, or righteousness. Our future hope does not depend on the quality of our education or the wisdom of the choices we have made. It is humbling to confess that no matter how wise and successful we are, our hope and security rest on this: God has placed his love on us and, because he has, he is with us in glory and grace forever. He will go with us wherever we go and will do for us what we have no power to do for ourselves—not because we deserve it, but because he is generous in love and mercy. It really is true that he is everything we need.

For further study and encouragement: 1 Peter 1:13–21

JANUARY 30

EXODUS 36–38

God not only kindly and generously gives us great gifts, but he also
works in our hearts so that we would offer those gifts back to him.

I greatly value my second career (or maybe it should be called a very serious hobby). As a painter, my art is very important to me, and I spend a lot of my time thinking about the painting I am working on at the moment. It's important for me to always keep in mind that this gift I have to create beauty on a large white canvas does not belong to me. If God is the Creator (and the Bible declares that he is), then he is the rightful and sole owner of my gifts. It's humbling to understand that I am not the owner; I am simply the resident manager.

When I am in my studio, I am very aware that the particular artistic gift I am exercising there belongs to my Lord. He is the source of anyone's ability to create art of any kind, and he is the one who decides to give a gift to a particular person. As Romans 11:36 says, "From him and through him and to him are all things. To him be the glory forever. Amen." I did not create my artistic abilities, and those abilities don't continue because of my power. Those gifts don't belong to me, and they have not been given for my glory.

In the Bible's description of the design and construction of the tabernacle, that house where the Lord would dwell with his people, the curtain is pulled back and we are given a glimpse of where human gifts come from and why they exist. God wants his house to be artfully designed, and if that is to happen, there must be artists to execute that design, as he gives specific gifts to specific men to do that work. "Moses called Bezalel and Oholiab and every craftsman in whose mind the LORD had put skill, everyone whose heart stirred him up to come to do the work" (Ex. 36:2).

We should notice two things in this verse about God's involvement in the giftedness of these men. First, we are told that God put skill in these men's minds. What an incredible statement of the power and presence of God. He has the power to place human ability, skill, and giftedness wherever he wishes. This is true not just of the building of the tabernacle, but this is always the case. It makes sense that creative ability comes from the Creator, and if it comes from the Creator, then it belongs to him. But this passage also tells us something else. It tells us that God not only gives gifts, but he stirs up our hearts to use the gifts he has given. So, today, whether you have mechanical ability, the skill to cook a beautiful meal, musical giftedness, carpentry skill, or the ability to make your surroundings beautiful, stop and give thanks to the owner and giver of your gifts.

For further study and encouragement: Colossians 3:12–17

JANUARY 31

EXODUS 39–40

*By grace we are not just accepted into God's family, but
the glory of his presence dwells in and among us.*

Then the cloud covered the tent of meeting, and the glory of the Lord
filled the tabernacle. And Moses was not able to enter the tent of meeting because the cloud settled on it, and the glory of the Lord filled the
tabernacle. Throughout all their journeys, whenever the cloud was taken
up from over the tabernacle, the people of Israel would set out. But if the
cloud was not taken up, then they did not set out till the day that it was
taken up. For the cloud of the Lord was on the tabernacle by day, and fire
was in it by night, in the sight of all the house of Israel throughout all their
journeys. (Ex. 40:34–38)

Reread that opening passage and let your heart be filled with the wonder that
is captured here. Here is one of the most magnificent moments of divine grace
in all of the Old Testament. We must never let words like these pass quickly
through our minds as we move on to the next thing. This moment has been
captured by God and written into his book so that today you and I would be
stopped by it and left in awe. This has been retained for us in order to rescue us,
change us, and produce in us a heart captured by a life shaped by God's glory.

It is hard for me to find words that properly express the wonder of this moment in God's redemptive narrative. The children of Israel have already proven
themselves to be sinful, complaining, rebellious, and doubt-filled people. They
have doubted God's presence and power, and they have questioned his wisdom.
Shockingly, they have already erected an idol, giving this lifeless image credit for
what only God, in his rescuing mercy, could have done (Ex. 32:1–6). Yet God had
a plan for his people: out of them the Messiah would come. That plan depended
on the Lord's constant presence with them. The Israelites were included in God's
plan not because they had done things to deserve it, but because in his sovereign
mercy he had chosen to place his love on them. It is humbling to understand
and confess that what we need most in life and death we have no ability to earn
or deserve. God with us, in us, and for us is always the result of one thing: grace.

The cloud and the fire were physical, visible symbols of God's presence with
his people. The cloud and fire pictured that Israel had been sanctified by God.
What do I mean by this? God had set Israel apart from every nation on earth
for his will and his glory. These visible symbols were to remind them again and
again that they were the children of God.

38

If you're God's child, his presence and glory have descended on you not because of what you've done, but because of what Jesus has done for you. God's glory resting on you means not only that he is with you, but that you belong to him, set apart for his purpose and his glory.

For further study and encouragement: Ephesians 1:15–23

FEBRUARY 1

LEVITICUS 1–4

No greater gift has ever been given than the gift of atonement for sin. We will be celebrating this gift of grace for all of eternity.

A sad awareness eventually washes over every parent. At some point, early in the life of your little loved one, you see sin rear its ugly head. It is obvious and unavoidable. You had hoped your child would be the exception, but it turns out she's not. She might refuse to do what you ask. She might shout "No!" to a command you have given. She might display selfishness or anger. You know the reason: your child is a sinner. It's not just that your child does things that are wrong. No, you are confronted with something profoundly deeper and more controlling. If the problem were just an occasional behavioral problem, perhaps some system of behavioral modification would work. But, as we look at every human being, we realize our problem is not just a matter of behavior; we have a problem with behavior because we have *a nature problem*. Sin is not only a matter of what we occasionally *do*. Sin, apart from the restorative power of God's grace, is *who we are*. We are sinners by nature, and that is why we have no ability to escape its power and penalty on our own.

I love the good news of Leviticus. This book in God's word is like a finger pointing us to where God's great redemptive story is going. Leviticus alerts us to the fact that God, in glorious grace, is very serious about providing atonement for sin. He makes a way for sin's penalty to be paid, so that gracious forgiveness can be granted. If sin is our deepest, most destructive, and most inescapable problem, then atonement for sin is the best, most-needed news ever. If you understand that every sin is a direct rebellion against God, then the gift of atonement becomes even more amazing to you. Sinners offend God in innumerable ways, yet, with a love that is almost too wonderful for words, God moves to make atonement for sin possible.

Leviticus 4 uses a refrain three times: "The priest shall make atonement for him, . . . and he shall be forgiven" (4:26, 31, 35). These are glorious, hope-filled words. There is hope for us, no matter how strong the hold of sin is on us and no matter what dark hallways of sin we have walked. In these words we are assured that an utterly holy God makes a way for thoroughly sinful people to have their penalty paid and their record wiped clean. But there is more. In these words we find a promise of the coming of the Great High Priest, Jesus. He will be the final sacrifice, the complete payment, and the ultimate means of eternal forgiveness. What better news could you ever want to hear?

For further study and encouragement: Hebrews 7:11–28

FEBRUARY 2

LEVITICUS 5–7

Sin leaves each of us guilty. The question is,
What will we do with our guilt?

My son had taken something that wasn't his. I watched him do it, even though he didn't know he was being watched. I called him over. He diverted his eyes as he walked toward me. His head-down walk was a picture of guilt. He knew that what he had done was wrong. He knew now that I had seen him. He knew he was in trouble, but, when I asked him if he had done what I saw him do, he denied it. I was an eyewitness, yet he would not admit his guilt.

My son, whom I love with all my heart, is not alone in his response. Since we are all sinners, we all stand guilty before God. We all deal with our guilt some-how, someway. Some of us live in denial, telling ourselves again and again that we are righteous. This is an exercise in self-atonement. Some of us deal with our guilt by comparing ourselves to others, concluding that we are not so bad after all. Some of us are good at minimizing our sin, working to make what we have done seem less than sinful. Some of us are skilled at pointing the finger and shifting the blame to someone or something other than ourselves. Some of us wallow in self-despising guilt, allowing shame to depress and isolate us. Some of us try to deal with our guilt by committing to a regimen of self-reformation, determining to set high, perfectionistic standards for ourselves.

All of these reactions to guilt are burdensome, dysfunctional, and disappoint-ing. They simply never work. They turn us into either proud legalists or fearful depressives, but they never produce good fruit in us or in our relationships with others. Since we are all born guilty, our guilt can't be denied or wished away. Our guilt must be confessed; it must be borne; and it must be removed, so that we can live in the light and without shame. This is why the institution of the guilt offering is both an essential gift and a great relief (Lev. 5–7). God declares that he has made a way for our guilt to be dealt with so that we don't have to get up every morning and put that huge, heavy backpack of guilt on our shoulders once again. The guilt offering tells us where the redemptive story is going. Embedded in every animal guilt offering is the promise that there will be a final Lamb of sacrifice (1 Cor. 5:7). He will carry the full range of our guilt and shame. Although perfectly spotless in every way, Jesus will take the heavy load of our guilt on himself. He will remove our guilt so that we can stand before God righteous and without fear or shame.

Since guilt is inescapable, the guilt offering is essential. Jesus is our guilt offering, so we deny our patterns of denial and confess to our guilt, knowing we will receive mercy and grace when we do. Celebrate today the guilt offering that God has so willingly and graciously made for you. Come out of shame's darkness and live in the light.

For further study and encouragement: 1 John 1:5–10

FEBRUARY 3

LEVITICUS 8–10

It is essential for us to take sin seriously, because
Scripture makes it clear that God does.

He was an angry, emotionally abusive, demanding, controlling, and physically intimidating husband. I have to admit that, when I sat with him in my counseling office, he intimidated me. He had destroyed all the sweetness, unity, peace, and joy in his marriage. His wife was emotionally broken. She had lived too long in fear of when she would anger him next. When she voiced her hurt, he mocked her for being weak and needy. The thing that struck me the first time I met with them was the smile on his face. His wife tearfully told me why she had begged him to come with her for counseling as he sat there with his arms folded and a grin of mockery on his face. He wasn't ashamed. He didn't feel guilty. He didn't think his behavior was that big of a deal. He surely wasn't in my office that morning because he thought he needed help. He was there to placate his wife, to get her off his back so that they could "move on." I wanted to think that he and I had nothing in common, but we did.

There are times when I too don't take my sin seriously. There are times when my pride and impatience don't seem such a big deal to me. There are times when I am defensive when approached about a wrong I have done. There are times when I work to make my sin look less than sinful to me. And I am sure there are times when you do the same. For most of us our problem is not that we take sin too seriously, feel its weight too much, or confess our wrongs too quickly and too often. No, for most of us our problem is that we often fail to see the seriousness of our sin and the gravity of its vertical and horizontal consequences. It is scary that we are able to call ourselves followers of Jesus Christ, and yet we minimize the very thing that led him to the cross. The whole content and motion of the grand redemptive narrative is a result of God's unwillingness to close his eyes to the pervasiveness and gravity of sin, which has infected every one of us. To God, no disease that has befallen humanity is more significant and destructive than sin. That's why, immediately after Adam and Eve sinned, our God promised that this dark thing would be once and for all defeated and eradicated (Gen. 3:15). Sin is so serious that it gets that kind of attention from the Creator Sovereign King.

This is why the story of Nadab and Abihu, who made an unauthorized incense offering, should get our attention (Lev. 10:1–3). A fire from the Lord consumed them, and they died. That's how serious sin is: "The wages of sin is death" (Rom. 6:23). Because God saw sin as serious, he set in motion a process to give us a Savior. The grace of new life is needed only if sin is as deadly as God says it is. Do you take sin seriously?

For further study and encouragement: Romans 3:9–20

———

FEBRUARY 4

LEVITICUS 11–13

*By the loving miracle of God's grace, unclean
hearts are made new and pure.*

Leviticus 13:45–46 says, "The leprous person who has the disease shall wear torn clothes and let the hair of his head hang loose, and he shall cover his upper lip and cry out, 'Unclean, unclean.' He shall remain unclean as long as he has the disease. He is unclean. He shall live alone. His dwelling shall be outside the camp." These words remind me of David's prayer after committing adultery: "Create in me a clean heart, O God, / and renew a right spirit within me" (Ps. 51:10). Although the laws surrounding leprosy had to do with God's lovingly and wisely protecting his people from a deadly infection, they also point us to something profoundly deeper.

Sin is the ultimate infection. No one escapes this disease. It renders us all unclean. It separates us all from our Maker. It cries out for the ultimate cure, one only the Messiah can provide.

Like a bad stain
on white linen,
like a black smudge
on pure vellum,
like wine spilled
on a new dress,
like paint drips
on window glass,
like mud
on a new shoe,
this stain won't just go away.
It won't fade into
nothing.
You won't wake up one
morning to discover
it has suddenly
disappeared.
The deepest, darkest,
most penetrating
stubborn stains
must be cleansed.
Denying that they're there
never works.
Doing your best to hide them
doesn't remove them.
Living with them
is foolishness.
Hoping no one will notice
is vain.
Worrying about them
changes nothing.
Whatever has been stained

must be cleansed
to be new again.
So it is with the human heart.
It is sad to admit,
but no one has a
pure,
perfectly clean,
unstained,
pristinely beautiful,
heart.
No one.
Every heart of
every person
comes into this world
stained by sin.
Sin is immorality's
permanent ink,
sinking into the deepest regions
of the thoughts,
desires,
motives,
purposes,
worship
of the heart.
This tragic sin stain is
humanly unremovable.
No matter what you try,
no matter how many times you try,
it is there to stay
without something that has
cleansing power.
You can look at your stains with hope

because
there is a cleansing stream.
It flows through the righteous life,
the substitutionary sacrifice,
the victorious resurrection of
Jesus.
He came so that sin-stained hearts
would have the hope
of being clean again,
new again,
spotless in his sight again,
ultimately pure again,
forever.
If we confess that we are
stained,
he is faithful,
he is righteous,
he will forgive our sins,
he will cleanse our hearts
and thoroughly wash us
from all unrighteousness.

Step out from the shame of your
stains.
Refuse to put your hope in things
that do not cleanse.
Walk away from a life of
denial.
Confess that you have no
cleansing power of your own.
Quit blaming your stains on
other people,
other things.
Humbly bring the garment of
your heart
to him.
Put your stains in his hands.
He will wash you in his grace.
He delights in doing for you
what you could never do for
yourself.
He delights in making you
clean.

For further study and encouragement: Psalm 51:1–12

———

FEBRUARY 5

LEVITICUS 14–15

*No detail of your life is outside of the watchful and
faithful care of your heavenly Father.*

Politicians on the campaign trail often communicate that they care for their
constituents, but their care is distant and impersonal at best. They don't know
you, they don't love you, and they have no idea what your personal life is like or
what burdens you bear. So when a politician says he cares, you don't tell yourself
that you can let go of your burdens and rest in this leader's care. Because you
hear his words of care in the most general sense, they make little difference in
your emotional or spiritual state or in how you live your life.

But imagine what it would be like to have the most powerful person in the universe set his love on you, commit to unleashing his power to bless you, and deliver amazing promises of guidance, protection, and provision. Wouldn't the care of that person change the way you think about yourself, your life, your hopes and dreams, your potential, and the hardships and burdens of life? This is exactly what the book of Leviticus is about; it's about Almighty God, the Lord of heaven and earth, setting his love on his children and making covenant promises to bless them and, through them, to bless the peoples of the earth. What Leviticus pictures for us is how deep, detailed, and pervasive the care of God is for his children. The specificity and detail of God's laws for his children show just how much he loves them. In these laws we see how much he cares about every detail of what we deal with as we live in this fallen world. The one who created us cares for us, and, because he created us, he knows just what we need.

Leviticus 15 includes a series of laws about bodily discharges. Now, you may not have known that this was in the Bible, or you may be wondering why it *is* in the Bible. Perhaps you have never heard a sermon on Leviticus 15 and bodily discharges. But there is a reason for these laws, and a reason they were preserved for us. They remind us that no human experience, no matter how personal or embarrassing, is outside the Lord's care. God's care is so insightful and thorough that he even cares about our most intimate bodily functions. He knows what men and women go through, and he meets us with his loving care. I am glad for Leviticus 15 and what it communicates about the specificity of God's love for his children. If he cares so much about the little things in our lives, you can be sure he cares about the biggest danger to us: our sin. If he works in the little things, you can rest assured that he will deal with this big thing: he will send one who will conquer sin and death and reconcile us to himself forever.

For further study and encouragement: Psalm 139:1–16

———

FEBRUARY 6

LEVITICUS 16–18

God's laws are not only for his glory; they are for our thriving as well.

You probably don't need me to tell you that we are living in a culture that has gone sexually insane. The anytime, anyway, and with-any-person culture of sexuality will not lead us anywhere good. The social philosophy of gender fluidity, based solely on spontaneous personal preference, must include the denial of biological and relational realities. Where we are as a society, when it comes to human sexuality, should remind us of the importance of God's wise and holy laws regarding sex. We should be grateful that God has spoken with such remarkable and memorable clarity about this important aspect of human desire and function. He has done so because he loves us.

Leviticus 18:5 introduces a list of laws pertaining to sexuality: "You shall therefore keep my statutes and my rules; if a person does them, he shall live by them: I am the LORD." First, this verse reminds us that the laws of God do not get in the way of the good life but are the tracks upon which the good life runs. "He shall live by them" means that life—abundant life—is found in a careful, life-shaping submission to the wise and holy laws of our Creator Lord. Second, this verse tells us that God is not sex-negative; in fact, the Bible makes it clear that God is not pleasure-negative. He has placed us in a world of glorious pleasures wherever we look. And he has created us with pleasure gates (eyes, ears, nose, etc.) so that we can participate in, absorb, and enjoy the physical pleasures that he has filled the earth with. But as an infinitely wise Creator, God knows that pleasure requires boundaries. A whatever-you-want, however-much-you-want, anytime-you-want, with-whomever-you-want approach to pleasure will always harm yourself and others in some way. A life controlled by the unbridled love of pleasure is a life heading for destruction. God wants us to enjoy sexual pleasure, and he wants our sexual lives to thrive, but he knows this will happen only when we submit our sexual desire to his wise commands.

Leviticus 18:5 reminds us of one final thing. As weak and wandering sinners, we have no power on our own to love God and his law more than we love the pleasure of sexual fulfillment. So our hope of thriving in this area lies with our God, who meets us by his grace and empowers us to desire and to do what is right in his eyes. Once again, we are pointed to Jesus. In Jesus, God not only reconciles us to himself, but he gifts us with his Spirit to guide, convict, and empower us, so that we can know the joy of living the good life, that is, living the way the Creator designed for us to live.

For further study and encouragement: Proverbs 7:1–27

FEBRUARY 7

There is no higher, grander purpose in life than to
accept God's call to be holy as he is holy.

Although Leviticus is filled with God's insight and wisdom, many people find it difficult to read through this Old Testament book. Many have confessed to me that, when using a daily Bible reading plan, they quickly skip through Leviticus to get to "more interesting and more helpful" parts of God's word. But I have come to love Leviticus, and to love the Lord who is revealed in this book, more fully and more deeply.

Note the words of Leviticus 20:26: "You shall be holy to me, for I the LORD am holy and have separated you from the peoples, that you should be mine." This verse points us to the call of God. To love God's law is to live for something vastly bigger than the comfort, pleasure, or ease of the moment. God calls you to live for something dramatically more fulfilling than your personal definitions of happiness. He calls you to live for something greater than material affluence, personal power and control, or acceptance, respect, or fame. He calls you to surrender every desire in every situation of your life to the holy will of the one who created you and then took you for his own. The call to holiness enjoins you to always ask in every situation, oration, or relationship, "What is the will of God for me in this place, or what thought, desire, or response would be pleasing to my Lord here?"

This verse clearly communicates what holiness is about. It's not first about what you and I do as the children of God. It is first about what God has done. Pay attention to these words: "You shall be holy to me . . . you shall be mine." In an act of divine sovereignty and grace God takes his children out of the mass of humanity and separates them for his own possession and purpose. Holiness is about being separated by God. It is about no longer belonging to ourselves but belonging to him. And it is about living, in every area of our lives, as if we really do believe that we have been separated by God for his possession and purpose. To be holy is to live in light of God's choice to make us his own.

Consider a New Testament passage:

The grace of God has appeared, bringing salvation for all people, training us to renounce ungodliness and worldly passions, and to live self-controlled, upright, and godly lives in the present age, waiting for our blessed hope, the appearing of the glory of our great God and Savior Jesus Christ, who gave himself for us to redeem us from all lawlessness and to purify for himself a people for his own possession who are zealous for good works. (Titus 2:11–14)

May we live as a people for God's own possession.

For further study and encouragement: Titus 2:11–14

———

FEBRUARY 8

LEVITICUS 22–23

The Sabbath is more than a religious duty; it is a gift of grace from a God who knows us and loves us.

It is tempting to live beyond your limits. It is tempting to work harder and longer than God has designed you to do. It is tempting to evaluate your life by how much you have experienced or achieved. It is tempting to exhaust yourself by working to acquire, and then working to maintain what you have acquired. But there is no limitless human being. God has created all of us with limits of time, energy, wisdom, and righteousness.

Think about time, for instance. You and I will never get ten days in a week or thirty hours in a day. We'll never have fifty days in a month or five hundred days in a year. We all have to live inside of the limits of time that God has set for us. This means that if something in your life commands more and more of your time, it will begin to eat into and take away time from some other area of your life. If you work eighty hours a week, it *will* encroach on your familial and spiritual callings. The same applies to physical energy. No person is an endless fount of energy and strength. It never pays to deny your body the need to rest and rejuvenate. Think of human wisdom. No human being is wise all the time and in every way. It is unwise to leave no time in your life to grow in wisdom and knowledge, to act as if you know it all.

So God, knowing the limits he has set for us, says, " 'Six days shall work be done, but on the seventh day is a Sabbath of solemn rest, a holy convocation. You shall do no work. It is a Sabbath to the LORD in all your dwelling places" (Lev. 23:3). In loving wisdom God calls us to stop each week for one day. Stopping is hard for some of us, because we have attached our identity, meaning, and purpose to always being in motion. God says, "You need to have a day when you do no work." I love the words "solemn rest." Here is a call to be serious about rest, because the one who made you and called you to himself is serious about it. But there is more. This stop-day is also a day of holy convocation. It is a time, because of sabbath, that God's people can gather for worship and remember who we are and what we have been given as the children of God.

"It is a Sabbath to the LORD." We don't belong to our material possessions. We don't belong to our achievements or successes. We belong to *the Lord*. By grace, he has made us his, and in living for him we experience life's greatest joys. And, finally, every Sabbath reminds us of the ultimate Sabbath of rest found only in our substitute and Redeemer, Jesus.

For further study and encouragement: Hebrews 4:1–13

FEBRUARY 9

LEVITICUS 24–25

We see the beauty and tenderness of God in his kindness toward the poor.

Because I live in the heart of the city, I walk everywhere. I am on the sidewalks almost every day, walking to meet someone for lunch, to pick up something at the store, or to go out to dinner with my wife. As do so many big cities, Philly has a heartbreaking homeless problem. We see people living and begging on the streets every day. Sometimes we literally have to step over someone to get to where we are going. It is easy to get used to diverting your eyes, to act like you didn't hear that cry for assistance, to harden your heart. It's easy to get mad at someone who is messing up the sidewalks or intimidating tourists. I admit that it is often hard to look upon a street person with eyes of love, remembering that, like me, he is made in the image of God, and, because he is, he has value and dignity.

This is why I am struck by the directives in Leviticus on how to treat the poor:

> If your brother becomes poor and cannot maintain himself with you, you shall support him as though he were a stranger and a sojourner, and he shall live with you. Take no interest from him or profit, but fear your God, that your brother may live beside you. You shall not lend him your money at interest, nor give him your food for profit. I am the LORD your God, who brought you out of the land of Egypt to give you the land of Canaan, and to be your God. (Lev. 25:35–38)

God's words here are touching and important. He is instructing his people to take in and provide for the poor in the community. This is a call to loving, radical hospitality. Then God addresses the motivation for such self-sacrificing kindness. God tells them, "Don't do this for personal gain, but because you fear me." God's children should remember how he responded to them when they were poor, needy, and unable to change their circumstances, and then show that same kindness to others. If you live in fearful awe of God's mercy to you, then you will be an agent of his mercy to others. Gratitude is the soil in which kindness grows. God makes the invisible mercy of his kindness visible by sending people of mercy to respond with kindness to people who need mercy. God calls his children to represent his character and will wherever he places them.

Now think about your life. The Bible says that Jesus became poor so that through his poverty we might become rich (2 Cor. 8:9). He looked on us with love and, in the mercy of kindness, did for us what we could never have done for ourselves. May God grant us the grace to show kindness to the needy people we encounter, with gratitude for the mercy we have been given.

For further study and encouragement: 2 Corinthians 8:1–15

———

FEBRUARY 10

LEVITICUS 26–27

Where would we be without God's forgiving and restoring grace?

It is important to have a well-oiled, activated gospel memory. It's important to require yourself never to forget. Few things are more spiritually benefiting than rehearsing the story of God's rescuing, forgiving, and restoring grace in your life. It's vital to remember that we not only experienced his forgiving grace at the moment of our conversion, but continually experience his grace as a lovingly patient process of restoration. God has forgiven you again and again, he has restored you to himself again and again, and he will continue to do so again and again.

God knows that between the "already" and the "not yet," living in a fallen world and with sin still inside of us, we will mess up. There will be times when we think, desire, and do wrong things. There will be times when we willingly step outside of God's holy boundaries. This side of eternity we will sin. This is why God's commitment to forgive us and restore us is so beautiful and hope-inspiring. If you are at all humble, then you know you're not perfect. You know no day in your life is totally sin-free. You know you are a person in need of daily forgiveness.

God's forgiving and restoring mercies didn't begin with the birth of Jesus but were baked into his law.

> If they confess their iniquity and the iniquity of their fathers in their treachery that they committed against me, and also in walking contrary to me, so that I walked contrary to them and brought them into the land of their enemies—if then their uncircumcised heart is humbled and they make amends for their iniquity, then I will remember my covenant with Jacob, and I will remember my covenant with Isaac and my covenant with Abraham, and I will remember the land. (Lev. 26:40–42)

How does a person enter into the blessing of God's forgiving and restoring grace? The answer, which is the same in the old covenant and the new, is clear: by humble, heartfelt confession. God will not turn his back on a sinner who comes to him with confession that is free from excuse or blame-shifting. He always greets the humble in heart with the fullness of his forgiving and restoring mercies. God has always been a God of grace, his people have always been in need of grace, and he has always reminded them of his willingness to respond to them with grace when grace is needed.

Leviticus 26 is yet another Old Testament passage that foreshadows the person and work of Jesus. These verses cry out for an ultimate and once-for-all purchase of forgiveness, for a sacrifice to be made that will forever restore us to God. Jesus has come to be that final sacrificial Lamb. In him our sins—past, present, and future—are fully forgiven. As a result of Jesus's work on our behalf, God is in us and we are in him forever, and nothing can separate us from his love. For sinners like you and me, there is no better, more beautiful gift than the gift of forgiving and restoring grace.

For further study and encouragement: Hebrews 10:1–18

FEBRUARY 11

In the beauty of his loving care, God numbers, orders, and prospers his
people so that through them all the peoples of earth will be blessed.

Hear what Paul says to Timothy about the gift of the word of God: "All Scripture is breathed out by God and profitable for teaching, for reproof, for correction, and for training in righteousness, that the man of God may be complete, equipped for every good work" (2 Tim. 3:16–17). This means that every single thing recorded for us in God's word is there for a reason. There are no superfluous, throwaway, or needless passages in your Bible. God recorded and preserved every passage in his word for our spiritual benefit. He retained every passage so that you and I would be spiritually complete and equipped to do what is good in God's sight, wherever we live. You will never encounter a passage, whether historical, didactic, poetic, or prophetic, that has nothing to do with you or your life and is therefore a waste of your time.

But your daily Bible reading plan brings you to the first few chapters of Numbers, where the children of Israel are being listed, numbered, designated, and ordered by tribes. You think, "What does this have to do with anything I'm facing or need in my life?" On the surface these accounts seem like unneeded historical detail, not very interesting, and easily forgotten. But the apostle Paul says that they are in your Bible for your spiritual maturation and readiness. So before you conclude that these particular chapters are unhelpful, ask yourself how your loving heavenly Father, who loves you with an everlasting love, wants you to be helped by what seems so distant and unhelpful.

Consider Numbers 2:32: "These are the people of Israel as listed by their fathers' houses. All those listed in the camps by their companies were 603,550." What do we need to hear from this passage? First, it reminds us of the intimate and specific care God has for his people. He numbers each one of them. God's care is so active and complete that he constantly knows the exact number of those he has taken as his own possession. God loves us so much that he never quits counting us, and he never loses track of one of his children. If a loving father counts his children as they get in the car after a day at the amusement park, how much more does our perfect heavenly Father number each and every one of his own? God's divine attention is constantly on his children.

Second, we learn from this verse that God is not only numbering and ordering his children, but is prospering them as well. This group of former slaves is now a growing nation. Why is this important to you and me? Because the hope of the universe is in the prospering of the children of Israel. Out of them will come the Savior, Jesus, who will provide forgiveness, reconciliation to God, and final renewal of all that sin has broken. It is good for us to know that God's children are always in good hands.

For further study and encouragement: 2 Timothy 3:16–17

———

FEBRUARY 12

NUMBERS 3–4

We should always live in life-shaping awe of the dangerous holiness of God.

If you and I were able to stand as we are in the presence of God, not only would we be overwhelmed with his incalculable holiness, but we would be filled with dread and grief at the extent of our unholiness. In fact, it is only in light of the perfectly perfect holiness of God that we can have a sense of the sinfulness of our sin. It is easy to have a casual attitude about things that are deeply offensive to our holy God. It is easy to rise to our own defense when accused of a wrong that, before God, should grieve us. It is easy to minimize the importance of God's holy standards for us in little moments of choice, little moments of behavior, and little moments of talk. God is so holy that he is unapproachably holy.

Hear the sobering warning of these words from Numbers 4:

> The LORD spoke to Moses and Aaron, saying, "Let not the tribe of the clans of the Kohathites be destroyed from among the Levites, but deal thus with them, that they may live and not die when they come near to the most holy things: Aaron and his sons shall go in and appoint them each to his task and to his burden, but they shall not go in to look on the holy things even for a moment, lest they die." (Num. 4:17–20)

In the kindness of his mercy, the Lord warned the Kohathites, who were tasked with taking care of the holy things in the tabernacle, that they could not enter the Holy of Holies and look around, or they would die. This was a warning to these tabernacle servants, but it has been retained as a warning for us, too. God's perfectly holy holiness is not something to be messed with. Ignoring the holiness of God and doing what you want to do led to death then, and it does so now.

If God is unapproachably holy (he is), and if he is the Creator and ruler of all that is (he is), and if he is the ultimate moral standard (he is), then everything in life is both moral and serious. There is no area of life where it is okay to take life into your own hands and do what you want to do. There is no room for writing your own rules. There is no time when your passions, pleasures, and desires are more important than God's holy standard. It is dangerous to deny or ignore the holiness of God. God is serious about his holiness, and we should be too.

This is why we today—and every day to come—should celebrate the life, death, and resurrection of Jesus. In our most holy moments, all of us would fall miserably short of the glory of God's holy standard. So humanity needs a substitute, one who lives a perfectly holy life in every way on our behalf. Because of Jesus's perfect substitutionary righteousness, we can enter into the presence of God without fear. Sinners in the presence of a holy God—what amazing grace!

For further study and encouragement: Romans 15:1–7

FEBRUARY 13

NUMBERS 5–6

*If you seek and celebrate God's forgiving grace, then your
life will be shaped by humble, heartfelt confession.*

Luella and I had just been introduced to a famous pop singer and his wife. They looked so young to us. They knew we had been married for a long time, and they were newlyweds, so their question was predictable: "What would you say is the key to a good, long-term marriage?" People often ask me this question, and I always give the same practical, biblically supported answer: "Confession and forgiveness." This is true not only of marriage, but it is true also of any other relationship you will ever have. You cannot have a relationship of any quality or longevity between one sinner and another sinner in a fallen world without committing to the humble habit of confession.

If this is true of human relationships, how much more is it true of a relationship between a far-less-than-perfect human being and a perfectly holy God? How can you acknowledge God's holiness and your sin and not be committed to confession? How can you meditate on the impossibly high standards of God's law and not be committed to confession? How can you believe in the presence of real evil and a real evil one and not be committed to confession? How can you confess that your life is not your own and that God has taken you for his own possession and not be committed to confession? Personal holiness and humble confession cannot be separated. As long as God calls us to be holy as he is holy, and as long as sin still lives inside of us, confession must be an essential ingredient in the life of every child of God.

Confession is baked into God's law, as we see in Numbers 5–6. The holy God who gave these wise and holy laws is a God of glorious grace. He knows his people, he knows the condition of the world in which they live, he knows the temptations they will face, and he knows that they will fall short of his commands. So he calls them to a humble life of confession. You cannot grieve what you don't see, and you cannot confess what you haven't grieved. So even this command to confess has redeeming grace built into it. If God doesn't grant his children eyes to see their sin for what it is, then they will never confess it as they should.

These chapters are another reminder that the Old Testament system was not all law and no grace. Embedded in God's holy law are offers of his forgiving and restoring grace. Is it any wonder, then, that the biblical story of God and his people would march toward the coming of the ultimate gift and giver of grace, the Lord Jesus Christ?

For further study and encouragement: Psalm 32:1–5

———

FEBRUARY 14

NUMBERS 7–8

The need for the Old Testament priests to be repeatedly cleansed should make us thankful for the coming of a priest who needed no cleansing.

Luella has been known to say, "I can't understand, with just the two of us living here, how things get so dusty." Have you ever noticed that nothing in your life stays clean? Your clothes don't stay clean; your house doesn't stay clean; your car doesn't stay clean; your teeth don't stay clean; your garage doesn't stay clean—the list goes on and on. We spend a large portion of our time working to keep things clean. Even more important to recognize is that your heart doesn't stay clean. Sin causes us to wander away from God's holy standards and expose ourselves to things that are not morally pure. Temptation seduces us into seeing as beautiful the things that God calls ugly. The dirt and dust of a heart not yet free of sin causes all of us to need a constant cleansing stream of God's grace.

So we find this directive in Numbers 8:5–6: "The LORD spoke to Moses, saying, 'Take the Levites from among the people of Israel and cleanse them.'" Before the priests could do their holy sacrificial work before God and on behalf of his people, they needed to be cleansed. It is important to understand that the priests did not stand above the need for sacrifices to be made to atone for their sins and to grant them forgiveness and cleansing before God. The priests did not live above a need for God's grace. They were men with sin still living inside of them, which meant they desperately needed for themselves what they had been called to offer to the rest of God's people. No one has ever lived above the need for a sacrifice for one's sin, just as no one has ever lived above the need for God's forgiving and cleansing grace. No one.

I think particularly of the leaders of Christ's church. This portion of God's word has been retained for you as a warning and a calling. There has only ever been one priest who needed no cleansing, the Messiah Jesus. He alone lived without the need for the forgiving and cleansing stream of God's grace. It is vital that you look at the people to whom you have been called to minister and see yourself as another person in need of God's grace. A seminary degree doesn't make you a grace graduate. A ministry calling doesn't make you a grace graduate. Ministry gifts don't make you a grace graduate. Ministry experience and success don't make you a grace graduate. Like the priests of old, it is important to recognize that, this side of eternity, the school of God's grace has no graduates. It is spiritually vital for you to humbly acknowledge that every part of the gospel that you hold before your people, you desperately need yourself. And it is good to remember that no one gives grace better than a person who knows he needs its cleansing stream himself.

For further study and encouragement: Hebrews 7:26–27

———

FEBRUARY 15

NUMBERS 9–10

The way to live in light of the grace of the constant presence of the Lord is to willingly and joyfully submit to his commands.

"On the day that the tabernacle was set up, the cloud covered the tabernacle" (Num. 9:15). This was not just another cloud in the sky. This was the most wonderful and important cloud ever. It was the cloud of the presence of God that hovered like a covering over the tabernacle. This cloud was a visible sign that the Lord God Almighty, the Creator and ruler of all that is, had set his love on these people and had chosen to dwell with them. This was so wonderful and amazing, it is hard for us to take it in. God had taken them for his own. He had made covenant promises to them. He had blessed them with his law. He had designed a system of sacrifices so that their sins could be confessed and forgiven and they could be cleansed and restored. And then the Lord of lords demonstrated that he would not be a distant monarch, with little attachment to his people. No, *he chose them so he could be with them.* The glory of his presence therefore hovered above the tabernacle, a constant reminder of the amazing grace of his presence.

But it is important to recognize that the cloud above the tabernacle was not just a cloud of presence; it was also a cloud of guidance. The God who dwelled with his people was the supreme guide of his people. The cloud of God's presence wasn't stationary. It moved, and, when it moved, the people of God were called to follow and move with it. They had to disassemble the tabernacle and their personal dwelling places, pack up their things, and follow. This cloud of presence and guidance moved not at a regular or predictable pace but according to the will of the Lord. When he decided to move, his people had to willingly move with him. When the cloud remained, they had to stay in that place. The children of Israel were called not only to celebrate the presence of the Lord but also to submit to his guidance: "At the command of the LORD they camped, and at the command of the LORD they set out" (Num. 9:23). The guidance of the cloud wasn't advice. The movement of the cloud represented the command of the Lord. For the children of Israel, the way to recognize and celebrate the Lord's presence was to follow his commands. The cloud represented not only the grace of his presence but also the call to submit to his rule.

So it is with us. The grand mystery of the Christian life is that we celebrate the grace of God's love and presence *and* accept his claim on our lives and the call to submit at all times and in every way to his commands. So we are thankful for the grace of Jesus, who empowers our resistant hearts to follow him, desiring and doing what he commands.

For further study and encouragement: Deuteronomy 30:15–20

FEBRUARY 16

Complaining is always dangerous because it causes us to be
willing to question the goodness and faithfulness of the Lord.

Every parent has experienced it. You get up every morning with a commitment to provide what is best for the spiritual, emotional, and physical help of your children. You actively do things every day because you love them, you know what they need, and you do what is necessary to provide it. You are not perfect, but your intentions are good-hearted and loving. But your children don't always appreciate you. They aren't always thankful for your loving attention or hard work. They often complain about what you feed them or schedule for them. They don't always think that your intentions are good, and they often find it easier to complain about you than to be thankful for you. But it's not just children, sadly, who do not praise, because complaining is the default language of fallen humanity.

The story recorded in Numbers 11 is striking, sad, illuminating, and convicting. The children of Israel were on a long journey through wilderness country to the land God had promised them. They were living what was essentially a nomadic life. It was therefore impossible for them to plant seeds, cultivate crops, or harvest food to eat. So God, in one of the most striking miracles of provision in Scripture, caused edible material to appear every morning like dew on the ground. This is both a visible demonstration of God's commitment to unleash his almighty power to provide for his people and a visual prophecy of his ultimate provision from above, Jesus. Jesus is the bread of life, the manna come down from heaven. Manna was nutritious, but here is God's dear children's response to this amazing provision: "Now the rabble that was among them had a strong craving. And the people of Israel also wept again and said, 'Oh that we had meat to eat! We remember the fish we ate in Egypt that cost nothing, the cucumbers, the melons, the leeks, the onions, and the garlic. But now our strength is dried up, and there is nothing at all but this manna to look at'" (Num. 11:4–6).

Notice what is happening here. You can't complain about God's provision without questioning his wisdom, goodness, faithfulness, and love. If you question his goodness, then you will stop relying on him for help; you don't trust someone you don't think is good. If you don't functionally trust God, you will take your life into your own hands, and, with a heart that's turning away from him, you will be susceptible to look at what is bad and see it as good. God's complaining children looked back at Egypt and didn't remember it as a horrible place of slavery and suffering; it looked more like a great Middle Eastern deli! Allowing your heart to complain and your mouth to grumble is always spiritually dangerous. The same heart that caused people to reject wilderness manna caused people thousands of years later to reject the ultimate provision of manna, Jesus. May God grace us with always-thankful hearts.

For further study and encouragement: 1 Corinthians 10:9–10

FEBRUARY 17

NUMBERS 14–15

God is perfectly glorious all the time and in every way, but we need grace to open our often-blind eyes to see the magnitude of his glory.

A glorious painting was on loan to the museum for a limited period of time, and I just had to see it. However, many other art lovers had the same response. When I arrived at the museum and found the gallery where the painting hung, so many people were already there that I couldn't even get into the room. I craned my neck to get a glimpse from the doorway, but all I could see was a brown corner of this masterpiece. If you had asked me then, with my limited view, to describe this glorious masterwork, I would have given you a description that was anything but glorious. The problem wasn't that the painting lacked artistic glory. No, the problem was mine. I had a vision problem that kept me from seeing, being in awe of, and celebrating the extent of the glory that the painter had laid down on that canvas.

I am convinced that one of the reasons the book of Numbers is in the Bible is to display the extent of the glory of God and, not only that, to demonstrate how God unleashes his glory to provide for his people. The glory of God and the glory of his love for his people shine in Numbers like a galaxy of stars in the night. Here we see the glory of his presence, the glory of his wisdom, the glory of his power, the glory of his patient love, the glory of his guidance, the glory of his forgiving grace, the glory of his discipline, the glory of his protection, the glory of his provision, the glory of the specificity of his care for each of his children, and the glory of his zeal to deliver what he has promised. Yet, when his children look at this portrait of his glory, they don't see glory. It is a sad picture of the tragedy of spiritual blindness. For this, all of humanity needs a Savior who has the power to open blind eyes to the grace and glory that are all around.

Just as God is about to deliver the land that he had promised to his children so long ago, a moment when his glory is about to shine its brightest, his people respond with this:

"Would that we had died in the land of Egypt! Or would that we had died in this wilderness! Why is the LORD bringing us into this land, to fall by the sword? Our wives and our little ones will become a prey. Would it not be better for us to go back to Egypt?" And they said to one another, "Let us choose a leader and go back to Egypt." (Num. 14:2–4)

Panic in the face of opposition blinds the Israelites from seeing the glory of God's almighty power that would rain down to deliver this promised place into their hands. This narrative asks this question of us: What blinds our eyes from this same God of awesome glory and the grace he daily provides in his Son, the Lord Jesus?

For further study and encouragement: Isaiah 6:1–7

———

FEBRUARY 18

NUMBERS 16–17

Jesus stands as the mediator between us and God. He takes God's judgment on himself, so that it will not fall on us. What amazing grace!

Some moments in Old Testament history summarize the entire redemptive narrative for us in one story. We need to pray that God would give us eyes to see these examples of redeeming grace and to understand that they are always about Jesus. In Numbers 16 we find ourselves at a shocking and sad moment in the story of God and his people. In holy anger God metes out judgment against his rebellious and complaining people. God will not compromise his high and holy requirements in order to have communion with his people. He will not allow challengers to his authority, faithfulness, or loving provision. In this moment we are reminded again that the wages of sin is always the same: death.

But this is not just a sad passage of holy judgment; it is also a beautiful portrait of God's provision of redeeming grace. Though 14,700 Israelites died, a tool of intervening grace spared the nation from being entirely wiped out. Aaron was the tool of this grace. He literally ran and stood between the dead bodies and those who were alive, with his censer filled with incense, to make atonement for God's people. Priests were never to come near dead bodies for fear of contamination, which would make them unclean and unable to do their priestly duties. But Aaron, as a tool of atoning grace, stood between the living and the dead, rescuing God's people from God's deadly and righteousness anger.

It should be impossible for us to look at Aaron here and not see Jesus. He is the greater Aaron, the Savior who comes to stand between the living and the dead. He not only makes atonement for the sins of his own; he *is* the atoning sacrifice. He not only is the Great High Priest; he is the Lamb of sacrifice. He not only stands between the living and the dead; he dies so that all who place their trust in him will live. Every act of atonement in the Old Testament is a finger pointing us to Jesus. The Old Testament is not simply a series of stories from which we can draw moral lessons. No, it is one story with many chapters. It is the story of the tragedy of sin and the progressive plan of God to provide a once-and-for-all sacrifice for sin, the Lord Jesus Christ.

The story of Numbers 16 confronts us with the fact that God takes sin seriously, and we should too. If sin is not serious, then there is no need for a Savior, but, if it is, then all of humanity is in need of Christ's willingness to stand between the living and the dead and make atonement for sin. There is never a day when you and I are free from our need for his atoning grace.

For further study and encouragement: Isaiah 52:13–53:12

———

FEBRUARY 19

NUMBERS 18–20

Not only is God the ultimate provider, but he is also the ultimate provision.

Nothing gives a person more security and rest of heart than knowing that the King of kings has promised to provide for him. God is the Creator, owner, sustainer, and ruler of all things. Nothing that exists is outside of his command. When he says he will provide, not only does he have the position and power to do so, but his storehouse is limitless. Because his eye is always on his children and his ears are always open to their cries, he never fails to provide just what they need, just when they need it. This is God's faithful commitment to all of his children.

But his promises to Aaron and the Levite priests were different and unique. Because of their priestly duties, they had no means of support and no inheritance in the land. God set up a system of tithing so that what they needed would be provided. Their security was not in this system, however, but in the unique and powerful commitment of the Lord. Note these words in Numbers 18:20: "The LORD said to Aaron, 'You shall have no inheritance in their land, neither shall you have any portion among them. *I am your portion* and your inheritance among the people of Israel.'" These words are meant to instill hope and security. When God says, "I am your portion," he is saying that he is their inheritance and their provider. But there is more. God is saying, in effect, "Your allotment, your portion, of what has been provided is *me*. I am not just your provider; I am the provision. You have hope and security, no matter what, because I, the Lord of heaven and earth, have given myself to you."

You may wonder what this has to do with you. Because of the life, death, and resurrection of Christ, we, God's children by grace, are a "royal priesthood," a "holy nation" (1 Pet. 2:9). By grace we can enter the Holy of Holies and stand before God unafraid. By grace we have been called and welcomed into the service of worship and we present our bodies as living sacrifices before him (Rom. 12:1). We are not just God's adopted children; we are a community of priests before him under the chief priest, Jesus Christ.

Not only does God say to us "I am your portion forever" and make provision for all our needs, but he *is* the ultimate provision. He has given us himself forever. We who were once poor are now rich because God is our inheritance forever. He not only provides for what we need; he is what we most desperately need. This gift is too huge in grace and glory for our limited minds to grasp. In the full range of his glorious glory, God has given himself to us. Could there be any better news than this?

For further study and encouragement: John 6:25–40

FEBRUARY 20

NUMBERS 21–22

God, the righteous Judge, is also a gracious Redeemer. Because sin exists and leads to death, both judgment and atonement are necessary.

You would not want to live in a city where there was no law, no punishment for crime, and no restoration for the criminal. Life in such a city would be dangerous and unbearable. In the same way, you and I should be thankful that God is a perfectly holy Judge who hates sin in all of its forms. You and I should be thankful that sin has consequences and penalties. You and I should be thankful that the one who sits on the throne of the universe takes sin seriously and is angry with sin every day. If God were to turn his back and let sin reign on the earth, we would have no hope. At the same time, you and I should never stop celebrating that, because God is who he is, he not only judges sin but also extends grace for sinners. This is the overarching plot of the biblical story: sin, judgment, and atonement.

That plot plays out in brief form in Numbers 21:4–9. The people of Israel attacked the very character of God: his goodness, his faithfulness, and his commitment to provide. They said they hated where God had led them and loathed what he had provided. There is no way that a holy God who loved his children could have turned his back on this rebellion. So God sent deadly serpents among his people. The serpents were both a discipline and a warning.

But God was not done. He had no intention of wiping out his children. As he disciplined them in righteous anger, he remembered his covenant to them and provided for them a way of escape. He commanded Moses to put a bronze serpent on a pole; those who looked upon it would live. Here again is the great plot of the biblical narrative: sin, judgment, and atonement. But here also is a foreshadowing of where the biblical story is headed. There would be another tree. Nailed to it was not a serpent but the Son of God. He hung there as the atoning sacrifice for my sins and yours (John 3:14–15). We, too, have questioned God's goodness. At times we have loathed what he has provided. We have rebelled against his authority, choosing to follow our own way. We have looked back longingly at the idols that once enslaved us. We deserved God's judgment, but he met us at that tree outside the city walls. His anger with sin and his grace toward the sinner drove Jesus to the cross.

Because of God's unrelenting anger with sin and because of the magnitude of his grace, there will be a day when sin will be no more. There will be no more rebellion. There will be no more questions of his goodness. There will be no more challenges to his authority. And we will be with him in a place of complete peace and righteousness forever. God takes sin seriously, and, because he does, we have hope now and for all of eternity.

For further study and encouragement: Psalm 96:10–13

FEBRUARY 21

NUMBERS 23–25

Hook your past, present, and future to a God who cannot lie.

The "prophet" Balaam is perhaps the most complex, complicated character in the Old Testament. Nothing good is said about this man in all of Scripture. He was probably more of a spiritualist medium than a true Old Testament prophet. He comes onto the scene in Numbers because Balak, king of Moab, was scared to death of the approaching armies of Israel. So he sought out Balaam, to hire him to pronounce curses on Israel. Numbers records four of Balaam's oracles (prophetic utterances). But they were not curses, because God had another plan. Although Balaam had taken the king's money to do his cursing work, Balaam's oracles were blessings. It is a weird but comforting story of how God uses whomever he will to do whatever he wants. Balaam was far from a righteous man, but he became a tool for good in the hands of a sovereign God.

In the middle of his second oracle, Balaam spoke these words of foundational hope and comfort:

> God is not man, that he should lie,
>   or a son of man, that he should change his mind.
> Has he said, and will he not do it?
>   Or has he spoken, and will he not fulfill it?
> Behold, I received a command to bless:
>   he has blessed, and I cannot revoke it.
> He has not beheld misfortune in Jacob,
>   nor has he seen trouble in Israel.
> The LORD their God is with them,
>   and the shout of a king is among them.
> God brings them out of Egypt
>   and is for them like the horns of the wild ox.
> For there is no enchantment against Jacob,
>   no divination against Israel;
> now it shall be said of Jacob and Israel,
>   "What has God wrought!" (Num. 23:19–23)

What King Balak hoped to be a curse became a righteous pronouncement. Balaam essentially said, "Balak, don't you understand? Nothing can stop these people, because God has promised to bless them, he has promised to be with them, and he will allow nothing to be against them. And *he is a God who cannot*

64

lie. What he has promised and what he has declared will be fulfilled." In these words the hope and help of Israel would be found. The God who covenanted himself to unleash his power for the blessing of his people *cannot lie*. Israel and the surrounding kings could be sure that he would do everything he had promised until the nations stood in awe and said, "What has God wrought!"

Remember that those of us who have been chosen by God and have put our faith in Christ are now the inheritors of those covenant promises. Our hope and security are not in the promises, however, but in the character of the one who made them. Our God cannot lie. All he has promised us in and through the life, death, and resurrection of his Son, he will do. And there will be a day when every knee will bow and every tongue will say, in submission and praise, "What has God wrought!"

For further study and encouragement: Titus 1:1–3

———

FEBRUARY 22

NUMBERS 26–27

*God not only blesses us with his great and precious promises,
but he also works by grace to prepare us to hear them.*

Imagine that an attorney informs you that a distant relative has left you an inheritance of property and money larger than you ever dreamed you would have. It's wonderful that you have been granted what you couldn't have achieved or earned on your own. But now you have a problem. How in the world do you manage your newfound wealth? It's one thing to be given an inheritance; it's another thing to be prepared to receive it. You now need property management and investment skills. You need qualified advisers to help handle your inheritance wisely. Imagine that you're in a state of panic, only to discover that your distant relative anticipated your need to receive and use your inheritance wisely, and he made provision for all of the necessary training and counsel.

This is what the final chapters of Numbers are about. God is about to fulfill his commitment to deliver the promised land to Israel, but they need to be prepared. Like a loving father who is about to send his children off on the adventure of a lifetime, God wants to make sure that they are prepared to receive what he promised so long ago. We see in these chapters that God is not distant, uninvolved, or uncaring. This transcendent one is intimately involved with his children. He is actively concerned for their welfare. He will not make promises and walk away. He not only promises; he also prepares. The numbering of the tribes and clans and the appointing of the next generation of leadership are God's preparing his children to receive all that he has promised them (Num. 26–27).

And this is what is happening right here, right now for all of God's children. Because of Christ's work on our behalf, we have been given a future and an inheritance beyond our wildest dreams. The Bible makes it clear that this broken world is our present address—not our final destination. What is going on right now is preparation. God is actively working to mold us into the image of his Son so that we will be ready for the destiny that is ours by grace—a new heaven and perfect new earth. This is how much God loves us. He not only blesses us with things we could have never created on our own, but he also works to prepare us to receive his gifts of grace. So when God takes you where you never intended to go, be thankful; you are being prepared for the awesome destiny that is yours because of the righteous life, the substitutionary death, and the victorious resurrection of Jesus. Your Lord not only promises, but he prepares. And it is a good thing that he does.

For further study and encouragement: Genesis 12:1–3

——

FEBRUARY 23

NUMBERS 28–30

*Hope for God's children is found not in their
remembering him, but in his remembering them.*

I had just spoken at a conference and was in the lobby of the church greeting the attendees, when a man approached me. He came toward me with a big smile on his face, like he knew me and was glad to see me. As he hugged me, he said, "It's so good to see you." His familiarity caught me off guard, because I didn't know who this person was. He clearly knew me and began talking about things he assumed I would remember. But as I searched through my mental file drawers, I couldn't place this man. He could tell I was lost and kindly reintroduced himself to me, jokingly saying he could tell he had really made a big impression on me. As he walked away, I knew he knew that I had no idea who he was. How could I fail to remember someone whom I apparently was supposed to know well?

Numbers 29 describes the blowing of the trumpets at the beginning of the holy convocation on the first day of the seventh month. The blowing of the trumpets was much more than an announcement that the convocation was beginning; it did more than call the children of Israel to attention. The blowing of the trumpets was a prayer, a specific and important prayer (see Num. 10:10). The trumpets were not blown for the people; they were blown to the Lord. The sound of the trumpet was a prayer for God to remember his people, and in remembering them to continue to guide, protect, and provide for them. The present security and the future hope of Israel rested on one foundation: that God would remember his people and all the promises he had made to them concerning his presence, his provision, his protection, and his forgiving grace. The children of Israel had no ability to control what they needed to be controlled, to conquer what needed to be conquered, or to provide what needed to be provided. They were wholly dependent on the Lord's remembering them and, in remembering them, working on their behalf. They would never grow into independence but would always need to rely on God's remembering and providing grace.

When God calls us to himself, he doesn't put us in a process that moves from dependence to independence. Christian maturity is not about independence, but about a growing willingness to be wholly dependent on the providing grace of the Savior. We can depend on him because we know that God never forgets or loses track of any of his children. With a loving heart he remembers all that he has promised us in Christ, and, because he does, we have both hope and help right now and a secure future waiting for us. It's good to always remember your Lord, but it is glorious to know that he always remembers you.

For further study and encouragement: Isaiah 49:8–16

———

FEBRUARY 24

NUMBERS 31–32

Our sins are never secret, because they never escape the watchful eye of the Lord.

Scripture tells us that sin is deceitful. We are often deceived into believing two lies, as we step outside of God's boundaries and do what he has forbidden. The first lie is that no one will know. That may be true of the people near us.

You can hide your sin so that those around you are unaware. But our sin is never hidden from the eyes of the Lord. His eyes are always on his children. You and I will never escape to a place where he is unable to see what we are doing. Hidden sin is a delusion. The second lie is that we can sin without consequences. I have sat with many adulterous men, with marriages in shambles, and thought to myself, "Where did you think this story was going? How long did you think you could have a relationship with a woman other than your wife and still have a healthy marriage?" I am amazed, in my own life and in counseling others, at our ability to convince ourselves that things are okay that are not and never will be okay.

Numbers 32:23 contains eight words of warning that not only were important for Israel, but are vital for us to hear as well: "Be sure your sin will find you out." Moses spoke these words because God had not only blessed Israel with the land of promise, but he had also called them to fight in his power to drive out all the enemy nations. The tribes of Gad and Rueben decided they didn't want to fight, so they settled outside of the promised land. This was not just an act of cowardice; it was direct rebellion against the commands of the Lord. What were they thinking? Did they actually think that God wouldn't care, or that he would say, "Okay, have it your way." God always sees, and he will never accommodate us by compromising his holy commands. Did the tribes of Gad and Rueben think that their refusal to do what God commanded wouldn't have consequences?

These words have been recorded and preserved for us by our loving heavenly Father. They have been recorded for us as a defense against sin's deceit. Just as with the tribes of Gad and Rueben, our sin is never secret or without consequences. It's wonderful to know that our Lord meets us in our weakness and not only warns us but also empowers us to live inside of his boundaries. It is encouraging to see that God's warning to Gad and Reuben was not in vain. They did finally heed God's warning and obey his command. It is also good to know that rather than hiding, because of the completeness of Christ's work on our behalf we can run to him, confessing our sin and receiving his forgiveness once again. Sin is deceitful, but God's grace is up to the task; it will expose sin's lies again and again until we're on the other side and sin is no more.

For further study and encouragement: Proverbs 15:3

FEBRUARY 25

*There is always a danger that the surrounding culture will
weaken your trust in and daily submission to your Savior.*

Most believers in Jesus Christ now deal with the pervasive influence of social media, a catalog of streaming services, and the twenty-four-hour infotainment cycle. We are constantly under the influence of voices that do not speak from a biblical perspective and have rejected the confrontation and comfort of the gospel of Jesus Christ. It's naive to think that, while our lives are dominated by a flood of constant noise, we are unchanged by them. I am convinced that the enemy of our souls will gladly give us our formal theology and our regular worship services, if he can control the thoughts and desires of our hearts at street level. Many of us can't be quiet for thirty seconds before pulling out our phones. Many us of reach for a digital device as soon as we wake up and check in with that device just before we go to bed. Are we aware that we have been changed, and are we grappling with the nature of that change?

What is culture? Here's my best answer. Human beings made in the image of God interact with God's world, and culture is what results. God's people have always lived in the midst of culture and its influence. So it makes sense that, as Israel enters the promised land, God gives them this stern but loving warning: "If you do not drive out the inhabitants of the land from before you, then those of them whom you let remain shall be as barbs in your eyes and thorns in your sides, and they shall trouble you in the land where you dwell" (Num. 33:55). These are the words of a jealous God who is unwilling to surrender to other gods the hearts of those he has set his love on and whom he has guided, protected, and provided for. He knows that his children have wandering hearts. They have demonstrated that they often have more allegiance to their own comfort than to his will. In light of the magnitude of God's love for them, they have at times been disloyal, even willing to question God's wisdom, faithfulness, and love.

All this means that, no matter how faithful God's people are in honoring the sacrificial and holy-day systems that God has laid out for them, their hearts are susceptible to wandering away from God and his plan for them. So God warns them against the danger of not driving out these pagan nations, of settling among them, of progressively assimilating their culture, and ultimately of serving their gods.

Although we are in a very different place than the children of Israel, this warning rings true for us today. We need Jesus's protecting grace so we can continue to seek and celebrate that very same grace, even though the story of this grace is seldom reinforced by the culture we live in. The warning in Numbers is repeated near the end of the biblical story: "Do not love the world or the things in the world. If anyone loves the world, the love of the Father is not in him" (1 John 2:15).

For further study and encouragement: 1 John 2:15–17

FEBRUARY 26

NUMBERS 35–36

It is vital to remember that Jesus is not just your Savior. Between your conversion and your homegoing, he is your refuge as well.

God's attributes never work in conflict with one another. His love does not weaken or negate his holiness. His justice does not derail his mercy. His sovereign plan does not work in conflict with his tender, patient heart. We see this clearly in Numbers 35:34: "You shall not defile the land in which you live, in the midst of which I dwell, for I the LORD dwell in the midst of the people of Israel." In these words we see the Lord's holy justice and patient mercy working in cooperation. Let me explain.

Note these words earlier in Numbers 35:

> The LORD spoke to Moses, saying, "Speak to the people of Israel and say to them, When you cross the Jordan into the land of Canaan, then you shall select cities to be cities of refuge for you, that the manslayer who kills any person without intent may flee there. The cities shall be for you a refuge from the avenger, that the manslayer may not die until he stands before the congregation for judgment." (35:9–12)

Now compare the two passages I have quoted and note that two things from the heart of God are operating here. First, God is uncompromisingly holy and will not have the land in which he dwells defiled by sin that is not properly dealt with. But that is not the only thing happening here. A city of refuge would provide mercy for the accused, a place where he could flee and stay until given a just trial. Although confined to a city of refuge, he would not be driven out of the land but, in mercy, could remain and be properly tried for his offense. In the creation of the cities of refuge, we see God's holiness and mercy acting not in conflict with one another but in perfect cooperation. In the cooperation of divine holiness and mercy we find hope right now, and hope to come.

We see God's holiness and mercy working in beautiful cooperation in a later account, too. The entire biblical narrative marches to a hill outside of the city, where, on a rough-hewn cross, God's uncompromising holiness and tender mercy would meet. The cross was necessary because God would not turn his back on the idolatry and rebellion of sin and act as if sin's offenses against him were okay. But the cross was necessary also because the God of mercy promised to provide a way for sinners to be forgiven and reconciled to him. This means that we, too, have a city of refuge to which we can run. Our city of refuge is not a place but a person, and his name is Jesus. It is beautiful to know that Jesus met all of God's holy requirements on our behalf and paid the penalty for our sin so that he could be a refuge for sinners like you and me.

For further study and encouragement: Nahum 1:6–9

FEBRUARY 27

DEUTERONOMY 1–2

You are in spiritual danger when you are able to convince yourself that God is not enough.

After setting his love on them and taking them as his own . . .
After unleashing his power to deliver them from slavery in Egypt . . .
After miraculously parting the Red Sea and defeating Egypt . . .
After thunderously giving the law at Mount Sinai . . .
After resting his glory cloud on the tabernacle . . .
After guiding his people with the cloud by day and the pillar of fire by night . . .
After providing daily manna to sustain them . . .
After all of God's mighty display that he was with Israel to guide, protect, and provide, the people of Israel are now separated from the promised land by just a mere river, and they refuse to go in because of the opposing forces there. This is much more than a military calculation based on information from surveillance of the land. No, the refusal of Israel is deeply spiritual. After all of God's displays of power and glory, his people stand looking at the land that has been promised to them and conclude that God is not enough. Their rebellious refusal to enter the promised land and fight battles in the power of the Lord is rooted in

unbelief. Unbelief is the ultimate rebellion. It gives you reason not to embrace God's promises or submit to his commands. Unbelief blames rebellion on God; that is, it asserts that he is not enough and has not done enough.

Pay careful attention to these words from Moses's first sermon in Deuteronomy.

> "The LORD your God who goes before you will himself fight for you, just as he did for you in Egypt before your eyes, and in the wilderness, where you have seen how the LORD your God carried you, as a man carries his son, all the way that you went until you came to this place." Yet in spite of this word you did not believe the LORD your God, who went before you in the way to seek you out a place to pitch your tents, in fire by night and in the cloud by day, to show you by what way you should go. (Deut. 1:30–33)

Let these words sink in: "The LORD your God carried you, as a man carries his son." This is how faithful, tender, and complete the guidance, care, and protection of the Lord were over his Israelite children. But Moses said that, in the face of all God had done, Israel still refused to believe that he would unleash his power to deliver the land he had promised.

The Savior of Israel is our Savior as well. In his incarnation, his miraculous ministry, his righteous life, his substitutionary death, his victorious resurrection, the miracle of his ascension, and the gift of his indwelling Spirit, he has shown us that he will do all that is needed to give us all he has promised. Yet, in the face of this display of redeeming grace, a question remains. Today, as you face opposition and trial, will you conclude that your Savior is not enough?

For further study and encouragement: 2 Corinthians 12:9–10

FEBRUARY 28

DEUTERONOMY 3–4

Sin is fundamentally idolatrous. It always puts something in God's place as the functional ruler of your heart.

It was weird and creepy to me. I didn't want to be there. I wanted to run outside and escape the spiritual darkness that enveloped that place. I was looking down at a Hindu priest, lying flat on his stomach with his arms and legs stretched out. He was lying in a posture of complete surrender and submission before an idol carved out of wood by human hands. He seemed to be emotional and in awe. It seemed as if he stayed in that position for an eternity. I wanted to yell at him, "It's just a piece of wood!" I wanted to reach down and yank him off the floor. I wondered what it would take to convince him that this idol was not a god, that it could do him neither harm nor good because it lacked life. The harm came from surrendering his heart, life, hopes, and dreams to this inanimate object.

In this sin-scarred world, which does not function as God intended, idolatry is a very-present danger. Idolatry is not just about how an idolatrous culture influences us; it is a matter of the heart. As long as artifacts of sin are still present in us, our hearts will be prone to wander. Idolatry always credits something other than God for what only God can do, causing us, then, to surrender to it our thoughts, desires, choices, and actions. The catalog of potential God-replacements is endless.

So it makes sense that as Israel entered the promised land, Moses warned them against this clear and present danger:

> Watch yourselves very carefully. Since you saw no form on the day that the LORD spoke to you at Horeb out of the midst of the fire, beware lest you act corruptly by making a carved image for yourselves, in the form of any figure, the likeness of male or female, the likeness of any animal that is on the earth, the likeness of any winged bird that flies in the air, the likeness of anything that creeps on the ground, the likeness of any fish that is in the water under the earth. And beware lest you raise your eyes to heaven, and when you see the sun and the moon and the stars, all the host of heaven, you be drawn away and bow down to them and serve them . . . Take care, lest you forget the covenant of the LORD your God, which he made with you, and make a carved image, the form of anything that the LORD your God has forbidden you. For the LORD your God is a consuming fire, a jealous God. (Deut. 4:15–19, 23–24)

The danger of surrendering our hearts to something other than the Lord is as great for us as it was for the children of Israel. May we be warned and comforted by the holy jealousy of our Lord, who will not share our hearts with anyone or anything. And may we remember that Jesus came to free us from idols, so we would bask in the freedom and blessings of what he is for us and what he will provide for us.

For further study and encouragement: Jeremiah 2:26–28

MARCH 1

God's commands are wisdom-drenched gifts of divine love. It would be foolish to resist their protecting and directing beauty.

God did not give his law as a means of gaining his acceptance; his standard is too lofty, too holy. No, God's law was a gift to those he had already chosen to love, so that they would know how to live and, in following his commands, thrive. That's why the psalmist can exult, "Oh how I love your law!" (Ps. 119:97). The words that follow are my celebration of the gift of God's commands and the grace that empowers us to love and keep them.

God's law is
perfect,
holy,
righteous,
good.
It is God's
gracious,
loving,
wise,
tender welcome
to the good life,
where sinful impulses
are restrained,
where we are protected
from our wandering hearts,
where we learn to live
as our Creator designed us to live.
God's protective boundaries,
the fences of his law,
are an expression of his love.
These laws have been given
not to earn his love,
but as a gift of grace
to those he has chosen
to love.
In an ever-changing
world—
valleys deep,
mountains high,
woods dark,
enemies abounding,
temptations whispering—
there is security
in God's unchanging law.
There simply is nothing to add
to his holy and righteous
commands.
Who would've thought,
who could've ever conceived,
who had the wisdom to design
such a plan,
such purpose,
such a moral structure
for human
help,
hope,
thriving?
It's an act of
arrogance,
confusion,
rebellion,
foolishness
to subtract things
from God's holy and loving

moral plan for us.
So settle in,
believe that God
always knows what is best,
and pray for grace
to surrender your

thoughts,
desires,
choices,
words,
actions,
to him.

For further study and encouragement: Psalm 1:1–6

———

MARCH 2

DEUTERONOMY 8–10

*Of all the things your mind needs to remember, nothing
is more important than remembering God.*

It was the morning of my first job. I was sixteen years old and very nervous. If you had asked me, I'm not sure I could have remembered my name. My dad had filled me with all kinds of advice about how to work, how to relate to my fellow workers, and how to relate to my bosses. I was clueless as to what I was facing, because I had never had a real job before. As I was about to leave my house, my dad stopped me and said, "Remember who you are representing." He didn't mean himself, or our family. No, he was reminding me that I represented the Lord. He had saved that bit of advice for last, because he wanted me to drive to my newfound world of work with this paramount issue in mind.

Of all the many laws God gave to his children, *the commandment to remember him* was perhaps the most important. If he was not at the center of all they thought, desired, said, and did, then they would not live in a way that pleased him, and their forgetful hearts would be susceptible to the allure of the idols of the nations around them. So Moses instructed the people:

Take care lest you forget the LORD your God by not keeping his commandments and his rules and his statutes, which I command you today, lest, when you have eaten and are full and have built good houses and live in them, and when your herds and flocks multiply and your silver and gold is multiplied and all that you have is multiplied, then your heart be lifted up, and you forget the LORD your God, who brought you out of the land of Egypt, out of the house of slavery. (Deut. 8:11–14)

Do everything you can not to forget me.
Do everything you can not to forget how I brought you out of slavery.
Do everything you can not to forget how I gave you my law.
Do everything you can not to forget how I chose to dwell in your midst.
Do everything you can not to forget how I sustained you in the wilderness.
Do everything you can to remember me.

When we are walking through the wilderness of life, feeling weak and dependent, we tend to remember and cry out to the Lord. But as Deuteronomy 8 warns, it is in seasons of comfort and ease that our minds become forgetful and our hearts begin to wander. May God give us the grace to remember our Lord and the magnitude of how he continues to bless us in his Son, the Lord Jesus Christ. And in remembering, may we worship and serve him with joy.

For further study and encouragement: 2 Timothy 2:8–10

———

MARCH 3

DEUTERONOMY 11–13

No blindness is more debilitating and life-shaping than spiritual blindness.

I used to think that no one knew me better than I knew myself. I looked at myself through the carnival mirror of my self-righteousness. When approached about a sin, weakness, or failure, I would list evidence of what a righteous man I was. I was defensive and self-protective, clearly more concerned about the sin of others than my own. I didn't know I was blind, because spiritually blind people are blind to their blindness. Even when Luella confronted me, I felt misunderstood and misjudged. I was headed for disaster and didn't know it until God, by grace, gave me eyes to see.

Deuteronomy 1–30 records for us three sermons preached by Moses to prepare the children of Israel for what they would face in the promised land. In those sermons no warning is more important than what we read in Deuteronomy 11:16: "Take care lest your heart be deceived, and you turn aside and serve other gods and worship them." This is and has always been a great danger to any child of God living in this fallen world. As long as sin remains in the world and as long as it still lives within us, our hearts are susceptible to being deceived. As the father counsels his son in Proverbs 4:23:

> Keep your heart with all vigilance,
> for from it flow the springs of life.

This is the best advice a father can give a son. The heart is the center of our thoughts, emotions, and will; it is the control center of our personhood. Whatever controls our heart will then control our choices, words, and actions. This means that the body will only ever go where the heart has already gone. The most dangerous aspect of the operation of sin is its ability to deceive. Sin is a liar. What it tells us is never true. It paints what is ugly as beautiful. It tells us that what God says is morally wrong isn't so bad after all. Moses warns that an even greater danger than the presence of physical idols is a deceived heart that would cause you to serve them.

Notice how sin works in Deuteronomy 11:16. It deceives us into believing its lies, and because we believe these lies, we turn away from God. And because we turn away from God, we end up worshiping and serving false gods. Sin's deception always leads to idolatry of some kind. Sin woos us to surrender the control of our hearts to something other than God. Moses's warning has been preserved for us because the danger of spiritual blindness is as great today as it's ever been. But we remember that Jesus is the light of the world, who came to give sight to blind eyes. When touched by his convicting grace, we are blessed to see ourselves with accuracy, to turn from sin's lies, to resist sin's allure, and to run to God for protecting and empowering grace. Yes, sin's deception is a great danger, but God's grace is greater.

For further study and encouragement: John 9:39–41

———

MARCH 4

DEUTERONOMY 14–16

*We see the beauty of the tenderness of the Lord
in his compassion for the poor.*

Philadelphia, where I have lived since 1987, has a homelessness problem. Thousands of homeless men and women live on the streets of my city. I encounter them almost everywhere I go. Sometimes they are begging for money, sometimes they have taken over a sidewalk with a temporary dwelling, sometimes they are angry and threatening, and sometimes they are asleep in a doorway or over the warmth of a grate. I wish I could say that I always meet them with compassion in my heart, but I can't. Sometimes I see them as a nuisance, in the way of what I want to do, and sometimes they make me angry. My problem isn't that homeless people exist; my problem is the coldness and selfishness of my heart. This means that I am not yet at the spiritual place where my heart mirrors the heart of my Lord.

That is why the following directives God gives Israel through Moses are instructive for me:

> If among you, one of your brothers should become poor, in any of your towns within your land that the LORD your God is giving you, you shall not harden your heart or shut your hand against your poor brother, but you shall open your hand to him and lend him sufficient for his need, whatever it may be. Take care lest there be an unworthy thought in your heart and you say, "The seventh year, the year of release is near," and your eye look grudgingly on your poor brother, and you give him nothing, and he cry to the LORD against you, and you be guilty of sin. You shall give to him freely, and your heart shall not be grudging when you give to him, because for this the LORD your God will bless you in all your work and in all that you undertake. For there will never cease to be poor in the land. Therefore I command you, "You shall open wide your hand to your brother, to the needy and to the poor, in your land." (Deut. 15:7–11)

Pay attention to God's compassion-call to Israel:

> "You shall not harden your heart . . . against your poor brother."
> "Take care lest there be any unworthy thought in your heart."
> "Your heart shall not be grudging when you give to him."
> "You shall give to him freely."
> "There will never cease to be poor in the land."
> "Open wide your hand . . . to the needy and to the poor."

Imagine what would happen if we acted with the compassion portrayed in God's call to Israel. Think of how our response to the poor would change if we remembered the words of the apostle Paul: "You know the grace of our Lord Jesus Christ, that though he was rich, yet for your sake he became poor, so that you by his poverty might become rich" (2 Cor. 8:9).

For further study and encouragement: Matthew 25:31–40

MARCH 5

*We should never underestimate the magnificent, life-giving
blessing that is ours by the fact that God speaks to us.*

It doesn't take long in the biblical narrative for God to speak. After creating everything by the power of his word, God speaks directly to Adam and Eve (Gen. 1:27–28). Here are perfect people in a perfect world, with a perfect relationship to God, yet they are completely dependent on his words to make sense out of life, to be what he designed them to be, and to do what he created them to do. Shalom is shattered early in the redemptive story, when Adam and Eve decide to disobey the words of their Creator, to take their lives into their own hands, and to step outside of the boundaries that God had set for them.

If Adam and Eve, in perfection, were completely dependent on the word of the Lord, how much more were the children of Israel? They lived in a world full of evil, where lies abounded. They were about to enter a place where false gods would greet them at every turn and where magicians, sorcerers, and divinators would vie for their attention. They needed the true, pure, and trustworthy word of the Lord to cut through all the noise of false voices, so that they would not be deceived but would live as God had called them to live. It was a huge blessing, then, that God promised them not just one prophet, but a continuing line of prophet after prophet, so that God's truth and will would guide, protect, and correct them.

> The LORD your God will raise up for you a prophet like me from among you, from your brothers—it is to him you shall listen— just as you desired of the LORD your God at Horeb on the day of the assembly, when you said, "Let me not hear again the voice of the LORD my God or see this great fire any more, lest I die." And the LORD said to me, "They are right in what they have spoken. I will raise up for them a prophet like you from among their brothers. And I will put my words in his mouth, and he shall speak to them all that I command him." (Deut. 18:15–18)

What protecting, guiding, and correcting love! This promise means that God's people will never be without the word of the Lord, no matter who they are, no matter where they are, and no matter what they might face. As I read these words, I think of myself. I wouldn't have a clue as to who I am, without the word of the Lord. I wouldn't know how to live, without God's word. I wouldn't know what is true or false, apart from God's word. I would have no wisdom to offer were it not for the word of the Lord. I wouldn't know how to live with others, how to make decisions, or where to look for spiritual help and hope, were it not for the word of God. It's hard to think of a more important promise than this. And remember, this is a messianic promise. Jesus is God's final Word to us; his words and work are life to us.

For further study and encouragement: Hebrews 1:1–2

MARCH 6

DEUTERONOMY 21–23

The biblical story marches slowly to a man hanging on a tree: Jesus, who died as our substitute, the perfect sacrificial Lamb.

I wake up every morning with hope and joy. It's not because I always feel great. As I write this, I am in unrelenting pain. Something has happened to my back, which makes everything I do painful. Getting out of a chair is torturous. Riding in a car is agonizing. But my hope and joy are not diminished. My hope is not based on what God has called me to do. It does not rely upon people's opinions of me or my financial security. My hope is not based on the fact that I am married to my hero or that I have four wonderful children. My hope really does look back to a tree, outside of the walls of an ancient city, where an innocent man willingly suffered the cruelest and most humiliating kind of death, crucifixion, for the sake of my forgiveness, my reconciliation to God, my adoption into his family, and my eternal place with him in glory. Jesus is my hope. Jesus is the source of my joy. His work on my behalf, his presence, and his grace—not my suffering, my work, or my family—define me. My chronic pain does not make me angry or bitter, because I am daily blown away by the knowledge of what he has done for me and of who I am in him.

In Deuteronomy 21 God gives directions for how to deal with a man who has committed a capital crime, that is, one punishable by death. Such a person is to be hanged on a tree. It's a hard passage to read, but it is there for our guidance and protection. This passage sits in the Old Testament to remind us that God takes sin seriously, so we better take it seriously too. In order to have a relationship with his people, God never ignores or minimizes sin. This passage has been retained to remind us that something has to happen that will allow sinners to have a relationship with a perfectly holy God.

Deuteronomy 21:22–23 points us to two trees. First, it looks back to the tree in the garden of Eden, where temptation and sin first entered the world and separated people from their Creator. Second, it looks forward to that tree on the hill of Golgotha, where Jesus willingly suffered and died for our justification and eternal adoption into the family of God. In Deuteronomy, one man hangs because of his sin; on Calvary, one man hangs for the sins of others. In Deuteronomy, one man suffers the penalty for his iniquity; on Calvary one man pays the penalty for multitudes. One tree is a tree of death; the other tree is, ultimately, a tree of life. On one tree hangs a man who has no hope; on the other tree a man's death gives eternal hope to a countless company of sinners.

We have hope because of what Jesus did on that tree, and because of what he continues to do for us with mercies that are new every day.

For further study and encouragement: 1 Peter 1:13–21

MARCH 7

DEUTERONOMY 24–27

We should never give God what is left over, but rather offer him the first and best of what he has provided.

We have to look back to creation to understand fully the importance of Deuteronomy 26:1–2:

> When you come into the land that the LORD your God is giving you for an inheritance and have taken possession of it and live in it, you shall take some of the first of all the fruit of the ground, which you harvest from your land that the LORD your God is giving you, and you shall put it in a basket, and you shall go to the place that the LORD your God will choose, to make his name to dwell there.

Genesis 1 and 2 tell us that God is the Creator of everything. As the Creator of everything, he owns everything. I am a painter. After I have gone to my studio and completed a painting, it belongs to me, because I made it. God, as Creator, is the rightful owner of all that is. This means he owns me and everything that I am and have. Nothing belongs to me; it all belongs to him.

As the Creator of everything, God not only owns everything, but he also determines everything's *purpose*. If you sit down to sew a garment, you don't start aimlessly, hoping that your sewing will turn into something. No, you sit down with a distinct purpose in mind. You make every stitch to accomplish that purpose. God not only owns everything, but he also has a purpose for everything he has created.

So when God asks his children to give him the firstfruits of their crops, he is not asking them to take what belongs to them and give it to him. He is asking them to return to him a portion of what already belongs to him. Nothing we own is ours to use however we choose to use it. It all belongs to God, and is to be stewarded as he directs. Now, this is important to understand: God does not want whatever is left over after we have satisfied ourselves with the fruit of our work. God wants us to make our offering to him first. When we do so, we acknowledge that all we are and all we have belong to him to be used as he pleases.

God is protecting his children from the idol of possession. He knows that the acquiring and maintaining of material things and the pleasure they give can rule our hearts and shape how we live. There's grace in this command to offer God our firstfruits. God is rescuing us from us, so that we can know the joy of worshiping the Creator rather than living in bondage to the creation. He made us. We belong to him. He is where true life is to be found. So, offer him your first and your best. You'll be glad you did.

For further study and encouragement: Genesis 4:1–7

———

MARCH 8

DEUTERONOMY 28–29

*Your physical eyes can be wide open even while
the eyes of your heart are sadly blind.*

During my time in seminary, Luella and I were houseparents at a school for the blind. We lived with about fifteen boys who either had been blind from birth or had become blind due to some kind of accident. We experienced firsthand the enormity of this physical deficit. We saw how it impacted every area of our boys' lives. We also witnessed the brilliant things our boys were taught so that they could do almost everything a sighted boy could do.

But there is a set of eyes dramatically more important than your physical eyes. A human being's most important sight comes from the eyes of the heart. Spiritual blindness is a life-destroying tragedy. If you are physically blind, you can forge a fairly normal existence, doing in your own way the things that sighted people do. But you cannot be spiritually blind and live well.

Hear the words of Moses:

Moses summoned all Israel and said to them: "You have seen all that the LORD did before your eyes in the land of Egypt, to Pharaoh and to all his servants and to all his land, the great trials that your eyes saw, the signs, and those great wonders. But to this day the LORD has not given you a heart to understand or eyes to see or ears to hear." (Deut. 29:2–4)

Moses makes a distinction that is important to understand. He points to a fault line that divides humanity. He says the Israelites saw with their physical eyes all that God had done for them, but they did not see these great wonders with the eyes of their heart. You can see and be blind at the same time. God's children saw the mighty wonders God had performed on their behalf, but they did not see (understand) the full spiritual significance of those wonders. Moses explains why they were blind to the spiritual glories behind the physical glories. When you are born, your physical eyes open; progressively, you gain clear vision. But it takes an act of divine grace to open the eyes of your heart to deep and wonderful spiritual mysteries.

Apart from an act of divine grace opening your eyes, you can look at wonderful things in creation but not see the glory of the one who has designed those things and set them in place. Without being visited by eye-opening grace, you can read the words on the physical page of the Bible but not understand the spiritual realities those words reveal.

If your eyes are open to the glories of God in creation and the spiritual mysteries revealed in God's word, know that you have been visited by divine grace. God has done for you what you could have never done for yourself. He has opened the eyes of your heart so that you would see him in all his glory, know his redeeming fullness, and surrender your life to him. It is an eternally glorious thing to be visited by the divine optometrist.

For further study and encouragement: Mark 8:22–26

Strength for the believer is not an independent accomplishment
but rather the result of the presence and power of God.

Though the life, ministry, and leadership of Moses comes to an end, God does not leave his children leaderless. He raises up leader after leader, until the train of God-appointed leaders culminates with the Messiah, Jesus Christ. As you work your way through the Old Testament, you encounter three kinds of leaders God raises up and through whom he guides his children. Leading Israel are prophets, priests, and kings. These three offices would be fulfilled by Jesus, who is the final and eternal prophet, priest, and king for the children of God.

At the end of Deuteronomy, God's people are in a significant moment of transition. They are preparing to enter the promised land—but without Moses. Who will fill the vacuum that Moses leaves behind? What kind of man will be able to deal with the grumbling, complaining, fearful, God-doubting, and often rebellious Israelites? Who will be able to handle the internal trouble in the Israelite camp, while at the same time leading them to conquer the nations that inhabit the promised land? Who can do this with hope and courage?

God appoints Joshua as the next leader of the Israelite children, but not because Joshua is a giant among men. God does not employ people in his work because they are able, but because he is infinitely able. Listen to the words that accompany Joshua's calling:

> Then Moses summoned Joshua and said to him in the sight of all Israel, "Be strong and courageous, for you shall go with this people into the land that the LORD has sworn to their fathers to give them, and you shall put them in possession of it. It is the LORD who goes before you. He will be with you; he will not leave you or forsake you. Do not fear or be dismayed." (Deut. 31:7–8)

It is clear that God doesn't choose Joshua because he is independent, strong, and capable. Then why can Moses say to Joshua, "Be strong and courageous"? Here is why: Moses understands the promises, resources, and power of the Lord. God never sends his children to do a task without going with them. When God sends his children, he doesn't leave his promises behind. When God sends his children to do his work, he empowers them to do the work he has called them to do. When God sends his children, he never turns his back on them or leaves them to the small resources of their own strength. God's children can go forward fearlessly, doing what God has called them to do, for one reason only: he is with them in his glorious presence and power.

The promises of God's presence and power are fulfilled in Jesus Christ, who took on flesh and exercised his power to do what we never could have done on our own—that is, defeat the enemies of sin and death. Remember: as you do what God calls you to do, you are never alone.

For further study and encouragement: Isaiah 40:28–31

———

MARCH 10

DEUTERONOMY 32–34

No one is like our God. Nothing compares to him. He is glorious beyond our ability to comprehend.

For a few summers I was a chaplain at a camp in the middle of Pennsylvania. The camp's ministry philosophy was to blow the campers away with the stunning glory of God in creation and give them an introduction to the glory of God as Savior. I loved my time there, as did my family. The camp was located in a valley between two mountain ranges. One afternoon I sat on the porch of the main building that overlooked the valley, and I watched dark clouds rise over the mountains as a storm began to build. In a few minutes the clouds broke, thunder roared, and lightning seemed to be everywhere. Rain came down with power like I had never seen before. I was transfixed, glued to my seat by the scary, thunderous glory I was viewing. The storm passed over us as quickly as it had risen, the sky brightened, and we could hear claps of thunder in the distance as the storm dumped its glory on another valley. Those of us on the porch spontaneously applauded. We were all blown away by the power we had just experienced, but our applause was about something deeper. We knew that what we had seen was a minute glimpse of the glorious glory of the God behind the storm.

Moses's final act as the great leader of the children of Israel was to pronounce a blessing on each of the tribes of Israel. The great prayer/poem of Deuteronomy 33 builds to this crescendo:

There is none like God, O Jeshurun,
    who rides through the heavens to your help,

through the skies in his majesty.
The eternal God is your dwelling place,
   and underneath are the everlasting arms.
And he thrust out the enemy before you
   and said, "Destroy."
So Israel lived in safety,
   Jacob lived alone,
in a land of grain and wine,
   whose heavens drop down dew.
Happy are you, O Israel! Who is like you,
   a people saved by the LORD. (Deut. 33:26–29)

Moses had witnessed incredible displays of divine glory. He had seen God unleash his power to deliver, protect, provide for, and guide the children of Israel.
From the plagues in Egypt, to the water walls of the Red Sea, to the glory display
on Sinai, to the cloud and pillar of fire, and finally to manna on the ground every
morning, God had displayed his glory on behalf of Israel. Moses summarized all
he had experienced with these two exultant statements: "There is none like God"
and "Happy are you, O Israel! Who is like you, a people saved by the LORD."

May we who have experienced the redeeming grace of Christ Jesus start each
morning with this twofold declaration: "There is no God like my God" and
"I am happy today because I am among that great company of people who have
been saved by the Lord."

For further study and encouragement: Psalm 86:8–13

———

MARCH 11

JOSHUA 1–4

*There is no greater act of courage than to obey the law of God, no
matter the opposition, the rejection, or the hardships you face.*

From age ten until about fourteen, I was obsessed with reading automobile-
racing stories. It didn't matter what kind of racing, or whether the story was
about race cars or race-car drivers. I was taken by the bravery of the drivers who
committed themselves to this perilous sport. They faced dangerous conditions,
endured physical injuries, and overcame discouraging defeats, but they never

gave up. As an awkward middle schooler, I was amazed by their courage, and I wondered if I would have that kind of courage when I grew up.

God had chosen Joshua to lead Israel. This man would need loads of courage to accomplish what God had called him to do. Joshua had been chosen to lead a difficult, often discontented people who were known to turn on their leader if they didn't like what they were experiencing. Joshua had been chosen to lead this group of people across the Jordan and into battle against the nations inhabiting the promised land. He had been called to be a wartime general leading an unhappy army into battle after battle. He would need courage for the internal and external battles he would face. I think it's important to recognize and understand how God defines that courage:

> Only be strong and very courageous, being careful to do according to all the law that Moses my servant commanded you. Do not turn from it to the right hand or to the left, that you may have good success wherever you go. This Book of the Law shall not depart from your mouth, but you shall meditate on it day and night, so that you may be careful to do according to all that is written in it. For then you will make your way prosperous, and then you will have good success. Have I not commanded you? Be strong and courageous. Do not be frightened, and do not be dismayed, for the LORD your God is with you wherever you go. (Josh. 1:7–9)

God defines courage as obeying his law no matter what, never allowing yourself to stray away from it to the right or to the left. We are to bathe in God's law day and night, so that it controls the thoughts of our minds and the desires of our hearts. As I read Joshua's commission, conviction sets in and the Spirit leads me to confess that I often fall short of God's standard. But I am not without hope, because a greater Joshua was sent to us. He was perfectly courageous on our behalf. He went about his mission to defeat sin and death, facing opposition, rejection, and torment of soul and body, yet he never wavered. He perfectly measured up to God's standard of courage. We now stand before God as righteous because of the courageous righteousness of Jesus. That's very good news.

For further study and encouragement: Acts 5:17–42

MARCH 12

*What do you do when the thing that God is
calling you to do seems absurd?*

It really is true that God's thoughts are not like our thoughts and his ways are very different from our ways.

I sat in my chair during a difficult and painful recovery from a surgery I had hoped to avoid. I was so weak that I could barely get out of that chair. I sat there doing nothing because medications had scrambled my brain enough that I couldn't do the writing I thought God had called me to do. It seemed absurd that at the moment of what I thought was my greatest gospel influence, I had been weakened almost to immobility and my world had shrunk to this chair in our loft in Philadelphia. On a human level, it didn't make any sense. I knew God wasn't toying with me. I knew him to be present, faithful, and right in every way. But I was impressed with the seeming absurdity of the moment.

Having read through the biblical narrative over the course of my life, I am tempted to write a book called *Divine Absurdities*. Please don't misunderstand the title. I don't think that God, in the complete perfection of his wisdom, ever thinks, says, or does anything absurd. But there are moments when God asks us to do something that, at a human level, seems absurd; that is, it's so hard for us to make sense of it that it leaves us confused or a bit scared. Biblical faith calls us to persevere through what may seem absurd and to hold on to our belief that God is holy and wise, that all of his ways are good, right, and true. If you stop at the absurd, you will abandon God's call and turn and run the other way.

Joshua 6 invites us to witness one of those seemingly absurd moments. God calls his children not to attack thick-walled Jericho with military strategy but to parade around it for seven days. On a human level, this doesn't make any sense. It seems like an act of military suicide. But God has a plan. On the seventh day, after the seventh time around the city, the Israelites blow their trumpets and scream at the top of their lungs. The walls collapse and the city is sacked. God's plan was to give his children a victory that they could not take credit for and, in so doing, to instill in them the belief that he would be present with them and that they would fight their battles in the promised land in his almighty power. The absurd was not absurd, but rather a gift of God's grace and glory.

The biblical narrative marches toward another moment that seems absurd. It seems absurd that the entire hope of humanity would rest on God becoming a man, living a perfect life, dying a substitutionary death, rising from the dead, and ascending in victory to sit at the right hand of the Father. But it wasn't absurd; it was the perfect plan, conceived before the earth began. By faith we embrace the plan, God-in-the-flesh, the ultimate gift and giver of grace.

For further study and encouragement: Matthew 4:1–11

MARCH 13

JOSHUA 9–11

God's sovereignty over everything, everywhere, all of the time isn't an invitation for you to live a passive life.

As we read through Old Testament history, we discover that the most important element in all that has been recorded and preserved for us is God's consistent revelation of himself. In these stories he reveals his wisdom, power, love, faithfulness, holiness, sovereignty, and patience. In these stories he progressively unfolds his redemptive plan. He reveals that he is willing to forgive, but there must be a sacrifice for sin. He shows that he will make a way for sinners to dwell in his presence and that he will be faithful to deliver every one of his promises. The Old Testament story is a divine glory display pointing to the Savior, Jesus.

Joshua 10:8 is one of many divine glory-revealing passages. It reveals something significant about who our God is, but it also reveals something important about who God designs us to be. God called Joshua to lead the Israelite army into battle against the five kings of the Amorites. Any sane leader would be a bit afraid when considering this task, but pay attention to what God said to Joshua: "Do not fear them, for I have given them into your hands. Not a man of them shall stand before you."

Do you see the stunning glory of God in this passage? These verses reveal the sovereignty of God in a way that should leave us in awe. God didn't say to Joshua, "Don't be afraid; I will be there for you." No, he said, "I *have given* them into your hands." Past tense. This means not only that God had decided, before the foundations of the earth were laid in place, to unleash his power in defense of his people, but also that his sovereign rule is specific to a certain time, place, and people. God wrote into his divine plan Joshua's victory over these particular kings in this particular place and at this specific moment before there was a

Joshua, Amorite kings, or a land of promise. God really does rule with specificity over all things for the sake of his own.

But something else is important to see in this account. Even though God had determined the outcome, he still called Joshua to do battle. God's sovereignty is no reason for our passivity. No, God exercises his sovereign rule through the vehicle of valid human choices and actions. It's not the sovereignty of God *or* the responsibility of people. It's *both operating together* to deliver God's preordained plan. God in his sovereign plan pours out his grace on us, while he calls us to trust, obey, and follow. The way to rest in his sovereignty is to give ourselves actively to what he has called us to do.

For further study and encouragement: Acts 20:17–24

MARCH 14

JOSHUA 12–15

In times that you wonder what God is doing, it's important to remember that he will unleash his power for the defense, protection, and guidance of his children.

We all go through times when God seems distant, passive, and maybe even uncaring. In these moments we can be tempted to believe that God has forgotten his promises to us or, even worse, has forgotten us. We may even get to the point at which we wonder whether God is who he's declared himself to be. In our fear, discouragement, and doubt, we may begin to wander away from him. We may begin to let go of habits of personal devotion and prayer, wondering what good they do. When we're in a spiritual desert or experiencing a dark night of the soul, we are susceptible to hearing the lie of the enemy, as Adam and Eve did in the garden. It is always the same lie: there is something better out there than trusting, worshiping, and obeying the Lord.

I am deeply persuaded that biblical history—and what it reveals of the glory of God's character, plan, and work on behalf of his people—is designed to speak with wisdom and hope when we are about to lose hope. In those moments, we need a fresh vision of the glory of God working on behalf of his people. When God's glory is clouded, we all need something that will break through the clouds. Joshua 12 is that kind of cloud-bursting passage. Stand back and take time to consider what it says about the power of God and his work for his people:

And these are the kings of the land whom Joshua and the people of Israel defeated on the west side of the Jordan, from Baal-gad in the Valley of Lebanon to Mount Halak, that rises toward Seir (and Joshua gave their land to the tribes of Israel as a possession according to their allotments, . . .): the king of Jericho, one; the king of Ai, which is beside Bethel, one; the king of Jerusalem, one; the king of Hebron, one; the king of Jarmuth, one; the king of Lachish, one; the king of Eglon, one; the king of Gezer, one; the king of Debir, one; the king of Geder, one; the king of Hormah, one; the king of Arad, one; the king of Libnah, one; the king of Adullam, one; the king of Makkedah, one; the king of Bethel, one; the king of Tappuah, one; the king of Hepher, one; the king of Aphek, one; the king of Lasharon, one. (Josh. 12:7, 9–18)

You may be thinking, "Paul, what in the world does this have to do with the hard thing I'm facing right now?" This passage should blow your mind and fill your heart with hope. King after king after king was defeated—not by Joshua and the Israelite army alone, but by the power of God. God will do whatever is necessary in his almighty power to provide for, protect, and defeat the enemies of his people. The ultimate example of this is Jesus, who came in divine power to defeat the ultimate enemies of sin and death, and is fighting now for you.

For further study and encouragement: Psalm 2:1–12

———

MARCH 15

JOSHUA 16–18

Hope in the Lord is not a wish or a dream. It is a confident expectation of a guaranteed result.

What gets me up in the morning is not that I think I have the wisdom, gifts, strength, and character to forge a good life for my family and myself. No, what gets me up in the morning are the promises of God. I wake up every morning with an unshakable joy; no matter what is going on, I am absolutely sure that God will do for me what he has promised. So morning after morning I reach up my hands and grab hold of what God has promised, and I do not let go until I am asleep. The following are just a few of the things God has promised me:

He will never leave or forsake me.

His Spirit will live inside of me, to convict me of sin and empower me to obey.

He will supply everything I need.

He is ruling over all things for the sake of his people.

He has forgiven and will forgive my sins.

He will give me strength.

He will give me rest.

He will bring good out of hardship.

He will never fail.

He will give me wisdom.

He will finally defeat sin and death.

He will reserve a place for me in the new heavens and new earth.

These promises of God get me up and give me hope and joy morning after morning. Because I cling to God, I cling to his promises every day. And I therefore don't find Joshua 16–18 boring at all. As I read about allotment after allotment of the promised land to the tribes of Israel, I feel peace and joy. You see, God recorded and preserved these passages for us with loving intentionality. We see that he will never forget, ignore, or turn his back on his promises. He will faithfully deliver just what he has said he will deliver. He will do for his people things that are so wonderful and amazing that they will never be able to say they deserved them or to take credit for them. We stand in amazement and wonder as we see Israel march through and possess the land in the power of God, just as he promised they would. Here is divine demonstration of sovereign power and authority, a rule and a power that cannot be stopped. Equally important, here is God's unfailing faithfulness. In a world where few things are sure and things and people fail us, it is so good to know that God never fails. The tribes of Israel settle in to their particular place in the promised land because God rules, and he is faithful.

There is a greater promise than the land of promise. Back in Genesis 3 God promised a conquering Savior who would crush the head of the enemy. Jesus came, because God is faithful. He conquered sin and death in his life, death, and resurrection. In him you find everything you need and a destiny that is secure. God makes promises. He always fulfills them, and that changes everything. So get up, reach out, and grab his promises; don't let go, but go out and live with hope.

For further study and encouragement: Hebrews 11:1–3

MARCH 16

When you bank on God's promises, you bank on truths
that were decided before the earth was set in place; you
therefore bank on truths that are absolutely sure.

What is absolutely sure in your life? People make a life commitment when they get married, but marriage isn't always sure. Sin can sneak in and destroy a marriage. Or your spouse may suddenly die, leaving you alone. Or perhaps you buy your forever home, with the intention of spending the rest of your life there. But the economy tanks, you lose your job, and you can no longer afford to live in that house. You may have found your best friend forever, the deep bond you were looking for, but sadly your friend betrays you, shattering that friendship forever. You join a church thinking it will be the gospel community you'll give yourself to for the rest of your life, but a new pastor comes in, the church radically changes, and you sadly have to face the fact that you can't be there anymore. Many things in our lives seem permanent and sure but end up failing us. Often we become either fearful or calloused, not willing to trust as we once did. I have heard people say, "I will never get a raise again," or, "I will never join another church," or, "I've been hurt too many times; it won't happen again."

Yet in our hearts we hunger for the peace, security, and rest of soul that come when we find something we can depend on, something that will never fail us. Every human being is on a lifelong search for a rock to stand on. This is why I love the words God preserved for us near the end of the book of Joshua. If you believe these words, you won't need to search for that rock any longer.

> Thus the LORD gave to Israel all the land that he swore to give to their fathers. And they took possession of it, and they settled there. And the LORD gave them rest on every side just as he had sworn to their fathers. Not one of all their enemies had withstood them, for the LORD had given all their enemies into their hands. Not one word of all the good promises that the LORD had made to the house of Israel had failed; all came to pass. (Josh. 21:43–45)

Please go back and read the last sentence again. God is declaring the utter surety, dependability, and reliability of his promises. God does for his children exactly what he has promised to do, right down to each and every word. He is the solid rock on which we can stand: "On Christ the solid rock I stand;

all other ground is sinking sand." The ultimate solid-rock promise God made is Jesus. He is our solid rock. The question is, Are you building your life on him?

For further study and encouragement: Matthew 7:24–27

———

MARCH 17

JOSHUA 22–24

Between the "already" of our conversion and the "not yet" of our homegoing, the big question is, Where the rubber meets the road in our daily lives, whom or what will we give our hearts to?

I have made many ministry trips to India. I have seen the dominating power of overt idolatry. I have experienced how idol worship forces itself into every area of a person's life. Those who worship physical idols in the temple also bow before idols in their homes, along the road, and in restaurants. The presence and power of idols cover every place and every activity like a dark and ominous cloud. The presence and influence of these things made of wood and stone seem inescapable.

In the book of Joshua, the children of Israel find themselves in a significant spiritual moment. They are in the place God had promised, but they are surrounded by the false gods of the nations around them. Will they surrender their hearts to God and God alone, being careful to keep his commands and resist idolatrous temptations? Or will they wander away from the Lord and progressively give their hearts away to false gods? Joshua gives the children of Israel this charge:

> Be very strong to keep and to do all that is written in the Book of the Law of Moses, turning aside from it neither to the right hand nor to the left, that you may not mix with these nations remaining among you or make mention of the names of their gods or swear by them or serve them or bow down to them, but you shall cling to the LORD your God just as you have done to this day. For the LORD has driven out before you great and strong nations. And as for you, no man has been able to stand before you to this day. One man of you puts to flight a thousand, since it is the LORD your God who fights for you, just as he promised you. Be very careful, therefore, to love the LORD your God. (Josh. 23:6–11)

Joshua reminds the leaders of the children of Israel that, by the display of his awesome power, God has again and again demonstrated that he is the one true God and that no one can stand against him. As the one true God, he gives power to his people so that just one Israelite can drive a thousand enemies away. The one true God has fought and will continue to fight for his people. So Joshua charges them to bow down to no other god and to surrender their lives to the moral code written in the Book of the Law.

Again, it's important to remember that this passage was preserved for our instruction, conviction, and guidance. You might think, "I don't serve any idols." That may be true of physical idols. But the broader definition of idolatry in Scripture includes anything that takes the place in your heart that only God should have. Anything can be an idol. What has the power to control your thoughts, emotions, and desires? May God alone lay claim to our hearts.

For further study and encouragement: Matthew 6:19–24

MARCH 18

JUDGES 1–2

The problem with partial obedience is that it is disobedience masquerading as obedience.

Do you find joy in obeying your Lord? Do you treasure his commands? Do you recognize the protective wisdom of the boundaries he has set for you? Do you really believe that God's way is always the best way? Do you pick and choose which commands you obey? Are there moments when your behavior is formed more by your passions than by God's commands? Regardless of how correct your theology might be, at street level do you love your way more than God's? In what ways are you tempted to debate the wisdom of God's law? Do you use the grace of forgiveness as an excuse for stepping outside God's moral boundaries? Are you content with partial obedience? Do you respond to or resist the conviction of the Lord?

At the beginning of the book of Judges, we are greeted with a problem that will haunt the children of Israel, cause them generations of difficulty, and necessitate the loving discipline of the Lord. The problem is *partial obedience*. God's children start down the moral pathway he had commanded them to walk, but they fail to complete the journey. There are a variety of excuses for partial obedience. Obedience is hard and requires personal sacrifice. It requires really believing that God is wise and that what he calls us to is always best. Obedience requires us to confess that we are not at the center of everything—God is, so life is about his will and his glory. Obedience requires resisting the temporary pleasures of sin. Partial obedience is not obedience at all; rather, it is dressed-up disobedience. Pay attention to what is said of Israel in Judges 2:1–3:

> Now the angel of the LORD went up from Gilgal to Bochim. And he said, "I brought you up from Egypt and brought you into the land that I swore to give to your fathers. I said, 'I will never break my covenant with you, and you shall make no covenant with the inhabitants of this land; you shall break down their altars.' But you have not obeyed my voice. What is this you have done? So now I say, I will not drive them out before you, but they shall become thorns in your sides, and their gods shall be a snare to you."

God had given Israel a job to do; they were to drive the pagan nations completely out of the promised land. But they did not complete the job. Yes, they fought many battles, but they ended up settling for living in and among these pagan nations with their false gods. In a real way, the rest of the drama, the spiritual struggle, and the discipline of the Lord that are so much of the content of the Old Testament have their roots right here. This passage also points us to the necessity of the gift of Jesus. He was sent to obey completely on our behalf, precisely because God knew that sin, somehow, someway, and at some time, makes us all too satisfied with partial obedience. He is our righteousness, because our righteousness is often incomplete.

For further study and encouragement: Philippians 2:1–11

MARCH 19

JUDGES 3–5

Nothing is sadder than when we exchange worship and service of the Lord for one of an endless catalog of God-replacements.

It is heartbreaking how blind and foolish we can be. It is sad to think of how we are often content to make bad moral bargains. It is hard to think about the times when we are willing to exchange God's good thing for the world's bad thing.

It is sad to watch someone grab hold of a temporary pleasure while letting go of eternal gain. It is tough to see someone begin to think of the enemy's lies as trustworthy while doubting God's truth. It is clear that the drama of the human community and of human history is all about one thing: worship.

The most significant function of any human being is his capacity for worship. Every human being is a worshiper. I don't mean this in the formal, religious sense. The most irreligious person is a worshiper, because that's how God designed him. This worship capacity is meant to drive us to the Lord, to offer ourselves to him, and to find our identity, meaning, purpose, and rest in him. Being a worshiper means you will always give over the rule of your heart, the causal core of your personhood, to something. Whatever controls your heart will then shape your thoughts, desires, choices, words, and actions. Nothing is more life-dominating than worship.

The children of Israel were blessed to be chosen to be the people of God. God blessed them with his presence, his grace, and his love. He poured out his almighty power to deliver, provide for, guide, and protect them. He made a way for their sins to be forgiven. He gave them his wise and holy law so that they would know how to live. He exposed them to his glorious glory. Quite apart from what they deserved, he lavished these blessings on them. They were set apart from all the other nations on earth to be his children, his possession. It's hard to overstate the generosity of the blessing that God poured down on them. And in the display of his glory, God made it clear that there is no God like him. You might think that God had done so much for his children that they wouldn't even think of serving other gods. But then we come to one of the saddest verses in the Old Testament: "And their daughters they took to themselves for wives, and their own daughters they gave to their sons, and they served their gods" (Judg. 3:6). Let the sadness of these words grip you: *"They served their gods."* They turned their backs on the God of glory and grace (who had placed his love on them and led them into Canaan) for gods of wood and stone, completely lacking life, love, or power. This idolatry, the epicenter of sin, is the sad drama of the human condition, and it is the reason for the coming of the Messiah, Jesus. He came to rescue us from us, and to free us from the bondage of the idolatry of our own hearts in order to worship God and God alone.

For further study and encouragement: Jeremiah 2:10–13

MARCH 20

Fear fails to rest in the power of the Lord and
looks too much at the ability of oneself.

Judges 6 is a master class on the anatomy of fear.

> Now the angel of the LORD came and sat under the terebinth at Ophrah,
> which belonged to Joash the Abiezrite, while his son Gideon was beating out
> wheat in the winepress to hide it from the Midianites. And the angel of the
> LORD appeared to him and said to him, "The LORD is with you, O mighty
> man of valor." And Gideon said to him, "Please, my lord, if the LORD is with
> us, why then has all this happened to us? And where are all his wonderful
> deeds that our fathers recounted to us, saying, 'Did not the LORD bring us
> up from Egypt?' But now the LORD has forsaken us and given us into the
> hand of Midian." And the LORD turned to him and said, "Go in this might
> of yours and save Israel from the hand of Midian; do not I send you?" And
> he said to him, "Please, Lord, how can I save Israel? Behold, my clan is the
> weakest in Manasseh, and I am the least in my father's house." And the LORD
> said to him, "But I will be with you, and you shall strike the Midianites as
> one man." And he said to him, "If now I have found favor in your eyes, then
> show me a sign that it is you who speak with me." (Judg. 6:11–17)

Pay attention to how fear operates in the face of the call of the Lord. Let me
set the scene for you. God calls Gideon, who is *threshing wheat in a winepress*,
to lead Israel against the Midianites. You crush grapes in a winepress, but wheat
needs to be threshed in an open, airy place so the wind can separate the grain
from the chaff. Gideon is doing something inside that needed to be done outside, because he is afraid of the Midianites. God knows exactly who he is calling.
God often chooses the most unlikely person to do the grandest thing, so that he
gets the glory and not some human hero. Note how God greets this fearful man:
"The LORD is with you, O mighty man of valor." Because the Lord is with him,
"mighty man of valor," is, in fact, Gideon's true potential. But Gideon misses the
point entirely and is afraid for two reasons.

First, *Gideon has come to doubt the presence, goodness, and faithfulness of the
Lord*, saying, "God, if you are with us, then why has all this bad stuff happened to
us?" The defeat of Israel by the surrounding nations had nothing to do with the
absence or weakness of the Lord; it was his discipline of Israel for their disobedience and idolatry. But a second thing contributes to Gideon's fear. *He looks too*

much to his own experience and ability. "Please, Lord, how can I save Israel? Behold, my clan is the weakest in Manasseh, and I am the least of my father's house."

Here's the plan. God calls the weak to be vessels for the display of his power, so that he will get glory and our hearts will turn to worship him.

For further study and encouragement: Exodus 4:1–17

———

MARCH 21

JUDGES 8–9

*Our God is a jealous God and will not share the
love of our hearts with anyone or anything.*

In the twenty years I spent as a counselor and counseling professor, I witnessed the devastation of adultery and divorce, up close and personal, countless times. I have heard shattered wives tearfully tell the sad story of progressively uncovering their husband's betrayal. I have sat with lost and afraid children who had been thrown into the chaos of the war of their parents' hurt and anger. I have listened to husbands, blind to the destruction of their lust, defend themselves and minimize their sin. I have seen homes become divided houses. I have watched the darkness of grief set in. But with all that I have experienced, I have come to understand that there is an adultery far more devastating than physical/marital adultery. Nothing leaves a legacy of deceit and darkness like spiritual adultery. It captures hearts, derails lives, and causes people to be comfortable with walking away from the one whom they were created to love, enjoy, and fellowship with forever.

Take note of the words of Judges 8:33–35:

> As soon as Gideon died, the people of Israel turned again and whored after the Baals and made Baal-berith their god. And the people of Israel did not remember the LORD their God, who had delivered them from the hand of all their enemies on every side, and they did not show steadfast love to the family of Jerubbaal (that is, Gideon) in return for all the good that he had done to Israel.

As you read this passage, one phrase jumps off the page: "and whored after the Baals." This is your Lord using strong language to help you understand what was going on with his people. Israel's relationship to God was not a kind of loose friendship where they could enjoy the company and love of many friends. No, they had been bound to God by an eternal covenant. Their pursuit of and worship of Baal was the spiritual equivalent of a man or woman pursuing, seducing, and sleeping with someone other than his or her spouse. The dramatic difference here is that the person they are being unfaithful to is God Almighty.

What is spiritual adultery? Any time I give the love of my heart to something other than God, so that this love controls my thoughts, desires, choices, and actions in the way that only God should, I have committed spiritual adultery. This passage tells us two of the roots of spiritual adultery. The first root is God-forgetfulness: "The people of Israel did not remember the LORD." The second root is unthankfulness: "They did not show steadfast love" to the family of Gideon.

Jesus came to restore us to the one love we were created to give our hearts to. Confess with me that you too can be God-forgetful and unthankful. Confess with me that you still have a wandering heart. Pray with me for strength to cling with all of your heart to your Lord. Be thankful with me today that Jesus lived, died, and rose again so that you can know both his saving and his keeping grace.

For further study and encouragement: Exodus 20:4–5

——

MARCH 22

JUDGES 10–12

Is your life its most spiritually vibrant when you are in times of trouble, crying out to God, or in times of ease, when things are going well for you?

Great spiritual wisdom and counsel are embedded in the narrative of Judges. These accounts, lovingly preserved for us, demonstrate the patient love of God and are meant to warn, protect, and guide us. They have been recorded for us so that we would not err in the ways that our spiritual forefathers did. The book of Judges is like a father's sitting down on the couch with his children, telling stories of the mistakes and failures of past generations of the family, because he wants his children to learn, live wisely, and not fall into the same errors.

But perhaps the most encouraging thing about this portion of God's word is its revelation of God's jealous heart. Think about it. In a marriage, jealousy can be a good thing. If I were to say to my wife, "Go ahead and find another lover;

that would be fine with me," she would be horrified. It is right for me to crave that Luella would give me the love of her heart to the exclusion of any other man. God's jealousy for the hearts of his people is a sign of the depth and faithfulness of his love.

The book of Judges is also helpful because it describes Israel's sad spiritual cycle. This is preserved for us as God's loving warning. Here is the cycle:

Israel experiences a time of ease and prosperity.
They forget the Lord.
They pursue other gods.
God uses the surrounding nations as tools of discipline.
Israel cries out for God's deliverance.
God sends a deliverer.
Times of ease return.
The cycle repeats.

Judges records this repeated cycle because God loves us and does not want us to wander away too. What is true for the children of Israel is true also for us. Times of comfort and ease are often the times when our prayer and devotional life weaken, our thankfulness for all of God's providing and protecting mercies wanes, and we begin to look for our identity, meaning, purpose, and inner sense of rest and peace horizontally rather than vertically.

It is also clear in Judges that God's discipline, no matter how harsh, is not his rejection. His discipline is a sure sign of his love. It is God's fighting for the love and loyalty of our hearts. It is God's wrenching us away from other lovers in order to claim us once again as his own.

In times of comfort and ease, does your pursuit of God weaken? Does your heart wander? The cross and tomb of Jesus tell us how far our jealous God will go to claim us as his own. Bask in the depth of God's jealous love for you today, and cling to him with your whole heart.

For further study and encouragement: Matthew 22:34–40

MARCH 23

*If you could watch a recording of your life from the past
six weeks, what influences would you conclude had
shaped your actions, reactions, and responses?*

Years ago I drove to the mall with my three-year-old son to complete an errand. It was a mundane journey on a mundane day. But the question the little voice in the back seat asked me was anything but mundane: "Daddy, if God made everything, did he make those light poles?" Now, what impressed me was not that my three-year-old son asked me a theological question. No, what impressed me was how deeply human it was to ask this question. God, in his creation wisdom, had designed my son to be an interpreter. He was created to think, that is, to try to make sense of his life, his surroundings, his relationships, and his own identity. When I heard the question, I knew that an interpretive process was happening and that the way my son made sense of the world would shape the direction of his life.

Before too long my son would be a young man, thinking about profoundly important moral and spiritual issues. Out of his moral conclusions would come a set of morally weighted desires, and out of those desires would come a set of choices, and those choices would form a lifestyle, and that lifestyle would carry with it a set of moral blessings and consequences. What I have described is the life cycle of every human being made in the image of God. That cycle is obvious in Judges 14:1–3:

> Samson went down to Timnah, and at Timnah he saw one of the daughters of the Philistines. Then he came up and told his father and mother, "I saw one of the daughters of the Philistines at Timnah. Now get her for me as my wife." But his father and mother said to him, "Is there not a woman among the daughters of your relatives, or among all our people, that you must go to take a wife from the uncircumcised Philistines?" But Samson said to his father, "Get her for me, for she is right in my eyes."

Samson desired a wife. This was entirely appropriate. God designed us to be social beings, and he created marriage for our thriving and our good. But the wife Samson wanted was a Philistine, and God had expressly forbidden such a marriage. Samson's parents protested because they knew that what Samson was thinking was wrong and that what he wanted was something God had forbidden. Samson's response to his parents' protest is telling: "Get her for me, for she is right in my eyes." You see, our God-given ability to think is always shaped by whatever rules our hearts. The big moral question is, Are our desires and choices ruled by what *we* think is right or by what *God* thinks is right? Our thought life is a place of spiritual warfare, a place of battle between God's will and our will, and for that we need God's rescuing and protecting grace.

For further study and encouragement: 1 Thessalonians 4:1–8

———

MARCH 24

JUDGES 16–18

Success in life and ministry isn't God's endorsement of
your character but rather a revelation of his.

God exercises his power for the sake of his people. He is faithful in guiding, providing for, and protecting his children. He unleashes his sovereign authority to deliver his promises at just the right time and place. He reigns in power and authority for his own glory and the good of his people. God does not let anything or anyone stand in the way of his wise and holy purposes on earth. In order to accomplish his purposes and fulfill his promises to his people, God raises up human leaders. He gives them wisdom and insight. He gives them power way beyond their natural strength. He grants them authority and success. He uses human instruments to advance his divine purpose.

But there are some important things that need to be said about the leaders God chooses to use. First, in his sovereign wisdom God uses whomever he chooses to use. When we read through the narrative of Scripture, we can be surprised by whom God chooses to use in order to move his purposes along and to fulfill his promises to his people. Samson is one of those surprising instruments. God gave Samson superhuman power and ability. On behalf of his people, God chose Samson to be a conqueror. But Samson was a mess. He disobeyed God and made regrettable moral choices. He was clearly driven more by his passions than by the clear will of God. This points to a second truth regarding the instruments God chooses to use for his glory and the good of his people. The fact that God gave Samson power and success does not mean God endorsed Samson's lifestyle or his moral choices. What is revealed in Samson's feats is God's character and faithfulness to the people upon whom he had placed his love.

Success in family, career, ministry, or any other endeavor should never be assumed to be God's endorsement of the way you live your life, the moral choices you make, the way you spend your money, your personal spiritual life, or the way you conduct yourself in relationships. God gives you success not to display your glory but to reveal his own. He gives to those to whom he chooses to give, he promotes those whom he wants to promote, and he empowers those whom he wants to empower—not so that they would receive honor and praise, but so that his people would give him the praise that is his due.

Because success tempts us to be proud—to think that we are something we are not—success is more spiritually dangerous than failure.

Only one instrument was perfect in every way and received God's complete endorsement: Jesus. "This is my beloved Son, with whom I am well pleased" (Matt. 3:17). Every other human instrument is flawed and dependent on God's rescuing, forgiving, and protecting grace.

For further study and encouragement: Psalm 127:1–5

———

MARCH 25

JUDGES 19–21

Even in the worst vacuums of human leadership, the people of God are never without a King.

When I stand up to speak or sit down to write, I feel as if a crowd of people stand up or sit down with me. These are all the teachers, pastors, professors, spiritual mentors, Christian leaders, writers, and friends whom God has used and is still using to form me. I am thankful for each one of them and for the lasting mark they have made on me. They have helped me to understand the gospel and to know what it looks like to teach and preach God's word, how to live a ministry-oriented life, what it means to be a good husband and father, what it looks like to lead others in ministry, and how to continue to grow in God's grace. God has blessed me with people to lead, teach, guide, and correct me. None of these dear people has been ever-present in my life. They have all come and gone, according to God's plan. But there is one who has always been present—leading, teaching, confronting, protecting, and providing. It is my Savior King. All the "kings" he has placed in my life are temporary representatives of Jesus's always faithful and eternal kingship.

The last verse of Judges says, "In those days there was no king in Israel. Everyone did what was right in his own eyes" (Judg. 21:25). This sad, dark, and disharmonious chorus is repeated throughout Judges. After being set apart as the people of God, after all of God's glorious display on their behalf, after God had raised up deliverer after deliverer, after all his loving protection and provision, and after warning after warning, the children of Israel are now in this sad state. Moral individualism reigns; each person sets himself up as his own moral authority. Although still a nation chosen by God, Israel now functionally ignores his presence and authority. These words should make us weep.

In this way Israel desperately needs a human king, one chosen by God to be his moral representative, not only to lead Israel in government and battle but also to call Israel back to functional worship and service of the one who had liberated them from slavery. He had given them his law, made provision for the forgiveness of sin, provided for them, and defeated their enemies. Israel desperately needs a godly leader who will lead them in a moral reformation.

But when I read this final verse, I think, "But Israel did have a King—the Creator, Sovereign, King of kings." The people of God not only desperately needed King David, a man after God's own heart, but ultimately they needed the perfect King, the Son of David, Jesus. They had the best King ever, yet they resisted him again and again and chose to be content with self-rule. No matter what "kings" are in our lives, may God grant us grace so we will joyfully surrender our wills to the will of the one perfect and eternal King, Jesus.

For further study and encouragement: Psalm 47:7–9

MARCH 26

RUTH 1–4

Often when God seems absent in moments of hardship, he is actually exercising his sovereignty to deliver good gifts of grace to his children.

We have all been through tough moments of suffering when we wonder where God is and are confused about what he is doing. If you read through the biblical narrative, you will soon have to let go of the conclusion that hardship means God is absent, distant, uninvolved, or uncaring. Behind dark clouds of difficulty is a God who is actively working for the good of his children. God regularly takes his children places they never would have planned to go in order to produce in and through them things they never could have produced on their own. It's important to recognize that the workings of God's grace aren't always predictable or comfortable. Often when we think grace has passed us by, God's grace is at work, just not in the way we expect.

The book of Ruth, one of the greatest biblical stories, contains a compelling and beautiful substory. On the surface Ruth is a beautiful love story, and one of the few biblical stories with women as main characters. But there is a deeper, more significant love story in the book of Ruth. It is the story of God's unshakable, unstoppable love for his children. This story of human hardship and human love is also God's assurance that he will exercise his wisdom and his sovereignty, he will remember his covenant promises, he will be faithful, and, through hardship, he will deliver gifts of kindness and grace to his own. Although the story of Naomi, Ruth, and Boaz is compelling, the one on center stage is the Lord. Through the vehicles of hardship and human love, God establishes the direction of the rest of the redemptive story.

At the end of the story, Ruth and Boaz have a son. We read, "Then Naomi took the child and laid him on her lap and became his nurse. And the women of the neighborhood gave him a name, saying, 'A son has been born to Naomi.' They named him Obed. He was the father of Jesse, the father of David" (Ruth 4:16–17). These words give us a sense of what this story has been about all along. God doesn't just deliver Ruth and unite her to Boaz, but he delivers to this family a son. This son, Obed, will have a son, Jesse, and Jesse will have a son, David, and ultimately out of David will come a son, the Son of David, Jesus. Through this little story of hardship and love, God sets things in place to deliver something anything but little: the ultimate promise, the gift of gifts, the Savior, Jesus Christ, through whom God's redeeming love will flow.

God will work and continue to work his redeeming plan until that plan is complete; this is the ultimate story behind every other story. Remember that it is at the intersection of God's sovereignty and his grace that life and hope are to be found.

For further study and encouragement: 1 Peter 1:3–12

MARCH 27

God's grace should make you sing. What better songs could you sing than ones about his power, his mercy, his forgiveness, and his love?

I grew up in a singing family. My sister played the piano, and I think my mom had memorized the entire hymnal. I grew up singing the great hymns of the faith, and I can still sing most of them without looking at the written words. I am thankful for the world of song. Songs give wings to the emotions of our hearts. With songs we celebrate, and with songs we mourn. With songs we remind ourselves of who we are and who God is. Songs commemorate huge victories and dark defeats. But the thing I like best about songs is their ability to paint in our minds the deep truths of the word of God in ways that are beautiful and memorable. Some of the most beautiful and penetrating theology ever written is found in the great hymns of the church. I love that the church will never stop writing and singing new songs of God's glory and redeeming grace.

First Samuel 2 records Hannah's song of thanksgiving and praise. She sang this song after God heard her cries as a barren woman and gave her a son, Samuel. Hannah's song is exuberant and joyful, and also theologically rich and deep. It reads much like a psalm and, as with the Psalms, we need to slow down, spend time in it, and let its content fill our minds and grip our hearts. In her song Hannah reminds us of who God is and where true and lasting hope and joy are to be found. Here is a portion her song:

> The Lord kills and brings to life;
>> he brings down to Sheol and raises up.
> The Lord makes poor and makes rich;
>> he brings low and he exalts.
> He raises up the poor from the dust;
>> he lifts the needy from the ash heap
> to make them sit with princes
>> and inherit a seat of honor.
> For the pillars of the earth are the Lord's,
>> and on them he has set the world.
> He will guard the feet of his faithful ones,
>> but the wicked shall be cut off in darkness,
>> for not by might shall a man prevail.
> The adversaries of the Lord shall be broken to pieces;
>> against them he will thunder in heaven.

The LORD will judge the ends of the earth;
   he will give strength to his king
   and exalt the horn of his anointed. (1 Sam. 2:6–10)

Hannah reminds us that life and death are in the Lord's hands. And, along with his awesome power, he meets the poor and hungry with mercy and tenderheartedness. I find the final words of her song striking: "He will give strength to his king / and exalt the power of his anointed." Here Hannah, speaking better than she knows, points us to the coming of the ultimate victorious King, Jesus. Every song of sovereignty and grace points us ultimately to him.

For further study and encouragement: Luke 1:46–55

———

MARCH 28

1 SAMUEL 4–8

Always remember that the Lord Almighty reigns in glory, and he will not give his glory to another.

I love good comedy. I love comedic moments that are unsettling and awkward, because in those moments the messiness of the personalities, intentions, and responses of human beings are being unclothed. There are moments in great comedies when I feel the awkwardness and think, "This guy is naked (metaphorically); everyone in the room knows it except him." You laugh as you cringe. You feel sorry for the guy, but you also like that he has been exposed. Comedy can break through our defenses, allowing us to examine and admit things that a lecture about the same things wouldn't allow. God gave us the ability to laugh. Humor is one of his good gifts, but even this gift is meant to point to God's existence and his glory.

There is divine comedy in the Bible. If you don't see it, then you have probably missed the power of the narrative that God has preserved for you. First Samuel 5 contains one of those moments. It is holy hilarity at its best. The Philistines have captured the ark of the covenant and, because they have, they are convinced that their god, Dagon, is more powerful than Jehovah, the Lord Almighty, the Creator and controller of everything that is. Now let yourself step into the cosmic ridiculousness of this. Could this god of stone, which at some point was crafted by human hands, ever be compared to the Lord of lords, let alone be greater than him? Watch what happens next; it should make you chuckle with awe:

> And when the people of Ashdod rose early the next day, behold, Dagon had fallen face downward on the ground before the ark of the LORD. So they took Dagon and put him back in his place. But when they rose early on the next morning, behold, Dagon had fallen face downward on the ground before the ark of the LORD, and the head of Dagon and both his hands were lying cut off on the threshold. Only the trunk of Dagon was left to him. (1 Sam. 5:3–4)

How awkward! Great, conquering Dagon now lies face flat before the ark of the Lord, as though in worshipful surrender (5:3). God will not give his glory to another. The scene should make you chuckle at the complete impotency of this idol in the face of the glory of the Lord. But the divine comedy of this moment isn't over. The Philistines, in a vain effort to hold on to the delusion of Dagon's power, prop him up again, only to find him toppled again, this time with his head and hands cut off, his powerlessness now rendered even more powerless. When I read this, I hear the heavenly host laughing. It's the laughter of praise. God won't give his glory to another. Psalm 2:4 tells us, "He who sits in the heavens laughs." There are moments when it is spiritually good for us to laugh, too, as we consider the ridiculous impotency of anything that would challenge the will and glory of our great and glorious Lord.

For further study and encouragement: Isaiah 42:8–12

———

MARCH 29

1 SAMUEL 9–12

God goes with the one he sends, and the one he calls he faithfully empowers.

The fool loves independence. Like a young child who wants to tie his shoe but does not know how and who slaps away his mother's hand when she reaches to help him, so is the foolish and spiritually immature person. By grace, the more you walk with the Lord, the more you come to know him and get to know yourself, the more you consider his high calling on your life, and the more you are struck by your own weakness and inability. Nothing God calls us to is possible in our own strength. Whether character or command, we have no ability whatsoever to independently live up to God's wise and holy standards. This is why you see this statement repeated throughout the biblical narrative: "I will be with you." We look to God not only for direction but also for empowerment.

So when Saul is being appointed and anointed as king of Israel, it makes sense that this would be recorded: "Then the Spirit of the LORD will rush upon you, and you will prophesy with them and be turned into another man. Now when these signs meet you, do what your hand finds to do, for God is with you" (1 Sam. 10:6–7). That the "Spirit of the LORD will rush upon" Saul means that God will fill him with the power he needs in order to do what God has appointed him to do. God's power is so significant that Saul will be "turned into another man." This does not mean that his physical appearance or personality will change; rather, God will so thoroughly equip him for the task to which he has been called that he will be like a new man. This empowerment is not *for* Saul but *through* Saul, for the good of God's people and for the glory of the Lord.

As we read separate parts of the grand biblical story, we must remember that the central character of every chapter of the biblical story is the Lord. The biblical story is his story. He is on center stage, and the spotlight is always on him. The human characters are the means by which God reveals who he is, how he works, and what his plan is. In the story of Saul's anointing, we see God's zeal for his plan and for his people and, through them, his plan for all the nations on earth. When God call us, he empowers us—not just because he is loving and kind and knows we are weak, but because we are the instruments through which he will accomplish his plan that he set in place before the world was created. He is the one who raises up kings, and he is the one who brings them down.

Saul was part of something infinitely bigger than himself, bigger even than Israel. Out of Israel would come another king, a Lamb King, who would shed his blood for the forgiveness of sins and secure the promises that someday everything damaged by sin would be made new again.

For further study and encouragement: Matthew 28:18–20

MARCH 30

1 SAMUEL 13–14

*When you sin, you have only two choices: either you
confess your sin to God or you create excuses that
make that sin acceptable to your conscience.*

"I forgot."
"I didn't understand you."
"He distracted me."
"I thought you meant later."
"I was gonna do it."
"Why didn't she have to do it too?"
"I ran out of time."
"Mom asked me to do something else first."

I could fill pages with the excuses my children gave when they failed to obey me. Now, don't be too hard on your children. If you're honest, you have to admit that sometimes you do the same thing. When you sin, you have two choices. The better choice is to admit that you have sinned, confess it to God, and rest in his forgiving grace. But often we opt for the second choice. We erect arguments that make our sins look not so sinful after all, and those sins then become acceptable to our hearts. Instead of confessing our sins, we argue for our righteousness with a litany of excuses meant to get us off the moral hook. We blame a bad attitude on not feeling well. We say our irritability and impatience are the result of busyness. We say our lust isn't sexual but just an enjoyment of beauty. We rationalize yelling at our children as righteous anger. The problem is that you and I can't minimize our sin without devaluing the gift of God's grace. The more you preach your own righteousness to yourself, the less you'll seek and celebrate God's grace.

In 1 Samuel 13, Saul is waiting for the prophet Samuel and, as he waits, he does something that God had forbidden him to do. He offers a sacrifice. In his law, God had forbidden anyone to independently make a sacrifice to him. He had appointed and set apart priests to offer sacrifices on behalf of his people. When Samuel confronts Saul with his sin, listen to where Saul's heart goes and what he then says:

> Samuel said, "What have you done?" And Saul said, "When I saw that the people were scattering from me, and that you did not come within the days appointed, and that the Philistines had mustered at Michmash, I said, 'Now

the Philistines will come down against me at Gilgal, and I have not sought the favor of the LORD.' So I forced myself, and offered the burnt offering." (1 Sam. 13:11–12)

In the face of his sin being exposed, Saul does two things: he blames Samuel for being late, and he sanctifies his sin by saying he was seeking the favor of the Lord. The kicker in Saul's system of self-excuse comes when he says, "So I forced myself . . ."

It is always biblical/gospel insanity to deny, minimize, or excuse your sin. Why? Because God reveals himself again and again as patient, kind, tender-hearted, and forgiving. He never turns his back on sinners who come to him in humble confession and with repentant hearts. Excusing sin never goes anywhere good; confessing sin always produces good fruit. So run to God in humble confession; he will greet you with mercy and bless you with his redeeming love.

For further study and encouragement: Psalm 51:1–19

———

MARCH 31

1 SAMUEL 15–17

We serve a God who is sure. He knows no mystery, never lies, makes no mistakes, and has no regrets.

Every human being is burdened at some point by regrets. We all look back and wish we hadn't said certain things. We are burdened by poor choices we made or by decisions we wish we could remake. As a dad, I wish I could remove some conversations with my children from history and from their memories. Sin mars our track record. The path behind us is littered with mistakes, weaknesses, failures, and sins. Along the way we've had to face our regrets, confess our sins, admit our weaknesses, and run again and again to our Lord's forgiving grace. There will be a day of no more regrets, no more sin to confess, and complete liberation from our weaknesses, but we regularly prove that we are not there yet.

This is why I find comfort and hope in the declaration Samuel made after he announced that God had rejected disobedient Saul as king: "The Glory of Israel will not lie or have regret, for he is not a man, that he should have regret" (1 Sam. 15:29). Repeat to yourself, "God is not like me. God is not like me. God is not like me," and then bask in the glorious comfort of those words.

Human relationships are messy, difficult, and hurtful because we fail, we do regrettable things, we carry weakness with us, and we are less than perfect. Every good premarital counselor warns the prospective husband and wife that they are marrying someone less than perfect. The shalom of a human community free from regret was shattered the moment Adam and Eve conspired to disobey God. But God is not like us. He is the absolute perfection of perfection. His every intention is completely pure. The complete perfection of his holiness means he cannot lie. He never needs a second chance or a fresh start. He never needs to be forgiven. He will forever have nothing to confess. He is the definition of what it means to be holy, right, and true all of the time, in every place, and in every way. No regrets, no lies—God is not like us.

In a moment of massive human failure (Saul's) with massively significant consequences (Israel is once again without a king), Samuel points Israel and us to where unfailing hope can be found. We live in a world where we—and everyone and everything around us—fail us in some way. But we can entrust ourselves to one who never lies and has no regrets. God is not like us; he is perfectly sure and eternally trustworthy. Preach to yourself the gospel of God's perfection, and rest in his unfailing care.

For further study and encouragement: Numbers 23:19–20

APRIL 1

1 SAMUEL 18–20

God is the giver of good gifts. Jealousy over the gifts and
successes of others never goes anywhere good.

God is the Creator of everything that exists. This includes the physical creation, which trumpets his glory and brings us such delight, as well as many nonphysical things that we depend on and celebrate. Beyond your physicality, God is the Creator of your mentality, personality, emotionality, and psychology. It is important to understand that God not only is the Creator of all things, but he also rules over how his creation is allocated. He dispenses the good gifts of his creation as he pleases and according to his divine plan. It is God who chooses a person's gifts and abilities. God allots these gifts and abilities for his glory, for the purpose of human thriving, and to advance his grand plan for his creation. A doctor with exquisite diagnostic skills has those skills not just because he studied hard and trained well, but because God gave him the set of gifts required to do his work. Picasso was working with God-given abilities. Mozart was employing God-allotted gifts.

When you are jealous of the gifts and successes of others, you're not just angry that you don't have what they have; you are angry with God. Jealousy questions the wisdom and goodness of God. Jealousy charges God with mistakenly giving to another what you should have. Jealous people claim to be smarter than God, thinking that they would have been better at managing creation's gifts. In 1 Samuel 18 and the chapters following, this is exactly where we find King Saul. God has rejected him as king, and David has been anointed as the next king of Israel. Because God calls David to be a warrior king, he empowers him with the gifts to be successful in battle. But Saul looks at David's success and is not thankful for God's loving protection of his people through David. No, Saul is consumed with jealousy, so much so that all he can think about is killing David.

David is not against Saul. In fact, he has been Saul's loyal servant. David is not in a contest with Saul; he is doing the work God has appointed him to do. Saul's murderous anger is not just against David; it is against his Lord. God, in his infinite wisdom and out of love for his people, chooses David as his instrument and gives him the power and ability to do his work. Jealousy rages against the wisdom and rule of God. It questions his wisdom and love. When you question God's wisdom and love, you don't go to him for help, because you've concluded he is not good. In choosing David, God is advancing his plan—not just for Israel, but for the whole world. The kingdom of David would never end, because out of him would come another King, Jesus. In David, God is working his saving plan, putting pieces in place that would lead to the final sacrifice for sins. What love! What wisdom! What grace!

For further study and encouragement: Luke 11:9–13

———

APRIL 2

1 SAMUEL 21–24

Biblical faith involves not just your mind; it also requires a commitment of your heart that radically changes the way you live.

Theology is a life activity. When you say you believe something, you are not just mentally assenting to that truth. True belief is always demonstrated by how you live. Every doctrine of Scripture is meant to set a culture for living. Every truth in the Bible calls you to a certain lifestyle. If biblical truth doesn't radically change the way you act, react, and respond, then you probably don't truly believe what you say you believe. This means that we should never be comfortable with a disharmony between our confessional theology (the things we declare that we believe) and our functional theology (the way we live). It surely is much easier to assent mentally to biblical truths than it is to carry those truths into your situations, locations, and relationships in a way that is life shaping. I am persuaded that the enemy of our souls would gladly concede our formal theology if he could control the way we live. Theology is much more than an intellectual world; theology is spiritual warfare. Our theology defines our identity, meaning, and purpose, and therefore it controls how we live.

The stakes are high because theological belief really is a matter of life and death. Because theology is not just a mental activity, but rather a set of life-shaping commitments, God has graciously given us practical, living examples of what true belief looks like. We see faith in action in how David responded to the murderous jealousy of Saul. Saul's anger against David was completely unjustified. Saul was so jealous that he lost his mind. Where did Saul imagine this story was going to go? Did he actually think that if he killed David, he would get the throne back? Did he think he could live with murderous intent and God wouldn't notice? Did he expect God to say, "Oops, you're right, Saul. I did give my anointing and power to the wrong man"? Truly, Saul was insanely jealous.

What about David? We find him in the same cave as Saul. His men think it's his chance to mete out vengeance against this man who had wronged him so. But David says, "The Lord forbid that I should do this thing to my lord, the Lord's anointed, to put out my hand against him, seeing he is the Lord's anointed" (1 Sam. 24:6). If you really do believe in the sovereignty, wisdom, presence, power, and love of the Lord, then you can be both resolute and at peace in the face of evil. God had met David with his grace, empowering him to continue to do what was right, even in the face of wrong. If you believe God rules and is with you too, then you can do what is right in the face of wrong, knowing that, by grace, he will empower you to live by faith as well.

For further study and encouragement: Ephesians 3:14–19

APRIL 3

1 SAMUEL 25–27

*The Bible is a chronicle of divine interruptions, an account
of how God intervenes to make a better way.*

Because God loves us, he interrupts us. He interrupted the human story with the great flood, stopping the flood of iniquity on earth. God interrupted Jonah as he ran away from God's call. He interrupted Nebuchadnezzar's glory-obsessed reign. He interrupted Paul and his violent persecution of the church. And he will interrupt human history to usher in the new heavens and the new earth. God regularly interrupts the lives and plans of his children, and not simply because he has the power to do whatever he wants to do. Every interruption of the Lord is the result of his wisdom, power, and love. Sometimes God interrupts his children to set them on a new and better pathway. Sometimes he interrupts their lives to reveal his presence and glory to them once again. God often interrupts his children to protect them from themselves. At other times, God interrupts their lives to protect them from others. Every divine interruption is wise and good. Every divine interruption reveals God's constant attention to and interaction with the lives of his children. He is constantly watching, he never withdraws his care, he always knows what is best, and he exercises his power and authority to flip the script whenever he chooses. And his timing in doing so is always right. These interruptions are never a change in God's sovereign will, but are often a significant disruption of our plans for ourselves.

First Samuel 25 records one of those divine interruptions. David and his men need provisions, so he sends ten men to ask Nabal, a wealthy man, whether he will give them what they need. Nabal doesn't just say no; he is insulting and rude. David is angry, and he is tempted to take vengeance into his own hands. But God interrupts David in the person of Abigail, a woman of great wisdom. Abigail steps in between David and Nabal, seeking first to calm David's anger by saying she will take the guilt on herself, and reminding him that he cannot take the life of a woman traveling by herself. Then she reminds David that the Lord is restraining him from bloodguilt. Because of Abigail's intervention, David calms down and realizes that what he intended to do was not only wrong but also far from the kind of response a future king should have (25:23–35). God interrupts David and the wrong path his anger would have led him down with the words and generosity of one wise woman.

We all belong to the Creator, and he will interrupt our lives as he wills and knows is best. There was no bigger or better interruption than the incarnation of Jesus. God invaded human history to do for us what we never could have done for ourselves. He sent his Son to conquer sin and death, so that rather than being slaves to sin we can know the freedom of his grace and life now and forever. May God, in wisdom and power, continue to grace us with divine interruptions until his final interruption, when all things will be made new again.

For further study and encouragement: Ephesians 2:1–10

———

APRIL 4

1 SAMUEL 28-31

Sin is a liar. It makes promises it will never keep, offering life, but leading instead to destruction and death.

It's important to realize that, until we are on the other side, with peace and righteousness reigning forever and ever, we will be told lies every day. When Satan first enters the scene in the garden of Eden, he proves himself to be a liar. The business of sin is deceit; its promises cannot be trusted. The good life that sin offers is the ultimate evil sleight of hand. I once watched card sharks on a street in Philadelphia. They made it look as though money were ready to be made, but the players always lost. I walked away wondering why anybody would ever play. But I knew the answer: the delusion of easy money drew players in. Similarly, we are deceived into thinking that blessing, benefit, and real life can be found somewhere outside of God's boundaries. Adam and Eve bought into that delusion, and people have been buying in ever since. Sin dangles, we reach, and nothing good happens in the end.

First Samuel 31 records the sad end of Saul's life. This final account of King Saul's life should make us weep:

Now the Philistines were fighting against Israel, and the men of Israel fled before the Philistines and fell slain on Mount Gilboa. And the Philistines overtook Saul and his sons, and the Philistines struck down Jonathan and Abinadab and Malchi-shua, the sons of Saul. The battle pressed hard against Saul, and the archers found him, and he was badly wounded by the archers. Then Saul said to his armor-bearer, "Draw your sword, and thrust me through with it, lest these uncircumcised come and thrust me through, and mistreat me." But his armor-bearer would not, for he feared greatly. Therefore Saul took his own sword and fell upon it. And when his armor-bearer saw that Saul was dead, he also fell upon his sword and died with him. (1 Sam. 31:1–5)

What a tragic end to this anointed king's life. The army of the king was completely defeated, his sons were killed in battle, and Saul died by suicide. When we read this account, we find it hard to remember the glory days when Saul was anointed as the first king of Israel. Saul has listened to and chased sin's lie. He knowingly stepped over God's boundaries, while excusing his transgressions. What was Saul thinking? Where did he tell himself the story would end? Did he really think he was smarter than God? Did he reason that God would simply ignore his rebellion?

I am persuaded that this account is in our Bibles because God loves us and wants to warn us. The wages of sin really is death (Rom. 6:23), and we all buy into sin's deceit. That's why we need to be rescued from ourselves, and why God in grace sent his Son to be the rescuer. Jesus offers us not only real life with a joyous end, but also power right here, right now to stand against sin's deceit. Run to him—he won't turn you away.

For further study and encouragement: John 8:39–47

———

APRIL 5

2 SAMUEL 1–3

Since we have been granted such grace from God, we should always respond to others with grace, even those who have mistreated us.

If I had been in Jesus's place—suffering the mistreatment, injustice, and torture he faced—I wonder what I would have done if I had had his power at my disposal. Even being tortured on the cross, Jesus expressed forgiveness for his torturers. Grace is the way of the cross. We cannot allow ourselves to take vengeance into our hands, by thought, words, or actions. We cannot allow ourselves to wish for or gloat over the demise of someone who has wronged us. It's wrong for us to celebrate grace while we wish condemnation on others. We cannot be content with loving our friends and hating our enemies when our Lord has called us to love our enemies, to pray for those who mistreat us, and to look for ways to do good to them. We all must fight the temptation to keep a record of wrongs, to allow bitterness to harden our hearts, and to fantasize about the suffering of others. Spite is not in our Lord's vocabulary of grace. To resist these things we need to be met by the very same grace that we are called to give.

We have an example of such grace in 2 Samuel 1:17–27, which records David's lament over the death of Saul and his son Jonathan. David chose to remember and recount the great things about this warrior king and his son. He wrote of might, valor, and conquests. He talked of how the children of Israel were blessed during Saul's reign. It's true that Saul made David's life very hard. Saul's jealousy made him long for and work toward David's death. But David did not use the occasion of Saul's demise to air all the evil that Saul had done to him and all the ways, in his pride and rebellion, that Saul had failed as God's appointed representative over Israel. This is not a poem written by a bitter man. David was a man of peace because he trusted in the Lord and, because he did, he was able to look at the life of Saul with grace. Here is a portion of David's lament:

Saul and Jonathan, beloved and lovely!
 In life and in death they were not divided;
they were swifter than eagles;
 they were stronger than lions.
You daughters of Israel, weep over Saul,
 who clothed you luxuriously in scarlet,
 who put ornaments of gold on your apparel.
How the mighty have fallen
 in the midst of the battle!
Jonathan lies slain on your high places.
 I am distressed for you, my brother Jonathan;
very pleasant have you been to me;
 your love to me was extraordinary,
 surpassing the love of women.
How the mighty have fallen,
 and the weapons of war perished! (2 Sam. 1:23–27)

May we, upon whom great grace has been poured, have such gratitude in our hearts and rest in our Lord that we find greater joy in granting grace than we find in fantasizing about or celebrating the demise of those who have troubled us.

For further study and encouragement: Matthew 18:21–35

APRIL 6

*Minimizing, ignoring, or doubting the perfect holiness of the Lord
will never produce anything good in you or through you.*

We don't have the vocabulary or categories to describe adequately the infinitely perfect holiness of our Lord. Nothing and no one is perfectly pure all of the time and in every way. The Hebrew word for *holy* means "other," set apart from everything else. In the complete holiness of his holiness, God is the great eternal other. There has never been and never will be anyone like him. His holiness is not a part of him; it is his essence. He is holiness through and through. He is holy in love, holy in wisdom, holy in power, holy in faithfulness, holy in anger, holy in grace, holy in patience, holy in judgment, holy in mercy, and so on. In all that he is, all of the time, he is perfectly holy. In this way he is unlike us. Here's why this is so important. Only when you understand the utter holiness of the Lord will you understand the horrible sinfulness of sin. Only in light of the holiness of God will you take his holy law seriously. Only when you understand the holiness of the Lord will you be blown away by the generosity of his gift of redeeming grace. Easy-believism and moral boundary-breaking begins with forgetting the shocking holiness of God.

I am convinced that this is why God, in protective love, has preserved for us shocking reminders of his uncompromising holiness. These stories are hard for us to read. As sinners, we are tempted to think that God is overreacting or that his anger has too much control over him. It is important to humbly admit that when we wince at accounts of God's acting in holy anger, we do so because we wish God were just a little bit more flexible, a little more like us, and maybe not so holy all the time and in every way. His otherness makes us uncomfortable—and it should, because confessing how unlike him we are is the doorway to seeking his grace.

One of these uncomfortable holiness stories is found in 2 Samuel 6. The ark of the covenant, over which God's presence rested, was being transported on a cart (6:1–11). This was a violation of God's law concerning transportation of the ark, a visible representation of God's presence. God had commanded that priests carry it with wooden poles. The cart began to tip, so Uzzah, walking beside the ark, reached out to steady it, touched the ark, and was immediately struck dead. Our holy God is serious about his law and will not compromise his holy standards. This is why the cross was necessary. God would not turn his back on our sin; a penalty had to be paid. Rather than making us question the goodness of God, the death of Uzzah should cause us to celebrate the grace of Jesus that allows sinners to stand in the presence of a perfectly holy God.

For further study and encouragement: Jeremiah 7:1–15

———

APRIL 7

2 SAMUEL 8–11

Besides Jesus, no human hero is the Messiah; no human hero is divine; no human hero is perfect; and no human hero has unlimited power. So, besides Jesus, no human hero is worthy of your worship.

When you read your Bible, it's important to know what you're reading. Although the Bible is full of doctrine, it is not first a tome on systematic theology. Your Bible is loaded with divine wisdom, but it is not merely a book of wisdom for everyday life. The Bible has many great and interesting stories, but it is not simply a collection of stories with morals for your daily life. The Bible is not solely a compilation of lives of great heroes for your admiration or imitation. The Bible is a story, God's story. It is his biography; he is the hero of every story, and he is always on center stage. Every part of the Bible is meant to reveal God to us, that is, his attributes, his character, his plan, and his redeeming grace. The Bible should cause us to fall on our knees in humble confession and willing submission before the great Creator, Sovereign, Savior King whose glory splashes across its pages.

The Bible confronts our tendency toward hero worship by reminding us of two things. First, the Bible reminds us of the one who is behind every form of human success. The credit for the amazing heroic feats the Bible records always goes to the Lord. Second, the Bible reminds us that every human hero is flawed in some way—except Jesus. David's story is a clear example of both of these facts. His feats of strength, courage, and battle are many and amazing. But David is not actually the hero of David's story; God is. Second Samuel 8 records a list of some of David's many conquests, but note the summary of David's heroics in 2 Samuel 8:14: "And the Lord gave victory to David wherever he went." None of these victories is independently David's. None of them are solely the result of his wisdom, strength, or military prowess. David is victorious because the Lord fights for him. Credit for the defeat of every enemy he faces belongs to the Lord.

But something else is revealed in David's story. Like every other human hero except one, David is a sinner, capable of succumbing to temptation and disobeying the clear commands of the Lord. How sad it is to read about David's lust for Bathsheba, his taking her for his own, his murder of her husband, and then his claiming her for his wife. This is the same conquering hero. It is hard to imagine. We find another summary statement about David in 2 Samuel 11:27, this one the polar opposite of the first: "But the thing that David had done displeased the LORD." Great victory and tragic failure in the same man. The story is told this way to remind us that only one great hero is worthy of our worship: the God whose glory is revealed in every biblical story. May we worship him and him alone.

For further study and encouragement: John 5:37–41

———

APRIL 8

2 SAMUEL 12–15

God's gift of forgiveness is not a guarantee of
the removal of sin's consequences.

The Bible is full of reminders that the one who sits on the throne of the universe is a God of glorious grace. It shows us God's grace in story form, in poetic utterances, and in doctrinal explanations. Grace is a central theme in every part of the biblical revelation. But the Bible never presents God's grace in a way that would cause us to be less than serious about sin. You can't read your Bible and walk away saying, "Because God is a God of grace, it doesn't make any difference how I live, because, no matter what I do, I will be forgiven." The Bible never presents God's grace in a way that would make you feel free to go out and do what is wrong in God's eyes. Grace is not God's being permissive. God's grace always takes sin seriously. If sin were okay, there would be no need for grace. The cross of Jesus Christ stands as a monument to the fact that sin has penalties because God takes sin seriously.

One of the ways that the Bible protects us from misunderstanding the grace of God is by reminding us of the consequences of sin. Because God loves us, because he is jealous for our love, and because he is always seeking to draw us near, he has ordained many biblical stories that portray the consequences of sin. But Scripture does even more. It makes it clear that the grace of God's forgiveness doesn't always mean the removal of the consequences of sin. God is ready, willing, and able to forgive us, but often, for our spiritual good and his glory, the consequences remain. In this way, God welcomes us to run to him for the forgiveness that he is ready to offer while also cautioning us to be serious about the destructive nature of sin.

Grace and consequences do not work in opposition, but are meant, together, to draw us into a life of deeper gratitude and greater surrender to God. We see the operation of grace and the consequences of sin in the life of David after he commits adultery and murder. The prophet Nathan confronts David after his sin, and King David repents. Note how forgiveness and consequences come together in Nathan's final words to David: "'The LORD also has put away your sin; you shall not die. Nevertheless, because by this deed you have utterly scorned the LORD, the child who is born to you shall die.' Then Nathan went to his house" (2 Sam. 12:13–15). Forgiveness and consequences in the same statement. God's message is obvious: grace is glorious, sin is serious, and we need to hear both notes loudly and clearly. May we never celebrate grace while our actions scorn the Lord. And may our celebration of grace be even more exuberant because we grasp, with seriousness, the utter destructiveness of sin.

For further study and encouragement: Philippians 2:12–18

APRIL 9

2 SAMUEL 16–18

The Bible does not present a sanitized world, but is graphically honest about the pains, losses, and griefs of life in a fallen world.

Scripture portrays a world that we find familiar. It's a broken world, not always functioning as the Creator intended. It's populated by less than perfect people. All the sad, disappointing dramas that we face are found in the pages of our Bibles. The Bible reminds us that God understands what we face and hears our cries, just like he heard the cries of the characters in his word who cried out in their weakness, fear, disappointment, pain, loss, and grief. The presence, power, promises, and grace of God that we read about in Scripture are all the more comforting to us because they occur in a world that is like ours, with the high mountains and deep, dark valleys that every human travels. As the blood and dirt of this fallen world splash across the pages of Scripture, the glories of God's kingdom of love and grace shine even more brightly and beautifully.

Your Bible contains stories of war, political intrigue, family betrayal, famine, religious persecution, suicide, injustice—the list goes on. This lets you know two things. First, God fully understands the broken world that is your address. Your world is accurately painted on the canvas of Scripture. Second, God's grace addresses all of the brokenness both inside and outside of you. Someday this broken world will be made completely new, free from all the sad things that you find in your Bible and in your own life.

One of the saddest stories in all of Scripture is the story of King David and his seditious son, Absalom. Absalom is obsessed with his father's power and begins to conspire to take his father's throne, the throne David had received by the anointing of God. In a monarchy, if someone is going to take the throne, the sitting king must die. David is forced to leave the throne and hide out in caves from the murderous intent of his own son. As you read this story, you know that there is no way it is going to have a good ending. Eventually, it is reported to David that Absalom has been killed, but there is no joy in David's heart. Hear the words of this distraught and grieving father: "O my son Absalom, my son, my son Absalom! Would I had died instead of you, O Absalom, my son, my son!" (2 Sam. 18:33). It's heart-wrenching to read.

The account of Absalom and David is in your Bible to tell you not simply that God will preserve the line of David out of which the Messiah will come, but also that God understands and hears our deepest cries of grief and dismay. David's cry represents the cries of thousands and thousands of grieving fathers and mothers, cries that do not go unheard by our tenderhearted and compassionate Lord.

For further study and encouragement: Psalm 44:1–26

APRIL 10

2 SAMUEL 19–21

*There will be a day when God will dry the last tear
from our eyes, and we will never weep again.*

When I got the call, the life almost went out of me, and it wasn't even concerning my own daughter. The girl's mom called and told me that, after calling and searching all over the house for her daughter, she had found her in their basement. She was dead, with her suicide note lying next to her. The depth of grief in this mother's voice, interrupted by haunting wails, would suck the life out of any caring human being. I knew I had to go to her, but I dreaded entering that house. I felt emotionally and spiritually empty. All of the things I rehearsed in my heart to say when I arrived seemed woefully inadequate or inappropriate. The theological things I knew that spoke to this horrible moment seemed distant, sterile, impersonal. When I entered the house, I could physically feel the grief. It was as though a horrible, heart-crushing cloud had filled that home. It made it hard to think and hard to breathe. The family cried and I cried. I held on to them in the silent awe of loss. I left them that night emotionally spent, but I knew they would never leave, never escape, never forget. Yesterday she was in the kitchen doing homework; today she was in the basement lifeless, a horror too powerful to grasp.

Absalom had been David's little boy. David had held him close to his heart as an infant. He had played with him as a toddler. He had watched his personality and gifts develop. He had experienced Absalom's searching mind and developing leadership gifts. David had enjoyed many loving, nurturing, wisdom-giving, discipling, fun-filled, and proud dad moments with his son. Nothing could have prepared David for what Absalom would do and the horrible way Absalom would die. David was overcome, controlled, and imprisoned by his grief (2 Sam. 18). It is right to feel and to cry out in grief, but it is dangerous to be ruled by it. So God raised up Joab to confront David, calling the king to return to the work God had anointed him to do.

Joab's words in 2 Samuel 19 may seem harsh and unloving, but grief is both appropriate and potentially destructive. It must never control our hearts, become our identity, or shape our future hope. Now, I am talking not about denying powerful and appropriate emotions, but about remembering who we are and what we have been given as children of God.

In horrible moments of tragedy and loss, we have four things from the Lord. We have his *presence*. He is with us and for us in our grief. We have his *power*. He blesses us with the same power by which Jesus was raised from the dead. We have his *promises*. These represent the present and future help that he has guaranteed each of his children. We have his *commands*. Scripture tells us how to live, no matter what we are facing. God meets us in the worst, most unthinkable moments with the grace of his presence, power, promises, and commands, and through them he gives us just what we need in our deepest times of need. What love!

For further study and encouragement: Isaiah 25:6–9

APRIL 11

When it comes to biblical truth, insightful people are
those not simply with the right answers but with the
right questions, which lead to the right answers.

The Bible is not just a book with life-changing answers; it is also a record of profound questions. In the garden of Eden, when God asks Adam, "Where are you?" we are confronted with the fact that something is terribly wrong and that the world will never be the same again (Gen. 3:9). Divine image bearers, Adam and Eve, are now hiding from their Creator; shalom has been shattered. Later Abraham asks a thunderously important question, appealing for God's mercy: "Shall not the Judge of all the earth do what is just?" (Gen. 18:25). How about the practicality of this question: "How can a young man keep his way pure?" (Ps. 119:9)? Paul's question in Romans 6:1—"Are we to continue in sin that grace may abound?"—exposes and addresses a significant misunderstanding of the gospel. The questions of the Bible are recorded to expose our hearts, enlighten our minds, guard and protect us, deepen our faith, stimulate a sense of spiritual need and hunger, and move us to love God more fully and deeply.

Near the end of King David's life, this poet and musician composes a lengthy and gloriously celebratory song of deliverance. In this song he celebrates the faithfulness of God's protection. Humbly, David makes it known that his enemies were defeated not because of his independent military prowess and power, but by the almighty presence and power of God. This song is not that of a conquering general, pumping out his chest and saying, "Look what I have done." No, it is a hymn of praise from start to finish. We would do well to stop occasionally and write our own songs of thanksgiving.

In the song David asks the best, most important questions ever. How you answer these questions will determine where your heart goes and how you will then live your life:

Who is God, but the LORD?
And who is a rock, except our God? (2 Sam. 22:32)

For David, these are rhetorical questions. His life is a narrative of the unparalleled majesty and splendor of his God. There is no one like the Lord. No one is righteous like the Lord. No one has power like the Lord. No one is faithful like the Lord. He alone is a rock of surety upon which life and hope can stand. "Who is God, except our God?" The resounding answer is, "No one."

As you encounter this particular question, you must understand that many gods are battling for the rule of your heart. Many lords want to be the lord of your life. The pool of God-replacements is as deep as our wandering hearts and as wide as the creation around us. False gods whisper lies in our ears every day. David's rhetorical questions speak to the heart of the great spiritual war: "Who will be your God?" May God's grace enable us to give the right answer to this most important question of all.

For further study and encouragement: Mark 12:28–34

APRIL 12

1 KINGS 1–2

*It is crucial that the children of God listen to
and follow their Father's counsel.*

My father was a broken, imperfect man. He didn't act or parent perfectly, but he left me with many words of counsel that I have carried throughout my life. So much of his counsel had to do with work. He told me that work was a dignity and not a curse. He said, "They can take away your job, but they can't take away your willingness and ability to work." He told me how important it is to always be willing to learn. He told me on one occasion that I could fool many people but that God is never fooled. True, my father could have made many better life choices, but I am thankful for the wisdom he imparted to me.

First Kings 2:1–4 records a father's final counsel to his son. David is at death's door; Solomon is going to succeed him as king. These are David's words of counsel:

> When David's time to die drew near, he commanded Solomon his son, say-
> ing, "I am about to go the way of all the earth. Be strong, and show yourself
> a man, and keep the charge of the LORD your God, walking in his ways and
> keeping his statutes, his commandments, his rules, and his testimonies, as
> it is written in the Law of Moses, that you may prosper in all that you do
> and wherever you turn, that the LORD may establish his word that he spoke
> concerning me, saying, 'If your sons pay close attention to their way, to
> walk before me in faithfulness with all their heart and with all their soul,
> you shall not lack a man on the throne of Israel.'"

It is hard to overstate the spiritual value of these brief words of wisdom from a dying dad. I especially appreciate how David defines what it will mean for Solomon to be a strong man. His definition is not about brash, bullying, big-personality, muscled machismo. No, David knows that true strength is about walking in the ways of the Lord, as defined by the law of Moses, no matter what. The strength that really makes a difference is spiritual strength. Everyone's life is directed and shaped by what one's heart values and serves. The big battle is an internal battle, the fight for control of your thinking, desires, and choices. There is no more important show of strength than to stand strong in the way of the Lord. And, because this is a high standard, too high for us to reach on our own, this strength is only ever the result of God's grace.

When I read David's words, I think not only of my earthy father, but also of my infinitely wise, kind, and loving heavenly Father. I am thankful that, by grace, he has chosen me to be his child and has made my heart receptive to his always-wise counsel. I am aware that I have no wisdom of my own; he is my wisdom. The question is, Will I submit to his wise counsel, or go my own foolish way?

For further study and encouragement: Ephesians 6:1–4

APRIL 13

1 KINGS 3–5

If God told you he would grant you one wish, what would you ask for?

We were in a big, flashy toy store. This place was any child's dream. I could see in my granddaughter's eyes that she was dazzled by everything around her. She let go of my hand as we walked down the first aisle. It was stocked to the ceiling with the latest and greatest toys. When she looked up at me, I said words to her that every child wishes to hear: "Pick one thing you want, and I will buy it for you." I had purposely set no limits of size or price. She looked up at me with a big smile on her face and said one single word: "Really?" I said, "Yes, whatever you want, but just one thing." We proceeded to take a rather long journey up and down the aisles of the toy store until I knew its geography by heart. She would stop for a minute and ponder. She would pick up an occasional toy, but she never made the big choice. Finally, she wandered to the back of the store and chose a book. She said, "Toys get boring real quick, but books stay interesting much longer." I walked away impressed at her little-girl values and wisdom.

If your heavenly Father said to you, "I will give you any one thing you want," what would you ask for? The question itself gets at the war that takes place in all of our hearts, between a life shaped by worship and service of the Creator and one shaped by love of and craving for the creation. As Solomon ascends to the throne, God says to him, "Ask what I shall give you" (1 Kings 3:5). Solomon doesn't ask for the best palace ever, for military power, to be loved by many, or to be fabulously rich. No, he asks for something that has more lasting value than all of those things combined. Solomon asks for the thing that is so valuable that money can't buy it and that is so humanly unnatural that only God can give it. Solomon asks for wisdom: "Give your servant therefore an understanding mind to govern your people, that I may discern between good and evil, for who is able to govern this your great people?" (1 Kings 3:9). It takes a heart for God in order to resist asking for material things; it takes true humility in order to admit that you're not wise enough to do the thing that God has called you to do; and it takes faith in order to believe that God is the only true source of wisdom you need. The next verse says that Solomon's request pleased the Lord.

My request today is that my Lord would be pleased by what my heart craves. For that to be true, I need his rescuing and empowering grace. I know that grace is mine because long after Solomon's request, these words were written: "[Jesus] died for all, that those who live might no longer live for themselves but for him who for their sake died and was raised" (2 Cor. 5:15).

For further study and encouragement: Mark 10:35–45

———

APRIL 14

1 KINGS 6–7

All of our religious habits and practices are empty if the Lord doesn't dwell in the temple of our hearts.

I was on a high mountain at a large Buddhist temple. Priests and iconic Buddhist images were everywhere. On an elevated platform in the main temple sat a huge golden Buddha, twelve to fifteen feet high. All around me were very sincere and religious people. They lit and strategically placed candles, got down on their knees, and bowed their heads nearly to the ground. You could sense their sincerity, awe, and joy at being there. The scene was both engaging and heartbreaking to me. The whole place was buzzing with religious fervor. Around me was the low drone of huge bells that the priests would ring. But, despite the religious activity and spiritual sincerity, the temple was, in reality, completely empty. It was empty of any divine presence, and the god that people worshiped was a sorry handmade replacement for the one true God.

Religion—spiritual habits, practices, and pursuits—is empty and meaningless if God is not the Lord who reigns over and is worshiped by the hearts of all its practitioners. True religion is about more than buildings, spiritual disciplines, or creeds. True spirituality is about the presence of God. If God isn't dwelling in the center of it, then despite all the visible elements of a religion, it simply isn't the real deal. In 1 Kings 6, as Solomon is building the temple (a huge time, money, and attention commitment), God reminds him of what is even more important than this historical religious edifice that he is about to construct. What is more important than this temple? God's dwelling in the midst of his people. That building would be empty of its meaning and purpose if the Lord did not dwell there. And the people of Judah would be without identity, purpose, power, or future hope if God didn't live in the midst of them as well.

This is true of every form of spiritual pursuit and practice. It all lacks purpose, power, and hope if God isn't central, dwelling as Lord in the midst of it. The thing that makes true religion true cannot be achieved by building edifices, achieving seminary degrees, or amassing large crowds. True religion is only ever a gift of God's grace, evidenced when a perfectly holy God dwells in the midst of his less than holy people and sanctifies them by his presence and power. In his presence we find identity, forgiveness, power for living, and future hope. Jesus paid our penalty so that we would be blessed to live in God's presence now and in the forever that is to come. God is not satisfied with buildings, degrees, or programs. He will settle for nothing less than being Lord of the temple that is our hearts.

For further study and encouragement: Psalm 50:7–15

APRIL 15

1 KINGS 8–11

God, who is infinite and omnipresent, cannot be limited by time and space.

Some of the most important and profound conversations with our children would just sneak up on us. They didn't come in scheduled moments. A side comment in the car on the way to practice opened up an important talk. A moment of reflection on the day started a significant interchange that went on into the night. We had to be prepared, looking for those moments and being ready and willing when they came. So it is with the word of God. Some of the most significant theological moments in Scripture seem to sneak up on us. They aren't preceded by a warning in all caps: WARNING: DOCTRINAL INSTRUCTION IN THE NEXT SENTENCE. They may come as an editorial comment in a historical passage or embedded in the verse of a poem or hanging in the middle of a prayer. Be looking for those moments when God pulls back the curtain, revealing who he is, how he works, or the nature of his plan.

We find one of these profound theological moments in the middle of Solomon's prayer at the dedication of the temple:

Will God indeed dwell on the earth? Behold, heaven and the highest heaven cannot contain you; how much less this house that I have built! Yet have regard to the prayer of your servant and to his plea, O LORD my God, listening to the cry and to the prayer that your servant prays before you this day, that your eyes may be open night and day toward this house, the place of which you have said, "My name shall be there," that you may listen to the prayer that your servant offers toward this place. And listen to the plea of your servant and of your people Israel, when they pray toward this place. And listen in heaven your dwelling place, and when you hear, forgive. (1 Kings 8:27–30)

It is important to understand that God is not physical like us. He is not limited by boundaries of space or time. He lives in an eternal now, and he is everywhere. This truth presents a bit of a spiritual quandary for Solomon. If heaven and earth are unable to contain God, how much less will the temple that Solomon has just built be able to contain him? Yes, the Lord is in the temple that he has attached his name to, but the temple is not able to contain him.

The limitless, everywhereness of God is a precious truth, but at the same time it is hard for us to conceive. We are physical people, living in a physical space and surrounded by physical things. We are limited, and we spend so much of our time coming and going. But not God. The promises of God are connected to his everywhereness. I can trust his promises because I know God will always be in the place where these promises need to be delivered. All of this makes the incarnation even more stunning. God takes on human flesh. The limitless one takes on human limits to provide what limited human beings cannot provide for themselves. What grace!

For further study and encouragement: Job 38:1–18

APRIL 16

No idol is more seductive, deceptive, or attractive than the idol of self.

A couple came to me for counseling because their marriage was a war zone. Normal conversations became verbal duels for power. They went after each other's motives, character, choices, and actions in ways that were deeply personal and hurtful. It was hard to find any area in their marriage that wasn't a battleground. They claimed to be believers and they went to a pretty good church, but there was no God in their marriage. Because there was no God in their marriage, there was no higher agenda than the wishes and happiness of self. Their marriage ethics were set by the lord of self. Selfishness ruled every aspect of their relationship. They were exhausted and discouraged, but never considered that hope for their marriage would be found not in attacking one another but in together attacking the idol that was at the core of all their problems.

Idol worship rears its ugly and destructive head early in the biblical story. In Genesis 3, Adam and Eve disobey God because they want to be like him. Worship of self, rather than worship of God, is the occasion of the very first sin on earth. Self-worship is the sad, discordant note that sounds throughout the entire biblical narrative. The great spiritual war is between the holy throne of God and the unholy deifying of self. Every act of vertical disobedience and horizontal cruelty is rooted in the dethroning of God and the enthroning of self.

We see this clearly in 1 Kings 12:25–29:

> Then Jeroboam built Shechem in the hill country of Ephraim and lived there. And he went out from there and built Penuel. And Jeroboam said in his heart, "Now the kingdom will turn back to the house of David. If this people go up to offer sacrifices in the temple of the LORD at Jerusalem, then the heart of this people will turn again to their lord, to Rehoboam king of Judah, and they will kill me and return to Rehoboam king of Judah." So the king took counsel and made two calves of gold. And he said to the people, "You have gone up to Jerusalem long enough. Behold your gods, O Israel, who brought you up out of the land of Egypt." And he set one in Bethel, and the other he put in Dan.

The kingdom is now divided. Jeroboam is king of Israel and Rehoboam is king of Judah. It is shocking to see Jeroboam set up calves of gold for his people to worship, but it is even more shocking to hear him credit these idols with the deliverance of the people of God out of slavery. However, if this is all you see in this passage, you miss its deeper warning. Jeroboam sets up this idol worship so that his people will no longer go to Jerusalem to worship. He is afraid of losing power. At the core of this religious idolatry is the idol of self. This account stands as a warning to us. May God, in grace, free us from our bondage to ourselves.

For further study and encouragement: Jeremiah 17:5–10

APRIL 17

1 KINGS 15–17

Nothing in the earth below or the sky above can stop the march of the plans and purposes of God. Nothing.

I was in the most vibrant, productive, influential, and exciting ministry period of my life. I had speaking engagements every weekend and several international trips each year. I was also writing a book a year. I was committed and determined, but I was not sovereign or without limits. All it took were some physical symptoms and a visit to the hospital, and my seemingly unstoppable plans stopped in an instant. I faced the fact that I would never again be capable of completing what I had committed myself to do.

Thankfully, God is not like me. Nothing can thwart his will, nothing can challenge his rule, and nothing can stop the march of his grand redemptive plan. The hope and spiritual security of every believer rest on the fact that our Lord cannot be stopped. His rule rules. This truth is clear and comforting in the following passage:

> Now in the eighteenth year of King Jeroboam the son of Nebat, Abijam began to reign over Judah. He reigned for three years in Jerusalem. His mother's name was Maacah the daughter of Abishalom. And he walked in all the sins that his father did before him, and his heart was not wholly true to the LORD his God, as the heart of David his father. Nevertheless, for David's sake the LORD his God gave him a lamp in Jerusalem, setting up his son after him, and establishing Jerusalem. (1 Kings 15:1–4)

The Lord of heaven and earth had set a redemptive plan in motion from before the world was formed, and he would not turn from that plan, no matter what. Here he established the throne of Abijam and his son in Jerusalem, not because Abijam was a God-fearing king but because God would not let anything stand in the way of his great redeeming plan. Out of Judah would come the King of kings whose throne would never, ever end. Don't misunderstand: God was not ignoring Abijam's sin, acting as though it were nothing. Abijam's sin against God is clearly proclaimed in this passage. What God was unwilling to do was to turn his back on the redemptive plan and the covenant promises he had made to David. Think about it for a moment. If our sin could thwart God's sovereign plan of grace, then there would be no hope for us. Hope for covenant breakers is found only in the perfect covenant-keeping zeal of the Lord. When we are faithless, he will remain faithful, because he cannot deny himself or the promises of grace he has made. So when you place your hope on him, your hope is secure. In a world where so many things disappoint us, that's very good news.

For further study and encouragement: Proverbs 19:21

APRIL 18

1 KINGS 18–20

The difference between true and false religion is clear. In false religion people fearfully reach up to somehow gain acceptance with their god. In true religion God reaches down and by grace grants his acceptance to those who do not deserve it.

There are more than three hundred and fifty "fear nots" (or similar expressions of that encouragement) in your Bible. There is a gloriously beautiful and comforting message in this central theme in Scripture. It splashes across the pages of your Bible to remind you that the faith you have given your heart to is a system not of fear but of grace upon grace. We do not wake up in the morning fearing our deity's wrath or wondering what we could do that day to ward it off. Our religious lives are not relegated to "do more and try harder." The story of the Bible is not an extended call for us to get our act together—or else. The primary theme of the biblical narrative is not divine condemnation but divine *grace.* Our consistent unworthiness doesn't make us hide in guilt and shame, but rather stands as a reminder of how much we need the grace that is our only hope. Acceptance by human effort vs. acceptance by a sacrifice of grace is the fault line between true and false religion.

We see this great spiritual fault line in the contest between the priests of Baal and the prophet Elijah to prove who the true God really is. It is clear that there is no restfulness of heart in the religion of these priests of Baal. They work as hard as they can, even to the point of self-injury, to try to get their god's attention and to make him willing to answer their prayers and consume their sacrifice. It's a sad display of fear mixed with delusion. After all their dancing, raving, and cutting themselves, they receive no answer. They are greeted with complete and utter silence, and their sacrifice sours in the sun.

Elijah has his sacrifice doused with water three times to prevent any charges of monkey business, and then he bows and prays a humble prayer for help: "O LORD, God of Abraham, Isaac, and Israel, let it be known this day that you are God in Israel, and that I am your servant, and that I have done all these things at your word. Answer me, O LORD, answer me, that this people may know that you, O LORD, are God, and that you have turned their hearts back" (1 Kings 18:36–37).

This is not a prayer of appeasement; Elijah does not say, "Haven't I done enough to get you to respond?" This is a prayer of glory and grace. He prays for God to answer, so that people would know that he is the one true God. His prayer is a request for grace. Elijah doesn't rave, parade, or cut himself. He simply bows his head and rests in God's gracious reply. God has called us not to a life of fear but to the rest of faith, made possible only because he is a God of amazing grace.

For further study and encouragement: Romans 5:6–11

———

APRIL 19

1 KINGS 21–22

The only hope for real sinners is real divine mercy.

Sin is real, it is destructive, and it always leads to death. Sin is humanity's greatest pandemic. No one escapes it. No mere human has ever defeated it. Systems of personal reform do not weaken its power. Every human being is born with this grave spiritual sickness and, apart from divine intervention, will carry it to the tomb. Sin rears its ugly head in your thoughts and desires. Sin colors your communication, both how you speak and how you listen. Sin corrupts every relationship, creating conflict where peace should dwell. Sin causes you either to deny God's existence or to rage against his rule. Sin makes us self-absorbed, self-righteous, and self-defensive. Sin makes us want to control more than to serve. Sin turns everything into an idol, as we fail to be in awe of the one who desires our worship. Sin is more deeply sinful than we can imagine—and that is why God's grace is more deeply essential than we tend to think. No matter how much you minimize your sin, you will still live under its power apart from divine intervention.

God's mercy is a constant theme of the biblical narrative. Again and again, as we read, we are confronted with real sin and real mercy. Sometimes you have to ask yourself, "How can God be so patient? How can he be so kind? Will his mercy ever run out?" You find one of those radical moments of mercy in 1 Kings 21:25–29:

> (There was none who sold himself to do what was evil in the sight of the Lord like Ahab, whom Jezebel his wife incited. He acted very abominably in going after idols, as the Amorites had done, whom the Lord cast out before the people of Israel.)
> And when Ahab heard those words, he tore his clothes and put sackcloth on his flesh and fasted and lay in sackcloth and went about dejectedly. And the word of the Lord came to Elijah the Tishbite, saying, "Have you seen how Ahab has humbled himself before me? Because he has humbled himself before me, I will not bring the disaster in his days."

It's important to pay attention to how Ahab is described. He "sold himself to do what was evil in the sight of the Lord. . . . He acted very abominably in going after idols." Not only was Ahab a wicked man, but in his wickedness and idolatry he encouraged others to be the same. You would think that God would exercise his righteous judgment against this evil king, but this is not where the story goes. Ahab has a moment of grief and contrition over his sin, and God's response is to treat him with mercy rather than judgment.

This passage points us to the cross of Jesus Christ. The cross is the ultimate demonstration that sin is real and has consequences, but also that God's mercy is real and will ultimately triumph over judgment. Because sin is the bad news we have to accept, grace is the good news we all need to hear and believe. No one is without a need for grace. No one.

For further study and encouragement: Exodus 34:6–7

APRIL 20

*No matter what we may face in this broken world, a bright
and glorious future awaits every child of God.*

I am not a prophet or the son of a prophet. It's not just that I cannot predict what will happen years down the road; I don't know what will happen in the next ten minutes. Fear of the future is a regular human affliction. We tend to fear what we do not know and have no ability to control. But this fear is weakened for the Christian, because grace has made us the sons and daughters of the one who is in complete control not just of our present, but also of all the tomorrows that follow on into eternity. The plan, over which God has complete control, has a glorious end written into it. We may weep with the pains of our present address, but there is glory in store for us.

Elijah had a rough life. He was called to his prophetic ministry during the reign of the abominable evil of Ahab and Jezebel. He faced opposition and threats. He proclaimed and defended the presence, power, and glory of God, while being surrounded by idolatry. At times he felt alone and forsaken, but a glorious homecoming was in God's plan for him:

> Now when the LORD was about to take Elijah up to heaven by a whirlwind, Elijah and Elisha were on their way from Gilgal. . . . And as they still went on and talked, behold, chariots of fire and horses of fire separated the two of them. And Elijah went up by a whirlwind into heaven. And Elisha saw it and he cried, "My father, my father! The chariots of Israel and its horsemen!" And he saw him no more. (2 Kings 2:1, 11–12)

The experience of going up into heaven after one's earthly life is over, without first experiencing physical death, is rare in the Bible, so there is something both unique and prophetic about the story of Elijah's end. Notice that he doesn't just disappear, and then is somehow in heaven with the Lord. No, chariots and horses of fire come to get him. It is important to understand that the chariots and horses of fire are a *theophany*, that is, a divine appearing. God didn't send an Uber to get Elijah. The Lord Almighty himself, whom Elijah served, came to carry Elijah to heaven, forever to dwell in his presence. This is almost too beautiful and amazing to grasp. What an incredibly and gloriously shocking scene for Elisha to witness! He saw the Lord come for his own, liberating him from the sin and suffering of this fallen world, and transporting him to a place where these things are no more.

What happened to Elijah stands as a prophecy of what is in store for all of God's children he has adopted by his grace. It is a finger pointing to Jesus's words to his disciples in John 14:3: "If I go and prepare a place for you, I will come again and take you to myself, that where I am you may be also." Here's the good news: the same Lord who came for Elijah will finally come in glory to take his children to be with him forever.

For further study and encouragement: Romans 8:18–21

———

APRIL 21

2 KINGS 4–5

Christianity rises or falls on whether God has the power to raise the dead.

No power can compare with resurrection power, which God alone holds. It is one of the things that separates him from everything else. We are used to death being the end. This may seem crass, but when you attend a funeral, you expect nothing from the deceased. You know that there is no life in that person, and that is that. The finality of death is why it is so painful. Nothing leaves us feeling more helpless than death. Because sin ushered death into our world, and because death is the inescapable end that every living thing eventually faces, God's power to raise the dead is the ultimate victorious comfort to his people. The apostle Paul argues that if there is no resurrection from the dead, then the resurrection of Jesus is a fake, and, if that is true, then we have been duped and our faith is in vain (1 Cor. 15:12–19). The power to raise the dead is the platform on which everything we believe rests.

Three times in the Old Testament and six times in the New someone is raised from the dead. Each of these has been recorded and preserved to remind us of the solitary power of God over life and death.[1] The account of the Shunammite's son in 2 Kings 4:18–37 is the second recording in the Old Testament of someone being raised from the dead. God works this miracle through his prophet Elisha.

These nine accounts not only remind us of the almighty power of God, a power that not even death can defeat, but they also foreshadow where the story

[1] 1 Kings 17:17–22; 2 Kings 4:18–37; 13:20–21; Matt 28:1–6; Mark 5:41; Luke 7:14; John 11:38–44; Acts 9:36–42; 20:7–12.

of redemption is going. Sin will not have the final victory. The story will not end in the unmoving stillness of death. Life will triumph over death. This is the plan of God.

The stories of individuals being raised from the dead that are sprinkled throughout the biblical story predict the necessity of two resurrections to come. The first is the resurrection of Jesus, after his death on the cross. He came not only to pay the penalty for our sin but also to defeat sin and death in his resurrection. Remember that the resurrection of Jesus is not the final resurrection; it is the firstfruit of resurrections to come. There will be a day when all of the dead in Christ will be raised (1 Cor. 15:20). Death will die, and the children of God will live forever with the Lord of life, dwelling in his presence and basking in his glory.

The stories of these individuals are a promise of the greatest ending to a story ever imagined. In the dark valleys and hardships of life in this groaning world, we remember again and again that sin, suffering, and death are doomed. Someday they will imprison us no more, because with our Lord we will rise and breathe in the perfect air of the new heavens and the new earth, never again to shed death's tears.

For further study and encouragement: Romans 8:1–11

———

APRIL 22

2 KINGS 6–8

It's sad when anyone is blind to the presence and almighty power of God.

It is vital for us to understand that the most important realities in all of life cannot be seen with our physical eyes. Our God, who sits on the throne of the universe, ruling with holy wisdom, absolute sovereignty, and awesome power, cannot be physically seen or touched. His existence, rule, and plan for his creatures are the most visible things in the world, but they are not physically visible. You can't use the scientific method or modern technology to prove the existence or character of God. You can point to physical evidences of his existence in the creation, but it takes another set of eyes to see the glorious one behind the glories of creation. This means that our most important vision system is not our physical eyes. When Luella and I worked at a school for the blind, we became aware of how devastating and life-altering physical blindness can be. But it is not the most destructive form of blindness. Nothing is more devastating than when the eyes of the heart are blind to the things of God.

The blindness in 2 Kings 6:15–17 is instructive:

> When the servant of the man of God rose early in the morning and went out, behold, an army with horses and chariots was all around the city. And the servant said, "Alas, my master! What shall we do?" He said, "Do not be afraid, for those who are with us are more than those who are with them." Then Elisha prayed and said, "O Lord, please open his eyes that he may see." So the Lord opened the eyes of the young man, and he saw, and behold, the mountain was full of horses and chariots of fire all around Elisha.

Elisha is under attack. The king of Syria has sent his troops to do him harm. Elisha's servant looks out and sees the Syrian army and panics. But Elisha assures him that they are being defended by an even greater army, one the servant cannot see. So Elisha prays that God would open the eyes of the servant to the spiritual realties right in front of him. The Lord answers Elisha's prayer, and the servant sees that the mountain is filled with horses and chariots of fire. Remember, horses and chariots are a theophany, that is, a divine appearing. God opens the eyes of Elisha's servant to his presence and his power.

This passage reminds us that spiritual sightedness is not natural. When the eyes of your heart "see" God in all his majestic power and glory, you can be sure that you have been visited by his grace. It took an act of divine empowerment for the servant to see the presence and power of God.

One of the prophecies regarding the earthly ministry of the Messiah, Jesus, said that he would give sight to blind eyes (Isa. 35:5). Since sin blinds and is still present in our hearts, we should never stop praying for the grace of spiritual sightedness. That's a prayer God delights in answering.

For further study and encouragement: John 9:1–41

APRIL 23

Like a father who warns his children about the dangers
of crossing the street, in his word God again and again
warns his children about the dangers of crossing his
boundaries and doing what he has declared to be sin.

It quickly became clear to me that our young children had no sense of the dangers that were all around them in the world they had been born into. Few days would go by that were not marked by repeated warnings about the steps, the stove, the electric sockets in the walls, what was edible and what was not, where sharp corners were, and the dangers of jumping off the back of the couch. I warned my children about dangers because I cherished them (I still do). I wanted them to grow, develop, and thrive, so I did everything I could to keep them safe.

God's righteous warnings are an expression of his love. If heeded, they are a spiritual safety system. The warnings in the Bible should be to us like alarms going off. They should get our attention and alter what we think and what we do. But God's warnings in Scripture are not always direct, as in "Don't do this" or "This is what will happen if you do that." God's warnings can sometimes be in poetic form or in story form.

If you don't understand God's zeal to protect his children from spiritual danger, to keep their hearts from wandering, to keep them from looking at what is evil and seeing good, and to claim them as his own, you might wonder why in the world 2 Kings 9:30–35 is in the Bible. You might think that this dark and gruesome story was unnecessary. It is the story of the death of the rebellious and horribly evil queen, Jezebel. God had prophesied through Elijah that dogs would eat her and there would be nothing left of her to bury:

When Jehu came to Jezreel, Jezebel heard of it. And she painted her eyes and adorned her head and looked out of the window. And as Jehu entered the gate, she said, "Is it peace, you Zimri, murderer of your master?" And he lifted up his face to the window and said, "Who is on my side? Who?" Two or three eunuchs looked out at him. He said, "Throw her down." So they threw her down. And some of her blood spattered on the wall and on the horses, and they trampled on her. Then he went in and ate and drank. And he said, "See now to this cursed woman and bury her, for she is a king's daughter." But when they went to bury her, they found no more of her than the skull and the feet and the palms of her hands.

Why is this passage important for us to read and contemplate? Because sin doesn't always seem sinful to us and because we sometimes tell ourselves that we can sin and things will turn out all right in the end. So, in loving and protective mercy, God lets his judgment for sin be seen. God exposes us to things we'd rather not see in order to keep us from going where he knows we shouldn't go.

For further study and encouragement: James 1:14–15

APRIL 24

2 KINGS 12–14

Our hope in life and death is found not in our faithfulness,
but in the perfect faithfulness of our Savior.

It was not my finest moment, by any measure. I was impatient and irritated. We had made plans, and I was watching my plans evaporate as Luella was waylaid by a phone call from work. The call seemed to last an eternity, and the delay seemed personal, although it wasn't. I paced the floor, making sure she knew I was not happy that we weren't leaving. When she got off the phone, I was cold and distant. But by God's grace, conviction set in quickly. It was all very humbling. I confessed my impatience, and Luella graciously forgave me. As we drove away, the gospel exploded in my brain. This is why my hope is never in my obedience, my faithfulness, my wisdom, or my righteousness. This side of eternity, I will never have a perfect track record to lay before the throne of God. I am not an intentional rebel against God or a heretic. I do not mock his existence or flaunt my transgression of his law. But even though I am a child of God, I am not yet sin-free. The longer I walk with the Lord, the clearer it is to me that my hope is not in my faithfulness, but in the absolute perfection of the faithfulness of my Lord.

You could argue that one of the main themes of the Old Testament is divine covenant faithfulness cast in contrast to human unfaithfulness. The story of the people of God is one of sin, repentance, and temporary obedience, followed by apostasy once again—and the cycle repeats. You want to scream, "Is there anyone faithful in Israel?" The answer is, "Yes, the Lord of Israel, Jehovah alone." You see this unfaithfulness/faithfulness contrast in an important passage in 2 Kings 13: "Now Hazael king of Syria oppressed Israel all the days of Jehoahaz. But the LORD was gracious to them and had compassion on them, and he turned toward them, because of his covenant with Abraham, Isaac, and Jacob, and would not destroy them, nor has he cast them from his presence until now" (2 Kings 13:22–23).

In spite of Israel's rebellion and idolatry, God keeps the Syrians at bay. He does so not because the Israelites have earned his favor through a track record of covenant faithfulness. No, the opposite is true. If their relationship to God had been based on their performance of the law, then God would have abandoned them long ago. Instead, God had compassion on Israel and turned toward them because *he is faithful* and will fulfill his covenant promises.

So it is with us. Our standing before God is based not on our righteousness but on the perfect righteousness of Jesus. He perfectly measured up for us in every way, because he knew that we never would. Here in 2 Kings, during the dark days of Israel's rebellion, the gospel is preached to us once again. Our hope in life and death rests on our Savior's faithfulness, not our own.

For further study and encouragement: 2 Corinthians 5:18–21

APRIL 25

2 KINGS 15–17

It is dangerous to minimize or forget the horrible sinfulness of sin.

It is easy to minimize, deny, or forget the evil that still lives within us and will continue to live there until God's redeeming work is complete and we are with him forever. Yes, he has given his children means of grace, such as his Spirit, his word, and his church, but we still must not minimize the presence or power of remaining sin. Think about the following realities:

We are still capable of going to where lust leads us.

We can still let anger drive our actions, reactions, and responses.

We are still able to be consumed by bitterness or jealousy.

We not only fail regularly to love our neighbor, but we also give way to contempt.

We often love our own way more than God's way.

We often seem to love the world more than we love our Lord.

This list could go on and on. It is clear that our struggle with sin is not over, but something else is just as clear. Sin doesn't always seem sinful to us. Sometimes what God says is ugly looks beautiful to us. We tell ourselves that we can sin and everything will be all right in the end. But sin is a liar. It never keeps its promises, and it never produces good in us or through us. Sin whispers to us promises of life, but it leads only to death. Sin is more deeply sinful than we tend to think or imagine. So God has recorded shocking moments of history in his word; he wants us to be confronted with the horrible nature of sin. One such shocking moment is recorded in 2 Kings 16:1–4:

> In the seventeenth year of Pekah the son of Remaliah, Ahaz the son of Jotham, king of Judah, began to reign. Ahaz was twenty years old when he began to reign, and he reigned sixteen years in Jerusalem. And he did not do what was right in the eyes of the Lord his God, as his father David had done, but he walked in the way of the kings of Israel. He even burned his son as an offering, according to the despicable practices of the nations whom the Lord drove out before the people of Israel. And he sacrificed and made offerings on the high places and on the hills and under every green tree.

When we read about these horrible idolatrous practices, including infanticide, we must remember that this passage is not describing some animistic, pagan nation. This is Judah, the tribe of David, out of which the Messiah will come. These are God's people, who have progressively, step by step, walked away from their Lord. They have walked so far away that they are now burning their children on altars to false gods!

This sickening passage screams to us of why the cross of Jesus Christ was necessary. Grace had to flip the script. A penalty for sin had to be paid, and sin had to be defeated. Today, remember the sinfulness of sin and celebrate the eternal victory of God's grace in Jesus.

For further study and encouragement: Jeremiah 7:30–34

APRIL 26

2 KINGS 18–19

*Nothing is more sure, faithful, and hope-giving
than the perfect goodness of the Lord.*

Years ago I came across a brief epitaph, but it was perhaps the best summary of a life one could give. In fact, I would like these five little words to be said of me: "He was a good man." More than being successful, more than being powerful, more than being rich, more than acquiring public acclaim, I aspire to live a life that is *good*. To be good is to be morally pure, patient and faithful, loving and generous. It means you live a Godward life. But as much as I am encouraged by a person's life that can be characterized as good, there is no goodness like the goodness of the Lord. God's word records Israel's moral wandering, the chaos of their idolatry, and the works of evil king after evil king. But what jumps off the pages of Scripture is the stunning goodness of the Lord. He will not return evil for evil, and he will not forsake his covenant promises.

You can't read this history without concluding that hope is never found in human plans or power. Hope is never found in human strength or wisdom. Hope is never found in human spirituality or righteousness. Hope is never found in dabbling in the philosophy or religions of the world. Hope is only ever found in one place: the goodness of the Lord. That goodness shines in 2 Kings 18:1–8:

> In the third year of Hoshea son of Elah, king of Israel, Hezekiah the son of Ahaz, king of Judah, began to reign. He was twenty-five years old when he began to reign, and he reigned twenty-nine years in Jerusalem. His mother's name was Abi the daughter of Zechariah. And he did what was right in the eyes of the LORD, according to all that David his father had done. He removed the high places and broke the pillars and cut down the Asherah. And he broke in pieces the bronze serpent that Moses had made, for until those days the people of Israel had made offerings to it (it was called Nehushtan). He trusted in the LORD, the God of Israel, so that there was none like him among all the kings of Judah after him, nor among those who were before him. For he held fast to the LORD. He did not depart from following him, but kept the commandments that the LORD commanded Moses. And the LORD was with him; wherever he went out, he prospered. He rebelled against the king of Assyria and would not serve him. He struck down the Philistines as far as Gaza and its territory, from watchtower to fortified city.

Just when you think things will only get darker for God's children, God raises up a righteous, faithful, and God-worshiping king—not because the people deserve it, but because God is that good. Because of Hezekiah, Israel experiences moral and spiritual renewal and renewed power against their enemies. When his children are faithless, God remains faithful. This was the hope of God's children of old, and it is our hope today.

For further study and encouragement: Colossians 2:8–10

APRIL 27

When you look at the moral, spiritual darkness around
you, you might wonder, Will evil win in the end?

When you read the following passage, it should make you weep. And it might
make you wonder, *Is this the end? Can it get any worse for God's children than this?*

Manasseh was twelve years old when he began to reign, and he reigned
fifty-five years in Jerusalem. His mother's name was Hephzibah. And he
did what was evil in the sight of the LORD, according to the despicable practices of the nations whom the LORD drove out before the people of Israel.
For he rebuilt the high places that Hezekiah his father had destroyed, and
he erected altars for Baal and made an Asherah, as Ahab king of Israel had
done, and worshiped all the host of heaven and served them. And he built
altars in the house of the LORD, of which the LORD had said, "In Jerusalem
will I put my name." And he built altars for all the host of heaven in the
two courts of the house of the LORD. And he burned his son as an offering and used fortune-telling and omens and dealt with mediums and with
necromancers. He did much evil in the sight of the LORD, provoking him
to anger. And the carved image of Asherah that he had made he set in the
house of which the LORD said to David and to Solomon his son, "In this
house, and in Jerusalem, which I have chosen out of all the tribes of Israel,
I will put my name forever. And I will not cause the feet of Israel to wander
anymore out of the land that I gave to their fathers, if only they will be careful to do according to all that I have commanded them, and according to all
the Law that my servant Moses commanded them." But they did not listen,
and Manasseh led them astray to do more evil than the nations had done
whom the LORD destroyed before the people of Israel. (2 Kings 21:1–9)

This is a hard passage to read. It seems as though righteousness has been
soundly defeated and evil now reigns. Manasseh had led God's children into a
level of evil that was worse than that of the surrounding pagan nations. He had
turned the house of the Lord into a place of idolatry, burned his own son as an
offering to a false god, sought the counsel of those who communicated with
the dead, and refused to heed the warnings of the Lord. Could this be the end?
Would evil finally have its way? The resounding answer of the biblical narrative
is, "No!" Righteousness will triumph because there is a holy one who sits on the
throne of the universe, and he will have his way in the end.

No matter how evil things get, the future of God's holy plan and his chosen people is not at stake. God will finally put the last enemy under his feet, and he will usher in peace and righteousness forever. In the darkness of the days we live in, do not panic. Our Lord is on his throne in power and glory, and he will win.

For further study and encouragement: Psalm 110:1–7

———

APRIL 28

2 KINGS 23–25

No matter how bad and spiritually dark things may seem,
don't ever stop praying for moral and spiritual revival.

Just when you get to the point where you want to stop reading the Old Testament because it has become so dark and discouraging, out of the darkness rises young King Josiah. Rather than reading about more idolatry, infanticide, desecration of the house of the Lord, or consultations with fortune tellers and necromancers, you find real spiritual revival. In the darkness a bright light shines through the moral commitments of a young and godly king. One of the first things this king does is to lead the children of Judah in a revival service. He leads the people in a covenant-renewing ceremony, in which they again vow their allegiance to the covenant of the Lord. Josiah then leads his people in a wholesale destruction of idol high places and idol practices. Out of utter spiritual darkness comes this moment of spiritual revival. God's law is observed and his covenant renewed. It had not seemed that this would be the next chapter for the people of Israel; and, yes, God would later raise up Babylon to purge his people and call them back to himself. But the beauty of this moment of revival should not be diminished.

A rallying cry for the Protestant Reformers was the Latin phrase *post tenebras lux*: "after darkness, light." Spiritual darkness had blanketed Europe, and the light and glory of the grace of the gospel of Jesus Christ seemed like a tiny flickering flame. But out of the darkness God raised up Martin Luther, John Calvin, and other gospel lights. The flames of the gospel burned bright in Europe, spread throughout the world, and burn brightly still today.

Between the "already" and the "not yet," *post tenebras lux* is and has always been the hope of God's people. This hope is rooted in the goodness, holiness, power, promises, and grace of God. It is about holding on to the belief that God will not let his grace die, that he will not let his plan fade away, and that he will keep every one of the promises he has made.

The birth of Jesus was a monumental *post tenebras lux* moment. He came into this dark world as the light shining in darkness (John 1:5). Jesus is the eternal light, the eternal torch that nothing or no one could ever extinguish. He shines into the hearts of all who put their trust in him.

The world might seem dark to you today, but another *post tenebras lux* moment is coming, when the light will come for his own, ushering them into his final kingdom of light, life, peace, and righteousness forever. Darkness will not ultimately defeat the light, and so, with the same hope as the Reformers, we say *post tenebras lux*.

For further study and encouragement: Lamentations 3:22–33

———

APRIL 29

1 CHRONICLES 1–4

It's important to remember that our hope in life and death is not our zeal for God, but his zeal to keep every one of his redemptive promises.

You should dedicate and discipline yourself to keep every one of God's commands. You should work to apply the wisdom of his word to every aspect of your life. You should be a student of his word. You should be committed to understanding the theology of Scripture and live that theology out in your daily life. You should use the resources God has entrusted to you to contribute to the work of his kingdom and to meet the needs of those he places in your path. You should be committed to sharing the gospel when God gives the opportunity. You should commit yourself to having a marriage and family life that are shaped by the comfort and call of the gospel. You should build a robust devotional life of worship and study. You should be committed to counting your blessings every day and resist numbering your complaints. You should live with gratitude, even when facing trials. You should do all of these things with joy. *But it is vital that you also remember that your zeal and discipline for God are not the rock of your spiritual hope.*

We must constantly remember that true, unshakable hope is only ever found in God's zeal for his own glory and the plan of redemption he set in place before the foundations of the world were laid. If you faithfully do all of the things above, which God clearly calls you to do, you do so only because you have been rescued and empowered by God's grace. It's true that not only is he faithful, but we can be faithful only because he has been faithful first. All of our desires to love, serve, and worship him are the fruit of his grace. We must always resist taking credit for things that are the fruit of his faithful grace. All human righteousness is the work of his convicting, rescuing, transforming, and empowering grace.

So, when you read the genealogies in 1 Chronicles, you should be impressed with something other than the long list of names. Your heart should go to the God behind the list. First Chronicles 1–4 takes us from Abraham and his descendants, to David and his descendants, and to Judah and his other descendants. These genealogies are a tribute not so much to human effort, commitment, wisdom, righteousness, or faithfulness, but to the perfect faithfulness of God to every covenant promise he had made. He called, empowered, guided, warned, and forgave. From the early promises to Abraham, to the redemption from Egypt, to the journey through the wilderness, to the entrance into the promised land, and to the establishment of a kingdom, God acted with power and grace on behalf of his people. This is why they exist. Romans 11:36 is the best summary of these genealogies: "From him and through him and to him are all things. To him be glory forever. Amen."

For further study and encouragement: Philippians 3:8–14

APRIL 30

1 CHRONICLES 5–9

We should be thankful that woven into the gospel is
the promise of fresh starts and new beginnings.

One of my favorite verses in all of Scripture is Jonah 3:1: "Then the word of the LORD came to Jonah the second time. . . ." God's patience and grace toward Jonah surprise me every time I read this book. In the face of God's call, Jonah ran in the other direction, not only to disobey God but to escape God's presence. I probably would have told Jonah that I was done with him, that I didn't need him because I had plenty of prophets to send in his place. But our God is a God of inexhaustible patience and grace. He pursued Jonah, rescued Jonah from himself, and then called him again to his mission to Nineveh. Jonah was granted a fresh start and a new beginning, even in the face of his rebellion, because God's grace is amazing. Once God has chosen you as his own, you cannot outrun his grace.

The history of the children of Israel was a chronicle of commitment, followed by rebellion and idolatry, followed by repentance, with the cycle repeating—but each time with a deeper falling away and deeper evil, until the sins of Israel were as great as those of the surrounding pagan nations. Because God loved his children, he could not sit by and dispassionately watch their wanton idolatry and immorality. Just as a father who truly loves his children will discipline them because of that love, God moved to discipline his own. This discipline was not a final condemnation. God was not turning his back on his own. He was not forsaking his covenant. He was not turning from all his promises. God was not casting his children away from his presence.

God raised up Babylon not as a tool of his final judgment against Judah, but as a tool of his purifying discipline. The captivity in Babylon would not be the final chapter for Judah because God is a God of inexhaustible patience and grace. There would be more chapters, culminating in the coming of the Son of David, Jesus Christ—the Lion of the tribe Judah.

So the words of 1 Chronicles 9:1–2 are heartening:

All Israel was recorded in genealogies, and these are written in the Book of the Kings of Israel. And Judah was taken into exile in Babylon because of their breach of faith. Now the first to dwell again in their possessions in their cities were Israel, the priests, the Levites, and the temple servants.

Judah was exiled because of their wholesale breach of faith, but it wasn't the end, because woven into God's grace is the promise of fresh starts and new beginnings. Judah returned to the promised land, led by those who would reestablish the centrality of the worship of God. Be thankful that, in spite of our sin, his grace offers us hope for a new day.

For further study and encouragement: Jeremiah 31:16–20

MAY 1

We should always hold our plans with an open hand, because
God is perfectly wise and sovereign and we are not.

What do you really want? Be honest with yourself and with God as you make this assessment. If you could have anything, what would it be? What personal dreams do you hold onto and revisit? Where do you wish you were sovereign and able to make the world do your bidding? What makes you dissatisfied with your life? Where are you tempted to doubt the wisdom or goodness of God? How do you handle disappointment? What do you tend to do when your plans are thwarted? What have you prayed for and later wondered why God failed to provide? Is there a struggle in your life between your plans for you and God's plans for you? Are you ever tempted to think that you are smarter than God?

The biblical story is God's story. It was written to introduce you to the magnificent glory of his glory. He is the character that dominates every narrative. The biblical story is meant to expose you to God's character, his will, and his plan for his own. He is the hero of every story. All the victories belong to him. Every great man or woman of faith is great only because of God's empowering presence and grace. In the biblical story, human plans fail, but God's never do. Human power is limited and temporary, but God's isn't. Human love is weak and fails, but God's love is strong and always prevails. But, despite God's zeal to reveal himself to us in such a way that should encourage us to trust him, follow him, and surrender our will to his, there is a constant struggle in the biblical story between what people want and what God knows is best for them.

Israel was dissatisfied with having no human king, even though God was an infinitely better ruler than any human king they could ever have. They looked at the nations around them and wanted a king like they had. So God gave them what they wanted. Sadly, Saul was a king like the other nations' kings. His repeated rebellion against God, his obsession with his own power, and his jealousy all led to his demise. God had planned something better for his children, something much better than what they envied in the surrounding pagan nations (see 1 Chron. 11:1–4). God wanted for his children a king after his own heart. He would covenant with this king to give him a throne that would never end. Out of this king's line would come Jesus, the Son of David, the Savior of the world. As a wise Father, God always knows what is best for his children. His plans are always best. His way is always right. We will never know more than he knows or be wiser than he is. Surrendering your desires, plans, and will to the Lord of lords is never a bad choice. Demanding your own way never produces anything good. The plan of the ultimate planner is always the wisest and best plan. Surrender your plans to him, and you will be glad you did.

For further study and encouragement: Psalm 37:1–6

MAY 2

1 CHRONICLES 12–14

When God calls you, he supplies everything you need to answer his call.

Sometimes God calls us into his service not because we are able, but because he is. When God calls us into his service, he is not necessarily endorsing *our* character, wisdom, power, or righteousness. His call reveals not how great or worthy we are, but how perfectly great and worthy he is. God knows we are sinners in need of grace. He knows that he has created us with limits. He knows we are still tempted to love what is foolish and to think that we are far wiser than we truly are. He knows how often our minds and bodies fail us. So every call and command of God is accompanied by his empowering grace. We need grace both to desire and to do what God calls us to do. I am convinced that we should never allow ourselves to forget that God's grace is designed to move us not from dependence to independence, but from independence to a greater and deeper dependence on him. Mature believers are mature because they have forsaken the delusion that independently they can be what God calls them to be and do what God calls them to do.

First Chronicles 11–12 records for us all the mighty men who come to King David and swear their loyalty to him in service and in battle. It is an impressive list of men of wisdom and valor. But as we read this history, we must understand what is happening here. These men gather around David in loyal service, surrendering their gifts and abilities to him, not simply because *he* is great. No, something grander and more encouraging is occurring. God has called David to unify and lead Israel, an extremely difficult task. To accomplish this, David is going to need lots of help. So God, in faithfulness to his servant, supplies him with what he needs. These men gather around David because when God calls one of his children into his service, he supplies what that servant needs. These men of valor are physical evidence that when God calls, he supplies.

God never calls us into his service and then walks away. He never calls you and then stands back to see how well you are doing. When God sends you, he goes with you. When he appoints you to a task, he supplies you with what you need to do that task.

David's Lord is your Lord; he will supply what you need, just as he did for his servant so long ago. Answer his call; he will supply.

For further study and encouragement: Ephesians 3:14–21

MAY 3

1 CHRONICLES 15–17

It is important to resist taking credit for what you never could have accomplished or produced on your own.

A spiritual leader's downfall can begin when he starts to take credit for what is actually the result of God's grace, faithfulness, and power. In this way, success in ministry can be far more dangerous than failure. Success has the power to change the way you think about yourself, who you are, and what you are able to do. Success has the power to make you self-congratulatory and seemingly self-sufficient. Success can steal away your daily worship and devotional life, as you begin to think of yourself as more capable than you actually are. You become less aware of God's presence and less mindful of his grace. Success has the power to make ministry seem like your show rather than God's work. It can cause you to think that your success is God's endorsement of your character, rather than a revelation of his own. Success can close you off from those whom God has sent to advise and confront you. Success can cause you to treat fellow workers as servants for your success, rather than acknowledging them as servants of God. But, most significantly, success can turn you into a glory thief, attempting to steal the spiritual limelight that rightfully belongs to your Savior King.

First Chronicles 16:8–36 records one of the Old Testament's most exuberant, humble, worshipful, and God-glorifying hymns of praise. With great rejoicing, the ark of the covenant of the Lord has been brought to the City of David and, as the crescendo of the celebration, David appoints Asaph and his brothers to sing this great hymn of praise. David has been hugely successful in battle, unified Israel, became a powerful reigning king, and brought the ark of the covenant back to Jerusalem. But David's heart isn't filled with his own glory. He doesn't want people to celebrate all that he has done. He knows that all he has accomplished is the result of the presence, power, grace, and covenant faithfulness of the Lord. David knows he is not the hero of his own story—the Lord is.

I am particularly taken by the final words of this hymn. They are a prayer:

Save us, O God of our salvation,
    and gather and deliver us from among the nations,
that we may give thanks to your holy name,
    and glory in your praise.
Blessed be the LORD, the God of Israel,
    from everlasting to everlasting! (1 Chron. 16:35–36)

"Save us, that we may glory in your praise." May this be your prayer and mine today. May we pray for relief from our trials and temptations not just so we would experience personal comfort, but so our lives would glorify God and lead others to do the same. May he give us the grace to glory in *his* glory and not our own.

For further study and encouragement: 2 Corinthians 10:13–18

———

MAY 4

1 CHRONICLES 18–21

No one extends grace better than a person who knows he needs it himself; therefore, humble prayers of confession tend to produce loving prayers of intercession.

Jesus told a parable about a man who stood in the temple and offered what he thought was a most humble prayer (Luke 18:9–14). In truth, his prayer wasn't a prayer at all. It lacked all the elements of true prayer: devotion, supplication, and intercession. This Pharisee essentially told God that he didn't need him, that he was righteous enough on his own. It is shocking that the most Godward-appearing act—prayer—can actually be just the opposite. The religious form may be there, but a prayer can be robbed, by human glory or selfish demand, of its devotion and submission. Not only was the Pharisee stunningly proud, but he also looked on a struggling tax collector with contempt. People who think themselves righteous tend not to be patient, compassionate, or gracious with those who appear to be less righteous than they have named themselves to be. It is, therefore, the grief of humble, heartfelt confession of sin that stimulates concern, compassion, and intercession for others who need the same grace you have just cried out for. Self-righteous pride is not the soil in which compassion grows.

We see this in the life of David. Take careful note of the two parts of David's prayer in 1 Chronicles 21:17: "David said to God, 'Was it not I who gave command to number the people? It is I who have sinned and done great evil. But these sheep, what have they done? Please let your hand, O LORD my God, be against me and against my father's house. But do not let the plague be on your people.'" David had succumbed to Satan's temptation to number his people. God didn't want David to grow proud and self-reliant. Because of his sin, God determined to send a plague upon the people of Israel. Note that David's guilt over and confession of his own sin prompted him to plead to God on behalf of God's people.

This is how prayers of intercession always work. Pride causes you to be less than compassionate or perhaps even condemnatory of other sinners. Uncaring judgment of lawbreakers is easy when you have named yourself a law-keeper. But constant confession of your need for God's rescuing, forgiving, and transforming grace is what softens your heart to extend that grace to others.

Sinless Jesus, who had no transgression to confess, was moved with compassion for sinners, so much so that he was willing to die to secure their forgiveness. His heart of grace for sinners like you and me is the hope of the universe. Although he needed no grace, he became the grace of God for all who believe. May we be tools of that same grace in the lives of those near us who need what only grace can give.

For further study and encouragement: Galatians 6:1–5

———

MAY 5

1 CHRONICLES 22–24

Grace transforms us from being those who live for our own glory to being those who find joy in living for the glory and fame of another.

The apostle Paul writes, "He died for all, *that those who live might no longer live for themselves* but for him who for their sake died and was raised" (2 Cor. 5:15). Here we see the center of the great spiritual war that rages in and around us. Sin causes us to shrink our world down to the tiny, self-focused scope of our wants, our needs, and our feelings. It really is true that the essence of sin is selfishness. We hold our wants, needs, feelings, dreams, and choices to be more important than God's existence, will, and glory. We ignore his existence, rebel against his commands, and step over his boundaries. We live as mini-sovereigns in constant conflict with other mini-kings and mini-queens. Think about times and situations when you have gotten angry. How much of your anger has anything whatsoever to do with God's law, glory, or kingdom? We tend to get mad at others not because they have broken God's law, but because they have offended the law of our wants, needs, and feelings. Only powerful, rescuing, and transforming grace can cause glory-seekers to live for the glory of God. This is why Jesus had to come; he rescued us from external evil as well as from our bondage to ourselves. Saving grace rescues us from our glory and changes us so that we might live for God's glory. That rescuing grace operates in you and me today.

This is why I am struck by David's zeal that the temple his son Solomon will eventually build must be a glory-of-God beacon—that is, a physical monument to the glorious glory of God. Whenever you encounter a biblical character or a person in your life whose goal is to show off the glory of God, you can be sure he or she has been visited by God's grace. Self-glory is natural for sinners, but it takes grace to have your heart consumed and your life shaped by the glory of God. Consider the words that expose David's heart: "David said, 'Solomon my son is young and inexperienced, and the house that is to be built for the LORD must be exceedingly magnificent, of fame and glory throughout all lands. I will therefore make preparation for it.' So David provided materials in great quantity before his death" (1 Chron. 22:5). David didn't want his fame to mar the temple. He wanted the temple to proclaim God's magnificence, fame, and glory. Notice the evangelistic zeal in David's heart. He wanted the temple to proclaim God's glory not to Israel alone but also to all the surrounding nations.

Even though you and I are not building a temple, we can have the same zeal. Our God is glorious beyond imagination and is worthy of our surrendering every aspect of our lives to the proclamation of his glory.

For further study and encouragement: 2 Corinthians 5:11–15

MAY 6

No human function is more important than worship. What
or whom you worship sets the direction for your life.

I once counseled a man who was hugely successful. But he was also driven, impatient, intolerant, and angry. In the corporate world he was an absolute star. Companies held bidding wars for his services. But the cost of his success was a shattered marriage and almost complete estrangement from his children. He had demanded, pushed, and bullied his way to a sad and lonely form of success. But he had no sense of personal guilt or remorse. He told himself that he had done it all for his family and that he was the victim of their ingratitude. He may have been the toughest person I ever counseled. I dreaded our appointments because they felt like hand-to-hand combat. He wanted me to fix everything, but he had no desire to change. I resorted to doing something I had never done before: I began reading him Scripture about worship. It irritated him, but one day he said, "Stop!" I thought, "Oh no, here we go. Another argument." But he had tears in his eyes. He said, "You're reading this to me because the only god I have worshiped for years is me." Then he began to weep. He was right—all the destruction in his life was the result of worship. He was his own false god; that is, he was the sovereign he demanded everyone to worship, or else pay the price for refusing to do so. Change for my friend had to come vertically before it could ever come horizontally.

Many believers fail to understand that not only are we called to worship, but *we are worshipers*. Worship is not just our most important function; it is our identity. Everything we do and say is the fruit of worshiping someone or something. This is why we need to pay attention to David's zeal in 1 Chronicles 25–27. He pours his power, influence, and gifts into one thing: the building of an awesome temple to the glory of God. David wants this temple to be a visible reminder of God's existence and presence. David wants it to remind the people of Israel that everything they have is the result of God's exercising his power on their behalf. This edifice will stand as a constant reminder that nothing in all of life is as important as the worship of God. David will not be the one to actually build the temple, but he wants to leave everything and everyone in place so that God's house will be a monument to God's glory and a constant reminder to worship him.

We do well to share David's zeal—not to build temples, but to live in a constant awareness of God's existence, presence, and power and always to remember that nothing in life is more important than worshiping him. As we do this, we need to remember that worshiping God is not natural for us. If our lives are to be shaped by the worship of him, then we need to be visited by his grace. It is his grace that rescues us from us and turns our hearts toward him.

For further study and encouragement: John 4:16–26

———

MAY 7

1 CHRONICLES 28–29

Your life is always shaped by the counsel you seek, listen to, and follow.

God creates people with the need for counsel. Immediately after creating Adam and Eve, God begins to talk to them. He does this because he knows that they need truth, which they will never discover on their own, in order to make proper sense of who they are and what they have been created to do. God has never stopped counseling his people. This is why he has given us his word, so that we would know him, ourselves, the nature of the world we live in, and how we are meant to live. We are meant to live under the guidance and counsel of the Counselor of counselors, as he speaks to us in his word.

Everyone is being counseled by someone all the time. You may be counseled by your parents, a friend, or a mentor. In fact, you can't really have a relationship without the give-and-take of counseling. Perhaps you are being counseled by Twitter, Instagram, and TikTok, and you don't even know what a huge shaping influence they are having on your life. The counsel that we hear, that captures our hearts and minds, and that we allow to shape our identity, meaning, and purpose is very important.

So I have a question for you. If you were about to die and your son were about to succeed you in the work you had given your life to, what would be your final words of counsel to him? What identity would you want to instill? What confidence would you like to give? What success would you like him to seek? What hope would you like to impart? First Chronicles 28:9–10 preserves for us David's final words of counsel to his son Solomon: "Know the God of your father and serve him with a whole heart and with a willing mind, for the LORD searches all hearts and understands every plan and thought. If you seek him, he will be found by you, but if you forsake him, he will cast you off forever. Be careful now, for the LORD has chosen you to build a house for the sanctuary; be strong and do it." There may be no better words of counsel in all of Scripture.

Here are the four life-shaping things that David wants Solomon to know and allow to shape his life:

1. Serve God with a whole heart and willing mind. Give your heart to the Lord, which will then shape everything you do.
2. The Lord searches hearts and knows every thought and plan. You will never fool the Lord. He knows your heart better than you do.
3. If you seek him, you will find him. The Lord is gracious, tenderhearted, loving, and kind, and he will never hide from those who seek him.
4. Be strong and do what the Lord has chosen for you to do. Don't let anything inside of you or outside of you keep you from doing what God has called you to do.

I can't think of better advice than this. Keep God central in all you think, desire, and do. Remember that he knows your heart, and don't let anything keep you from serving him. May God give each one of us the grace to follow these wise words of counsel. And may our lives be a hymn to the glory of our Lord as we do.

For further study and encouragement: Proverbs 15:22

MAY 8

2 CHRONICLES 1–4

Pride is the soil in which every other sin grows.

Pride is the enemy of every single human being. It is the disease of diseases, the pandemic that infects and destroys everyone, apart from divine intervention. It is the reason every day is a spiritual war. It causes us to be shockingly self-righteous. It turns relationships of love into battlegrounds. It causes you to excuse your sin while being all too focused on the sin of others. Pride makes you rebel against authority, while desiring way too much power and control. It causes you to be eaten up by bitterness and envy. It makes you want to be first, and it makes waiting feel painful. It causes you to get mad when people disagree with you, and it makes you think your ideas are always the best. It makes you think you are religious, when the only thing you really worship is yourself. Pride led to the fall in the garden of Eden and has caused every fall ever since. It is the root cause of every transgression of God's law, every moment when someone tries to steal his glory.

There is only one solution to the universal pandemic of pride: the sight-giving, convicting, rescuing, forgiving, and transforming power of God's grace. Only divine power can rescue us from our obsession with ourselves and our desire to be central. Only God's grace can cause you to mourn your pride and cry out for God's help. Only grace can humble you and release you from your bondage to your kingdom of one. Only grace can keep you from constantly taking credit for that which you never could have done in your own wisdom and strength. Pride destroys. Its roadway always leads to one destination: spiritual death. Essentially, pride is about wanting the acclaim, glory, power, and control that belong to God alone.

Second Chronicles 1:1 offers a thunderous summary of Solomon's power, wisdom, and wealth: "Solomon the son of David established himself in his kingdom, and the LORD his God was with him and made him exceedingly great." Solomon is not the focus or the hero of his own story. Solomon is not the one in the narrative that we should be amazed by. Solomon is not whom our awe and praise should land on. Everything that Solomon has and has accomplished is ultimately the work of someone greater. Glory belongs to the one who chose Solomon and who exercised divine power to make him great. Why was Solomon great? Because God was with him and made him great. May this also be true of us and of every good and great thing in our lives. Humility begins when we confess that behind every form of human grandeur is the incalculable grandeur and glory of the King of kings and Lord of lords. May God give each of us the grace to make that confession again and again.

For further study and encouragement: 1 Peter 5:5–11

MAY 9

2 CHRONICLES 5–8

We all tie our hope to something, and what controls your hope controls your heart. And what controls your heart controls you and everything you do.

Hope is in the heart and language of every human being.

"I hope you're doing well."

"I hope I get the job."

"I hope the weather is good."

"I hope my marriage problem will be solved."

"I hope he grows up to love Jesus."

"I hope to get over this sickness."

"I hope that what God says is true."

"I hope I can afford it."

Hope is an expectation tied to a particular object or outcome. Everything we do every day is fueled by some kind of hope in something or someone. We are motivated and guided by hope in ways we might not even recognize. The problem is that so much of what we hope in fails us. Hope in marriage is often dented and weakened because marriage is an intimate relationship between two people who still battle with sin. Hope for our children weakens as we realize that, even though we can guide, provide for, and discipline them, we have no power whatsoever to control their hearts. Hope in your job is rocky since you can't control your boss, the corporation you work for, or the economy. Hope in your physical strength wanes as age and illness weaken you. The failure of our horizontal hopes makes commitment to vertical hope (hope in God) even more important.

In 2 Chronicles 5 Israel is in a moment of national celebration. They are celebrating not because of political or military victories. No, the festivities are deeply spiritual; they get to the core of who these people are and why they continue to exist. Solomon has completed the building of the temple; the ark of the covenant and all the furnishings for the Holy Place are now in the temple; and the glory-cloud of the Lord has descended on his house. It is a glorious moment, setting Israel apart from every other nation on earth. The temple, the ark of the covenant, and the visible indication of God's dwelling with his people together remind the people not only of who they are, but of where lasting, faithful, and trustworthy hope is to be found. In response to God's faithfulness, the people sing, "He is good, for his steadfast love endures forever" (2 Chron. 5:13). Israel was delivered from Egypt because the steadfast love of the Lord endures forever. They were sustained in the wilderness because the steadfast love of the Lord endures forever. They conquered the nations in the promised land because the steadfast love of the Lord endures forever. They are a nation with a temple filled with the Lord's presence because the steadfast love of the Lord endures forever.

Nothing we put our hope in for this life will last forever, except the steadfast love of the Lord. Putting your hope in him is never a risk. He is sovereign, he is almighty, he is holy, he is faithful, and he is good. Rest your hope in your Lord; he is worthy of your trust.

For further study and encouragement: Psalm 42:1–11

MAY 10

God makes people great—not for their glory, but for his.

I watched as a gifted pastor not only lost the plot but lost himself. He had been blessed with a quick mind and awesome communication skills. He was a natural leader. He began his ministry knowing that his gifts were for a much higher purpose than his own success and glory. He had lived with a deep sense of gospel calling and dedicated his abilities to discipling people in the life-transforming truths of the gospel of Jesus Christ. But he became lost in the middle of his own story. What had been all about his Lord, was now about him. He was successful and powerful, and he knew it. Pride closed his heart to the counsel of others that he so desperately needed. He loved hanging with "people that matter." He loved telling the story of the rise of his ministry, and he loved giving people tours of his ministry kingdom. This once tenderhearted man became angry and controlling. Where once he led by encouragement and vision, he now led by intimidation and threat. His was a story of spiritual decline, and soon everything he had built crumbled.

When I witness the spiritual decline of pastors, I ask myself, "Why does God choose to make certain people great? Why does he bless them with great gifts? Why does he provide them with great resources? Why does he surround them with smart and dedicated people?" The answer in Scripture again and again is that human greatness is not an end in itself but a means to an end. God does not pour his greatness into people so they can bask in their own glory and be worshiped by others because of it. He knows the dangers of greatness. He is aware of how quickly pride in oneself replaces humble gratitude. He knows that success is far more spiritually dangerous than failure. So why *does* God make people great?

The answer to this question is found in the words of the Queen of Sheba as she reflects on the greatness of King Solomon: "Blessed be the LORD your God, who has delighted in you and set you on his throne as king for the LORD your God! Because your God loved Israel and would establish them forever, he has made you king over them, that you may execute justice and righteousness" (2 Chron. 9:8). The queen gets it right. Solomon's greatness is not about Solomon; it's about God's love for and faithfulness to his people. Human greatness is not a possession. It is an instrument given by a God of grace and glory for the sake of his people and the proclamation of his own glory.

May we willingly and joyfully surrender every gift and ability we've been given to him, for his purposes and for his glory.

For further study and encouragement: Matthew 20:20–28

MAY 11

2 CHRONICLES 13–16

Your Lord is the ultimate warrior. He always battles on
behalf of those whom he has chosen to be his own.

Picture two young boys about to fight. Although they project a kind of pugilistic bravado, they are both more afraid than they would ever admit. So their taunts move quickly from *their* strength to the size and ability of their fathers. "My dad is bigger than your dad." "Oh yeah? My dad is stronger than your dad." "My dad is really strong. He played football in college." "My dad is even stronger than that. He's a marine." The father-taunts that fly back and forth are both silly and very sweet. Neither dad is going to fight with a neighbor because of some petty quarrel between two nine-year-olds. So the father-threats are meaningless. But the safety that both boys feel in the strength of their fathers and the belief they have that their fathers would battle on their behalf is quite endearing.

This mundane but deeply human scene reminds me of deep spiritual truths. I cannot defeat many of the broken and evil things in this world. So much temptation comes at me that I cannot resist on my own. Even when I successfully turn from evil outside of me, I have little power on my own to liberate myself from the sin inside me. But confessing my weakness and inability does not depress me, because I have a heavenly Father who battles on my behalf. I can look evil in the face and say, "My Father in heaven is bigger and more powerful than your father, the devil." How encouraging it is to know that this is not a meaningless and silly taunt, but one rooted in the truth of God's covenant faithfulness.

In 2 Chronicles 13:13–16 evil King Jeroboam has amassed a huge army because he intends to defeat King Abijah and destroy Judah. The much smaller army of Judah is surrounded on all sides by Jeroboam's troops. But what Jeroboam doesn't understand is that he is not fighting just Judah, but Judah's Father, the Lord Almighty. God will not let Judah be destroyed because Judah has a place in his redemptive plan. With trumpet blasts and shouts, Jeroboam is defeated and five hundred thousand of his men die. And what is recorded of that victory? "God defeated Jeroboam and all Israel before Abijah and Judah. The men of Israel fled before Judah, and God gave them into their hand" (2 Chron. 13:15–16).

God never abandons his covenant promises, which means he will battle on behalf of his people until the final victory is won. There is no spiritual battle that we fight on our own, because our Savior is the ultimate warrior. He will continue to put enemies under his feet until the last enemy is finally destroyed. Then he will welcome us into his final kingdom, where war will be no more.

For further study and encouragement: Exodus 15:1–18

MAY 12

2 CHRONICLES 17–20

There is no greater form of courage than when you act with moral boldness because of your trust in the wisdom, commands, presence, power, and grace of the Lord.

We love tales of courage. We are inspired when we read of a soldier who puts his own life at risk in order to preserve the lives of his fellow soldiers. We love the stories of people who have suffered through physical disabilities to accomplish great physical feats. We are moved when we hear of the firemen who climbed the steps of the burning World Trade Center as everyone else was running down and trying to get out. We marvel at the stories of bold elderly people who have stood up to thieves. Recently I read of firemen who left the warmth and safety of their firehouse to go out into a historic blizzard to save families trapped in their cars. Although we are thrilled and encouraged by these stories, they often leave us haunted by a question: If I were in any of those situations, would I be able to muster up the same kind of courage?

Courage is something we all admire, but perhaps few of us think we are truly courageous. We wonder where true courage comes from, or what real courage looks like. Second Chronicles 17 gives us a clue. Here's how the reign, life, and character of King Jehoshaphat are summarized:

> The LORD was with Jehoshaphat, because he walked in the earlier ways of his father David. He did not seek the Baals, but sought the God of his father and walked in his commandments, and not according to the practices of Israel. Therefore the LORD established the kingdom in his hand. And all Judah brought tribute to Jehoshaphat, and he had great riches and honor. *His heart was courageous in the ways of the LORD.* And furthermore, he took the high places and the Asherim out of Judah. (2 Chron. 17:3–6)

For all of the greatness of his riches and honor, the most important thing about Jehoshaphat is captured in ten words: "His heart was courageous in the ways of the LORD." Here was a king who believed so deeply in the presence, power, and commands of his Lord that he acted with courage in the face of evil. He tore down all of the high places of idol worship, standing against the entirety of the spiritual culture of Judah, and therefore God established his kingdom and gave him great success.

There is no greater form of courage than moral courage. But moral courage is not natural for us. Faith in a God we cannot see or hear is not natural. So, in order to stand with courage of heart in the midst of this idolatrous world, we need to be visited by grace. That grace is readily available to us because of the life, death, and resurrection of the Lion of Judah, our Savior, the Lord Jesus Christ. He hears our cries and grants courage to those who seek him.

For further study and encouragement: Daniel 3:8–30

MAY 13

2 CHRONICLES 21–24

Reigning above the chaos of this fallen world is a sovereign God whose will will be done and whose plans will succeed.

Sometimes I tell myself that I should quit reading the news. So many distressing political, cultural, and ecclesiastical events occur every day. If the news were the primary force shaping your view of life, then of course you would conclude that the world is an out-of-control moral mess. From the vantage point of popular media, it often seems as though evil has won. Good people—that is, people of moral conviction—don't seem to be honored, but rather are rejected and dismissed. Entertainment often promotes what God prohibits. It is all quite discouraging. This is why we must make sure that modern social and information media are not the key influencers of the way we think about life and the world around us. It is vital that every day we put on biblical glasses that help us see the truth despite the chaos around us. What is that truth? It is that the world is not out of control but rather is under the firm, wise, and holy control of the Lord Almighty. He has not and never will be dethroned. Nothing can thwart the march of his sovereign plan. No evil is powerful enough to defeat our God, the Lord of hosts.

Buried in 2 Chronicles 22:7 are a few words that change the way you read and understand the history of God's people in the Old Testament. When you read the history of evil king after evil king, detestable idol practices replacing the true worship of God, babies being sacrificed, and kings killing their own to solidify their power, it seems as though God has lost control of his people. Yes, there are brief moments of repentance and a return to following the Lord, but the march back toward evil seems to happen too quickly. Ahaziah was one of those evil kings. He did what was evil, and he led God's people to do what was detestable in the sight of God. In the chronicle of Ahaziah's reign we find these words: "It was ordained by God that the downfall of Ahaziah should come about through his going to visit Joram." Let these words sink in. Ahaziah, with all of his evil pride and immoral power, was not the one in charge. For all of his desire to shake his fist in the face of God and go in the opposite moral direction from God's commands, Ahaziah did not possess the power to determine his own fate. His life, reign, and fate were in the hands of one of infinite power and glory.

Verse 7 tells us two things. First, the movement and success of God's plan for his world were determined before he formed the world. Second, God has the power at every moment to assure that what he has ordained actually happens. So do not fear; it is never risky to trust the Lord. Take heart. He reigns, and he always accomplishes his will.

For further study and encouragement: Isaiah 46:8–11

———

MAY 14

2 CHRONICLES 25–27

It is right to mourn our failures, but it is also important to remember that spiritual dangers lurk in our successes.

God wastes no words in Scripture. Every part of his word is profitable (2 Tim. 3:16). There are no needless historical accounts. There are no stories that didn't need to be told. There are no unnecessary moral observations. Every wisdom principle is important and life-shaping. There are no poetic passages that should have been edited out of the final manuscript. Every passage has been recorded and preserved by the source of all wisdom, for our benefit. There is wisdom, hope, rescue, grace, and life in every portion of God's word. We should read with enthusiasm, even when the going is tough. We should read with spiritually inquisitive hearts. We should approach God's word like spiritual archeologists, digging into every mound and looking for the artifacts of grace that God has buried there. Scripture isn't a book to be skimmed. We are to meditate upon and luxuriate in it. As we do, not only will our view of life change; *we* will change. Our thoughts and desires will change, our hope will deepen, and our worship will be more consistent and heartfelt. God's word will undo and rebuild us. Approach Scripture with an expectant heart; it is filled with life-altering treasures.

Second Chronicles 26 presents a contrast in the life of one man. I am deeply persuaded that it is there for our instruction and warning. Chapter 26:4–5 says this of king Uzziah: "He did what was right in the eyes of the LORD, according to all that his father Amaziah had done. He set himself to seek God in the days of Zechariah, who instructed him in the fear of God, and as long as he sought the LORD, God made him prosper." Whenever you read of a king of Judah who commits himself to fear, seek, and follow the Lord, you breathe a sigh of relief. Finally, a godly king rules over Judah. But then as you read on, you encounter another statement of the life and character of Uzziah: "But when he was strong, he grew proud, to his destruction. For he was unfaithful to the LORD his God and entered the temple of the LORD to burn incense on the altar of incense" (2 Chron. 26:16). The words *but when he was strong, he grew proud* should jump off the page. The success of Uzziah's reign contributed to his spiritual demise. The man who once feared the Lord feared him no longer, arrogantly going into the Holy Place to do what he had no right to do. He grew proud, to his own destruction. Strength, success, accomplishments, and acclaim have the power to change us. In terms of our relationship to God, they can make us feel less dependent and grateful. We begin to take credit for our successes, and we attempt to take our lives into our own hands. May we heed God's warning and affirm, once again, our constant dependency on his wisdom, his power, and the everflowing resources of his grace.

For further study and encouragement: Psalm 119:1–8

———

MAY 15

2 CHRONICLES 28–31

Your present, past, and future rest on the Lord's incalculable patience.

I stood in a line at the end of a busy day with just one thing in my hand. I was already late in picking up the one thing we needed to complete dinner. In front of me was a woman with a full cart and a fist full of coupons. Nothing in her actions communicated that she was in a hurry. The longer she took at the checkout counter, the more irritated I got. As I fidgeted, she took her time. The few minutes I had to wait seemed like an eternity. It's quite embarrassing to look back at myself in that scene. The few minutes I lost were not important at all. As I left the store and walked to my car, I was confronted by how impatient I am, how hard it is for me to wait.

I am thankful that God is not like me. One thing that jumps off the pages of the Old Testament, particularly Kings and Chronicles, is the amazing and incalculable patience of the Lord. The entire future of Israel, the completion of God's redemptive plan, and the hope of the nations rest on the foundation of the patience of God. Considering Israel's legacy of covenant-breaking immorality and idolatry, we would expect that at some point God would rise up and say, "Enough. I am done with your wickedness. I will be patient with you no more. I withdraw my covenant promises, and you will face my final condemnation." But that does not happen. God is not like us. He does not act in divine haste. He does not turn quickly from his covenant promises when his people offend him. It's not that God treats sin lightly. No, it's that he knows the only thing that will defeat it once and for all is his grace. So, in grace, he again and again gives his people the opportunity to confess and turn to him in repentance and renewed worship.

God's patience is demonstrated powerfully in 2 Chronicles 29. After using pagan nations as tools of his discipline and after all the destruction, defeats, and captivity, he is not done with his children. He raises up righteous Hezekiah, who appoints messengers to do the work of the Lord and to restore the temple to its God-honoring glory. Here are Hezekiah's words: "Now it is in my heart to make a covenant with the LORD, the God of Israel, in order that his fierce anger may turn away from us. My sons, do not now be negligent, for the LORD has chosen you to stand in his presence, to minister to him and to be his ministers and make offerings to him" (2 Chron. 29:10–11).

It is important to understand that Hezekiah reigns as king and makes this covenant commitment only because God is patient and does not abandon his covenant promises. That same patience is your hope today and all the days to come. His patience gives room for his grace to flow.

For further study and encouragement: Exodus 34:1–8

MAY 16

In a world that mocks the existence of God and his plan for humanity,
how tempted are you to doubt him, his wisdom, and his grace?

Your belief in God will not be supported and encouraged by the culture that surrounds you. News services, social media, and streaming platforms tend to ignore the existence of God, mock the concept of his existence, or promote lifestyles that rebel against his will. Many Christians are susceptible to having their trust in God weakened by the voices of media influencers who lay out arguments against a biblical worldview, biblical theology, biblical morality, and the essentiality of the church. How about you? Is your faith in God up for grabs in any way? Do you read things that shake your trust in him? Has your theology been corrupted by worldly philosophies? Are you ever tempted to abandon your faith? Are you fearful of letting people around you know that you are a Christian and that the Bible is your theological and moral guide? Do you find it hard to take a moral stand? To what extent is your faith mixed with doubt?

In 2 Chronicles 32 Sennacherib, the powerful king of Assyria, is threatening to lay siege to Judah, so he sends messengers to warn Hezekiah, the king of Judah, with these words.

> Thus says Sennacherib king of Assyria, "On what are you trusting, that you endure the siege in Jerusalem? Is not Hezekiah misleading you, that he may give you over to die by famine and by thirst, when he tells you, 'The Lord our God will deliver us from the hand of the king of Assyria'? Has not this same Hezekiah taken away his high places and his altars and commanded Judah and Jerusalem, 'Before one altar you shall worship, and on it you shall burn your sacrifices'? Do you not know what I and my fathers have done to all the peoples of other lands? Were the gods of the nations of those lands at all able to deliver their lands out of my hand? Who among all the gods of those nations that my fathers devoted to destruction was able to deliver his people from my hand, that your God should be able to deliver you from my hand? Now, therefore, do not let Hezekiah deceive you or mislead you in this fashion, and do not believe him, for no god of any nation or kingdom has been able to deliver his people from my hand or from the hand of my fathers. How much less will your God deliver you out of my hand!" (2 Chron. 32:10–15)

These words are a direct and blasphemous assault on the almighty power and infinite glory of the God of Judah. But they create no doubt whatsoever in

Hezekiah. Sennacherib's messengers shout out their contempt for God, comparing him to the gods of the nations that are made by human hands. But Hezekiah is not afraid. He responds with an act of faith—prayer—and the Lord delivers Judah.

May God's grace meet us, so that nothing can weaken the vitality of our trust in him. And when we are afraid, may we run to him in prayer, trusting his delivering grace.

For further study and encouragement: 1 Peter 3:13–17

MAY 17

2 CHRONICLES 35–36

God often uses unlikely and unusual instruments
to advance his eternal mission of grace.

I had a hard talk with my teenage son. It was late at night, and I think both of us just wanted to go to sleep. It had been hard going, but I thought the talk had ended on a good note. As I walked out of his room, I said, "I am so glad we talked." But I heard my son say, "I didn't." "You didn't what?" I asked. He said, "I didn't talk, because you didn't give me a chance." I walked back in his room, sat down on his bed, and said, "Talk to me now." He said, "When you came in this room, you had already made your judgment. We weren't having a conversation; you were just announcing my punishment. I didn't have an opportunity to explain why I did what I did because you weren't interested." His words pierced my heart. He was exactly right. He had made me angry, and I had judged him without any facts. I had gone into that room to enact discipline, but I had totally missed the opportunity to hear my son, to see into his heart, and to love him with fatherly and gospel love. In that moment there was a bit of a role reversal. God, in his faithful grace, raised up the son to parent the father. I am thankful that God is so unrelentingly committed to his redeeming work that, in his infinite wisdom, he uses whatever instrument at whatever time is best.

We should never be so proud that we reject whomever or whatever God intends to use to continue his work in us. Every tool God uses in our lives has been preappointed by him. There are no accidents. There are no divine last-minute decisions. There are no wrong choices. God always uses the right person or thing to take us where he has decided we will go.

For most of us, Cyrus, king of Persia, is an unlikely tool in God's hands to release God's people from captivity and secure the rebuilding of God's temple in Jerusalem. That is why the following words are so important:

> Now in the first year of Cyrus king of Persia, that the word of the LORD by the mouth of Jeremiah might be fulfilled, the LORD stirred up the spirit of Cyrus king of Persia, so that he made a proclamation throughout all his kingdom and also put it in writing: "Thus says Cyrus, king of Persia, 'The LORD, the God of heaven, has given me all the kingdoms of the earth, and he has charged me to build him a house at Jerusalem, which is in Judah. Whoever is among you of all his people, may the LORD his God be with him. Let him go up.'" (2 Chron. 36:22–23)

God, the owner and ruler of all things, uses whatever instrument he knows is best to do whatever is best for his children. That is called amazing grace.

For further study and encouragement: 1 Corinthians 1:18–31

————

MAY 18

EZRA 1–5

God promises to supply what you need—not necessarily what you want.

Years ago my wife and I helped plant a little church. We were very poor, but it was a wonderful and encouraging time for us. We look back on those days not with bitter memories, but with fondness. Our poverty didn't leave a bad taste in our mouths, because the lack of riches made us fully conscious of God's faithful provision. We can't remember any situation where we lacked what we truly needed. Sure, there were lots of things we wanted and wished for that we could not afford, but our daily needs were met by a God who promises to provide for his people. We lived then—as we do now—with the awareness that our heavenly Father has a better sense of what we really need than we ever could. Because we believed this to be true during those hard years, we were able to rest in God's providing care. Don't get me wrong: living in poverty wasn't always easy for us, but God gave us the grace to trust his goodness, faithfulness, and love.

King Cyrus of Persia released God's people from captivity in Babylon and allowed them to return to Jerusalem to rebuild the temple, because God had stirred up his heart to do so. But there was a huge and looming problem. These former captives had nothing; they had lost everything when Jerusalem was ravaged and burned. Where would they get the materials to rebuild the temple and remake all the implements and furnishings that were needed to fill the temple, so that worship could once again commence? Here is where the history of Judah's return to Jerusalem shines a bright light on the character and promises of God. God is a generous giver of grace. He had not turned his back on his people, even in the face of their rebellion and sin. He was calling them to return, and he would provide what they needed in order to do what he was calling them to do. If God sends you, he goes with you, and, if he calls you to a task, he will provide what you need to do it.

God raised up King Cyrus to provide everything needed to rebuild and furnish the temple, even things that Nebuchadnezzar had stolen from the temple and placed in his home. Who would have thought that the temple would be rebuilt because of the generosity of a Persian king? I love Ezra's accounting of God's provision: "And this was the number of them: 30 basins of gold, 1,000 basins of silver, 29 censers, 30 bowls of gold, 410 bowls of silver, and 1,000 other vessels; all the vessels of gold and of silver were 5,400" (Ezra 1:9–11). How great was God's provision!

God is faithful and generous and will provide just what his people need. You can trust that he will do that for you. Cry out to him in need and then rest in his providing grace.

For further study and encouragement: Philippians 4:14–20

———

MAY 19

EZRA 6–10

*Our God of unrelenting grace always offers us
fresh starts and new beginnings.*

You get angry with a coworker; you need a fresh start and a new beginning. You are needlessly impatient with one of your children; you need a fresh start and a new beginning. You are unlovingly critical of your spouse; you need a fresh start and a new beginning. You view internet material that you never should have seen; you need a fresh start and a new beginning. Success has become your functional idol; you need a fresh start and a new beginning. You allow yourself to fight with your neighbor; you need a fresh start and a new beginning. You cheat on a university exam; you need a fresh start and a new beginning. You are wrongly dismissive of your pastor; you need a fresh start and a new beginning.

It is wonderful to know that, if you are God's child, no sin is spiritually fatal. God's grace is more powerful than any compelling sin. So, in the bounty of his mercy, God offers to each of his children the grace of fresh starts and new beginnings.

This is the truth that gets me up in the morning. I am aware that I have never lived a perfect day. My actions are influenced by both my desire to please God and the presence of remaining sin. So it is precious to me that every morning I am greeted with new mercies, and with those new mercies comes the promise of fresh starts and new beginnings. I am not encased in the concrete of my sin, because I am in Christ and his grace lives with power in me.

This theme of fresh starts and new beginnings runs throughout the biblical narrative. The Bible is a record of God's again and again picking up his failing followers, dusting them off, blessing them with forgiving grace, and granting them new beginnings. For every human failure there is plentiful restoring grace. The Bible is honest about the powerful tragedy of sin, but it doesn't leave you there. It consistently points you to restorative grace.

After all of Israel's sin, idolatry, and rebellion, God calls his children back from captivity to participate in the fresh start and new beginning of rebuilding and refurnishing the temple. I find the following words so encouraging: "The people of Israel, the priests and the Levites, and the rest of the returned exiles, celebrated the dedication of this house of God with joy. They offered at the dedication of this house of God 100 bulls, 200 rams, 400 lambs, and as a sin offering for all Israel 12 male goats" (Ezra 6:16–17). When you read of the burning of Jerusalem and the captivity of God's people, it seemed as though the end had come. But it was not the end, because of the loving mercy of the God of Israel. God offered his people a brand-new physical and spiritual start in Jerusalem, not because they earned it but because he is a God of grace.

God offers the same to you today. Come to him in confession and hope. He will dust you off with his grace and grant you a new day in which to love and serve him.

For further study and encouragement: John 21:15–17

MAY 20

It is important to know that the power of prayer is not in the beauty of the words you pray, but in the character of the one to whom you pray.

You might think that the better your theology and phraseology in prayer, the better chance you have of getting a hearing. Prayer is not about proving yourself to God. It is not about establishing worthiness. Prayer is about what the Puritans called "importunity," that is, poverty of spirit. It is coming to God acknowledging that he has every right not to hear me, that my only hope is found in the bounty of his love and the extent of his mercy. The power of prayer is not in the beauty of my language or in my track record of righteousness, but in the character of the one to whom I pray. He hears me with ears of redeeming love—love that I could never earn, achieve, or deserve. We are not called to clean ourselves up so we can pray. No, we are called to pray, asking God to continue his work of cleaning us up.

Hear the words of Nehemiah's prayer in the face of the destruction of Jerusalem:

As soon as I heard these words I sat down and wept and mourned for days, and I continued fasting and praying before the God of heaven. And I said, "O Lord God of heaven, the great and awesome God who keeps covenant and steadfast love with those who love him and keep his commandments, let your ear be attentive and your eyes open, to hear the prayer of your servant that I now pray before you day and night for the people of Israel your servants, confessing the sins of the people of Israel, which we have sinned against you. Even I and my father's house have sinned. We have acted very corruptly against you and have not kept the commandments, the statutes, and the rules that you commanded your servant Moses. Remember the word that you commanded your servant Moses, saying, 'If you are unfaithful, I will scatter you among the peoples, but if you return to me and keep my commandments and do them, though your outcasts are in the uttermost parts of heaven, from there I will gather them and bring them to the place that I have chosen, to make my name dwell there.' They are your servants and your people, whom you have redeemed by your great power and by your strong hand. O Lord, let your ear be attentive to the prayer of your servant, and to the prayer of your servants who delight to fear your name, and give success to your servant today, and grant him mercy in the sight of this man." (Neh. 1:4–11)

Nehemiah knows he cannot commend God's people to God based on their righteousness, so he confesses sin on their behalf and appeals to God's character and covenant promises. When we pray, may we do the same, knowing that the power of prayer is found in the glory and grace of the one to whom we pray.

For further study and encouragement: Matthew 6:5–13

———

MAY 21

NEHEMIAH 4–7

*When you're doing the Lord's work, the best
defense against opposition is prayer.*

They were exciting days. God had returned his people to Jerusalem and restored them to himself; they were rebuilding the city wall. It was a powerful victory for God and an enormous fresh start for his people. But whenever God works in these ways, evil opposition rears its ugly head. Sanballat and Tobiah the Ammonite mocked and taunted God's people as they worked on the wall. When you are ridiculed for your faith, mocked for doing what is right, or taunted because of a moral stand that you have taken, how do you respond? Do you wallow in discouragement? Do you abandon your calling? Do you lash out in anger? Or do you run to God in prayer? There is no better defense against opposition to the work of God than prayer. Nehemiah's response is prayer: "Hear, O our God, for we are despised. Turn back their taunt on their own heads and give them up to be plundered in a land where they are captives" (Neh. 4:4).

May these words be your prayer:

Lord, when I am about your work,
giving my heart and hands
to your calling,
when your way
is more important than
my way
and when opposition comes,
please give me the grace
to resist fear,
to not return evil for evil,

to fight discouragement's darkness,
to not forsake your work,
but to run to you
in confidence and hope.
You are my refuge.
You are my defender.
You are my confidence.
You defeat what I cannot.
You give power when I am weak.
You quiet my fears.

You comfort and encourage.
I never do your work alone.
You are always with me
in power,
with grace,
fulfilling your promises.
Help me to remember
that though the opposition is great,
in the glory of your glory

you are infinitely greater.
I run once more to you,
my Lord and defender,
asking you to do in me and for me
what I cannot do for myself,
and to do to my opposers
what you in your holiness
know is right to do.

For further study and encouragement: Ephesians 6:10–20

———

MAY 22

NEHEMIAH 8–11

God responds to the sin of his children with the discipline
of a Father and the restorative mercy of a Savior.

The summary of God's love for his children, their sin and rebellion, and his discipline and mercy that is recorded for us in Nehemiah 9 is both convicting and encouraging:

> And you gave them kingdoms and peoples and allotted to them every cor-ner. So they took possession of the land of Sihon king of Heshbon and the land of Og king of Bashan. You multiplied their children as the stars of heaven, and you brought them into the land that you had told their fathers to enter and possess. So the descendants went in and possessed the land, and you subdued before them the inhabitants of the land, the Canaanites, and gave them into their hand, with their kings and the peoples of the land, that they might do with them as they would. . . .
>
> Nevertheless, they were disobedient and rebelled against you and cast your law behind their back and killed your prophets, who had warned them in order to turn them back to you, and they committed great blasphe-mies. Therefore you gave them into the hand of their enemies, who made them suffer. And in the time of their suffering they cried out to you and you heard them from heaven, and according to your great mercies you gave them saviors who saved them from the hand of their enemies. . . . And you

warned them in order to turn them back to your law. Yet they acted presumptuously and did not obey your commandments, but sinned against your rules, which if a person does them, he shall live by them, and they turned a stubborn shoulder and stiffened their neck and would not obey. Many years you bore with them and warned them by your Spirit through your prophets. Yet they would not give ear. Therefore you gave them into the hand of the peoples of the lands. Nevertheless, in your great mercies you did not make an end of them or forsake them, for you are a gracious and merciful God. (Neh. 9:22–24, 26–27, 29–31)

God was faithful in his defense of and provision for his people. Yet they consistently rebelled against him and gave their hearts to other gods. Even in the face of his people's repeated betrayal, God was astoundingly patient, sending prophet after prophet to give warning. But because the people did not heed God's warnings, he responded by exiling them from their land. Their suffering and captivity were not God's final condemnation, but rather the grace of a Father's disciplinary hand. God was not done with his people, so after his discipline, in mercy he restored them again.

God's discipline and his mercy do not oppose one another. They are both tools of grace in the hands of a Redeemer, to draw his children close and keep them near.

Confess today that you too have a wandering heart and, because you do, that you too need both God's discipline and his mercy. Be thankful for both his uncomfortable grace and the tender mercies that follow. He is willing and able to do what you can't do for yourself.

For further study and encouragement: Proverbs 3:11–12

MAY 23

NEHEMIAH 12–13

A life well lived is a life lived for the glory and the kingdom of God. Will that be your legacy?

My new acquaintance was very successful according to the world's standards. He was admired. He had wealth and acclaim. He had power and position. From a distance it appeared he had done everything right. But he had lived for himself. He was obsessed with the accoutrements of success. He was preoccupied with image and control. He made sure that no matter the occasion or endeavor, he was in the center and in charge. But in his selfishness he lost his way. He lost all that he had worked for, and eventually he even abandoned his faith. He had gotten it all wrong. Life wasn't designed to be about us. We were created to live for something vastly bigger than us. My friend claimed to be a believer, but functionally God wasn't his focus. The only glory he lived for was his own, and the only kingdom he sought to build was his kingdom of one. What looked like success was actually massive personal, moral, relational, and spiritual failure.

What, right now, are you living for? What gives you your highest joy and has the power to produce your deepest sadness? How do you define personal success? What gets you up in the morning and motivates you throughout the day? What is the grand vision behind the choices and decisions you make? Do God's glory, purpose, and kingdom shape the way you live, work, relate to others, and invest your time, energy, and resources? Is your life an expression of the two Great Commandments? What really do you live for?

Nehemiah's final prayer reflects the zeal he had for the Lord throughout his life: "I cleansed them from everything foreign, and I established the duties of the priests and Levites, each in his work; and I provided for the wood offering at appointed times, and for the firstfruits. Remember me, O my God, for good" (Neh. 13:30–31).

Nehemiah had dedicated his life to one central thing: the worship of God. God's children had abandoned this very thing, and that abandonment had led to their demise. They had pursued the gods of the surrounding nations, to their shame and destruction. But, after disciplining them, God, in mercy, had restored them to their home, where they rebuilt the temple. Nehemiah had focused on removing all the foreign spiritual influences, reestablishing the priesthood, and providing everything needed for the worship of God to continue. Nehemiah's labor of love had been not just for his people but, more importantly, for his Lord. And he had one final request: that God would remember.

At the end of your life will you ask God to remember all that you have done in his name, or will you hope he forgets the life you have lived? A life well lived is a life lived for the glory and kingdom of God. Is that what you're living for?

For further study and encouragement: Matthew 6:31–33

MAY 24

ESTHER 1–5

The God who works in the light also works in the shadows. If you do not see his hand, don't conclude that he isn't working.

When I counseled people, they would tell me their stories. Often they would recount their lives and express no sense of God's presence or influence. I found this jarring. So I would act as a tour guide, walking them back through their stories and pointing out evidence of God's presence, care, provision, and grace. Sometimes God works in the bright light. His hand is obvious, and his care is clear. But sometimes it is hard to "see" God. In these moments, it's tempting to wonder whether he is near and whether he is doing anything. So it is important to understand that the God who works in the light also works in the shadows. His sovereign power and redeeming care are not always clear, but we ought not think he is absent, distant, inactive, or uncaring. God never forsakes his own, and he never fails to deliver what he has promised. The assumption that we can't see evidence of his presence or care does not mean he is not present and at work.

I think one of the reasons the book of Esther is in the Bible is to teach us this lesson. Esther is one book of the Bible that does not mention God's name. This has troubled many people, but it shouldn't because there are evidences of God's power, presence, and care for his people throughout this little Old Testament book. God works in the shadows to cause Esther to rise to prominence in order to preserve his people. In so doing, God gives hope to the world, because out of those people the Savior would come and ultimately make new again everything broken by sin. Without Esther, the Jewish people would have been destroyed, and there would have been no birth of the Messiah in Bethlehem, no righteous life of Jesus, no substitutionary death, no victorious resurrection, and no ascension to the Father to intercede for his own. The world would have been trapped in sin and doomed with no hope.

The amazing outcome of the story of Esther cannot and should not be attributed to human initiative, wisdom, and ingenuity alone. Behind everything, God is controlling circumstances, working in people's hearts, and determining outcomes. We should be thankful for Mordecai and Esther, but God is the ultimate hero of this portion of Scripture. His providential care guarantees that his people and his work of redemption will have an eternal and glorious future.

You may not always see God's hand, but you can rest assured that your Lord never ceases working for your good and his glory. Remember that the God who is active in the light is just as active in the shadows. Even though his name might not appear to be plastered all over your story, he is with you, in you, and for you—and that is reason to rest in his care and give yourself to his work.

For further study and encouragement: Exodus 3:7–9

MAY 25

ESTHER 6–10

The Bible never presents the sovereignty of God in a way that erases human responsibility.

If someone told you, "I am just trusting God to reconcile my broken relationship with my brother," how would you respond? The person's statement reveals flawed and unbiblical thinking. God's absolute sovereignty over everything and everyone all of the time never excuses me from doing the things he has called me to do. If I am in an unreconciled relationship with my brother, I am to go to him with the hope of reconciliation. The Bible presents the truth of the interrelationship between the sovereignty of God and his people's responsibility. *God often exercises his sovereign will through the means of the true validity of the choices and actions of secondary agents (people).* Our actions and choices are means by which God works out his sovereignty. He is in control not only of the final end of things, but also of the means to the end. This means that our choices and actions matter. God's absolute rule in every situation and location never lets us off the hook. He is sovereign and we are responsible; these truths work in cooperation and never in opposition.

The crucial importance of human responsibility is the second great theme of the book of Esther. In the last devotional I wrote that Esther presents to us a God who works not only in the light but also in the shadows. He always works to ensure that what he has ordained—for his glory and the good of his people— will come to pass. He is never distant or uninvolved. He never takes a vacation or sleeps on the job. The hope of the universe rests in the fact that God's rule is universal and unstoppable.

But Esther presents us with another theme. The way God often works his will, assuring that what he has ordained actually comes to fruition, is through the choices and actions of real people, who have actual power to choose, decide, and act. This is illustrated clearly and powerfully in the faith, courage, and actions of

Mordecai and Esther. Through their brave and wise choices, God's plan—to preserve his people so that out of them would come the Savior of the world—continues undeterred. God's people are preserved and God's plan marches on. This is exactly what God has ordained, but everything comes to pass because of the crucial decisions and actions of Mordecai and Esther.

So today you can rest in the fact that God's will *will* be done. His perfect plan will march on to completion. But you must also understand that resting in his rule is not an excuse to be passive or inactive. The one who rules everything calls you to believe, obey, fight, proclaim, repent, love, and follow. He works his rule through your work. So rest and work; this is the lifestyle of the redeemed.

For further study and encouragement: Isaiah 64:1–5

—————

MAY 26

JOB 1–3

There is but one God, who is without an equal and rules over all.

My friend had endured a tough life. From childhood her life had been marked by disappointment, difficulty, and suffering. Her closest loved ones had failed her, and she was a disappointment to herself. Her marriage was marred by hurt and distrust. When I sat with her and her husband, I observed little warmth between them; in fact, it seemed as though they really didn't like each another very much. Their marriage was more of an attempt at civility than a story of love. She wanted to talk to me because she was severely depressed, to the point of being almost paralyzed spiritually, emotionally, and relationally. Her depression was not just the result of the physical and relational woes she had suffered. No, she was haunted by something much deeper, which made her world seem inescapably dark and dangerous. She was haunted by a particular question: *Can the one who sits on the throne of the universe be trusted?* You could argue that no question is more theologically profound or morally practical than this. Where the rubber meets the road in daily life, can I trust God? My friend's answer was, "I just don't know."

As I talked with her week after week, I realized she couldn't answer the question with a hardy yes because her theology was defective. She described the world as being inhabited by two awesome and powerful deities (although she never used that word). The good deity is named Jehovah and the bad deity is named Satan, and they battle for control of the universe. If this were true, then of course you couldn't be sure that God could deliver what he planned and promised. But in the very beginning of the book of Job, God rescues us from this false view of the power and authority of Satan.

Job was a rich and God-fearing man. So Satan came to God and essentially said, "Look, the only reason this guy fears and serves you is because he has everything. But if you allow me to remove it all from him, he will forsake you." It is incredible that we are invited to eavesdrop on this conversation. And one of the reasons it has been recorded and preserved for us is so that we can be sure that Satan is not, and never has been, God's equal. In order to trouble Job, Satan has to go to God for permission, because God alone is the ruler of the universe (see Job 1:6–12).

Even in this fallen world, we can rest assured that God can be trusted, because he rules with absolute authority over every situation, location, and relationship in order to execute his plan and deliver on his promises. He has no equal. The throne is his, unchallenged. And for every believer everywhere, that is the best news.

For further study and encouragement: Genesis 22:1–14

MAY 27

JOB 4–7

Not all counsel is wise counsel. Be careful of whose "wisdom" you open your heart and mind to.

I've worked with countless people whose troubles have been magnified by unwise and unbiblical counsel. Most foolish advice is dispensed by caring and well-meaning friends. And the people receiving the unwise counsel aren't aware that they are being counseled because they receive the advice in a casual setting, not in a therapist's office. We all need to be aware that friendships *are* counseling relationships. In a friendship you share yourself and your life, and your friends are always interacting with your story, giving their perspective on how you're feeling and doing. You can't have a close friendship without the giving and taking of advice. This is why it is important to realize that not all counsel is good counsel. A well-meaning friend may not be offering you wise advice.

When Job went from having everything to having nothing, his friends gathered around him to comfort him and to sit with him in mourning. Eliphaz the Temanite, Bildad the Shuhite, and Zophar the Naamathite had good intentions. They did what true friends do. And as good friends do, they had a lot to say about Job and what he was going through. Their counsel was based on a significant question: Is Job right with God? The friends answered this question inaccurately, which meant their counsel was unwise and unbiblical and therefore terribly unhelpful for Job in his time of severe suffering.

The counsel of these three friends is summarized by Eliphaz in Job 4:8–9:

As I have seen, those who plow iniquity
  and sow trouble reap the same.
By the breath of God they perish,
  and by the blast of his anger they are consumed.

Eliphaz is saying to Job, "You do right—you get blessed. You do wrong—you get cursed. Since you have been cursed, you must have committed iniquity before God." There are two problems with this counsel. First, we know from the first chapters of Job that this trial was brought upon Job because he was a righteous man. The question of the trial was, Will a righteous man continue to follow God if he loses everything? Second, this counsel does not come from a valid understanding of the character and purposes of God. It is based on a legalistic worldview that is absolutely devoid of grace, one that believes we must earn God's favor by living a righteous life. It's about performing one's way out of judgment.

If it were possible to gain God's favor by independent righteousness, then the whole redemptive narrative in the Bible, culminating with the death and resurrection of Jesus, would not have been necessary. If sinners are always cursed and never the recipients of God's grace, then there is no hope for any of us. Jesus came to bear our curse, so that we would bear it no more.

May the counsel you receive into your heart and mind be in tune with God's character and his glorious narrative of grace for sinners. That grace is our only hope, just as it was Job's ultimate hope.

For further study and encouragement: Psalm 1:1–6

MAY 28

Few things are more spiritually dangerous than allowing yourself
to think you're smarter than God, even for a moment.

It might be hard for you to admit, but sometimes you are tempted to think you are smarter than God. Anytime you step over God's moral boundaries, you are acting as though you're smarter than God. Anytime you question his revealed wisdom, you are telling yourself you're smarter than God. Anytime you get mad at him for what he has brought into your life, you are acting as though you know more and know better. Anytime you try to take your life into your own hands and do what pleases yourself rather than what he says is best, you are acting as though you have greater wisdom than he. It is important to always remember that God, in his infinite glory, is the ultimate source of everything that is wise, good, and true. He may confuse you, he may confound you, and he may disturb you, but he is never in error, and what he says and does is never wrong. God knows everything. It is the height of spiritual delusion to think that we could ever mount wise arguments against him and what he has done.

Job, dealing with the confounding nature of his suffering, understands these truths about God.

> Truly I know that it is so:
>   But how can a man be in the right before God?
> If one wished to contend with him,
>   one could not answer him once in a thousand times.
> He is wise in heart and mighty in strength
>   —who has hardened himself against him, and succeeded?—
> he who removes mountains, and they know it not,
>   when he overturns them in his anger,
> who shakes the earth out of its place,
>   and its pillars tremble;
> who commands the sun, and it does not rise;
>   who seals up the stars;
> who alone stretched out the heavens
>   and trampled the waves of the sea;
> who made the Bear and Orion,
>   the Pleiades and the chambers of the south;
> who does great things beyond searching out,
>   and marvelous things beyond number.

Behold, he passes by me, and I see him not;
  he moves on, but I do not perceive him.
Behold, he snatches away; who can turn him back?
  Who will say to him, "What are you doing?" (Job 9:2–12)

As Job stands before the glorious glory of the wisdom and power of God, he is deeply aware that, although his suffering is confusing and confounding, he cannot call God into question. Like Job, we all must rest in God's wisdom, goodness, and power, even though we can't always understand what God is doing or why he is doing it. It is wonderful that he is a God of wisdom and power as well as grace. When your understanding fails, cry out for grace not just to endure but to rest in God's rule, knowing that he is wise in ways you and I never will be.

For further study and encouragement: Isaiah 55:6–9

MAY 29

JOB 11–13

*What do you do when it seems as though the bad guys
are prospering and the good guys are suffering?*

We look around, and it doesn't seem that justice and righteousness are prevailing. Often it looks as though the bad guys are winning and the good guys are losing. Evil seems to be on the rise and good seems to be waning. Those who stand for biblical morality are characterized as hateful and unloving, while those who pridefully blow through all of God's boundaries are looked upon with respect and esteem. In our discouragement, we can wonder what God is doing or whether he is in control. Why do the righteous suffer? Why do the unrighteous prosper? Why do bad things happen to good people? Why do bad people seem to be blessed? You can't live between the "already" and the "not yet" of this broken world without being haunted by these questions at some point.

Job, a righteous man, feels the weight of these questions deeply:

I am a laughingstock to my friends;
  I, who called to God and he answered me,
  a just and blameless man, am a laughingstock.

In the thought of one who is at ease there is contempt for misfortune;
   it is ready for those whose feet slip.
The tents of robbers are at peace,
   and those who provoke God are secure,
   who bring their god in their hand. (Job 12:4–6)

Job is saying, "I have trusted God, yet look at my life. I have lived a blameless life, but my suffering has turned me into a laughingstock. Robbers are better off than I am. Those who provoke God seem to be more secure than I am. Idolaters have more peace than I have." It is the age-old dilemma: Why does the world seem upside down? Why do the bad guys seem to have it so easy?

Now, if there were no God and the world were on a mechanical moral scale, where right living would balance you toward a good life and bad living would balance you toward a bad life, these questions would make sense. But we do not live in a mechanical world. We live in a world ruled by one who is holy in every way, wise beyond our knowing, and faithful to every covenant promise he has ever made. He is ruling not for our comfort and ease, but for his glory and our eternal good. The one who rules over our suffering gave us his Son who, in his life, death, and resurrection, eternally connected us to God and assured an end to all suffering and to the questions that haunt us. God has not lost control. In those moments when it looks as though evil is winning, God is working his wise redemptive plan. Even in your confusion, you can still trust him, for he is worthy of your trust. And he gives you the grace to do so.

For further study and encouragement: Psalm 73:1–28

———

MAY 30

JOB 14–16

It is spiritually healthy to always remember that God,
in his infinite wisdom, has set limits for us.

Working beyond God-ordained limits is always spiritually debilitating and destructive. We will never be able to go two weeks without sleep. We will never be able to work eighty hours a week and not see a negative impact on our family. We will never have so much wisdom that we will be free of God's. We will never be so righteous that we will no longer need God's grace. We will never grow so strong that we will no longer require God's power. We will never have so much control that we will no longer need to rest in God's sovereignty. If you deny the limits God has set for you, you then begin to live with a self-sufficiency and independence that never go anywhere good.

Job in his suffering—over which he has no voice or control—is powerfully confronted with his limits. Note Job's words:

Since his days are determined,
and the number of his months is with you,
and you have appointed his limits that he cannot pass . . . (Job 14:5)

Job is faced with the reality that not only does he have limits and not only do those limits set boundaries for him that he cannot pass, but those limits have been preordained and predetermined by God. If you think back to Genesis 1 and 2, you realize that the only being in the entire creation account that is without limits is God himself.

The limits God has set for us are not unloving or unkind. He does not intend them to handicap or incapacitate us. God's boundaries are not meant to stifle us, to make life hard and frustrating. No, the wise God who made us knew what was best for us. He specially designed us, knowing exactly what we needed. In his wisdom, he did not create us to be limitless, self-sufficient, independent beings. The limits he set for us drive us, in humility, to surrender to and depend on him and to find in him our wisdom, strength, righteousness, and power. We push against our limits when we forget the meaning and purpose for which we were created: to know God and to rest in and enjoy him forever.

Nothing confronts us with our limits more than the cross of Jesus Christ. We cannot bridge the gap between ourselves and God on our own. Because of our limits, we needed the Redeemer, Jesus, to come as our substitute, to do what we could never do, and by grace to unite us to God forever. The limitless one took on limits, so that we would someday know the glory of a limitless eternity with God. Accept your limits and rest in the wisdom and grace of the one who put those boundaries in place for his glory and your eternal good.

For further study and encouragement: Proverbs 3:5–6

MAY 31

*Amid all the questions, stresses, disappointments, and hardships of life,
it is heartening to be able to say, "I know that my Redeemer lives."*

Everybody has it, even people who consider themselves to be completely irreligious. It gets you up in the morning and motivates you throughout the day.
It comforts you when you are sad. It gives you hope when your dreams have
been dashed. It causes you to endure when suffering enters your door. You
use it to encourage others. What am I talking about? Faith. Everyone looks to
someone or something for security. Everyone has some kind of rock of hope. Everyone hooks his life to something he thinks is secure and will always be there.
Everyone has faith in something. What makes Christians different is not that we
live by faith. No, what makes us different is the *object* of our faith.

The things that most people have faith in ultimately will fail them. Only one
source provides unshakable security and hope in this fallen world. If you want
sturdy peace of heart and mind, quit looking horizontally and lift up the eyes
of your heart. God is the only reliable, unfailing, never-changing, and always-
faithful rock of security and hope. You can put your hope in him—not just
because he has awesome power and makes wonderful promises, but because he
rules over every situation and relationship you will ever have in your life.

This is where Job's heart goes in the middle of horrible suffering and loss, the
faulty counsel of friends, and confusion about what God is doing. The words he
speaks in the midst of his hardships have given strength and courage to generation after generation of believers. Job might not know and understand much at
this point in his life, but one transformative thing he knows for sure:

I know that my Redeemer lives,
 and at the last he will stand upon the earth.
And after my skin has been thus destroyed,
 yet in my flesh I shall see God. (Job 19:25–26)

Speaking as a prophet, uttering words that have meaning beyond his understanding, Job reminds himself where unshakable hope and help can be found.
What gives Job hope? God is alive and will never go away. After everything else
has passed away, God will still stand. But there is more. Job knows that even
though he is suffering, even though God has confused him, and even though
God seems distant, God has not forsaken him and there will be a day when Job
will see God.

Even if you're not facing hardship now, you will someday. In your tears and loss, may you look up with confidence and hope and say, "I am unsure of many things right now, but this I know for certain: I know that my Redeemer lives!"

For further study and encouragement: Psalm 121:1–8

———

JUNE 1

JOB 21–23

*We face spiritual danger when we think God
is distant, inactive, or unreachable.*

I have counseled many people during times of trouble and difficulty. Their problems loom so large, dominating their thoughts and clouding their hearts, that they are tempted to believe that God doesn't exist or that he has forsaken them. They think their prayers are not powerful enough to penetrate the ceiling, let alone reach God. What do you do when you're in times of intense suffering? What do you say to yourself? What happens to your spiritual life? We live in a world that is broken, and so bad things happen to us. Times of trial turn our lives dark. We face physical suffering, relational disappointment, and situational struggles. These problems seem so big that they confront us as soon as we awake, dominate our thoughts during the day, and make sleeping difficult at night. Suffering is the universal experience of people living in a world that is groaning, waiting for its final redemption.

The book of Job invites us into the sacred space of a suffering man's struggle with God. We get to eavesdrop on the private conversations between Job and God. We get to walk down the corridors of Job's heart. As we look in and listen to Job, we realize that our struggles are not new or uncommon. We experience the same kinds of struggles that God's children have always endured. In his suffering, Job puts words to our questions and our cries:

Behold, I go forward, but he is not there,
    and backward, but I do not perceive him;
on the left hand when he is working, I do not behold him;
    he turns to the right hand, but I do not see him. (Job 23:8–9)

As part of the travail of living in this fallen world, we all go through times when it seems as though God has left us alone in our suffering. If you have suffered deeply, if loss has changed your life forever, or if something has come into your life that you did not expect and did not want, then you can relate to Job's words.

Why has this private conversation been recorded for us? Why have we been invited into the sacred space of a man's struggle with God? The answer is that God loves us. In the tenderness of his love and mercy, and with his knowledge of the brokenness of the world we live in, God lets us know that he sees and cares about what we are going through. And, because he does, he will make everything new again. Your Lord knows—and has already set in motion—our final, glorious renewal.

For further study and encouragement: Psalm 88:1–18

JUNE 2

JOB 24–28

In times of trouble, it is important to protect
and stimulate your awe of God.

Your heart is always being captured and shaped by the awe of something. God has hardwired us for awe in order to drive us to him in worship and surrender. He placed us in an awesome world, where created glories greet us everywhere we look. Perhaps you stand in awe of a snowcapped mountain peak or a bubbling stream. Maybe you're awestruck by a huge ribeye steak. Perhaps you're amazed by the beauty and intelligence of another person, or a feat someone has accomplished. Maybe money or the pleasures of sexuality capture your wonder. All of the awesome glories and pleasures of life have been created by God. Rightfully enjoyed, they serve an essential purpose in God's wise plan for us. They are signs that point us to his presence and glory. God does not intend for his created glories to be objects of our worship. Rather, they should excite and deepen our awe of God, so that his majesty captures us and sets the agenda for the way we live.

Particularly when trouble looms large and seems inescapable, we must protect and stimulate our awe of God. If awe of God doesn't shape our lives when times are hard, then awe of something else will. When we are suffering, we must work to gaze upon the glory of the Lord; that is, we meditate on him, not on our trouble. Biblical faith never asks us to deny reality. But it does require that we meditate on the glory of God in the midst of overwhelming trouble.

This is exactly what Job does in the middle of horrible suffering and loss:

[God] stretches out the north over the void
and hangs the earth on nothing.
He binds up the waters in his thick clouds,
and the cloud is not split open under them.
He covers the face of the full moon
and spreads over it his cloud.
He has inscribed a circle on the face of the waters
at the boundary between light and darkness.
The pillars of heaven tremble
and are astounded at his rebuke.
By his power he stilled the sea;
by his understanding he shattered Rahab.
By his wind the heavens were made fair;
his hand pierced the fleeing serpent.
Behold, these are but the outskirts of his ways,
and how small a whisper do we hear of him!
But the thunder of his power who can understand? (Job 26:7–14)

May God give us the grace in times of trouble, even when he seems distant, to preach to ourselves the glory of his majesty, so that trouble doesn't overwhelm us and rob us of our awe of him.

For further study and encouragement: Psalm 46:1–11

———

JUNE 3

JOB 29–31

When darkness comes, do not spend your days grumbling to yourself or complaining to others, but rather cry out to the Lord.

Job provides us with powerful descriptions of the dark night of the soul, including the following:

And now my soul is poured out within me;
days of affliction have taken hold of me.

The night racks my bones,
and the pain that gnaws me takes no rest.
With great force my garment is disfigured;
it binds me about like the collar of my tunic.
God has cast me into the mire,
and I have become like dust and ashes.
I cry to you for help and you do not answer me;
I stand, and you only look at me.
You have turned cruel to me;
with the might of your hand you persecute me.
You lift me up on the wind; you make me ride on it,
and you toss me about in the roar of the storm.
For I know that you will bring me to death
and to the house appointed for all living.
Yet does not one in a heap of ruins stretch out his hand,
and in his disaster cry for help?
Did not I weep for him whose day was hard?
Was not my soul grieved for the needy?
But when I hoped for good, evil came,
and when I waited for light, darkness came.
My inward parts are in turmoil and never still;
days of affliction come to meet me.
I go about darkened, but not by the sun;
I stand up in the assembly and cry for help.
I am a brother of jackals
and a companion of ostriches.
My skin turns black and falls from me,
and my bones burn with heat.
My lyre is turned to mourning,
and my pipe to the voice of those who weep. (Job 30:16–31)

Notice that Job here is not grumbling to himself or complaining to others. When trouble overtakes us, it is natural for complaint to be our default language. And this default language tends to silence prayer. Complaining to yourself does not change your circumstances, and it surely doesn't lift your soul or motivate you to persevere in the darkness. Grumbling to ourselves or others becomes a doxology of bitterness, replacing the language of prayer with the language of spiritual dissatisfaction.

Prayer acknowledges the harsh realities of the moment. It confesses an inability to alter what is not under our control, and it cries out to the one who is in control and has the power to intervene. Prayer builds the soul. It reminds us of God's existence and presence, the very things that darkness seems to cloud.

May God give us grace in the darkest moments of trouble to lift our cries and complaints to him, and may he use our prayers to remind us that he is near, that he hears us, and that our hope is found in him.

For further study and encouragement: Philippians 4:4–13

JUNE 4

JOB 32–34

Remember that God's primary concern is not earthly comfort but eternal rescue.

Sometimes we struggle with God not because he is unloving or unfaithful (he never is!), but because our values don't match his. When we read through the biblical narrative, we realize that God's primary agenda is not that we would achieve a comfortable and pleasurable life between the "already" and the "not yet." Think about what makes you frustrated, irritated, disappointed, or sad. Think about what makes you happy, satisfied, or content. What causes these feelings? How many of your joys and sorrows have anything whatsoever to do with the kingdom and purposes of God? How often do you mourn your lack of conformity to his perfect and wise will? How often do you celebrate the outpouring of daily grace? How often are you grieved because your heart still wanders? How often are you grateful that God meets you every day with rescuing and restraining mercies? Many of us don't need a disaster in order to feel frustration and disappointment; no, a flat tire or missing the subway on the way to work can wreck our day.

We experience sturdy joy—the kind that does not rise or fall with our circumstances—when what we want most for ourselves matches what God wants for us. But if what we want is not the thing that God wants most for us, then we are living at cross-purposes with him and struggle to see him as kind, good, faithful, and loving. And when we begin to question the goodness of God, we stop going to him for help and instead we seek help only from those who we think are good and trustworthy.

In Job 32, Elihu enters the scene of this great moral drama to correct Job's three counselors. Although in some ways Elihu is as legalistic as Job's other friends, he has moments of wisdom and insight:

God speaks in one way,
and in two, though man does not perceive it.
In a dream, in a vision of the night,
when deep sleep falls on men,
while they slumber on their beds,
then he opens the ears of men
and terrifies them with warnings,
that he may turn man aside from his deed
and conceal pride from a man;
he keeps back his soul from the pit,
his life from perishing by the sword. (Job 33:14–18)

Elihu is on to something. Why do we fail to see God? Why do we fail to hear his words? It is not because he has forsaken us. It is not because he is silent. It is because while we are worrying about why our lives have been so hard, God is working on something much more significant and glorious than the comforts of the moment. With wisdom, faithfulness, and rescuing grace, he is securing our eternal rescue. And that is a reason to celebrate!

For further study and encouragement: Matthew 18:7–9

———

JUNE 5

JOB 35–37

Few things are more spiritually revitalizing than getting off the treadmill of life and taking time to meditate on the wondrous works of the Lord.

We are addicted to distraction. We seem to be unable to resist the next hit. Accustomed to endless information, entertainment, and controversy, we hate even a few moments of silence. We get anxious after we've been disconnected for a while. I remember when the cell phone was a new and seemingly unneeded novelty. I said that there was no way I would ever carry a phone around with me. But the device we carry with us now is not primarily a phone. When Steve Jobs gave us a portable touch screen, life began to change. Now we can access any form of entertainment or information—no matter how healthy or spiritually dark—wherever we go and whenever we want. We all feel the need to be connected, but our digital connectivity keeps us constantly distracted. Many of us spend hours a day on our devices, but less than twenty moments in personal devotion and prayer. We leave ourselves little time to stop, think, consider, and meditate.

Why does this matter? It matters because the central fact of human existence—that which gives understanding and purpose to everything we encounter—is the existence, character, purpose, and glory of God. The truth of the existence of God is the lens through which you and I need to look to properly understand everything in our lives. God's existence and glory give us identity, meaning, purpose, moral boundaries, and lasting peace. His will should guide every one of our thoughts, desires, choices, words, and actions. His glory can rescue us from living for our own glory. His holiness can expose our sin and cause us to seek and celebrate his grace. We need time every day to stop and gaze upon the glorious glory of the Lord. Consider these words from Job 37:

Hear this, O Job;
  stop and consider the wondrous works of God.
Do you know how God lays his command upon them
  and causes the lightning of his cloud to shine?
Do you know the balancings of the clouds,
  the wondrous works of him who is perfect in knowledge,
you whose garments are hot
  when the earth is still because of the south wind?
Can you, like him, spread out the skies,
  hard as a cast metal mirror? . . .
The Almighty—we cannot find him;
  he is great in power;
  justice and abundant righteousness he will not violate.
Therefore men fear him;
  he does not regard any who are wise in their own conceit.
    (Job 37:14–18, 23–24)

We need to heed these words. We need to silence our devices and stop to consider, gaze upon, and meditate on the wondrous works of God. When we do so, we find life, hope, and help. May the Lord's majesty supersede everything else in our lives, and may it give shape to how we live.

For further study and encouragement: Psalm 63:1–8

JUNE 6

God willingly and generously reveals himself to us. What a gift!

I remember the theological questions our children would ask. The concept of a God who was in charge of everything, but whom you couldn't see, touch, or hear, amazed them. Our family devotions were freewheeling question-and-answer times. What is God like? Where does he live? Is he nice? Why is he invisible? How can we trust him? Does he really hear us when we pray? I loved the natural inquisitiveness of our children, and I loved that I had answers for their questions. I had loads of things that I could, with confidence, say about God, because he says so much about himself in his grand self-revelation, the Bible.

We should never underestimate the spiritual importance of God's willing and generous revelation of himself to us in his word. The Bible is his autobiography, penned by the hands of those he directed by his Spirit. God wants to be known. He does not hide from his creatures—the opposite is true. He goes to great extents over long periods of time, through many situations, and through many spokesmen, to reveal to us his existence, character, grandeur, rule, and plan for the world he has made. He lavishly reveals himself in his creation, defines himself in his word, and breaks through our spiritual blindness, by his Spirit, so that we can "see," understand, and come to know and love him. The fact that God shows himself to people who naturally worship anything in creation *but* him is a sure sign of the magnitude of his love for us.

In Job 38–39 we find one of Scripture's most expansive descriptions of God's glory, power, and rule. Employing beautiful word pictures and focusing on his own creation and rule of the natural world, God rips back the curtain so that Job can experience the magnitude of who God is and what he does. There is uncomfortable grace in this self-revelation, as God lets Job know that, given who God is and who Job is, Job has little cause to question or debate one of such glory.

We, too, find comfort and confrontation in this awesome self-description God has preserved for us. Our ruler and Creator is also our rock of salvation. What comfort! But God's revelation of himself also confronts us with the fact that everything in life is not about our glory—it's about his.

Celebrate today that God has made himself known to you, and that this changes everything about you now and forever. God's grace in your life began with his willing and generous self-revelation.

For further study and encouragement: Psalm 19:1–11

JUNE 7

The story of God's grace is about new beginnings. In fact, what seems like the end of the story is actually a new beginning that lasts forever.

As you walk through God's great redemptive story, you see that it is a story of fresh starts and new beginnings. The sin of Adam and Eve seems like the end of a very short story, but God promises that a fresh start is coming. The global flood seems like the end of the earth, but God makes a covenant with Noah, and God's plan marches on. The enslavement of the children of Israel in Egypt seems like the end of the people of God, but God exercises his power to give them freedom and a land of promise. David's sins of adultery and murder seem like the end of David's line, from which the Messiah was to come, but God forgives and restores his king. The destruction of Jerusalem and the temple, along with the captivity of Judah, seem like the end of God's people once again, but God leads a remnant back, restores his people, and rebuilds the temple. The crucifixion of Jesus seems like the final end of all hope, but then comes the resurrection, Christ's ascension, and the growth of his church. This fallen world will someday be burned up, but it will not be the end, because the new heavens and earth will rise and peace and righteousness will reign forever. This is what powerful redeeming grace does. It cannot and will not be defeated. God's grace will have its way. God's grace will win. You are wise to build your life, hope, and dreams on the sure foundation of God's amazing grace.

So it is with the story of Job. He loses so much, including his own health. It is clear that he and his friends don't fully understand what is going on. As you read Job's sad story, you realize that he is not going to dig himself out of his mess and regain all that he has lost. But this is what is so important to remember: *Job's future is not in his hands.* It is in the hands of his Lord, and his Lord is the definition of wisdom, power, love, and grace. Why does Job have a future? Because God exists and he is gloriously good. Why is there any hope for this poor suffering man? Because God's grace is restorative grace.

So the story of Job doesn't end with suffering. It ends with God's restoring to Job more than he lost: "And the LORD restored the fortunes of Job, when he had prayed for his friends. And the LORD gave Job twice as much as he had before" (Job 42:10). How lavishly generous is God's grace. Job lives to see four generations of his family bloom and grow.

What seemed like the end for Job was not the end, because God had a plan for him. Your struggles today are not the end either. Your Lord has a plan for you. His grace guarantees a future for you. Rest in his grace, trust, and obey. His plan marches on.

For further study and encouragement: Revelation 22:6–21

———

JUNE 8

PSALMS 1–8

God is never too busy, distracted, or distant to hear our cries.

Everybody sings. Even the most tone-deaf person sings. We sing songs of praise, songs of wonder, songs of hope, songs of love, songs of protest, songs of joy, songs of sorrow, and songs of anger. We sing birthday songs, Christmas and Easter songs, children's songs, political songs, folk songs, advertisement jingles, and national anthems. Human beings are always singing. Songs are a window into our hearts. They reveal what is important to us, what our hearts resonate with, what group we identify with, and what grabs our attention and emotions at a given moment. That which captures our hearts comes out in our songs. It makes sense, then, that the Bible talks a lot about singing. In fact, right in the middle of the Bible is a songbook, the Psalms. The Psalms portray all kinds of songs, from exultant anthems that celebrate the awesome power of the Lord to laments that mourn the sadness of life on this fallen earth.

I have a particular affection for the Psalms, because they exalt someone who hears each and every one of our cries. And the one who hears all of our cries happens to be the King of kings and Lord of lords, who sits on the throne of the universe ruling with almighty power, incalculable wisdom, and transforming grace. He not only is able and willing to hear the cries of his children whenever they cry out, whoever they are, and wherever they are, but he also has the power to answer. He listens not because we deserve his attention, but because he is good, faithful, loving, and kind. We can have hope when we cry not because we have cleaned ourselves up enough to get his hearing, but because he has boundless compassion and limitless mercy.

See how the psalmist's tone turns from grief to hope in Psalm 6:

I am weary with my moaning;
every night I flood my bed with tears;
I drench my couch with my weeping.

My eye wastes away because of grief;
  it grows weak because of all my foes.
Depart from me, all you workers of evil,
  for the LORD has heard the sound of my weeping.
The LORD has heard my plea;
  the LORD accepts my prayer. (Ps. 6:6–9)

Why can you have hope in the middle of grief? You can have hope because someone is listening. God hears your weeping, even when it's without words. God hears each and every one of your pleas for help. God never closes his ears to your prayers.

Today you do not have to suffer in silence. Say to yourself, "My Lord hears, my Lord hears." God never shuts his heart to your weeping, and he never closes his ears to your prayers. From his throne he will hear and, with wisdom and grace, he will answer.

For further study and encouragement: Psalm 150:1–6

JUNE 9

PSALMS 9–16

The Lord, who rules over everything, is perfectly just all the time and in every way. Therefore, justice and righteousness will never end.

In the heart of every human is a desire for justice. All of us have felt the pain of injustice. A child sees someone cheat in a game on the school playground and says, "That's not fair." A worker gets accused by his boss of doing something he did not do. A person is rejected because of his skin color and wonders how he will ever escape racial injustice. An elderly woman is cast aside because of her age. A family arrives home from vacation to discover that they've been robbed. A man living in poverty feels as though everything is against him, making success impossible. A family attends the funeral of a dad and husband who lost his life because of a drunk driver. A wife watches her unfaithful husband build a new life that seems much easier and better than the one she's left with. A criminal system is too light on crime, and the bad guys seem to win while the good guys struggle.

We all have moments when we cry out for justice. We all wish that right would win more often. When you read the Psalms, you find your cries for justice there. I often think that the book of Psalms is in the Bible to keep us honest about the true nature of faith between the "already" and the "not yet." The grittiness of faith—its doubts and fears, its battles and enemies, and its dark valleys and mountain peaks—is graphically depicted in the Psalms. Here we are confronted with the fact that a life of faith isn't easy; it's more of an arduous journey than a paid vacation. But the book of Psalms, with all of its stark realism, doesn't leave us discouraged, depressed, or hopeless. It doesn't ask you to deny reality, nor does it allow you to let the fallenness of this sin-scarred world dominate your meditation, because in the middle of all the realism is a God of righteousness, justice, and grace. Psalm 9:7–9 makes this very clear:

> The LORD sits enthroned forever;
>   he has established his throne for justice,
> and he judges the world with righteousness;
>   he judges the peoples with uprightness.
> The LORD is a stronghold for the oppressed,
>   a stronghold in times of trouble.

Justice can be found, because the Lord of lords has established his throne for justice. Even if we can't always see his justice, he judges his world in righteousness and, because he does, he is a stronghold of safety for his people. Your cries for justice are heard, and there will be a glorious day when righteousness will win. Don't give up. God will act in righteousness on behalf of the children of his love.

For further study and encouragement: Amos 5:18–24

———

JUNE 10

PSALMS 17–20

You can pray that, by the power of the Holy Spirit, the thoughts and desires of your heart would be completely acceptable to your Lord.

Prayer can be a fickle and deceptive thing. Though prayer appears to be a pure act of faith in God—speaking words to one you cannot see or hear—it can also be an occasion for our idols to rear their ugly heads. Prayer empty of praise and worship, lacking confession of sin, devoid of an attitude of surrender, and dominated by a list of wants and desires is shaped by something other than devotion to God. Prayer is not about bringing your list of wants or perceived needs to God and asking him to sign off. No, prayer is surrendering all your wants and desires to the perfect plan and will of your heavenly Father. Often in prayer, worship and service of the Creator battle with worship and service of the creation. In prayer, do you sit in restful awe of your Lord, gazing upon his beauty and placing your life in his hands? Does a surrender to his perfect will shape the way you bring your requests to him? Do you long for his kingdom to come and his will to be done right here, right now—in your marriage, at work, in your friendships, with your money, in your children, and in your home—as it is in heaven?

Because prayer is spiritual warfare, we do well to echo the words of Psalm 19:14:

Let the words of my mouth and the meditation of my heart
  be acceptable in your sight,
  O LORD, my rock and my redeemer. (Ps. 19:14)

This simple prayer goes right to the core of our spiritual battles. *We live out of the heart.* That which rules your heart exercises inescapable influence over your thoughts, desires, choices, words, and actions. A God-honoring life does not begin with acts of obedience. Godward living results from a heart captured by love for and worship of God. Your mouth goes where you heart has already gone. Your choices are the result of the desires and decisions of your heart. We honor God when we ask him to recast every meditation of our heart so that they will be acceptable to him, by his grace.

We pray this because, on our own, we cannot create hearts that are acceptable to God. We pray for rescuing, forgiving, transforming, and delivering grace. But something more needs to be said about Psalm 19:14. This prayer cries out for and has its perfect fulfillment in the person and work of Jesus. His heart was perfectly acceptable to his Father all of the time and in every way. And he lived this way for us. In the perfection of Jesus, we are made perfectly acceptable to our heavenly Father. So, as you pray for a heart that is acceptable to God, rest in the acceptance that is yours because of the perfect life, acceptable sacrifice, and victorious resurrection of his son, Jesus.

For further study and encouragement: John 15:16–17

JUNE 11

The Bible graphically depicts the hardships of life in this fallen world,
assuring us that God sees, knows, and understands our suffering.

When suffering enters our door—when we are weakened and distressed by the unexpected, the unplanned, the unwanted—we are susceptible to listening to the lies
of the enemy. One lie is that we have been singled out; that is, that our suffering is
unique. This is the lie that God has favorites, and we are not one of them. Another
lie comes in the form of a question: "Where is your God now?" This is the lie that
God has abandoned us and doesn't always keep his promises. In our moments of
weakness, the enemy wants us to doubt the love, goodness, and covenant faithfulness of the Lord. The enemy knows that when we begin to doubt God's goodness,
we stop going to him for help, because we seek help only from someone whom we
know we can trust. If we doubt the love of God, then we won't follow him by faith.

In its honesty about the dangers, hardships, and trials of life in our broken
world, the Bible silences these lies. Over and over, the Bible shows us the struggles of people like you and me. Scripture doesn't give us a sanitized depiction of
life, one free of disappointments and hardships. This assures us that God sees,
knows, understands, and cares about what we are going through. He reminds
us that his promises do not depict some unreal world that none of us live in.
Rather, he gives us hope in the middle of the real world of hardship. One place
where the cries of the sufferer are graphically depicted is Psalm 22:

> My God, my God, why have you forsaken me?
>   Why are you so far from saving me, from the words of my groaning?
> O my God, I cry by day, but you do not answer,
>   and by night, but I find no rest. . . .
> I am poured out like water,
>   and all my bones are out of joint;
> my heart is like wax;
>   it is melted within my breast;
> my strength is dried up like a potsherd,
>   and my tongue sticks to my jaws;
>   you lay me in the dust of death. (Ps. 22:1–2, 14–15)

Psalm 22 not only accurately depicts our struggles in times of hardship; it also
welcomes us to take our cries to our Lord. Jesus applies this psalm to himself,
reminding us that he is one with us in our suffering (Matt. 27:46; Heb. 5:7). But

there is more. Jesus came to earth, willing to suffer on our behalf, to purchase for us the guarantee that someday we would suffer no more. In him we find comfort as we suffer now and hope for a future when we will be free from suffering forever.

For further study and encouragement: Hebrews 4:14–16

———

JUNE 12

PSALMS 26–31

Theology can be deeply personal. It concerns our identity,
our need, our provision, and our hope for the future.

Many believers associate the word *doctrine* with academics, intellectuals, and seminary students. They think of abstract theological concepts discussed and debated by the Christian elite. A counselee once told me, "Don't lecture me with that doctrinal stuff. Just tell me how Jesus can help me." She failed to understand that nothing is more practical for daily living, times of suffering, and spiritual struggles than the theology we find in the word of God. The beautiful doctrines presented in God's word are intensely personal. They help us think through who we are, why we do the things we do, how we should live, and how our hearts and lives can change. Most importantly, those doctrines introduce us to our Creator, our Lord and Savior, for whom we are meant to live and in whom we find redemption and eternal hope.

In reality, everyone is a theologian. Everyone seeks to make sense out of life. Everyone develops an identity and assigns meaning to life. Everyone carries around a system of "doctrine" that helps us interpret and respond to situations and relationships. You get your theology either from the Bible or from somewhere else, but you have a theology.

Psalm 27 is one of my favorite psalms. Consider the theology of the first verse:

The Lord is my light and my salvation;
  whom shall I fear?
The Lord is the stronghold of my life;
  of whom shall I be afraid? (Ps. 27:1)

David wrote Psalm 27 when he was in the middle of heart-crushing trouble. He was trying to escape either the jealous anger of Saul or the violent betrayal of his son Absalom. But Psalm 27 doesn't begin with trouble; it begins with theology. In times of trouble, theology is meant to be our comfort and guide. We also see how doctrine is presented in this psalm. David doesn't say the Lord *is* light, the Lord *is* salvation, or the Lord *is* a stronghold, as though these doctrines are distant and removed from David's life. No, he writes, "The LORD is *my* light . . . the LORD is *my* salvation . . . the LORD is the stronghold of *my* salvation." These truths are deeply personal for David. They define his identity and depict where his help and hope are found. He is saying, "I have been connected to this glorious one by grace, and therefore he is all of these things for me." The theology expressed in Scripture introduces us to the one in whom life is found. It gives life to all who put their trust in the one who sits at the center of every doctrine in the word of God.

For further study and encouragement: Colossians 2:6–10

———

JUNE 13

PSALMS 32–35

*As a child of God, you receive the blessing of
complete and final forgiveness.*

What is the biggest blessing in your life? I know that I have been blessed in many ways. I have been blessed with a long-term marriage to my hero, my counselor, and my best friend, Luella. I cannot imagine what my life would have been without her. I have been blessed with four children, now adults, and the relationships of love we share with them. I have been blessed with six wonderful grandchildren. I have been blessed with a ministry life that has been more motivating and exciting than I ever could have dreamed. I have been blessed to always have food to eat and homes in which to stay. I have been blessed to be in wonderful churches that are committed to the gospel. I have been blessed with many faithful friends. I could go on and on with the undeserved and unearned blessings in my life, but one blessing is so amazing and life-transforming that I will celebrate it for the rest of eternity. This blessing gets me up in the morning and gives me hope. It has captured my heart and set the direction for my personal life and my ministry life.

What is this amazing blessing that outshines every other on my list? Psalm 32 captures it well:

I acknowledged my sin to you,
   and I did not cover my iniquity;
I said, "I will confess my transgressions to the Lord,"
   and you forgave the iniquity of my sin.   *Selah* (Ps. 32:5)

We are all born in a condition so deep, dark, and destructive that it always leads to death. This darkness pervades every aspect of our personhood. We have no power whatsoever to escape it. It captures our heart and controls every thought and desire. It is the cause of every moral and relational human dysfunction. It makes life hard and sad. Sin is the worst thing that could have ever happened to us. Therefore, God's forgiveness is the best thing that could ever happen to us.

David uses three words to characterize this dark condition: *sin*, which is falling short of God's holy standard; *transgression*, which is the rebellion that causes us to step over God's boundaries; and *iniquity*, which is moral uncleanness. God's forgiveness covers each aspect of what sin is and what sin does.

It's an amazing blessing that we don't have to work to clean ourselves up or try to make ourselves acceptable to God in order to earn his forgiveness. No, he meets us as we are, asking us to come to him with humble words of confession and trust his forgiving mercies. Minimizing, denying, or excusing our sin never defeats it. Arguing for our own righteousness has never made us righteous. Comparing ourselves to others never breaks the hold that sin has on us. Our only hope in the face of this terminal disease is divine forgiveness. Psalm 32 looks forward to how that forgiveness will be finally secured for us by Jesus.

For further study and encouragement: Psalm 103:6–14

———

JUNE 14

PSALMS 36–39

Willing and humble patience is a significant aspect of faith in God.

In his infinite wisdom, God faithfully delivers, in his own time, what he has ordained and promised. God's timing is never wrong. Not only does he give us what is best, but he gives it at the very best time. This means that if, by faith, we place our lives in God's hands, then we must be willing to wait. Waiting is an essential element of biblical faith. This is hard for me. For reasons I don't completely understand, I am very time-oriented. I hate being stuck in traffic. I don't like waiting in long lines. I dislike waiting for my name to be called in the waiting room of a doctor's office. I have a hard time being patient as I am waiting to go somewhere with my wife and she is not quite ready. I do understand that impatience is prideful. It puts my needs, wants, and schedule first. Impatience is frustrated self-sovereignty, a desire for greater control over people and situations than God designed us to have.

Because patience is such a significant function of biblical faith, and because it is a personal struggle for me, I have found Psalm 37 to be both convicting and motivating:

> Fret not yourself because of evildoers;
>   be not envious of wrongdoers!
> For they will soon fade like the grass
>   and wither like the green herb.
> Trust in the LORD, and do good;
>   dwell in the land and befriend faithfulness.
> Delight yourself in the LORD,
>   and he will give you the desires of your heart.
> Commit your way to the LORD;
>   trust in him, and he will act.
> He will bring forth your righteousness as the light,
>   and your justice as the noonday.
> Be still before the LORD and wait patiently for him;
>   fret not yourself over the one who prospers in his way,
>   over the man who carries out evil devices!
> Refrain from anger, and forsake wrath!
>   Fret not yourself; it tends only to evil.
> For the evildoers shall be cut off,
>   but those who wait for the LORD shall inherit the land. (Ps. 37:1–9)

What does waiting look like? It looks like not giving in to fear even when it seems as though the bad guys are winning. It looks like not envying the prosperity of those who break God's rules. It looks like delighting in the Lord while you are waiting. It looks like willingly committing your life to the wise rule of the Lord. It looks like not giving way to anger and believing that God blesses those who are willing to wait. Now, none of these aspects of waiting is natural for us. So, in order to wait with joyful, fear-free patience, we need God to meet us and empower us with his grace. If waiting is an essential aspect of true faith, then it is also a fruit of divine grace.

So, we wait. Ultimately, we wait for the fulfillment of the promise that we will be with our Savior face-to-face.

For further study and encouragement: Galatians 6:6–10

––––––

JUNE 15

PSALMS 40–45

Your body always moves toward what your heart has been longing for.

If I could eavesdrop on the longings of your heart, what would I hear? Maybe you're single and long for the lifelong companionship of marriage. Maybe you have a job, but what you long for is a satisfying career. Perhaps in the midst of extended family chaos, you long for the sweetness of family peace. Maybe you're sick and long for physical health and strength. Perhaps you long for enough money to pay your bills or to afford a dependable car. You may be a student who longs for success in your upcoming exams. Our hearts are never free from longing and, as the Bible reveals, our bodies follow after the longings of our hearts.

Psalm 42 is about the beautiful and life-giving longing that God designed to rule our hearts and shape how we live. What is this longing? It is longing for God himself. Longing for God involves longing for his presence, his fellowship, his wise rule, his rescuing grace, and the gathering of others who long for him as well. But in order to long for God, grace must first inspire and empower that longing. At the center of what sin is and does is a longing to *be* God. This desire goes all the way back to the fall in the garden of Eden. And because we are born in sin, we are born with idolatrous longing. Rather than naturally longing for God, we long for his position, power, and rule. We all need grace to rescue us from idolatry of self, so that our hearts may reach up to the one who first reached down to us.

Psalm 42 is both convicting and encouraging:

As a deer pants for flowing streams,
    so pants my soul for you, O God.
My soul thirsts for God,
    for the living God.
When shall I come and appear before God?

My tears have been my food
    day and night,
while they say to me all the day long,
    "Where is your God?"
These things I remember,
    as I pour out my soul:
how I would go with the throng
    and lead them in procession to the house of God
with glad shouts and songs of praise,
    a multitude keeping festival. (Ps. 42:1–4)

Be honest today: Do you hunger after and long for God? Are you like a parched deer, panting for water? Does longing for God propel your devotional life, your relationships, and your participation in public worship? Longing for God will always produce love for the people of God and joyful participation in the public worship of God.

If you lack that longing, remember that Jesus came to restore what sin robbed you of. Pray that God would place longing for him in your heart. God delights when his people long for him, so he delights in answering our prayers for that longing.

For further study and encouragement: Matthew 5:1–12

———

JUNE 16

PSALMS 46–50

Your world is not spinning out of control, careening toward chaos, because we have a King who rules over all the earth.

Does it feel as though your life is out of control? Family drama, violence in the world, the rapid coarsening of the surrounding culture—chaos appears to be all around us. Perhaps you're dealing with a physical sickness that you can't seem to get on top of. Maybe you suddenly lost a job or a friendship, or experienced a life-altering accident. Perhaps your daily responsibilities are a burden too heavy to bear. The unexpected, unplanned, and unwanted confront us with how little power and control we actually have. They reveal our delusion of self-sovereignty. When you must face how few things you rule, you either spin off into depression, fear, or panic, or you remember that you can rest, knowing that though your life is out of *your* control, it is not actually out of control. We have a King who sits on his throne above the earth. He rules with wisdom, holiness, power, and grace. His rule is always right, his plan cannot be thwarted, and his will is done in heaven and on earth. Nothing escapes his rule. Everything he ordains, he accomplishes. He delivers on every promise he has made. He is King.

Psalm 47 calls us out of our fear and panic and welcomes us to peace and rest of heart:

> Clap your hands, all peoples!
> Shout to God with loud songs of joy!
> For the LORD, the Most High, is to be feared,
> a great king over all the earth.
> He subdued peoples under us,
> and nations under our feet.
> He chose our heritage for us,
> the pride of Jacob whom he loves.   *Selah* . . .
> God reigns over the nations;
> God sits on his holy throne.
> The princes of the peoples gather
> as the people of the God of Abraham.
> For the shields of the earth belong to God;
> he is highly exalted! (Ps. 47:1–4, 8–9)

Psalm 47 tells you that you will never be in a situation, location, or relationship that is not ruled by your Lord. You will never wander outside of his rule. Not only does he rule, but he exercises his sovereign rule over all things for the sake of those whom he has chosen to be the objects of his love. Your world is ruled by one who loves you and exercises his infinite power for your eternal good. This does not mean that you will always understand what happens in your life, but, in the failure of your understanding, you can know that your life is in good hands.

Does your life seem out of control? Run again and again to Psalm 47. Remember, rest, and rejoice. The one who rules loves you and is exercising his kingship for your good and his glory.

For further study and encouragement: 1 Chronicles 29:10–13

JUNE 17

One of the best things you can ask of God is a clean heart.

Psalm 51 is beautiful prayer of confession and repentance:

> Purge me with hyssop, and I shall be clean;
>   wash me, and I shall be whiter than snow.
> Let me hear joy and gladness;
>   let the bones that you have broken rejoice.
> Hide your face from my sins,
>   and blot out all my iniquities.
> Create in me a clean heart, O God,
>   and renew a right spirit within me. (Ps. 51:7–10)

David wrote these words after his sins of adultery and murder. He makes no excuses in this psalm, he does not minimize what he has done or shift the blame elsewhere, and he does not argue for his own righteousness. In verses 1–6 David acknowledges his sin and even confesses that this sin was not just a technical breaking of God's law; it was an offense against God himself. This is what true confession looks like. But at verse 7, the psalm takes a turn.

David has come to understand that he doesn't have just a temptation problem or a behavior problem; he has a heart problem. His actions went where his heart had already gone. So David needs the sort of forgiveness that only God can give—the kind that cleanses the heart. His problem was not that Bathsheba was beautiful; no, his problem was he looked on her beauty with an unclean heart. So he prays for something he cannot create on his own, something that requires divine intervention: a clean heart.

But David asks for something else. He prays, "Let the bones that you have broken rejoice." David acknowledges that, in order to reclaim and purify our hearts, God often leads us through pain and hardship. He does what we can't do for ourselves—create in us a clean heart. David is talking here about God's hammer of grace. Grace is not always a cool drink or a soft pillow. God's grace often leads us into difficulty and pain, not because God is evil or lacking in love, but in order to recapture our hearts. So, in perfect redeeming love, God may break things in our lives that capture our hearts and our worship. The beauty of a clean heart before God is far more valuable than bones that have to be broken to cleanse and free us.

Like all of the psalms, Psalm 51 points us to Jesus. God was willing to bruise, break, and sacrifice his Son so that it would be possible for us, in Christ, to stand before him perfectly clean. Now he works so that we will be not just positionally clean before him, but actually clean. And he will not relent until every atom of sin is removed from every cell of every heart of each of his children. What grace!

For further study and encouragement: 1 John 1:5–2:2

JUNE 18

PSALMS 58–65

Between the "already" and the "not yet," life is one big and continuing battle of trust. Your actions serve what your heart trusts.

It is inescapably true that you are always putting your trust in something. Your decisions might be shaped by your trust in a friend. Maybe you are fearful and anxious because you don't trust your boss. Marriages rise and fall according to the level of trust that spouses have in one another. Maybe you act in certain ways because you trust your feelings. Perhaps you have too much trust in your culture and, because you do, you allow it to counsel and guide you. You might struggle to trust what your church teaches or the worldview that your parents sought to instill in you. Maybe you're discouraged and depressed because you don't trust anyone or anything.

Because our lives (our thoughts, desires, choices, words, and actions) are shaped by whom or what we trust, life on this side of eternity is an unceasing war of trust. An army of God-replacements constantly battles for our trust. So we must ask ourselves, "Trust in what or whom will shape my actions, reactions, and responses today?" Every scripture was given for our conviction, instruction, and transformation.

Regarding trust, Psalm 62 is insightful and practical:

For God alone, O my soul, wait in silence,
    for my hope is from him.
He only is my rock and my salvation,
    my fortress; I shall not be shaken.
On God rests my salvation and my glory;
    my mighty rock, my refuge is God.
Trust in him at all times, O people;

pour out your heart before him;
  God is a refuge for us.   *Selah*
Those of low estate are but a breath;
  those of high estate are a delusion;
in the balances they go up;
  they are together lighter than a breath.
Put no trust in extortion;
  set no vain hopes on robbery;
  if riches increase, set not your heart on them.
Once God has spoken;
  twice have I heard this:
that power belongs to God,
  and that to you, O Lord, belongs steadfast love. (Ps. 62:5–12)

Do you have this kind of unbending trust in the Lord? Does God alone rule your heart? What causes you to question his goodness, thereby weakening your trust in him? Is your trust in the Lord built on the foundation of your experience or on his word? Psalm 62 calls us to "trust in him at all times." That includes the times when he seems distant and uninvolved as well as when he seems near.

The "steadfast love" of the Lord is seen most clearly in the person and work of his Son. In Christ we have the grace we need to defeat our fears and to give our hearts to trusting God, no matter what. Today, look up and trust God.

For further study and encouragement: Jeremiah 17:5–8

———

JUNE 19

PSALMS 66–69

*Only God's grace keeps us from reducing our lives to a
pursuit of our own comfort, pleasure, and glory.*

Most of my happiness and joy come from experiencing things that give me pleasure or comfort. I tend to grumble when things get in my way, when I have to wait, or when I feel weakness or pain. I love when people quickly agree with me, and I enjoy being in control. The battle for glory still rages in my heart, confronting me with difficult questions: Will I shrink life to the size of my own glory, or will I live for the expansive and eternal glory of God?

Psalm 67 confronts us with the grand purpose of God's grace:

May God be gracious to us and bless us
  and make his face to shine upon us,   *Selah*
that your way may be known on earth,
  your saving power among all nations.
Let the peoples praise you, O God;
  let all the peoples praise you!
Let the nations be glad and sing for joy,
  for you judge the peoples with equity
  and guide the nations upon earth.   *Selah*
Let the peoples praise you, O God;
  let all the peoples praise you!
The earth has yielded its increase;
  God, our God, shall bless us.
God shall bless us;
  let all the ends of the earth fear him!

God pours his grace on us, both for the good of our redemption and so that, through us, his glory would be seen and known throughout the whole earth. The ultimate end of the gift of God's grace is his own glory. God's grace was never intended to stop with us. He desires that all people everywhere would see his glory and give him the praise that is his due: "May God be gracious to us and bless us and make his face to shine upon us, that your way may be known on earth" (67:1–2). Why does God bless us with his grace? *So that* his way might be known on earth. God's grace drafts us into an army of people who live, work, relate, and speak in order that the plan, purpose, and glory of the Lord would be known around the entire earth. Embedded in the gift of God's grace is a call to live as his evangelists. His grace doesn't end with our justification and sanctification, because through us he wants his presence and glory to be seen everywhere.

And remember, God gives us all the grace we need to be ready and willing evangelists of the glory of his grace wherever we go.

For further study and encouragement: Matthew 5:13–16

JUNE 20

Life looks radically different when we view it
from the perspective of eternity.

Sometimes life doesn't make sense. In these moments it's hard to understand what God is doing. It's difficult to see the blessings of his presence, promises, and grace. Sometimes trouble overwhelms us and solutions escape us. This is when we can be tempted to look around and conclude that those who do not acknowledge God and who rebel against his commands have comfortable and successful lives. In these moments life doesn't seem right or fair.

This was the experience of Asaph, who penned Psalm 73:

> As for me, my feet had almost stumbled,
>   my steps had nearly slipped.
> For I was envious of the arrogant
>   when I saw the prosperity of the wicked.
> For they have no pangs until death;
>   their bodies are fat and sleek.
> They are not in trouble as others are;
>   they are not stricken like the rest of mankind. . . .
> Behold, these are the wicked;
>   always at ease, they increase in riches. (Ps. 73:2–5, 12)

Asaph essentially says, "God, I don't understand what is going on. Why do the wicked seem to have such easy and prosperous lives, while my life is hard?" Then Asaph says,

> All in vain have I kept my heart clean
>   and washed my hands in innocence. (73:13)

He essentially says, "God, I've believed in you and obeyed you—and this is what I get?" But Asaph makes a significant theological mistake that deepens his discouragement and weakens his trust in God. Asaph is in a state of functional eternity amnesia. When you forget eternity, your view of the present becomes distorted. Notice what causes Asaph's heart to change:

> But when I thought how to understand this,
>   it seemed to me a wearisome task,

until I went into the sanctuary of God;
  then I discerned their end. . . .
Whom have I in heaven but you?
  And there is nothing on earth that I desire besides you.
My flesh and my heart may fail,
  but God is the strength of my heart and my portion forever.
For behold, those who are far from you shall perish;
  you put an end to everyone who is unfaithful to you.
But for me it is good to be near God;
  I have made the Lord God my refuge,
  that I may tell of all your works. (Ps. 73:16–17, 25–28)

Asaph comes to understand that, when viewed from the vantage point of eternity, God's moral scales are not imbalanced. The wicked may have pleasure now, but their ease is as impermanent as a dream that evaporates when you awake (see Ps. 73:20); their lives of prosperity will be followed by eternal doom. God's children may experience brief trouble now, but we are promised a never-ending eternity with our Lord in a place where peace and righteousness reign forever.

When life seems difficult, don't give way to eternity amnesia. This present moment is like an evaporating dream in comparison to the endless glory to come, which is yours because of the presence and power of God's eternal grace.

For further study and encouragement: James 5:1–12

JUNE 21

PSALMS 74–77

*May the gospel be the song that wakes us up in the morning,
carries us through the day, and puts us to bed at night.*

No matter who you are, where you are, how old you are, or what you believe, you will sing. And whether you are aware of it or not, the songs that dominate your personal playlist are a window into your soul. What songs do you love to sing the most? What songs bring the greatest joy to your heart? What songs do you sing in times of sorrow? What songs do you sing in times of joy? What songs wake you up in the morning and put you to bed at night? What songs best express what you hold dear? What songs provide you with the most comfort? What songs capture your heart?

Most of the songs in the Psalms were for public worship; many were written to be sung as people were going up to the temple in Jerusalem. But I love these verses of Psalm 77, which take us into the private world of an Old Testament believer:

> I cry aloud to God,
>   aloud to God, and he will hear me.
> In the day of my trouble I seek the Lord;
>   In the night my hand is stretched out
> without wearying;
>   my soul refuses to be comforted.
> When I remember God, I moan;
>   when I meditate, my spirit faints.   *Selah*
> You hold my eyelids open;
>   I am so troubled that I cannot speak.
> I consider the days of old,
>   the years long ago.
> I said, "Let me remember my song in the night;
>   let me meditate in my heart." (Ps. 77:1–6)

Notice that the psalmist composes these lines in a time of trouble. He is so distressed that he cannot speak. But rather than meditating on his troubles or complaining silently in his heart, he sings. Remembrance in song is a means of finding comfort in distress.

Do you complain your way to sleep? Do fearful thoughts drive your sleep away? Do the pressures of the next day capture your thoughts? Do disappointments haunt you as you attempt to rest? May God meet us in the night. May he remind us of his presence and care. And may he place a night song in our hearts, one that puts us to sleep with the comfort of the gospel of his goodness and grace. Tonight, remember your Lord, and sing yourself to sleep.

For further study and encouragement: Colossians 3:16–17

JUNE 22

More important than children's education, socialization,
or physical development is the nurture of their souls. May
their hearts be captured by the things of God.

When our children were small, they asked probing questions based on their keen observations. Luella and I knew we were parenting thinkers. If you are a parent or caregiver of little ones, it is vital to understand that these little theologians, philosophers, and archeologists will dig through the mountain of their experiences in order to make some kind of sense out of life. Sometimes we accuse our children of not thinking, but, in truth, they never stop thinking. Our children are meaning makers. They will develop ways of thinking about their identity, about what is important in life, about what is right or wrong, and about relationships. And the sense that they make out of life will then determine how they live. Every day our children are observing, learning, interpreting, connecting, concluding, associating, and developing a view of life that will guide every word they say, every action they take, and every decision they make.

Because this is true, it is important for parents to start early and work often to instill in their children a view of life that has God in the center and on the throne. It is important that your children begin to understand that everything comes from the Lord, exists through him, and was made for him and his glory (see Rom. 11:36). Parents, hear the instructions of Psalm 78:5–8:

[God] established a testimony in Jacob
    and appointed a law in Israel,
which he commanded our fathers
    to teach to their children,
that the next generation might know them,
    the children yet unborn,
and arise and tell them to their children,
    so that they should set their hope in God
and not forget the works of God,
    but keep his commandments;
and that they should not be like their fathers,
    a stubborn and rebellious generation,
a generation whose heart was not steadfast,
    whose spirit was not faithful to God.

Don't miss the vision here. We are called to faithfully teach our children the things of the Lord so that their children, yet unborn, will set their hope on God, remember his commands, and not rebel against him.

You may be thinking, "It's all we can do to keep our kids under control and put three meals on the table." But remember this: every one of God's commands is accompanied by his grace. He will meet you in your weariness and weakness and help you to do what he's called you to do.

Someone will answer your children's questions. Some system of thought will capture their hearts and minds. May God use you, parent, to lead them to the one who is wisdom, so that they follow him, and their children and their children's children do as well.

For further study and encouragement: Deuteronomy 6:4–9

———

JUNE 23

PSALMS 80–85

The grace of the gospel promises us both forgiveness and restoration. God will restore us to himself, and he will restore what sin has broken.

Workers were restoring a house across the street from us, and I couldn't resist checking it out. I asked whether I could look around. They told me I was welcome, but that I should be careful. A man in the kitchen was swinging a sledgehammer, knocking down walls. A guy on scaffolding in the living room was carefully prying old crown molding off the wall with a small hammer and little wedges. Elsewhere an electrician was using a meter to test the condition of the wiring. I loved that this grand old house, once barely habitable, was going to be made new again. But it wasn't just going to be restored; it would end up in better condition than when it was first built. I've thought about that house throughout the years, because it was a beautiful picture of God's restorative grace. Just as a carpenter uses a variety of tools to restore a house, God uses a variety of means of grace to restore what sin has damaged. The great divine restorer knows exactly what tool to use at exactly the right moment in order to restore what sin has broken. Because sin has wreaked such damage, we are all broken-down people living in a broken-down world, so the restoration themes in the Bible are precious and comforting.

Psalm 80 is a prayer for restoration, one that we would do well to pray again and again until God makes all things new again. "Restore us, O God. Let your face shine, that we may be saved!" is its main cry. It's repeated three times throughout the psalm:

> Turn again, O God of hosts!
>   Look down from heaven, and see;
> have regard for this vine,
>   the stock that your right hand planted,
>   and for the son whom you made strong for yourself.
> They have burned it with fire; they have cut it down;
>   may they perish at the rebuke of your face!
> But let your hand be on the man of your right hand,
>   the son of man whom you have made strong for yourself!
> Then we shall not turn back from you;
>   give us life, and we will call upon your name!
> Restore us, O Lord God of hosts!
>   Let your face shine, that we may be saved! (Ps. 80:14–19)

The psalmist asks God to turn his face of rescuing grace toward his children and restore them. "Give us life," he pleads.

Where do you need restoration? Where in your life do things need to be made new? The great restorer offers you his restorative grace today. He has the necessary skills and always uses the right tool. Cry out today for his restorative craftsmanship, and watch what he, in mercy, will do.

For further study and encouragement: Ephesians 2:8–10

———

JUNE 24

PSALMS 86–89

*Where does your mind go and your heart
run when life doesn't make sense?*

I counseled a woman who had enjoyed a wonderful life. She and her successful husband had two wonderful children. She attended a good church and was surrounded by a group of devoted friends. But in an act of unfaithfulness and betrayal, her husband forsook her, and she lost everything. After she realized the extent of her loss, she had no life in her eyes, no spring in her step, and no hope in her heart. She was burdened by the uncertainty of her future. Where would she live? How would she survive? I couldn't answer all of her questions, but I knew one thing: she was not without hope. I told her that even in the face of all the grief and loss, she would stand. I told her this not because she was strong, wise, and capable, but because the most important person in her life, the one who was near to her and who would give the grace to continue, had not forsaken her. We talked about the rock of hope that was hers in the steadfast love of the Lord, a love that never fails. I did my best to help her see that his steadfast love was as real as all of the loss that had so devastated her. Then we talked about the decisions she needed to make to move forward in her new circumstances.

When our comfortable plans for our life come crashing down, God can seem distant and inactive. Psalm 89 paints a picture for us of two colliding realities. It first celebrates God's steadfast love:

> I will sing of the steadfast love of the LORD, forever;
>   with my mouth I will make known your faithfulness to all generations.
>   (Ps. 89:1)

This is the rock of hope for believers of all generations, for Old Testament Israelites as well as people in the pews in Chicago. We all experience the bright mountain peaks and dark valleys of life. Things happen that make us think life is over. In our trouble, we can be tempted to think that God has withdrawn his presence and his promises. But nothing can break his commitment to love his own.

When we read the first verse of this psalm, we might think that it's going to be a happy psalm, but it's not. Psalm 89 is a lament. It was written in a moment when it seemed as though God had turned his back on his children, rejecting them and withdrawing his love. But his discipline in the face of their sin was not a sign that he had withdrawn his love.

The surest indication of the steadfast love of the Lord is the birth, life, death, and resurrection of Jesus. His sacrifice assures us that our sin will not cause God to withdraw the grace of his love. Today, in your trouble, remember where your hope is found: in the steadfast love of the Lord. That love is forever.

For further study and encouragement: Psalm 56:1–4

JUNE 25

It is important to understand and live within the limits
that God, in his infinite wisdom, has set for us.

One of the most significant limits that God, in his wisdom, has set for us is the limit of time. You and I will never enjoy a ten-day week. We will never experience the luxury of a forty-day month or a five-hundred-day year. We will never be granted a thirty-five-hour day, and none of us will physically live forever on this fallen earth. It is the height of foolishness to deny the limits of time that God, in his infinite knowledge, has set for us.

God has hardwired us with the limit of time. Denying this reality will only get you into difficulty. Psalm 90:12 reveals how we should approach this limitation:

Teach us to number our days
that we may get a heart of wisdom.

Notice that the psalmist connects numbering your days with gaining a heart of wisdom. Acknowledging the limits of the life God has given you is a significant part of living wisely. When you live with your limits in view, you don't waste your time. You don't load your schedule with things that don't matter. You value your time, and you want to invest it wisely. When you live with your limits in view, you want to understand what is important to God and you spend your days pursuing those values.

Wasting time is easier now than it ever has been before. With the twenty-four-hour infotainment media, social media platforms, network television, and streaming services—most of this content available on your phone—it is possible to waste hours every day without even being aware of how much time has blown by. It takes humility and discipline to say no to visual noise that greets you from the time you wake up until the time you go to bed.

Here's our problem. Humility and discipline aren't natural for us. We love what is comfortable and pleasurable. Most of us would rather be entertained than study, learn, work, and serve. So, like every other psalm, Psalm 90 preaches the gospel to us. It confronts us with the fact that our biggest problem in life isn't outside of us. No, our biggest problem in life *is us*. Psalm 90 reminds us that Jesus lived, died, and rose again both to rescue us from the external evils of this fallen world and *to rescue us from us*. He offers us not only forgiveness but also empowering and transforming grace. In the power of his grace, we can humbly admit our limits and live with the discipline of wisdom, investing ourselves in that which has eternal value. Our days are numbered; may we reach for the grace to invest in them well.

For further study and encouragement: Psalm 39:4–5

———

JUNE 26

PSALMS 96–102

*Sadly, for many of us, a dangerous gap lies between
what we say we believe and how we live.*

When I regularly counseled people, I found that the most difficult clients were those who had a high level of theological knowledge. It was hard to talk to them about biblical commands and principles because, in their theological prowess, they would quickly tell me that they already knew what I was telling them. But what they failed to understand was that I wasn't giving them an abstract, impersonal theological lecture. No, I was attempting to help them understand the real-life implications of the theology that they so confidently said they understood and believed. Theology is not just a pursuit of the mind; it is something that you do with your whole life. The theology that you actually believe is always exhibited by the way you live. For too many of us, a disconcerting gap lies between what we say we believe and the way we live.

You may say you believe in grace, but the way you treat your family lacks grace.

You may say you believe in God's call to love, but you respond impatiently and unlovingly to those around you.

You may say you believe in the sovereignty of God, but you give way to anxiety and fear.

You may say you believe in the theology of God's forgiveness, but you are self-righteous and unforgiving.

You may talk about God's generosity, but you invest your resources selfishly.

You may preach the doctrine of God's holiness, but in your private world you give in to temptation and sin.

In this struggle between formal confession and our daily living, we turn to Psalm 101:

> I will sing of steadfast love and justice;
> to you, O Lord, I will make music.

222

I will ponder the way that is blameless.
   Oh when will you come to me?
I will walk with integrity of heart
   within my house;
I will not set before my eyes
   anything that is worthless.
I hate the work of those who fall away;
   it shall not cling to me.
A perverse heart shall be far from me;
   I will know nothing of evil. (Ps. 101:1–4)

These verses offer a prayer of commitment and a cry for help. The commitment is to a life of integrity. Integrity exists when there is no gap between what you say you believe and your actions, reactions, and responses. But this is what we must understand. If integrity were natural for us, we wouldn't need Jesus. So, embedded in these verses is a cry for the promised Messiah. Only through his person and work can we close the gap between what we say we believe and our daily actions, reactions, and responses.

The perfect integrity that we long for—when there is no gap—will be ours only when we're on the other side. Until then, our Savior meets us with his patience, his kindness, and his inexhaustible grace.

Make the commitment to integrity today, and cry out for the grace that is yours in Jesus. You will be glad that you did.

For further study and encouragement: James 1:19–27

JUNE 27

PSALMS 103–105

*No greatness in the universe compares to the awesome,
magnificent, expansive greatness of the Lord.*

Take time to allow your heart to grasp and luxuriate in the words of Psalm 104 and in the grandeur of the God they portray:

Bless the LORD, O my soul!
   O LORD my God, you are very great!

You are clothed with splendor and majesty,
    covering yourself with light as with a garment,
    stretching out the heavens like a tent.
He lays the beams of his chambers on the waters;
he makes the clouds his chariot;
    he rides on the wings of the wind;
he makes his messengers winds,
    his ministers a flaming fire.
He set the earth on its foundations,
    so that it should never be moved.
You covered it with the deep as with a garment;
    the waters stood above the mountains.
At your rebuke they fled;
    at the sound of your thunder they took to flight.
The mountains rose, the valleys sank down
    to the place that you appointed for them.
You set a boundary that they may not pass,
    so that they might not again cover the earth. (Ps. 104:1–9)

We use the word *great* too casually. We talk about great games, great burgers, great shoes, and so on. We use this word so frequently and casually that it has nearly lost its meaning. But the God portrayed in Psalm 104 is magnificent and glorious. Nothing compares to him. He sits in majesty above all that he has created. He controls everything that exists. If anything were to bring you to your knees in awe, wonder, and worship, it should be him. Nothing else possesses his splendor. No one rivals his wisdom. Nothing compares to his power. No one can challenge his rule. The created world does his bidding. The Lord Almighty defines greatness. May awe of him shape and direct everything you think, desire, and do. And though I have quoted a few verses here, I encourage you to read the entire psalm.

Because God is this magnificently glorious, then what follows should be the response of each and every one of us:

May the glory of the Lord endure forever;
    may the Lord rejoice in his works,
who looks on the earth and it trembles,
    who touches the mountains and they smoke!
I will sing to the Lord as long as I live;
    I will sing praise to my God while I have being.
May my meditation be pleasing to him,
    for I rejoice in the Lord.

Let sinners be consumed from the earth,
and let the wicked be no more!
Bless the LORD, O my soul!
Praise the LORD! (Ps. 104:31–35)

How do you know when your heart has been captured by the glorious greatness of God? He will own your songs, he will be the subject of your meditation,
and you will hate evil. So what makes you sing? How often do you meditate on
the grandeur and glory of your Lord? Do you hate sin and what it does to your
life? Happily, his empowering grace makes you able.

For further study and encouragement: Jude 24–25

———

JUNE 28

PSALMS 106–107

*The life of faith can be summarized with three words:
confession, remembrance, and proclamation.*

I once spoke on the nature of true faith at a retreat, where I tested the attendees'
understanding of this bedrock Christian life concept. As Romans 1:17 tells us,
"The righteous shall live by faith." Faith is the oxygen of the Christian life; you
can't be spiritually alive without it. Consequently, you must understand what
true biblical faith is. So I asked the group to define faith for me. One person
said, "It means you believe." So I said, "What does it means to believe?" Someone
in the back shouted out, "It means to trust." So I said, "What does it means to
trust?" And from somewhere the answer came: "It means to have faith." We had
ended up where we had begun, without much further illumination. Scripture is
clear that faith is something more than mental assent. It is more than agreeing to
a theological creed. Faith is not just an exercise of the mind. It is a commitment
of the heart that fundamentally changes the way you live your life.

Embedded in Psalm 106 is a helpful summary of what true faith looks like:

Both we and our fathers have sinned;
we have committed iniquity; we have done wickedness.
Our fathers, when they were in Egypt,
did not consider your wondrous works;

they did not remember the abundance of your steadfast love,
   but rebelled by the sea, at the Red Sea.
Yet he saved them for his name's sake,
   that he might make known his mighty power. (Ps. 106:6–8)

Three essential elements of a life of faith are laid out in these verses.

Confession. Our sins have been forgiven, but they have not yet been completely eradicated. The Christian life, therefore, is a life of humble, heartfelt confession. The closer we walk with the Lord, the clearer our sin becomes. So, the life of faith demonstrates a daily commitment to confession.

Remembrance. Faith involves fighting to remember the life-transforming magnitude of God's steadfast love. We resist the temptation to forget God, and instead strive for ever-increasing gratitude. Biblical faith replaces complaint with praise and demand with worship.

Glory. The life of faith acknowledges that we live in the midst of a glory war. We don't want to be glory thieves. We commit to live for a glory greater than our own. Faith finds joy in praising God's name and in making his mighty power known. In faith, we humbly acknowledge that God works for the sake of his own glory.

Do you have regular habits of confession? Do you meditate on the gift of God's steadfast love? Do you live for his glory to be displayed? You don't have to deny the truth or wallow in shame. The Lord meets you in your weakness and failure with his forgiving and empowering grace. Faith is a gift from him. Reach out for that gift once more today.

For further study and encouragement: Hebrews 11:1–6

———

JUNE 29

PSALMS 108–114

You have a bright future because Jesus now reigns at the right hand of the Father, and he will defeat the final enemy and usher in his final kingdom of peace and righteousness forever.

Psalm 110 is both prophetic and grand:

The Lord says to my Lord:
   "Sit at my right hand,

until I make your enemies your footstool."
The LORD sends forth from Zion
　　your mighty scepter.
　　Rule in the midst of your enemies!
Your people will offer themselves freely
　　on the day of your power,
　　in holy garments;
from the womb of the morning,
　　the dew of your youth will be yours.
The LORD has sworn
　　and will not change his mind,
"You are a priest forever
　　after the order of Melchizedek."
The Lord is at your right hand;
　　he will shatter kings on the day of his wrath.
He will execute judgment among the nations,
　　filling them with corpses;
he will shatter chiefs
　　over the wide earth.
He will drink from the brook by the way;
　　therefore he will lift up his head. (Ps. 110)

These claims couldn't possibly be fulfilled by an earthly king. Psalm 110 looks to the final reign and ultimate victory of the Messiah, Jesus. He is the final priest. He is the reigning King. He will make his enemies his footstool. He will execute universal judgement. God will expedite his plan, he will accomplish his victory, and no power or person can stop him.

You live in a world broken and damaged by sin. Evil still lurks, bad things happen, and temptation seems to be everywhere. Because this world is groaning and waiting for redemption, you face the unexpected, the unwanted, and the unplanned. Difficulty, pain, suffering, and loss invade your story. You wonder, "Why this? Why now?" You long to escape things that you can't escape and control things that you can't control. And, in your suffering, you might be tempted to wonder where God is and what he is doing.

Psalm 110 speaks into your story, offering you security and hope. You haven't been left to yourself. The Messiah, to whom you've given your life, now reigns. His reign guarantees the end of all evil, the cessation of all suffering, the defeat of every last enemy, and the drying of all tears. He knows exactly what you are going through because he came to earth and walked in your shoes.

Written thousands of years ago, this bright song of security and hope points to the coming reign of Jesus and says to you, "Dear one, do not lose heart, and do not give up hope, though things are hard now. Everything you now suffer is under my rule. I will bring it all to an end, defeating what you lack the power to defeat. Your future is bright beyond your ability to conceive. So live with hope, courage, and joy. Your Lord reigns."

For further study and encouragement: 1 Corinthians 15:20–28

———

JUNE 30

PSALMS 115–118

Every idol is a liar and full of deception. Placing your hope in idols never goes anywhere good.

Often when people think of idolatry, they picture formal religious idols, like those you find in Buddhist or Hindu temples. And yes, that kind of idolatry is a powerful spiritual evil. But it is important to understand that the Bible has a much wider and bigger explanation of what idols are and how idolatry operates. Scripture defines an idol as anything that exercises rule and control over your heart, which God alone should have. Because your heart is the operational core of your personhood, anything that controls the worship of your heart will then control your thoughts, desires, choices, words, and actions. Because God designed us to be worshipers, we are always surrendering the control of our hearts either to God or to something he created. This means that literally anything can become an idol. Idols are not always evil things, although idolatry is always sin. A desire for even a good thing becomes a bad thing when it becomes a ruling thing.

As sin turns us away from God, it also turns us into idol worshipers. We all allow things in our lives to become more important and necessary than they should be and, because we do, they begin to control how we live. This never goes anywhere good. Psalm 115:1–8 tells us why:

Not to us, O LORD, not to us, but to your name give glory,
    for the sake of your steadfast love and your faithfulness!
Why should the nations say,
    "Where is their God?"
Our God is in the heavens;
    he does all that he pleases.
Their idols are silver and gold,

the work of human hands.
They have mouths, but do not speak;
  eyes, but do not see.
They have ears, but do not hear;
  noses, but do not smell.
They have hands, but do not feel;
  feet, but do not walk;
  and they do not make a sound in their throat.
Those who make them become like them;
  so do all who trust in them.

Don't miss the mocking humor in this psalm. When it comes to worship, we have only two options. We can worship the one true God, who reigns over heaven and earth and has the power and authority to do whatever he pleases. Or we can worship something made with human hands that is devoid of life or ability of any kind. The psalmist highlights the absurdity. These idols have eyes, but cannot see; ears, but cannot hear; and noses, but cannot smell. It's as though he is saying, "*This* is what you choose to worship? This is what you choose to replace the all-sovereign, Almighty God?"

What rules your heart today? What controls your desires and actions? Run to the throne of grace, confess your idol wanderings, and pray for power to resist counterfeits and to worship the one true God.

For further study and encouragement: Exodus 20:1–6

JULY 1

PSALM 119:1–88

*Those who humbly and joyfully submit to God's
wise and holy commands are truly blessed.*

A man came to me to discuss the sad state of his marriage. His first words were, "I know God says that we should be known for our gentleness, but sometimes you just have get into someone's face and give him what for." Don't react too harshly to my friend. We all experience times when we think we are smarter than God and disobey his clearly revealed commands. Maybe you're thinking, "Paul, I know God is infinitely wiser than I will ever be." But, when we step over

God's boundaries, we tell ourselves that somehow, someway things will work out okay, even though we haven't obeyed God's commands. We convince ourselves that disobedience of thought, decision, word, or action will produce good fruit. These are "I-know-better-than-God" moments. The deceitfulness of sin causes us to think that there is blessing on the other side of God's moral boundaries. Satan tempts us to believe that we will achieve the good life when we take our lives into our own hands and do what we feel is best, rather than what God says is best. On this side of eternity, we all face situations where we are tempted to think that our way is better and smarter than God's way.

Psalm 119 is a celebration of God's word in the context of a world where temptation, difficulty, and suffering exist. Think carefully through the beginning of the psalm:

> Blessed are those whose way is blameless,
>   who walk in the law of the LORD!
> Blessed are those who keep his testimonies,
>   who seek him with their whole heart,
> who also do no wrong,
>   but walk in his ways!
> You have commanded your precepts
>   to be kept diligently.
> Oh that my ways may be steadfast
>   in keeping your statutes!
> Then I shall not be put to shame,
>   having my eyes fixed on all your commandments.
> I will praise you with an upright heart,
>   when I learn your righteous rules.
> I will keep your statutes;
>   do not utterly forsake me!
> How can a young man keep his way pure?
>   By guarding it according to your word.
> With my whole heart I seek you;
>   let me not wander from your commandments! (Ps. 119:1–10)

Psalm 119 reminds us that our way is never better than God's way, and that we are never smarter than the King of heaven. The message is clear. Our lives are blessed when we live in wholehearted obedience to God's law. Obedience is always the better way. And in our struggle to obey, God meets us with his empowering grace, enabling us to find joy in doing his will. Pray now for the blessing of that grace.

For further study and encouragement: Psalm 1:1–6

JULY 2

PSALM 119:89-176

*God's word can reshape how you think and
should guide every step you take.*

Sadly, for many Christians, a troubling gap lies between what we say we believe
and the way we live. Our functional theology doesn't match our confessional
theology. We say we believe in God, but we live as though life were all about
us. We confess to believe in God's sovereign rule over all things, but we live in
anxiety and fear or we crave being in control. We sing songs of grace, but we
are unloving and ungracious with others. We confess we believe in the reality
of eternity, but we live only for the present moment. We say we believe in the
importance of the body of Christ, but in our churches we act more like consum-
ers than participants. If I were to watch a video of a week in your life, would
I conclude that your life is shaped by the commands, principles, promises, and
overall mission of God's kingdom as they are unfolded in Scripture?

Almost right in the middle of your Bible is its longest chapter: Psalm 119. It is
longer than some books of the Bible. The main topic of this psalm is the blessing
of God's word. God dedicated the longest single passage in all of Scripture to
reminding us of the inescapable importance of his word. In the middle of this
lengthy reflection on the beauty of God's word, the psalmist says something that
we must not miss:

Your word is a lamp to my feet
and a light to my path. (Ps. 119:105)

Pretend that you are walking at night down a path through the woods to get back
to your summer rental cabin. You're unfamiliar with this path, so of course you have
your flashlight with you. Your flashlight is pointed not at your head, but at your feet.
To make your way in the darkness, you need light on the path and on your feet. Your
flashlight guides you in the darkness. So it is with the word of God. If you shine it
only on your mind and fail to shine it on your life, you may get lost or fall. It is sad
to see how many of us have big theological brains but wandering hearts and lives.

God intends his word to completely rearrange the way you think, but he also
wants it to guide and direct every aspect of every single thing you do. Belief in
the truths of Scripture is expressed in the way you live your life.

In this darkened world, God has blessed you with his word to light your way.
Do you shine its light on your everyday life?

For further study and encouragement: Joshua 1:6-9

231

JULY 3

*The Sunday gathering of the church for worship is not so much
a duty as it is one of God's kind and essential gifts to us.*

Though the ostensibly Christian home I grew up in was troubled in many ways, one thing marked my family out, for which I am thankful. My mom and dad were committed to the Sunday gathering of the church for worship, and because my father had hearing loss, we sat right up front. On Saturday night or Sunday morning, there was never a debate about whether we would go to church. For my parents, that decision had been made by their Lord, so their part was not to decide but to obey. Nothing got in the way of Sunday worship. I clearly remember my parents discussing where we would attend church even while on vacation. In fact, many of our vacations were at a summer Christian conference, where there were worship services every day! As a boy, I wasn't particularly spiritually insightful, but I knew that, for whatever reason, my parents thought gathering with fellow believers for worship and instruction was essential.

It's no wonder, then, that I love the words of Psalm 122:1–4:

> I was glad when they said to me,
>   "Let us go to the house of the LORD!"
> Our feet have been standing
>   within your gates, O Jerusalem!
> Jerusalem—built as a city
>   that is bound firmly together,
> to which the tribes go up,
>   the tribes of the LORD,
> as was decreed for Israel,
>   to give thanks to the name of the LORD.

As the psalmist anticipates the journey up to Jerusalem and to the temple, he expresses four attitudes:

Gratitude. The psalmist is not being dragged up the road to Jerusalem. No, he is thankful for this opportunity to give thanks to the Lord. "Our feet have been standing within your gates, O Jerusalem!"

Anticipation. The psalmist is propelled by the anticipation of what is to come: "Let us go!" He knows what awaits him, and he cannot wait to get there.

Enthusiasm. There is no sense of boredom in this psalm. No sense of lifeless duty. There is only joy over what is to come.

Privilege. "Our feet have been standing within your gates, O Jerusalem!" The writer is saying, "I have been blessed with the privilege of being welcomed into the presence of the Lord for worship."

Are these the attitudes that you carry into Sunday worship? Do you view corporate worship as a gift? Or have you lost sense of the grace it took for you to be included? May God give us hearts that are glad when we approach the gathering of God's children for the most important thing a human can do—*worship.*

For further study and encouragement: Psalm 84:1–12

JULY 4

PSALMS 133–139

Your interpretation of your history is never neutral. May you always view your life through the lens of the grace of the gospel.

You live your life based not on the various facts of your experiences, but on your *interpretation* of those facts. That's why two people in the exact same situation can have completely different experiences—they interpret the moment differently. So, the way you make sense of the situations, locations, and relationships that make up your personal history is never neutral. You always look at your life through some kind of lens that helps you make sense of who you are, where you have been, what you have experienced, what you have done, and where you are going. Sadly, as we look back on our lives, many of us omit the most important fact of human existence: the being, character, and rule of God. The existence of God is the ultimate fact that makes sense of every other fact in the universe. If you leave him out of your assessment of your life, you will never properly understand who you are.

If you are a child of God, the most important interpreter of your life is grace. God's grace was operating for you long before you knew anything about grace. In fact, it was working before you knew anything. God's work of grace in your life was written into his sovereign plan before the foundations of the earth were set in place. The author of your story decided that your story would be one of rescuing, forgiving, transforming, providing, empowering, and delivering grace. You have been showered with inexhaustible and eternal love, which you never could have earned. In every situation in which you have found yourself, in every location you have lived, and in every relationship you've been a part of, God's love and grace have been operating. You may not have seen or felt that love and grace, but they were there. God was working so you would know him, and, in your communion with him, that you would have everything you need now, in the days that follow, and on into eternity.

Recounting the history of God's people, Psalm 136 views the high-mountain victories and deep-valley struggles through a single lens: the steadfast love of the Lord, which endures forever. In fact, that statement is repeated in every verse. Twenty-six times! It's written to get your attention, echo in your brain, and change the way you, as a child of God, think about your life. You will walk through dark valleys, but your identity and future are secured by the fact that the steadfast love of the Lord endures forever. May this shape the way you think about your life as a child of grace.

For further study and encouragement: 1 Chronicles 16:28–34

———

JULY 5

PSALMS 140–145

We are little specks on a tiny planet in a vast universe, but God cares for us and unleashes his sovereign power for our good.

I cherished the moments when one of our children would ask a question about the most important things in life. "Why do we go to church every week?" "Why do we pray before we eat?" I wanted my children to know God and the stunning glory of his grace. I wanted them to know that following him was the best decision of their lives. I wanted them to develop an identity and view of life that had God in the center. So I wasn't irritated by their questions. They were doorways leading to the gospel.

Consider the important question King David asks in Psalm 144:

Blessed be the LORD, my rock,
    who trains my hands for war,
    and my fingers for battle;
he is my steadfast love and my fortress,
    my stronghold and my deliverer,
my shield and he in whom I take refuge,
    who subdues peoples under me.

O Lord, what is man that you regard him,
  or the son of man that you think of him?
Man is like a breath;
  his days are like a passing shadow. (Ps. 144:1–4)

David calls upon God to bless his reign and those of his sons who will come after him. And then he asks the key question: "O Lord, what is man that you regard him, or the son of man that you think of him? Man is like a breath; his days are like a passing shadow." This question fills you with wonder and can change the way you think about your life.

Think of how little and insignificant we are. We are tiny dots, living somewhere on a tiny little planet that is spinning around in the vastness of the universe. In light of the enormity of time and eternity, our lives are the definition of brevity. Each of us is just one of a billion little dots that shines for a moment, but then quickly burns out. Yet God regards each one of us. Stop and take it in. The King of kings, the great Creator who set everything in motion, the sovereign Lord who sits on the throne of the universe *cares about us.* The essence of human significance is rooted in the fact that God thinks we are worth caring for. Not only does he think about us, but he meets us in our lostness with his rescuing, forgiving, and transforming grace. If you matter this much to God, then you matter. You are more than a dot in the universe; you have worth in the mind of the Lord. That is enough to get you up in the morning. No matter what you're facing, you can live as God intended because you matter to him.

For further study and encouragement: Isaiah 40:6–8

———

JULY 6

PSALMS 146–150

You always put your trust in someone or something. Whoever or whatever holds your trust also controls the way you live.

Psalm 146 is about trust. God created us to be trusting beings. This means that we continually entrust ourselves to someone or something. When we trust someone or something, we ask that person or thing to deliver what we think we want or need. Even the most fearful or cynical people trust something.

Our capacity to trust was woven into us by God. It is supposed to drive us to him; we are to give our hearts to him and believe that what he says is true. The first horrible moment of sin and rebellion in the garden of Eden was a drama of trust. Would Adam and Eve continue to trust God and live as he commanded, or would they trust the serpent and step over God's boundaries? Adam and Eve made a terrible trust decision, and we continue to deal with the results today.

Read the psalm carefully:

Praise the LORD!
Praise the LORD, O my soul!
I will praise the LORD as long as I live;
   I will sing praises to my God while I have my being.
Put not your trust in princes,
   in a son of man, in whom there is no salvation.
When his breath departs, he returns to the earth;
   on that very day his plans perish.
Blessed is he whose help is the God of Jacob,
   whose hope is in the LORD his God,
who made heaven and earth,
   the sea, and all that is in them,
who keeps faith forever;
   who executes justice for the oppressed,
   who gives food to the hungry.
The LORD sets the prisoners free;
   the LORD opens the eyes of the blind.
The LORD lifts up those who are bowed down;
   the LORD loves the righteous.
The LORD watches over the sojourners;
   he upholds the widow and the fatherless,
   but the way of the wicked he brings to ruin.
The LORD will reign forever,
   your God, O Zion, to all generations.
Praise the LORD!

Why trust a powerful prince, whose life fades away quickly and who cannot offer you salvation? Why trust any created thing? Compare the trustworthiness of created things with the psalmist's description of the Lord, what he has done, what he continues to do, and what he offers those who put their trust in him. The attributes and works the psalmist assigns to God are awesome and glorious and true of no one or nothing else. God alone knows what we need. He alone provides. In the majesty of his character and work, he alone is worthy of our trust. If we put our trust in him, we have hope that will never fail us or fade away. Why would we entrust our lives to anyone or anything else?

For further study and encouragement: Genesis 3:1–6

———

JULY 7

PROVERBS 1–4

It's impossible to be independently wise, because true wisdom always begins with the fear of the Lord.

When you ask people whether they think they are wise, many will answer, "Of course!" Few answer, "No, I'm a fool. I've been foolish all my life. I have made foolish decisions and have lived foolishly. No one would look at my life and think that I am wise." Yet, true wisdom is an elusive treasure that can be found in only one place. Scripture tells us that since all of us are born in sin, we are born fools. That's why "folly is bound up in the heart of a child" (Prov. 22:15). This means that wisdom is not natural for us—foolishness is. We are born fools who desperately need to acquire wisdom. But the Bible tells us more. Pay attention to the words of Proverbs 1:2–7:

> To know wisdom and instruction,
>   to understand words of insight,
> to receive instruction in wise dealing,
>   in righteousness, justice, and equity;
> to give prudence to the simple,
>   knowledge and discretion to the youth—
> Let the wise hear and increase in learning,
>   and the one who understands obtain guidance,
> to understand a proverb and a saying,
>   the words of the wise and their riddles.
> The fear of the Lord is the beginning of knowledge;
>   fools despise wisdom and instruction.

You can't buy wisdom or earn a wisdom degree. You can't take a wisdom pilgrimage. You can't independently make yourself wise. Wisdom is found only in fearing the Lord. This fear is not terror, which would drive you from the Lord, but rather awe that causes you to listen to his words and offer your life to him in willing sacrifice and service. The reason a fool is a fool is because he does not fear the Lord: "The fool says in his heart, 'There is no God'" (Ps. 14:1).

Therefore, true wisdom is always the result of the grace of divine rescue. The fool needs to be rescued from *himself*. We have no capacity for wisdom unless God radically transforms the character and content of our hearts. Do you want insight, righteousness, and justice in your life? Do you want knowledge and discretion? Do you want to obtain guidance and increase in learning? Do you want to understand the deep riddles and questions of life? All of these things are the fruit of true wisdom, and they are yours for the taking. God welcomes you to come to him, confessing your foolishness and crying out for the wisdom he alone can give. Let go of your awe of your own wisdom and bow in awe and wonder before him. He generously gives wisdom to those who seek it, because he is tenderhearted, generous, and kind. Why live foolishly, when God graciously offers you the treasures of his wisdom?

For further study and encouragement: James 3:13–18

———

JULY 8

PROVERBS 5–9

*God created us to work, and he gives us his presence, promises,
and grace so we can work diligently and faithfully.*

I was sixteen years old, and it was the night of the last day of school. My father called me into the living room and said, "Sit down. I want to talk to you." He proceeded to tell me that the next day I was to get up, put on a suit coat and tie, and go out and look for a job. He told me that if I didn't get a job the first day, I would have to do the same thing day after day until I found a job. I look back on that conversation with gratitude. I learned the value of work at a young age, and it has served me well throughout my life.

From the beginning, God designed us for and called us to work. Labor is not the result of the fall. Adam and Eve were called to certain work in the garden of Eden. Sin's effect on the physical creation makes work hard, but work was always God's plan for us. Work is part of our identity as human beings. And people who work hard are blessed by the fruit of their labors. One of the ways God cares for, maintains, and develops his creation is by the work of those made in his image. Consider Proverbs 6, where God points us to the industrious discipline of the ant:

> Go to the ant, O sluggard;
> consider her ways, and be wise.
> Without having any chief,
> officer, or ruler,
> she prepares her bread in summer
> and gathers her food in harvest.
> How long will you lie there, O sluggard?
> When will you arise from your sleep?
> A little sleep, a little slumber,
> a little folding of the hands to rest,
> and poverty will come upon you like a robber,
> and want like an armed man. (Prov. 6:6–11)

Why does God call the ant wise? The ant works without a boss forcing him to work, and he knows the value of planning; therefore, the ant never pays the price for being lazy. It's humbling to have your attitude toward work compared to an ant's, but maybe that's the point. If an ant works faithfully, without needing to be prodded, how much more should we, who have been called to care for what God has made?

It's not natural for sinners to love work; we are inclined to do little while hoping for much. So, if we're going to love work and live a disciplined and faithful life of work, God must meet us with his grace. Divine grace has the power to turn sluggards into people who work with joy as unto the Lord. Reach out for that grace today.

For further study and encouragement: 2 Thessalonians 3:6–12

———

JULY 9

PROVERBS 10–11

You can't read the Bible without coming to the convicting and motivating conclusion that words matter.

Words have fierce power. Read and meditate on what Proverbs says about the power of our words:

Whoever walks in integrity walks securely,
  but he who makes his ways crooked will be found out.
Whoever winks the eye causes trouble,
  and a babbling fool will come to ruin.
The mouth of the righteous is a fountain of life,
  but the mouth of the wicked conceals violence.
Hatred stirs up strife,
  but love covers all offenses.
On the lips of him who has understanding, wisdom is found,
  but a rod is for the back of him who lacks sense.
The wise lay up knowledge,
  but the mouth of a fool brings ruin near.
A rich man's wealth is his strong city;
  the poverty of the poor is their ruin.
The wage of the righteous leads to life,
  the gain of the wicked to sin.
Whoever heeds instruction is on the path to life,
  but he who rejects reproof leads others astray.
The one who conceals hatred has lying lips,
  and whoever utters slander is a fool.
When words are many, transgression is not lacking,
  but whoever restrains his lips is prudent.
The tongue of the righteous is choice silver;
  the heart of the wicked is of little worth.
The lips of the righteous feed many,
  but fools die for lack of sense. (Prov. 10:9–21)

Our words matter. They produce either a good or a bad harvest. You can give a person joy with words. You can crush a person's spirit with words. With words you can help others see God and understand their need of him. With words you can create division or restore unity. You can use words to let people know you love them, or to tell them they are deeply hated. With words you can give people a vision and expand their imagination. Your words can impart wisdom or can drag a person down into your foolishness. With words you can lovingly rebuke or hatefully condemn. Words are the way we communicate the most beautiful truths, and also how we deceive with the ugliest lies.

We cannot let ourselves minimize the power of the words we speak. Our problem is that most of our words aren't spoken in dramatic or important moments. We let words fly in many mundane moments, without thinking that our words matter and always leave behind some kind of effect. Scripture reminds us that no one is able to tame the tongue (see James 3). With humble hearts, we need to ask our Lord to meet us with his powerful grace, so that the words we speak would be like choice silver. May God help us to remember that words matter, and may he help us to speak words that produce a harvest of righteousness.

For further study and encouragement: James 3:1–12

JULY 10

PROVERBS 12–13

It takes rescuing and empowering grace to love reproof and to understand that, on this side of eternity, we regularly need it.

When my good friend and I sat down to talk, I didn't know that he planned to confront me about something I had said and the attitudes behind my words. As I got a sense of where he was going, I felt my chest tighten and my ears grow warm. As he was talking, I thought of all the ways I could defend myself and show him that he was wrong. I didn't like being in that moment, and I didn't like what he was saying to me about me. But something else was going on in my mind. I knew then, as I know now, that I am not perfect. I knew that the things I had said had been fueled by anger. He had made me mad, and my anger had shaped my words. As much as I hated being in that moment, I knew my friend was right and what he was saying to me about me was true. By grace, I resisted my self-justifying internal arguments, listened to his words, and asked for his forgiveness.

I know I need to read the following words again and again. What about you?

> Whoever loves discipline loves knowledge,
>   but he who hates reproof is stupid.
> A good man obtains favor from the LORD,
>   but a man of evil devices he condemns.
> No one is established by wickedness,
>   but the root of the righteous will never be moved. (Prov. 12:1–3)

If I called you up on a Friday night and told you that I wanted to come over to rebuke you, how would you respond? When we think of reproof or rebuke, we often think of pointed fingers, a loud voice, and inflammatory accusations. But this is not what Proverbs has in mind at all. Reproof in Proverbs is such a good and necessary thing that you would have to be stupid not to want it in your life. Why? Scripture teaches that sin blinds us, and, because it does, we often don't see or hear ourselves with accuracy. The doctrine of the deceitfulness of sin teaches us that we do not know ourselves well. So I need help, and since God is the helper of helpers and is unwilling to leave me to my blindness, he sends helpers my way. He puts people in my life who love me enough to step into hard moments with me, helping me see what God wants me to see. When I am properly rebuked, I am not experiencing human disrespect. No, I am experiencing divine rescue, a rescue I will need repeatedly until sin is no more. Jesus came to give sight to blind eyes, and he sends people into our lives as his instruments of seeing.

For further study and encouragement: Revelation 3:14–22

JULY 11

PROVERBS 14–15

Only one fear gives us life, hope, and courage: the fear of the Lord.

I stood transfixed before what may be Barnett Newman's greatest painting, *Vir Heroicus Sublimis* (*Man, Heroic and Sublime*). Newman applied layers and layers of thin red paint, creating a hundred square feet of red. When you stand before the painting, you feel as though you could walk into this sea of red. If you stand there for long, it feels as though the painting is absorbing you. It is magnificent and awe-inspiring, and there is nothing else like it. But, though this work of art momentarily captures your awe, it cannot change the character or content of your heart, and it surely has no power whatsoever to bring you from death to life. *Vir Heroicus Sublimis* is a lifeless glory hanging on the wall of a museum, and nothing more.

The world around us is filled with created glories: a sunset painted across the early evening sky; the undulating dance of poppies in the wind; the glistening white purity of new-fallen snow; the melody of a multihued songbird; the thrill of standing on top of a mountain you have just climbed; or the rush of accomplishment as a diploma is placed in your hands. Each of these things captures our awe for a moment, but does little more than that. The world God made is wonderful and inspiring, but it has no power to address and meet our deepest longings and needs. Earth will never be our savior.

That's why the words of Proverbs 14:26–27 should not be glossed over:

In the fear of the LORD one has strong confidence,
  and his children will have a refuge.
The fear of the LORD is a fountain of life,
  that one may turn away from the snares of death.

God has hardwired us to fear. No, I don't mean he intends us to live in terror. Here's what this fear is about. Our hearts are awe centers. This means that
something always captures the awe of our hearts, and what captures the awe
of our hearts will then control the way we live. Fear of God—life-shaping,
worship-producing, and obedience-motivating awe of God—is the only thing
that can capture our heart and has the capacity to give us life. Fear of God
produces confidence, because it has the power to disarm all the other things
we may be afraid of in this life. Fear of God is a fountain of life, renewing our
lives day after day.

Do you fear the Lord? Has awe of him protected you from awe of other things
that have no ability to give you what only God can? What shapes the way you
live? What gives you the confidence to get up in the morning to face another
day? May we fear the Lord.

For further study and encouragement: Psalm 111:1–10

——————

JULY 12

PROVERBS 16–18

*The unshakable sovereignty of God does not nullify the
importance of the choices and decisions of his creatures.*

As I look back over my life, with all of its twists and turns and highs and lows,
I can be sure of one thing: I never could have written my own story. I am constantly surprised by my own journey. Even typing words that will become a book
is something I never thought I would do. That writing would be the primary
way I would work to serve and bless the church of Jesus Christ amazes me. I am
not the author of my story; God is. Every aspect of it—every location, situation,
relationship, triumph, defeat, sunny day, and dark night—was written into his
sovereign book before I took my first breath.

My story has been written by the wise, powerful, and gracious hand of the King of kings. But something else is equally true. I have not been passive. I have made countless mundane and dramatic decisions along the way, each one contributing to who I am, where I am, whom I am with, and what I do. I would not be here if I had made different decisions. Each choice was formative. Every decision contributed to the shape, content, and direction of my life. I was desiring, thinking, meditating, choosing, conversing, and acting all along the way. Nothing about my journey has been robotic.

Are you confused? Do these two ideas seem to contradict one another? Here is the question that many people ponder: If God determines everything, then do my decisions matter? The Bible teaches us that our decisions are important, and it teaches us that God is sovereign. So how do we put these two seemingly contradictory truths together? Scripture teaches us that God accomplishes his unalterable sovereign plan through the means of the valid choices and decisions of the people he has created. It is never a question of God's sovereignty *or* our responsibility. No, it is always *both-and*. God is completely sovereign *and* we are always responsible for how we act and what we chose.

One little verse in Proverbs captures this well:

The heart of man plans his way,
   but the LORD establishes his steps. (Prov. 16:9)

You can rest in God's wise and gracious plan. Nothing can stop what he has already written in his holy book. But resting doesn't mean living passively or being careless with your choices and decisions. God designed you to plan your way. He calls you to have righteous desires and to make wise choices. He calls you to look to Scripture as your authority for what is right and true. As you do so, you can rest assured that God's wise and holy will for you will be done.

God rules and you choose—rest and responsibility. This is the life of faith.

For further study and encouragement: James 4:13–17

JULY 13

The questions that divide humanity are: Do I think I'm okay
as I am, or do I see myself in desperate need of a Savior?

Once a child is able to communicate in words, an endless stream of questions starts pouring out. *Why, Mommy? Why not, Daddy? What is that? How does it work? Why can't I go?* The questions you ask and the answers you accept influence the content, character, and direction of your life. Insightful, wise people are not those who have the right *answers.* They are the people who have the wisdom to ask the right *questions.* You can't get to the right answers if you spend your life asking the wrong questions.

The greatest questions have reflected humanity's philosophical and theological search since creation. God designed us to think, wonder, and interpret, and in the center of our thinking lie innumerable small and hugely consequential questions. But one question marks the human fault line. It is humanity's great dividing question, because how you answer it will put you into one of two camps. It is a question that offers no neutral in-between. This question is deeply moral, and your answer sets the spiritual direction of your life. This fault-line question is found in the last third of the book of Proverbs:

Who can say, "I have made my heart pure;
I am clean from my sin"? (Prov. 20:9)

One group answers this question by saying, "I am basically a good person, with the power to be as righteous as I need to be. Sin isn't something I need to worry about." Now, maybe most people wouldn't say it that way explicitly, but most of the people you live near, work with, or encounter at the store or the park think this way about themselves. They are not haunted or anxious about their sin. They think they do not have an evil heart, and, because they think this way, they don't feel any need for the rescuing grace of the Savior.

The other group answers this question this way: "I know I cannot have a pure heart on my own, and I surely know that I am not free from sin." These people recognize the presence and power of indwelling sin and spend their lives crying out for the help of the grace of the Savior, Jesus. May we never become so used to minimizing or explaining away our sin that we no longer have a daily hunger for what he alone can give us.

For further study and encouragement: Genesis 6:5–7

JULY 14

*The ultimate goal of parenting is not behavior
management. It is heart realignment.*

So much of what we need to know and understand about the task of parenting
is captured in this passage from Proverbs 22:15:

> Folly is bound up in the heart of a child,
>   but the rod of discipline drives it far from him.

This short proverb is helpful in many amazing ways. Consider the following:

1. *When God calls you to parent, you become his tool in the formation of a
child he made in his image.* This passage makes it clear that what is at stake in
parenting is bigger than whether a child will do well at school, get a good job,
or have a happy married life. No, what is at stake is the heart of the child. Will
your child be rescued from his or her foolishness and live a life shaped by the
fear of the Lord?

2. *The root problem with your children is not their misbehavior but the condition of their heart.* Disobedience, rebellion, and disrespect stem from a heart
condition: foolishness. A fool's world is upside down and inside out. A fool looks
at wisdom and sees foolishness, at truth and sees falsehood, and at right and
sees wrong. This means that the little one whom you love so much is a natural
danger to himself.

3. *A well-designed system of clear rules and punishments will not address a
child's deepest needs.* The word *discipline* in this passage confuses many parents.
Most parents think discipline is only about making sure children receive consequences for their wrong behavior. But the biblical picture of discipline is bigger than that. It includes loving instruction about what is important in life and
helping your child view life from God's perspective. Biblical discipline provides
constant gospel instruction that points children to the rescuing grace of Jesus.

4. *You have no power at all to change the heart of your child.* Because your
child's problem in life is the heart, good parenting begins by humbly acknowledging that you can't give your child what he or she desperately needs. This
means that you are never the change agent. Rather, you are an instrument in the
hands of the one who has the power and the willingness to do in and for your
child what you are unable to do.

5. *The rod is a word picture for the importance of loving discipline of your
children.* You discipline your children not because they have made you mad,

but because you love them. Loving discipline teaches them that sin has consequences and softens the heart to hear the gospel.

God meets parents with his rescuing and transforming grace. He works to change your heart so that you can become a tool of change in the heart of your child. You can have confidence that God is in you, with you, and for you as you help your child to understand that his or her hope in this life and the one to come is found only in the person and work of the Lord Jesus Christ.

For further study and encouragement: Ephesians 6:1–4

JULY 15

PROVERBS 24–26

*If your heart has been softened by God's grace, you will
find no joy in anyone's fall—even an enemy's.*

If you're a regular user of social media, you have witnessed too much curiosity, interest, and enjoyment in someone else's fall. Posts about the good someone has done receive little interest, but if the news breaks that a well-known Christian leader has fallen, it doesn't take long for hundreds of people to jump on the controversy. We want to know what happened, when it happened, and how it happened. We want the inside details about this person's life. We are quick to give our opinion about the person's character, what he did, and how it was handled. We'll go back to Twitter or Facebook, searching to see whether more has been uncovered. We want to know what other people are saying, and we contemplate adding our own two cents' worth. All of this chatter by people who don't know the person involved and have no ability to help is fueled by a perverse interest, and, yes, a delight in the falls and failures of others. We have particular interest and enthusiasm when the person who has fallen is part of a tribe other than our own. But Proverbs 24:17–18 warns:

> Do not rejoice when your enemy falls,
>   and let not your heart be glad when he stumbles,
> lest the LORD see it and be displeased,
>   and turn away his anger from him.

This is not just a social media problem, although social media makes this piling-on dynamic much easier. Digital delight in another's sin and digital gossip are sins of the heart before they are words typed on a screen. When it comes to how we should respond to the fall of another person, even one whom we would consider an enemy of what is right and true, *God himself is our model.* God, who is perfectly holy in every way and all of the time and who has never compromised his righteous standard, says this about how he views the death of a wicked person:

> Say to them, As I live, declares the Lord GOD, I have no pleasure in the death of the wicked, but that the wicked turn from his way and live; turn back, turn back from your evil ways, for why will you die, O house of Israel? (Ezek. 33:11)

God never takes pleasure when a wicked person dies. He responds to the ultimate fall of a person with tenderhearted grace and mercy. He does not delight in the details of anyone's sin. He finds no pleasure in the fact that someone has finally gotten what he deserves. No, he pleads that the wicked would turn from their ways and find his forgiveness and transforming power. Do we model the heart of God? Have our hearts been made tender by his grace? No one gives grace better than one whose heart and life have been changed by its transforming power.

May we not delight in another's fall. With broken hearts, may we pray for an outpouring of God's rescuing grace for ourselves and anyone who has fallen. And may God work in our hearts so that we'll find greater delight in what is good than in what is evil.

For further study and encouragement: Romans 12:9–21

———

JULY 16

PROVERBS 27–29

There isn't a person alive who doesn't need God's rescuing, forgiving, empowering, transforming, and delivering grace.

The writers of Proverbs often use graphic word pictures to make important gospel points. Consider how the following argues for the power of God's grace:

> Crush a fool in a mortar with a pestle
>   along with crushed grain,
>   yet his folly will not depart from him. (Prov. 27:22)

Imagine that we are in my kitchen, and on my counter stands a mortar and pestle, made of stone. You watch me put a few ounces of wheat grains into the mortar and begin to pound and grind them with the pestle. After a few minutes of physical exertion, I invite you to look into the mortar. What will you see? You will still see wheat. It may have changed its shape and become a fine powder, but it will still be 100 percent wheat, just as it was when it was a whole grain. You could watch me pound on that wheat for ten days, but it would still be wheat, because wheatness is its fundamental nature and all the pounding in the world will not change it.

So it is with every fool ever born—and that includes all of us—because sin reduces all of us to fools. Since foolishness (sin) is a matter of nature and not just behavior, external manipulation will not change us at the level of the true nature of our hearts. God's law is important, but rigid enforcement of his law alone will not change the character of our hearts. Education cannot change our nature. Threats of consequences have no power to change our hearts. Changes of situation and location do not address what is foundationally wrong with us. If our sin were just about behavior, then behavioral control and retraining would take care of our problem. This proverb is in the Bible to help us understand that nothing has the power to address the deepest of human problems—except the grace of the Savior. If any of the external forces I mentioned had the power to change the fundamental composition of our hearts, then Jesus would not have had to come.

Rather than discourage you, this proverb should cause you to reflect with gratitude on the amazing gift of the glorious grace of Jesus. God, in love, refused to leave us in our natural state. He had a plan to give us the help that he alone could give. Jesus's life, death, and resurrection offer us the promise of real change, which reaches the very character of our hearts.

The mortar and pestle teach us that external forces cannot change us, and this is why we daily seek and celebrate the grace of Jesus. He alone breaks the power of sin and sets the captive free. Celebrate his grace today.

For further study and encouragement: Ephesians 2:1–10

JULY 17

We should be quick to be grateful for and give honor to women
whose lives picture what it means to fear the Lord.

Charm is deceitful, and beauty is vain,
    but a woman who fears the LORD is to be praised.
Give her of the fruit of her hands,
    and let her works praise her in the gates. (Prov. 31:30–31)

When you read through the book of Proverbs, it might seem as though it addresses a cast of male characters. But then you get to its final chapter. Proverbs gives special time and attention to the character and accomplishments of an excellent woman, that is, one whose whole life is shaped by her awe of God.

The verses of this portrait of the godly woman follow the letters of the Hebrew alphabet, as though the writer wants to reinforce the wide-ranging nature of her gifts, character, and accomplishments. In so doing, Proverbs 31 speaks to present cultural mistakes when it comes to women. The culture around us often gets womanhood all wrong. If you examine the websites of female social media influencers, the dominant theme is that physical beauty is everything. And, in fact, it is even worse than that. Our culture's definition of physical beauty is not naturally attainable. By today's definition, you can become truly beautiful only with the help of chemical injections and surgery. So many young girls are depressed, and some even suicidal, because they have no way of reaching this beauty standard.

But the church doesn't always get the definition of beauty right either. If there is any place where godly women should receive "praise in the gates," it is in the church. We are to recognize gifted and accomplished women, because we know that God chose them to be examples of what his grace can do. We see the work of the Spirit in women's lives, and we see in them what God's gifts can accomplish. Proverbs 31 argues that in God's economy we need these women, and we should be quick to rise and thank God for their presence and contributions to the health of the community of faith.

I have spent half a century married to a woman who fears the Lord. She has a legacy of accomplishments inside and outside of the home. She is a comforter and mentor to younger women and has been the most consistent spiritual influence in my life. Proverbs reminds us that women like my wife are worthy of our corporate gratitude and public praise. We should always remember that women who fear the Lord are good gifts to the church and to the world.

For further study and encouragement: 1 Peter 3:1–6

JULY 18

A devastating emptiness of life results when you remove
God from your journey on this side of eternity.

No other book of the Bible begins as Ecclesiastes does. We are given no introduction, but are immediately thrown into a discouraging world of endlessly repeating vanity:

> Vanity of vanities, says the Preacher,
>   vanity of vanities! All is vanity.
> What does man gain by all the toil
>   at which he toils under the sun?
> A generation goes, and a generation comes,
>   but the earth remains forever.
> The sun rises, and the sun goes down,
>   and hastens to the place where it rises.
> The wind blows to the south
>   and goes around to the north;
> around and around goes the wind,
>   and on its circuits the wind returns.
> All streams run to the sea,
>   but the sea is not full;
> to the place where the streams flow,
>   there they flow again.
> All things are full of weariness;
>   a man cannot utter it;
> the eye is not satisfied with seeing,
>   nor the ear filled with hearing.
> What has been is what will be,
>   and what has been done is what will be done,
>   and there is nothing new under the sun. (Eccl. 1:2–9)

It is as though the Preacher were standing in the middle of the cosmos and screaming, "What is all of this about? There has to be more to my life than this. What in the world am I missing?" In this way, Ecclesiastes is a huge comfort to the thousands of people who have stood in the middle of their lives and asked the same questions. As the Bible so often does in its honesty about the struggles of life on this side of eternity, Ecclesiastes welcomes the reader to be honest with God about the seeming meaninglessness of life.

Though it might seem that these verses are communicating meaningless hopelessness, the Preacher's aim is more profound. To get his deeper point, you have to understand the phrase "under the sun." What does he mean when he says that life is vain "under the sun"? This phrase reinforces the central message not only of Ecclesiastes, but of the entire word of God. It is impossible to find a life of unshakable identity, meaning, purpose, contentment, and joy if you look only horizontally. Nothing in the world God created has the power to give you the satisfaction and joy of heart that every human longs for. Everything in life will fail you. Imperfect people, places, and things can't give you what you long for.

Where is life to be found? Above the sun; that is, in God alone. Knowing him and being known by him give our lives meaning and purpose. Having a relationship with him gives even the most menial tasks purpose and dignity. It is only in, with, and through him that contentment is possible and our hearts are satisfied.

By grace we can rise above the vanity. God not only exists, but he has made himself known and taken us as his own. That changes everything.

For further study and encouragement: Philippians 3:1–11

JULY 19

ECCLESIASTES 5–8

A life of gratitude and joy grows in the soil of contentment.

I have a wonderfully blessed life, yet I still find reasons to complain. On this side of eternity grumbling seems to be the default language of the human community. There is a reason for this. Selfishness is in the DNA of sin. Sin causes us to put ourselves in the center of our world and make life all about us. Life gets reduced to our wants, our needs, and our feelings. And there is no end to the catalog of things we find dissatisfying. We complain about the weather, traffic, and waiting in line. We whine that there's nothing to eat, nothing worth watching, and too much to do. We're bored, we don't feel well, and everything costs too much. We're tired of dealing with our kids, our parents, our spouses, and our churches. A life of complaint is a life shrunken to the size of one person. It's a life of entitlement. It's God-forgetful. This life robs you of your joy. Complaint crushes glad-hearted worship. God did not design us to be lifelong complainers. Note the Preacher's take on contentment:

Behold, what I have seen to be good and fitting is to eat and drink and find enjoyment in all the toil with which one toils under the sun the few days of his life that God has given him, for this is his lot. Everyone also to whom God has given wealth and possessions and power to enjoy them, and to accept his lot and rejoice in his toil—this is the gift of God. For he will not much remember the days of his life because God keeps him occupied with joy in his heart. (Eccl. 5:18–20)

Contentment is not the product of an affluent and easy life. This passage talks about enjoyment both in toil and in wealth. Contentment depends not on your situation but on the heart that you bring to each situation. Fabulously wealthy people complain. Poor people complain. People in between complain. Joy in labor is possible only when you are thankful that God has provided you with a job and the ability to work. Toil is a good gift from God, as is every opportunity I get to enjoy the fruit of my labor. Every day of my life is a gift from God, and every day is filled with more gifts from him.

This passage teaches us one more important thing. Contentment itself is a gift from God. It's not natural for sinners to be content. When I'm content, the joy in my heart protects me from finding things to grumble about. Are you content? Confess your discontentment, and God will give you grace for the struggle.

For further study and encouragement: Philippians 4:10–13

JULY 20

ECCLESIASTES 9–12

The life of faith always begins with recognizing your need for wisdom.

Habakkuk 2:4 says that "the righteous shall live by his faith." But what does that mean? What does a life of faith look like for a single adult? What does it look like for a married couple? What does a life of faith look like for a teenager or an elderly person? What does it look like at your work? What does a life of faith look like when it comes to sex and money? What does it look like when it comes to making decisions? What does a life of faith look like when you are suffering? What in the world is a life of faith?

Like many people, Luella loves Ecclesiastes for both its honesty and its wisdom. She tells people all the time to study their way through this wonderful book. The wisdom of Ecclesiastes perhaps shines brightest in its final paragraphs:

The words of the wise are like goads, and like nails firmly fixed are the collected sayings; they are given by one Shepherd. My son, beware of anything beyond these. Of making many books there is no end, and much study is a weariness of the flesh.

The end of the matter; all has been heard. Fear God and keep his commandments, for this is the whole duty of man. For God will bring every deed into judgment, with every secret thing, whether good or evil. (Eccl. 12:11–14)

The life of faith begins with recognizing your need for wisdom and recognizing that the wisdom you need is found in one place. Because of sin, wisdom is not natural for us. We have to humbly admit that, in our foolishness, we are a danger to ourselves. Notice the protective and life-shaping nature of true wisdom. Wisdom is like a goad. A goad is a long stick used to keep oxen moving straight when pulling a plow. Wisdom is also like a nail on which you can hang aspects of your life. We all need goads to keep us straight and nails on which to hang our decisions and actions. The good shepherd, in grace and in his wisdom, offers us both.

What does this wisdom tell us about the life of faith? First, the life of faith is shaped by the fear of the Lord. That means we do not allow any other thing to rule the thoughts and desires of our heart. Second, the life of faith commits to obeying God's commands, no matter what situations you find yourself in.

So run today to your good shepherd, confess your need for his wisdom, and cry out for the desire and strength to keep his commands. By grace, he will bless you with his goads and nails.

For further study and encouragement: Proverbs 1:1–7

JULY 21

SONG OF SOLOMON 1–8

One of God's beautiful gifts to us is love—not just his perfect love, but also the beauty and pleasure of marital love.

I will never forget the first time I told Luella that I loved her. We had been dating for a while, and I was convinced that I was deeply, madly in love with her. I was searching for just the right moment to say those powerful words: *I love you.* An evening came when the moment seemed right. I looked into her eyes and said,

"Luella, I love you." What happened next was not in my romantic plan. She said, "You what? You love me? What do you know about love? Don't ever say that to me again." Now, Luella wasn't being mean to me. She was looking into the face of a seventeen-year-old boy. She was right; I had little knowledge of what real love was. This was my God-given wake-up call to be more serious about one of the most beautiful things God has created: the love, romance, passion, and commitment between a man and a woman. By the way, things turned out quite well after that disaster of an evening. Luella and I have enjoyed our love relationship for over five decades, and are going strong.

God dedicated an entire book of the Bible to painting a stunning picture of the love relationship between a man and a woman—highlighting its pleasure, passion, and commitment. There is no other book of the Bible like Song of Solomon. It is beautiful, graphic, poetic, and wise. You can't read this book and think that God is against pleasure or views sex as negative. God put us in a world where pleasurable things are all around us, and he designed us with eyes, ears, mouth, nose, and touch—pleasure gates so we could enjoy the pleasures he created. God gets glory when his creatures enjoy the pleasures he has created, within the boundaries he has set and with the understanding that these gifts come from him. God delights in the loving sexual pleasure of a married couple. He created it, after all.

> You have captivated my heart, my sister, my bride;
>> you have captivated my heart with one glance of your eyes,
>> with one jewel of your necklace.
> How beautiful is your love, my sister, my bride!
>> How much better is your love than wine,
>> and the fragrance of your oils than any spice!
> Your lips drip nectar, my bride;
>> honey and milk are under your tongue;
>> the fragrance of your garments is like the fragrance of Lebanon.
>> (Song 4:9–11)

There it is, right in the middle of God's revelation to us: a beautiful expression of a man's love for his wife. She has not only excited his passion; she has captivated his heart. His words remind us that, except for the love of God, there is no human experience like heart-committed, long-term marital love. When lived God's way, nothing really is better than love.

But, as with any other pleasure God created, we need to be rescued from ourselves so that we can be free to love another as God has designed. Human love is a gift from God, but it takes his grace to enjoy it as he designed.

For further study and encouragement: Ephesians 5:22–33

God is not content with your apathetic participation in the
formal rituals of the church; he wants to rule your heart.

God has gifted us with the local church, where we can be instructed in the gospel, lift our voices in songs of praise, give out of the treasures he has provided for us, and enjoy the community of his people. The church, with all of its rituals, is a precious gift from the God of grace. Your participation in the life and activities of the church is meant to flow from a heart that has submitted to your Redeemer. But that is not always what happens in worship. *Formalism* is one of the gospel's most seductive and deceptive counterfeits. It looks like real Christianity on the surface, but it lacks that which Jesus came to redeem and rule: the heart.

Formalism is not new. It was around in the Old Testament, where we see how seriously God responded to this counterfeit worship:

> Hear the word of the LORD,
>   you rulers of Sodom!
> Give ear to the teaching of our God,
>   you people of Gomorrah!
> "What to me is the multitude of your sacrifices?
>   says the LORD;
> I have had enough of burnt offerings of rams
>   and the fat of well-fed beasts;
> I do not delight in the blood of bulls,
>   or of lambs, or of goats.
> "When you come to appear before me,
>   who has required of you
>   this trampling of my courts?
> Bring no more vain offerings;
>   incense is an abomination to me.
> New moon and Sabbath and the calling of convocations—
>   I cannot endure iniquity and solemn assembly.
> Your new moons and your appointed feasts
>   my soul hates;
> they have become a burden to me;
>   I am weary of bearing them." (Isa. 1:10–14)

Everything that God here calls an abomination—sacrifices, burnt offerings, coming to the temple, the Sabbath, convocations, appointed feasts—are practices he ordained and commanded his people to participate in. But they were to flow from hearts that were faithful to him, producing a life of willing obedience to his commands.

This passage is a warning to us. We must not pride ourselves on the consistency of our church attendance, the regularity of our giving, or the degree of our theological knowledge. God designed us to live out of the heart, that is, everything we do and say is controlled by the thoughts and desires of our heart. And he will settle for nothing less than the ownership and true worship of our hearts. He will not be satisfied with our singing songs of grace on Sunday if throughout the rest of the week we respond gracelessly to the people we live and work with.

How about you? Is there a disconnect between what you say you believe, what you celebrate on Sunday, and how you live your life on the other days of the week? Thankfully, God gives forgiving and empowering grace for this struggle.

For further study and encouragement: 1 John 3:16–24

JULY 23

ISAIAH 5–8

*God has revealed his perfect holiness not only to tell
us who he is, but to redefine who we are.*

The prophet Isaiah invites us to witness his vision of standing before the throne of the Almighty God:

> In the year that King Uzziah died I saw the Lord sitting upon a throne, high and lifted up; and the train of his robe filled the temple. Above him stood the seraphim. Each had six wings: with two he covered his face, and with two he covered his feet, and with two he flew. And one called to another and said:
>
>> "Holy, holy, holy is the LORD of hosts;
>> the whole earth is full of his glory!"
>
> And the foundations of the thresholds shook at the voice of him who called, and the house was filled with smoke. And I said: "Woe is me! For I am lost; for I am a man of unclean lips, and I dwell in the midst of a people of unclean lips; for my eyes have seen the King, the LORD of hosts!"

Then one of the seraphim flew to me, having in his hand a burning coal that he had taken with tongs from the altar. And he touched my mouth and said: "Behold, this has touched your lips; your guilt is taken away, and your sin atoned for." (Isa. 6:1–7)

This is one of the most amazing and awe-inspiring scenes in Scripture. Seraphim stand on either side above God's throne and call to one another, "Holy, holy, holy is the Lord of hosts; the whole earth is full of his glory!" God is so infinitely holy that it takes the threefold use of the word to express the expansive nature of his perfection. But that's not all. God is so holy that the glory of his holiness fills the whole earth.

Pay attention to Isaiah's response. He doesn't say, "This is so amazing. I am so glad I was chosen to see this!" No, he is immediately aware of the gravity of his sin. This is what the revelation of God's holiness should do to each of us. When you let your heart meditate on the glory of the perfect holiness of God, you cannot help but feel the weight of your sin. The revelation of God's holiness redefines how we think about ourselves.

In the beauty of grace, God doesn't leave Isaiah weighed down by the gravity of his sin. For a moment the chant stops, and a seraph flies to Isaiah and offers him atonement for his sin. In seven verses the whole gospel is preached. God is holy, we are sinners, and there is no hope for us apart from his atoning grace.

Has God's holiness had this effect on you? Has it opened your eyes to the tragedy of your sin? Has it caused you to cry out for his grace? Sin is real and powerful, but it has been defeated in the life, death, and resurrection of Jesus. And, because it has, forgiving, empowering, transforming, and delivering grace is ours when we humbly repent and call upon the name of Jesus.

For further study and encouragement: 1 Peter 1:13–21

JULY 24

ISAIAH 9–12

Jesus is the grace of God come to earth.

Once on a speaking trip, I stayed at the home of a wealthy family. This family had been wealthy for generations. One room featured a wall full of portraits of past generations of family members. My host explained to me that, in the days before the camera, itinerant painters would travel from city to city in search of well-to-do clients who would sit for a portrait. Since painting a portrait takes time, the painter would typically live with the family, in a guesthouse or guest room, until the painting was complete. In so doing, the painter would get to know the family, particularly the person he was painting. His knowledge of the person influenced his composition of the portrait. Good painters were known for their ability to capture the essence of the lifestyle, personality, position, and work of their subjects.

If you were to "paint" a verbal picture of Jesus, what words would you use to capture who he is, what he came to do, and what he continues to do in and for those who put their trust in him? It may surprise you, but one of the most beautiful and best-known verbal portraits of Jesus is found not in the New Testament Gospels or Epistles, but rather in the beginning of one of the Old Testament Prophets. For generations, students of the Bible have wondered at, meditated on, and attempted to understand the meaning and implication of the words of this portrait. Perhaps you have already figured out that I am referring to the picture of Jesus painted by Isaiah:

> To us a child is born,
>   to us a son is given;
> and the government shall be upon his shoulder,
>   and his name shall be called
> Wonderful Counselor, Mighty God,
>   Everlasting Father, Prince of Peace.
> Of the increase of his government and of peace
>   there will be no end,
> on the throne of David and over his kingdom,
>   to establish it and to uphold it
> with justice and with righteousness
>   from this time forth and forevermore.
> The zeal of the LORD of hosts will do this. (Isa. 9:6–7)

What an incredible portrait of the one who is our only hope in life and death.

Jesus is everything Isaiah depicted. Jesus is our source of wisdom, the power by which sin is defeated, the one who adopts us into the family of God forever, and the means by which we have peace with God and with one another. And his kingdom of peace and righteousness will never end. He is the hero at the center of God's plan of redeeming grace, and nothing will impede God's zeal to complete his plan.

It is right to say that in Jesus you find everything you need in order to be what you were meant to be, to do what God designed you to do, and to enjoy life as God meant for you to enjoy it. Jesus is life. Jesus is hope. Jesus is the grace of God. We will spend eternity worshiping and celebrating him. Why not start now?

For further study and encouragement: 1 Corinthians 1:26–31

JULY 25

ISAIAH 13–17

God, in grace, not only forgives us, but he also restores the things sin has damaged or destroyed.

There are many wonderful old homes in Philadelphia. I get excited when someone purchases an old broken-down house and, instead of tearing it down, chooses to restore it. I love watching the slow progress of the damage being undone, piece by piece. I try to imagine what the house looked like in its former glory, and I love seeing that former glory progressively return. Even though I don't own the home, I find myself celebrating the fact that time and disrepair have not won. When the work is finally done and the house stands regal and beautiful, I celebrate the victory. But as much as the restoration of any physical thing is a victory over time and decay, it doesn't compare to the eternal glory of restorative grace. We must understand and celebrate the truth that God's grace doesn't end with forgiveness; it extends and extends until all that sin has damaged or destroyed is fully and finally restored.

We get a glimpse of God's restorative mercy in Isaiah 14:1: "For the LORD will have compassion on Jacob and will again choose Israel, and will set them in their own land, and sojourners will join them and will attach themselves to the house of Jacob." God was not willing to leave his children in captivity and defeat. Even though they had not earned it, nor did they deserve it, God would restore the glory of his people—not just for their good, but for his own glory. He would demonstrate that nothing could get in the way of his eternal redeeming plan for a world so damaged by sin. He would restore and preserve his people, so that out of them could come the ultimate restorer, the Lord Jesus Christ.

Passages like Isaiah 14 are not in the Bible just to record the progress of redemptive history. They are also there to help you understand God's character and plan. These restorative moments are God's reminders that he cares about the damage sin has done to us, our families, the natural environment, our neigh-borhoods and cities, and our systems of education, industry, and government. Everything has been damaged by sin, somehow and in some way. God's love for us is so vast that he forgives us *and* restores us.

Your Lord begins by restoring you so that you can live as he designed you to live. But there will be a day when he will make all things new. In almighty mercy, he will reverse every bit of damage sin has done, and we will live forever, in peace and righteousness, in a totally new world. This broken-down house that we call home will not be broken forever.

You live in the middle of the brokenness now, but there is hope, because the divine restorer has entered the house, and very good things are on the way.

For further study and encouragement: Revelation 21:1–5

———

JULY 26

ISAIAH 18–22

The Lord is sovereign over the affairs of nations, and ultimately his holy and wise will shall be done.

You might look around at the chaos of this world, and wonder whether anybody is in charge. It looks as though things are going from bad to worse. The church's influence seems to be shrinking, while evil seems to be prospering. Unthink-able things that are against God's creation plan are not just tolerated, but are celebrated as the new norm. As grandparents, it makes us sad to think about the condition of the world that our grandchildren will grow up in. The culture around us seems to be in constant and rapid change, and the changes aren't for the good. You look around, and the world seems out of control.

The Bible consistently reminds us that, yes, the world is out of our control, and we are often powerless to effect the changes it desperately needs—but our world is, in fact, under control. God holds the whole world in his hands. The one who is the definition of holy, wise, and good sits on the throne as the ruler over everything. He is the ruler of rulers. He controls everything, everywhere, all of the time. Rest and peace of heart come not from trying to understand it all, but from trusting the one who understands it all and rules it all for his glory and our ultimate good.

We find one of Scripture's "I am in charge" moments in Isaiah 21:16–17:

Thus the Lord said to me, "Within a year, according to the years of a hired worker, all the glory of Kedar will come to an end. And the remainder of the archers of the mighty men of the sons of Kedar will be few, for the LORD, the God of Israel, has spoken."

Kedar (Arabia) will be humbled in defeat and trouble God's people no more. But it is important to note why this will happen. This defeat will not be the result of military might. It will not happen because of the power of an earthly king. It will happen because the Lord, the God of Israel, has spoken. God's power is so infinitely great and his rule so complete that whatever he speaks comes to pass. Not only does God declare that this defeat will happen, but he declares exactly when it will take place. Now that is control!

God's sovereign rule over the nations is our hope. Every promise he has made to us is only as good as the extent of his rule, because he can guarantee the sure delivery of his promises only in the places where he rules. But since he is in total control everywhere, we can rest in the knowledge that he will deliver all that he has promised. The work of the Son will be completed, he will win the final victory, and we will live with him forever. The Lord has spoken.

For further study and encouragement: Psalm 2:1–12

JULY 27

ISAIAH 23–27

Sin defiles the perfectly beautiful world that the Lord created.

The prophet Isaiah captures the sad, destructive, and defiling legacy of sin:

The earth mourns and withers;
   the world languishes and withers;
   the highest people of the earth languish.
The earth lies defiled
   under its inhabitants;
for they have transgressed the laws,
   violated the statutes,
   broken the everlasting covenant.
Therefore a curse devours the earth,

and its inhabitants suffer for their guilt;
therefore the inhabitants of the earth are scorched,
and few men are left.
The wine mourns,
the vine languishes,
all the merry-hearted sigh.
The mirth of the tambourines is stilled,
the noise of the jubilant has ceased,
the mirth of the lyre is stilled.
No more do they drink wine with singing;
strong drink is bitter to those who drink it.
The wasted city is broken down;
every house is shut up so that none can enter.
There is an outcry in the streets for lack of wine;
all joy has grown dark;
the gladness of the earth is banished. (Isa. 24:4–11)

Sin never produces anything good. It never leaves a harvest of good fruit. It never builds or reconciles. It never restores what is broken or creates unity and peace. Sin never enhances a culture or makes human government serve its people better. Sin never causes marital love to deepen or grow. Sin never makes people kinder, more content, or wiser. Sin is always destructive; it always leaves a bitter harvest. Sin is the ultimate pandemic. It infects everyone and everything. Its defilement is inescapable. Sin is the ultimate enemy of all that is good. It is a spiritual cancer without a human cure. Sin has one destination: death.

It is easy for us to minimize the presence, power, and destructiveness of sin. Yet Isaiah 24 reminds us of its destructive and defiling nature. Even so, it's easy to tell ourselves that what God says is wrong isn't so bad after all. But sad, hard-to-read passages are in the Bible because God is a God of tender, loving, and protecting grace. He knows our hearts. He knows that sin doesn't always look sinful to us. So he lovingly warns us.

May we ask for forgiveness for the times we have named as beautiful the things God says are defiled. And may we seek him for the grace to see sin in all its ugliness, to have the power to say no to its seductive draw, and to find joy in the wisdom and good fruit of God's commands.

For further study and encouragement: Mark 7:14–23

JULY 28

Jesus is our sure foundation. He is the cornerstone
upon which the house of God stands.

When you're reading a well-written novel, you have no trouble identifying the main character. He will be there on page after page. He will dominate chapter after chapter. Although the book will contain many other characters and sub-plots, the novel really is his story. Everything in the book is somehow about him. If you were to take him out of the novel, the whole story would fall apart and make no sense, because he is the story.

So it is with the Bible. It is the story of Jesus. He is the hero of the story. His presence looms over every book of the Bible. You don't encounter him first in the New Testament. No, he is present from the very first chapter of Genesis (see Col. 1:16). As the history of the people of God is told in the Old Testament, sometimes it's clear that an author can be speaking only of Jesus, even though his name isn't mentioned. Isaiah 28:16–17 is such a passage:

Thus says the Lord God,
  "Behold, I am the one who has laid as a foundation in Zion,
  a stone, a tested stone,
a precious cornerstone, of a sure foundation:
  'Whoever believes will not be in haste.'
And I will make justice the line,
  and righteousness the plumb line."

The apostle Peter applies these words to Jesus (see 1 Pet. 2:6). In Isaiah, God is speaking into his people's present situation, but the words look beyond any human leader of the moment and find their fulfillment in Jesus Christ. Consider Peter's amazing description of Jesus. He is the tested stone. He faced Satan's temptations, the rejection of those he had created, plots against him, torturous suffering, and the general hardships of life in this fallen world, and he was without sin. Jesus is the precious one. There is no one like him. He is the gift of infinite value, the rarest of diamonds. He is the cornerstone of the house of God, the temple for the people of God, where his presence dwells. He is the definition of righteousness, and through his righteousness we are redeemed. He is the ultimate judge, who will restore perfect justice to the earth. When you entrust your soul to Jesus, he gives you everything you need.

Many of us live with cornerstone amnesia. We live in functional confusion and fear. The demands and busyness of life cause us to forget the sure foundation upon which our lives as his children are built. We forget that we are part of the surest edifice that has ever been built—the church, the household of faith. Although we face hardship, disappointment, and suffering, our lives are built on Jesus the sure foundation. We have a security that can never be shaken.

Jesus is your cornerstone. What amazing grace!

For further study and encouragement: 1 Peter 2:4–10

JULY 29

ISAIAH 31–35

*God's presence and promises give us reason to
get up in the morning and persevere.*

Sometimes I suffer through extended periods of intense physical pain. It's very hard. During the day, there is not a painless moment. At night my sleep is regularly interrupted by pain. Because of other physical issues, I am unable to take medication that could alleviate my suffering. It makes everything difficult and many things impossible. Sometimes the pain is so severe that I can barely concentrate. On many occasions, the pain brings me to tears. But I never consider giving up or caving in to the pain. I get up every day and do the things God calls me and blesses me to do. Please know that I do not press forward because I am a hero. Sometimes my suffering gets me down. Only one thing causes me to persevere, and it is captured by the prophet Isaiah:

> The wilderness and the dry land shall be glad;
>   the desert shall rejoice and blossom like the crocus;
> it shall blossom abundantly
>   and rejoice with joy and singing.
> The glory of Lebanon shall be given to it,
>   the majesty of Carmel and Sharon.
> They shall see the glory of the LORD,
>   the majesty of our God.
> Strengthen the weak hands,
>   and make firm the feeble knees.

Say to those who have an anxious heart,
    "Be strong; fear not!
Behold, your God
    will come with vengeance,
with the recompense of God.
    He will come and save you." . . .
And the ransomed of the LORD shall return
    and come to Zion with singing;
everlasting joy shall be upon their heads;
    they shall obtain gladness and joy,
    and sorrow and sighing shall flee away. (Isa: 35:1–4, 10)

How do you respond when you lose your job? How do you deal with the rebellion of one of your children? What do you think as you're being rejected at your university, simply because you are a Christian? How do you face physical suffering? How do you respond to financial need? What do you do when death enters your family's door? How much is anxiety a regular part of your emotional life? How much of your life is shaped by fear and not by faith? What do you do to cope? This passage from Isaiah is in the Bible to get your attention and to give you reason to continue to do the things God calls you to do. As his children, we have reason to get up day after day and persevere: his glorious presence and his unshakable promises. He is with us in glory now, and his promises guarantee that our sorrow and sighing will one day end, forever.

You have a reason for rest of heart now and hope for a bright future, which give you a reason to get up tomorrow. With faith, courage, and a glad heart, you can do the things God has chosen you to do.

For further study and encouragement: Psalm 30:1–12

JULY 30

God answers our prayers not because we are worthy, but because
he is a God of grace and is zealous for his own glory.

I probably couldn't get an audience with the president of the United States at the White House, no matter how hard I tried. In fact, I probably couldn't get an appointment at City Hall. These people of power, where decisions are made that affect my life in many ways, are for the most part closed to me. No one there wants to hear me talk about what I need. No one there is open to my opinion or cares for me personally. When it comes to the rooms of human power, where significant decisions are made, no one hears me when I cry out. In those places, the life and cares of Paul Tripp mean little. Such is life for most of us.

But, without even rising from the place where I am now seated, I can speak to the King of kings, the one who made and rules this world. He hears every word, knows me, understands me, cares for me, and always answers. He is never too busy, too distracted, or too disappointed in me to hear and answer. In the places of human power, I am not received or heard because those leaders have no incentive to receive or hear me. Yet the ruler of the universe welcomes me whenever and wherever I cry out. I come into his presence without an appointment and without having to argue for my worthiness. Why would God ever listen to my prayers?

In Isaiah 37 King Hezekiah receives a letter that mocks God's presence, power, and promises. The king doesn't respond, but spreads the letter out before the Lord and prays:

> O Lord of hosts, God of Israel, enthroned above the cherubim, you are the God, you alone, of all the kingdoms of the earth; you have made heaven and earth. Incline your ear, O Lord, and hear; open your eyes, O Lord, and see; and hear all the words of Sennacherib, which he has sent to mock the living God. Truly, O Lord, the kings of Assyria have laid waste all the nations and their lands, and have cast their gods into the fire. For they were no gods, but the work of men's hands, wood and stone. Therefore they were destroyed. So now, O Lord our God, save us from his hand, that all the kingdoms of the earth may know that you alone are the Lord. (Isa. 37:15–20)

What gives Hezekiah the confidence to rush into God's presence and ask for his help? There is no indication that he appeals to his own righteousness.

He comes to God trusting in his covenant promises, and he appeals to God's zeal for his glory to be known.

Our confidence in prayer is the same as Hezekiah's. It's based not on who we are, but on who God is and what he has promised his children.

For further study and encouragement: Luke 11:1–13

––––

JULY 31

ISAIAH 40–43

*Nothing in heaven or on earth compares to the
infinitely glorious greatness of our Lord.*

I think the word *great* has lost much of its meaning. We talk about a great piece of cake. We celebrate a great pair of shoes. We talk about how great a game was. We tell people we had a great vacation. But true and incomparable greatness belongs only to the Lord. Attempting to capture the grandeur and greatness of the Lord, Isaiah stretches the boundaries of language and word pictures. Even under the inspiration of the Holy Spirit, Isaiah seems to understand that there is no way to capture the greatness of our God inside the limits of human language. Our Lord's infinite greatness cannot adequately be described or understood. And so Isaiah offers a true but limited portrait:

> Who has measured the waters in the hollow of his hand
>   and marked off the heavens with a span,
> enclosed the dust of the earth in a measure
>   and weighed the mountains in scales
>   and the hills in a balance?
> Who has measured the Spirit of the LORD,
>   or what man shows him his counsel?
> Whom did he consult,
>   and who made him understand?
> Who taught him the path of justice,
>   and taught him knowledge,
>   and showed him the way of understanding?
> Behold, the nations are like a drop from a bucket,
>   and are accounted as the dust on the scales;

behold, he takes up the coastlands like fine dust.
Lebanon would not suffice for fuel,
    nor are its beasts enough for a burnt offering.
All the nations are as nothing before him,
    they are accounted by him as less than nothing and emptiness.
To whom then will you liken God,
    or what likeness compare with him?
An idol! A craftsman casts it,
    and a goldsmith overlays it with gold
    and casts for it silver chains.
He who is too impoverished for an offering
    chooses wood that will not rot;
he seeks out a skillful craftsman
    to set up an idol that will not move. . . .
To whom then will you compare me,
    that I should be like him? says the Holy One. (Isa. 40:12–20, 25)

This description of the glorious greatness of our Lord is in the Bible so that everyone reading it will know with certainty that placing your heart and life in his almighty hands is never risky. Because he is this great, God is able to keep every one of his promises and to push his redemptive plan to its final and glorious conclusion.

Because this is true, Isaiah ends his "God is great" poem with these lines:

He gives power to the faint,
    and to him who has no might he increases strength.
Even youths shall faint and be weary,
    and young men shall fall exhausted;
but they who wait for the Lord shall renew their strength;
    they shall mount up with wings like eagles;
they shall run and not be weary;
    they shall walk and not faint. (Isa. 40:29–31)

In his greatness, God has more than enough power to meet you in your weakness and to empower you to be what he has redeemed you to be and to do what he has redeemed you to do.

For further study and encouragement: Romans 11:33–36

AUGUST 1

God often uses the hardest things in life to produce the best things in us.

We love comfort. If we were in charge, we would make sure that our lives were easy and predictable. We don't want to be sick. We don't want our lives to be unsettled by less-than-perfect people. We want to be financially secure. We want clean houses and dependable cars. We want plenty of food in the refrigerator and lots of money in the bank. We want comfortable jobs and memorable vacations. We want control over our lives. We want our opinions affirmed and our viewpoints respected. We want a good night's sleep, and we want to feel refreshed in the morning. We don't want to get old. We don't want to feel afraid or anxious.

It is not sinful to want these things, but if our desire for comfort rises in importance in our hearts and becomes the thing we live for, then we will find ourselves at cross-purposes with our Lord. God often compromises our comfort in order to produce something even better in us: godly character. God exercises his power over us with redeeming zeal. His plan is not just to forgive us, but also to refine us by his grace. We have been made positionally righteous by the work of Christ, but we are not yet purely righteous in terms of the character of our hearts. So, with refining grace, God works to make us what he has declared us to be in Christ. We need sanctifying grace far more than we need comfortable lives.

It's important to know that the theology of God's refining and transforming grace is not just a New Testament theology. This has always been God's plan for his people. We see this clearly in Isaiah 48:9–11:

> For my name's sake I defer my anger,
>> for the sake of my praise I restrain it for you,
>> that I may not cut you off.
> Behold, I have refined you, but not as silver;
>> I have tried you in the furnace of affliction.
> For my own sake, for my own sake, I do it,
>> for how should my name be profaned?
>> My glory I will not give to another.

God sees our weakness, immaturity, and failure, but he withholds his anger so that his refining grace has more time to work. How does he refine us? He uses the furnace of affliction to make us stronger vessels so that our souls will shine for his glory. Why does he do this? He refines us so that our lives will not profane his name, but rather give him the glory he is due. He refines us so that the only explanation for the way we live is that we have been touched by the power of his refining grace. May we love refining grace more than we love our comfort. And may he grant us the grace to live not for our own glory but for his.

For further study and encouragement: James 1:2–4

———

AUGUST 2

ISAIAH 49–53

Jesus willingly bore the penalty that we deserve, so that we can live forever in a reconciled relationship with God.

Familiarity with biblical passages is a good thing. By grace and through his Spirit, God works in us so that we will know and remember his word. But there can be a downside to familiarity. When we have read something many times, we might stop taking time to examine, consider, and be grateful.

You might be familiar with the following passage, but I ask you to slow down and take another look with me:

Who has believed what he has heard from us?
    And to whom has the arm of the LORD been revealed?
For he grew up before him like a young plant,
    and like a root out of dry ground;
he had no form or majesty that we should look at him,
    and no beauty that we should desire him.
He was despised and rejected by men;
    a man of sorrows and acquainted with grief;
and as one from whom men hide their faces
    he was despised, and we esteemed him not.
Surely he has borne our griefs
    and carried our sorrows;
yet we esteemed him stricken,
    smitten by God, and afflicted.
But he was pierced for our transgressions;
    he was crushed for our iniquities;
upon him was the chastisement that brought us peace,

and with his wounds we are healed.
All we like sheep have gone astray;
  we have turned—every one—to his own way;
and the LORD has laid on him
  the iniquity of us all. (Isa. 53:1–6)

If this passage doesn't shock you, I think you've missed its power. This passage is in the Bible so that you can understand Jesus's radical willingness to go through radical suffering in order that we could experience the radical intervention of God's grace. Jesus was willing to be "crushed for our iniquities" in order to secure our salvation. None us would have accepted this job. But the King of kings was willing to be pierced, chastised, crushed, and wounded for us. He willingly carried the collected weight of all our sin to the cross. The eternal one was willing to die so that we could live forever.

Here's why remembering all of this is so important. If you forget or minimize the extent to which Jesus had to suffer in order to deal with your sin, then you will forget or minimize the gravity of your sin. If you want to know how serious, powerful, dark, and destructive sin is, then read Isaiah 53. Jesus had to endure all that he endured, including death, because that is how serious sin is. It requires a perfectly righteous substitute, one willing to face the temptations of life in this fallen world, suffer for crimes he did not commit, and die as a sacrifice for our sins.

Our hope in this life and the one to come hinges on the willingness of Jesus to endure what none of us would be willing to endure. He was willing. What grace!

For further study and encouragement: Matthew 26:36–46

AUGUST 3

ISAIAH 54–58

Nothing you experience on this side of eternity
is more amazing than God's grace.

I love to watch the Food Network. I enjoy watching gifted chefs work with the plants and animals that God created to produce beautiful, tasty, and satisfying food on the plate. I have learned so much about cooking good food as I have watched, and I love that God has given us such a wide variety of things to eat.

The world he has created is a wonderful banquet table. Perhaps it is my love for the culinary arts that helps me appreciate the beauty of the word pictures in Isaiah 55:

> Come, everyone who thirsts,
>   come to the waters;
> and he who has no money,
>   come, buy and eat!
> Come, buy wine and milk
>   without money and without price.
> Why do you spend your money for that which is not bread,
>   and your labor for that which does not satisfy?
> Listen diligently to me, and eat what is good,
>   and delight yourselves in rich food.
> Incline your ear, and come to me;
>   hear, that your soul may live;
> and I will make with you an everlasting covenant,
>   my steadfast, sure love for David. (Isa. 55:1–3)

God knows that people are spiritually hungry. People are constantly look-ing for life and for peace and satisfaction of heart. God has wired this spiritual hunger into us, so that it would drive us to him.

This passage is a gracious invitation to the spiritually hungry and thirsty to come to the one and only place where your heart can be filled. The physical things of this earth are not designed to satisfy your spiritual hunger. The most wonderful experiences or relationships or possessions in this life will not fill your heart. So, with a tender and compassionate heart, God says, "Come to me. I have prepared for you the one meal that will fill and satisfy that hunger in your heart." He says, "And you don't have to pay for the food I give you. It is free!" Then he asks the question of questions: "Why would you work hard for and spend money on what cannot satisfy?" People do this every day. At great cost and with hard work people run after and consume things that will never satisfy the hunger that drives them.

What about you? At what table do you sit, hoping that your hungry heart will be satisfied? Do you hear the Lord's invitation to you to come to him, eat from the banquet of his grace, and live? What he offers is free, because the Son has paid the cost.

May we come again and again to the only one who has the bread that will satisfy our hearts.

For further study and encouragement: Psalm 63:1–11

AUGUST 4

*Humanity was created to live in a loving, worshiping, and
life-giving relationship with God, but sin separated us
from the one we were created to live with and for.*

Most of us hate to be separated from those we love. Luella and I have three married children and six grandchildren in Southern California. So, though we live in Philadelphia, we have become bicoastal. We spend about half of our time in California and half with our married son and his wife in Philly. We love being with our grandchildren out west, and there are always tears shed when we leave. While we are in California, we miss our East Coast son and his wife and anticipate our time with them as we are flying home to Philly. Because we are not omnipresent, we are always happy to be with those we're with, yet sad because other loved ones are so far from us. Few things are more joyful than being among those with whom you share a deep bond of love.

But, even when we consider the immense sadness that human separation brings, nothing in life is sadder than being separated from God. Of all of the tragedies we face in life, this is the tragedy of tragedies. Not only were we made *by* God, but we were made *for* him. Every person you see on the street, in a store, at work, at a conference, at a reunion, at church, or at a concert was made for a relationship with God. God designed us to find our highest end and purpose in him. Our relationship with him was meant to be the way we understand our identity. Worship of him was meant to be the deepest and most abiding motivation of our hearts. It was in relationship with him that we were meant to find our humanity and our sanity.

Therefore, the greatest tragedy is that people who were made in the image of God became separated from him:

Behold, the LORD's hand is not shortened, that it cannot save,
    or his ear dull, that it cannot hear;
but your iniquities have made a separation
    between you and your God,
and your sins have hidden his face from you
    so that he does not hear. (Isa. 59:1–2)

God hid his face from those he had made. How tragic! Separation from him means losing not only true spirituality but also true humanity. We cannot be what we were meant to be apart from him. Separation from him is our eternal doom. Sin is not just the breaking of moral law; it is the breaking of a relationship with God that was meant to be the core of who we are.

This is why we celebrate the life, death, and resurrection of Jesus. Through him our sins are atoned for, we are reconciled to God, and sin separates us no more. By grace he is ours and we are his forever. Sin has been defeated, so those who believe are separated from God no more. Now, that's very good news!

For further study and encouragement: 2 Corinthians 5:11–21

———

AUGUST 5

ISAIAH 63–66

As children of God, we are marching toward the new heavens and the new earth, where every last effect of sin will be erased forever.

The Bible is honest about the sorry condition of this fallen world, but it doesn't leave us sad or without hope. The purpose of the grand redemptive story is not to leave us in suspense, without a clue as to where this great narrative is going. Although our Lord is wise not to tell us everything—because our finite little minds could not fathom the whole body of his secret will—God does tell us where his story is going. Dotted throughout his narrative are visions of what is to come. It's as though for brief moments God pulls back the curtain and gives us a glimpse of the glory he has planned for all who put their trust in him. This is meant to give us hope, one that purifies the way we live and motivates us to persevere through life's most severe hardships. Parents know how difficult long trips can be for children; sometimes we show them pictures of the glories awaiting them at the end of their mobile travail. Similarly, God gives us a look at what is to come.

We find one of those curtain-pulled-back moments in Isaiah 65:

Behold, I create new heavens
    and a new earth,
and the former things shall not be remembered
    or come into mind.
But be glad and rejoice forever
    in that which I create;
for behold, I create Jerusalem to be a joy,

and her people to be a gladness.
I will rejoice in Jerusalem
    and be glad in my people;
no more shall be heard in it the sound of weeping
    and the cry of distress. (Isa. 65:17–19)

These words describe our ultimate destination as the children of God. Let me point out three things that God promises to everyone who has been redeemed by the power of his grace.

1. God will make a new heavens and a new earth. The disastrous damage sin has done to God's creation will be eradicated. God is going to create new heavens and a new earth, where there will be no sin, no suffering, no corrupt government, no ecological pollution, no abuse, no racism, no falsehood. Sin will be permanently defeated.

2. The former things will not be remembered. We will not be weighed down by what we experienced in our sinful past. We will live with renewed minds, free to experience the glory of our new home.

3. The sound of weeping will no longer be heard. God will dry every last tear of each of his children, and they will have no reason to weep ever again. Imagine a sorrow-free existence forever.

This is not an unreal science fiction fantasy. No, this is the promise of the Lord who, because of the glory of his perfection, cannot tell a lie. Things may be hard now, but the hardships will end and God will usher in a new order that will be more beautiful than human words can describe. You have reason to look up and persevere.

For further study and encouragement: 1 Corinthians 2:6–10

———

AUGUST 6

JEREMIAH 1–3

Although we are not always naturally capable of doing the work to which God calls us, he grants us the gifts, wisdom, and strength we need.

Jeremiah 1 records the moment when God called Jeremiah to be a prophet:

Now the word of the LORD came to me, saying,

"Before I formed you in the womb I knew you,
and before you were born I consecrated you;
I appointed you a prophet to the nations."

Then I said, "Ah, Lord God! Behold, I do not know how to speak, for I am only a youth." But the Lord said to me,

"Do not say, 'I am only a youth';
for to all to whom I send you, you shall go,
and whatever I command you, you shall speak.
Do not be afraid of them,
for I am with you to deliver you,

declares the Lord."

Then the Lord put out his hand and touched my mouth. And the Lord said to me,

"Behold, I have put my words in your mouth.
See, I have set you this day over nations and over kingdoms,
to pluck up and to break down,
to destroy and to overthrow,
to build and to plant." (Jer. 1:4–10)

God called Jeremiah to serve him at a very difficult time in Israel's history. God's people had forsaken him and his commands. They worshiped other gods and participated in the detestable practices of the surrounding nations. So, as a wise and holy Judge, God disciplined his people—and his discipline was severe. God did not eradicate his people, but called them back to serve him and him alone. Jeremiah needed to know that God would give him everything he needed in order to do what God was calling him to do.

Although Jeremiah's calling was individual and unique, we can learn from it, since all of us have been called into the service of our Savior.

Before we were born, God set us apart to receive both the comfort and the call of the gospel. God decided what part we would each play in his kingdom work before we took our first breaths. He chose us for his work not because we are worthy, but because he is sovereign, loving, and wise.

We cannot let weakness or fear keep us from God's work. Each of us is a bundle of weaknesses held together by divine grace. God calls us not because we are able, but because he is.

God will touch us with his power and give us what we need to do his work. God's call to his kingdom work is always accompanied by his empowering grace. He gives what we need when we need it. He even fills our mouths with the right words, as he did for Jeremiah.

What a picture of God's grace. He chooses us to go, and he goes with us, providing everything we need to do what he's chosen us to do. This means that ministry success isn't necessarily God's endorsement of our wisdom and power, but rather a revelation of his.

For further study and encouragement: Philippians 2:12–13

AUGUST 7

JEREMIAH 4–6

God is so loving and so committed to his plan of rescue that he will not settle for anything less than the total surrender of our hearts to him.

If someone were to ask you what God requires of you, what would you say? Would you point to the Ten Commandments? Would you talk about Sunday worship and regular giving? Would you talk about Christian ministry? What does God require of those who follow him?

An adequate answer has to begin with acknowledging that whatever God asks of us is *good* for us. The one who made us knows us and the world in which we live. He knows why he made us and how he designed us to live. He understands what sin has done to us and how we need to be rescued and restored by his grace. He understands every temptation we face. He knows the blessings that come when we follow him by faith. His infinite wisdom and knowledge, coupled with his perfect holiness, mean that it is impossible for him to ask anything of us that is not wise or good. His way is always the best way.

Knowing that God always wants what is best for us, we get back to our question, What is it that God requires? We find a clear answer to this question in Jeremiah 4:

Thus says the LORD to the men of Judah and Jerusalem:

> "Break up your fallow ground,
>   and sow not among thorns.
> Circumcise yourselves to the LORD;
>   remove the foreskin of your hearts,

O men of Judah and inhabitants of Jerusalem;
lest my wrath go forth like fire,
and burn with none to quench it,
because of the evil of your deeds." (Jer. 4:3–4)

The seriousness of this passage should get our attention. Remember, God's warnings of judgment are not judgment itself; they are a gift of grace. Because he loves us, he warns us. His warning is a mercy, giving us time to consider, examine ourselves, confess, and repent. God will not compromise his holy will, and that is good for us, because what he wills for his children is always what is best.

God requires nothing less than the *circumcision of our hearts*. What in the world does this mean? Remember that the physical act of circumcising every male Israelite was a sign that they were separated from the rest of humanity for the Lord. It was the sign of the unique blessing of being in the company of people whom God had chosen to be his people. But God was not satisfied with the outward sign; he wanted circumcision of the heart—that is, its complete surrender to him.

He wants complete control of our thoughts, desires, will, and emotions, because that which controls the heart controls everything else in our life. Only a circumcised heart can offer God true, loving obedience to his commandments. It is a blessing that God will settle for nothing less than the surrender of our hearts, because in requiring this he rescues us from us. Have you experienced the grace of this surrender?

For further study and encouragement: Deuteronomy 30:1–11

AUGUST 8

JEREMIAH 7–9

Hypocrisy is the mortal enemy of the work of God's amazing grace.

Hypocrisy confuses many of us. It is not hypocritical to commit to live as God commanded but to fail. On this side of eternity all of us have done and will continue to do this. That's why we always need God's forgiving and restoring grace. Hypocrisy always involves *intentionality*. Hypocrisy is making a public confession of allegiance to God while having no intention of living out that public confession. Hypocrisy settles for public religious displays while the heart is far from God. The hypocrite makes public confessions of sin while pursuing the very sins he confesses. The hypocrite throws around his theological knowledge without any real intention of surrendering to the one who is at the center of that theology. The hypocrite demands of others what he has no intention of doing himself. The hypocrite is quick to point out another's sin, while carefully hiding his own. The hypocrite claims to worship God while living in constant pursuit of God-replacements. Hypocrisy is the enemy of the work of God's grace because the hypocrite is satisfied with external religiosity rather than the true surrender of heart that grace alone can produce.

Jeremiah 7 records God's redemptive anger and discipline of his people. One thing God charges his children with—something that he will not tolerate—is hypocrisy:

> If you truly amend your ways and your deeds, if you truly execute justice one with another, if you do not oppress the sojourner, the fatherless, or the widow, or shed innocent blood in this place, and if you do not go after other gods to your own harm, then I will let you dwell in this place, in the land that I gave of old to your fathers forever.
>
> Behold, you trust in deceptive words to no avail. Will you steal, murder, commit adultery, swear falsely, make offerings to Baal, and go after other gods that you have not known, and then come and stand before me in this house, which is called by my name, and say, "We are delivered!"—only to go on doing all these abominations? Has this house, which is called by my name, become a den of robbers in your eyes? Behold, I myself have seen it, declares the LORD. (Jer. 7:5–11)

God makes strong charges here in order to instruct and convict us. His children do not offer love, which he has given to them, to those around them. His children benefit daily from his holiness, but have no commitment to holiness in their own lives. And those who stand before God in the court of the temple make offerings to false gods at the same time.

Here's the danger of hypocrisy: it leads you to forsake God, while doing enough "good" things to convince yourself that you haven't truly forsaken him. Hypocrisy is rooted in the deceitfulness of the heart.

May we pray for rescuing and empowering grace, so that we will never become comfortable with the spiritual duplicity of hypocrisy. It is only by convicting, rescuing, and empowering grace that we are able to surrender our hearts solely to God.

For further study and encouragement: Matthew 23:1–36

AUGUST 9

God mocks the complete inability of idols to do
what only he as Creator King is able to do.

The Old Testament contains a bit of divine humor, mockery, and sarcasm. It is hard for us to mock another person and not to sin. But God, who is perfectly holy in every way and all of the time, can mock in a way that is righteous and pure. Few passages drip with more sarcastic humor than Jeremiah 10. God mocks the idols that have captured the hearts of his people. He compares their lifeless inability to his creation power and sovereign authority. It's as though God were saying to his people, "Seriously, this is whom you have forsaken me for? Do you really understand who they are, compared to who I am?"

> "Learn not the way of the nations,
>> nor be dismayed at the signs of the heavens
>> because the nations are dismayed at them,
> for the customs of the peoples are vanity.
> A tree from the forest is cut down
>> and worked with an axe by the hands of a craftsman.
> They decorate it with silver and gold;
>> they fasten it with hammer and nails
>> so that it cannot move.
> Their idols are like scarecrows in a cucumber field,
>> and they cannot speak;
> they have to be carried,
>> for they cannot walk.
> Do not be afraid of them,
>> for they cannot do evil,
>> neither is it in them to do good."
> There is none like you, O Lord;
>> you are great, and your name is great in might.
> Who would not fear you, O King of the nations?
>> For this is your due;
> for among all the wise ones of the nations
>> and in all their kingdoms
>> there is none like you.
> They are both stupid and foolish;
>> the instruction of idols is but wood! . . .

Thus shall you say to them: "The gods who did not make the heavens and the earth shall perish from the earth and from under the heavens."

> It is he who made the earth by his power,
>   who established the world by his wisdom,
>   and by his understanding stretched out the heavens.
> When he utters his voice, there is a tumult of waters in the heavens,
>   and he makes the mist rise from the ends of the earth.
> He makes lightning for the rain,
>   and he brings forth the wind from his storehouses.
> Every man is stupid and without knowledge;
>   every goldsmith is put to shame by his idols,
> for his images are false,
>   and there is no breath in them.
> They are worthless, a work of delusion;
>   at the time of their punishment they shall perish. (Jer. 10:2–8,
>   11–15)

I have quoted this long passage so that you can more fully grasp the power of God's idol-mockery. You have to nail idols to a post or else they'll tip over; you have to carry them since they can't walk; they are about as powerful as scarecrows in a cucumber patch, and they are stupid because they're lifeless, made of wood.

May God's mockery remind us that no idol could ever do what our Almighty Lord can do. He alone deserves our worship.

For further study and encouragement: Psalm 135:13–21

——

AUGUST 10

JEREMIAH 14–17

One of God's good gifts of grace to us is the Sabbath of rest and worship.

The truth that God knows who we are and what we need is taught throughout Scripture. The creational establishment of the Sabbath is a perfect example. God knows that he created us with limits, so it is physically and spiritually unhealthy for us to work 24/7. He knows that our hearts are prone to wander, losing spiritual focus and allowing created things to gain power in our hearts that challenges the rule God deserves. So, in loving mercy, he created the Sabbath and commanded his children to observe it. The Sabbath is for us. It gives us regular times of rest without feeling guilty that we are not being productive. It calls us out of the distracting clamor of our daily lives into worship, reminding us that our identity, meaning, purpose, and hope are found in the Lord alone. How loving it is that God designed for us to have times of regular physical and spiritual retreat, refreshment, and renewal.

> Thus says the LORD: Take care for the sake of your lives, and do not bear a burden on the Sabbath day or bring it in by the gates of Jerusalem. And do not carry a burden out of your houses on the Sabbath or do any work, but keep the Sabbath day holy, as I commanded your fathers. Yet they did not listen or incline their ear, but stiffened their neck, that they might not hear and receive instruction.
>
> But if you listen to me, declares the LORD, and bring in no burden by the gates of this city on the Sabbath day, but keep the Sabbath day holy and do no work on it, then there shall enter by the gates of this city kings and princes who sit on the throne of David, riding in chariots and on horses, they and their officials, the men of Judah and the inhabitants of Jerusalem. And this city shall be inhabited forever. (Jer. 17:21–25)

God is saying, "Don't you understand? I have given you a day when you can lay down your work burden without guilt." God calls his children to keep the Sabbath *holy*, which means "separated unto him." He wants us to set apart a day to rest from work and to worship. God says, "If you do this, then you will prosper—not just now, but forever."

Nowhere in the surrounding culture is Sabbath recognized or reinforced. No matter what your specific theological views of the Sabbath might be, you too need to set aside a day for rest and worship and to resist powerful cultural influences that want to control your weekly schedule.

Don't fool yourself into thinking that you have unlimited energy or strength. Don't deceive yourself into thinking your heart is free from the temptation to wander. Receive God's gift of Sabbath with gratitude and joy, and celebrate the physical rest and spiritual renewal that come with this gift.

For further study and encouragement: Mark 2:23–28

AUGUST 11

God's stern warnings are not judgment, but rather extensions
of his mercy. We are to examine ourselves, confess, repent, and
experience the grace of fresh starts and new beginnings.

Through his prophet Jeremiah, God warns his people to turn from their sin, with a threat of dire consequences if they don't:

> Go down to the house of the king of Judah and speak there this word, and say, "Hear the word of the LORD, O king of Judah, who sits on the throne of David, you, and your servants, and your people who enter these gates. Thus says the LORD: Do justice and righteousness, and deliver from the hand of the oppressor him who has been robbed. And do no wrong or violence to the resident alien, the fatherless, and the widow, nor shed innocent blood in this place. For if you will indeed obey this word, then there shall enter the gates of this house kings who sit on the throne of David, riding in chariots and on horses, they and their servants and their people. But if you will not obey these words, I swear by myself, declares the LORD, that this house shall become a desolation. For thus says the LORD concerning the house of the king of Judah:
>
> > 'You are like Gilead to me,
> >   like the summit of Lebanon,
> > yet surely I will make you a desert,
> >   an uninhabited city.
> > I will prepare destroyers against you,
> >   each with his weapons,
> > and they shall cut down your choicest cedars
> >   and cast them into the fire.'" (Jer. 22:1–7)

Do you struggle to think of these words as being consistent with a perfectly holy God of infinite love? Do they seem to you to contradict the gospel of his grace? Do they make you afraid to entrust yourself to him? How do you understand divine warnings and threats?

Here's the first thing that we need to understand. None of us would want to live in a world whose ruler wasn't angry with evil. If he wasn't, there would be no hope of justice, righteousness, security, or peace. In actuality, God's anger with evil is the hope of the universe. It is his anger with sin that sent

Jesus to the cross to provide for us forgiveness and the deliverance found in the ultimate defeat of sin. God also knows that, because of sin's deceptiveness, we convince ourselves that we can do what is wrong without consequences. So, in rescuing love, God punctuates his warnings with the threat of dire consequences.

When parents warn their children not to do something wrong and add a threat of consequences if they do, it's not because they lack love but because their children are dear to them and they want to rescue them from whatever may harm them. So it is with our Lord. He knows what can harm us, and so he speaks with the stern voice of a loving Father. He reveals the potential consequences of our sin not because he despises us, but because we are precious to him.

For further study and encouragement: Proverbs 3:11–12

AUGUST 12

JEREMIAH 23–25

We have no righteousness of our own; therefore, we place our hope in the presence and reign of the perfectly righteous one, Jesus.

Are you tired of another day of devastating news about some horrible thing happening somewhere in the world? Does your battle to cobble together a marriage of unity, understanding, and love discourage you? Are you exhausted by friendship hassles and family drama? Are you sick of hearing about the power of corrupt politicians or failed church leaders? Does your struggle to parent your children get you down? Does the moral state of the surrounding culture make you weary? Are you tired of all of the pain and loss around you? Do you look at all of these things and wonder what can be done? Sometimes it seems as though there's more darkness than light in our world. Sometimes we find ourselves wondering where the true, wise, and moral leaders are. Often we wonder whether there's anything that can be done to right the course.

Into the darkest of days in the time of the prophets, when it seemed as though things were about as bad as they could get and the end of the people of God was near, Jeremiah delivered words of hope. These words were not about human wisdom, human intervention, or new human solutions. When it comes to eradicating evil and setting the human community on a new course, human wisdom, strength, and righteousness fall short. This does not mean that we shouldn't fight for what is right or fight against what is wrong, but it does mean that we are not the hope that we need. This is why the words of hope in the Old Testament—promises of what is to come—are so important. They speak comfort into sad and tired hearts:

> Behold, the days are coming, declares the LORD, when I will raise up for David a righteous Branch, and he shall reign as king and deal wisely, and shall execute justice and righteousness in the land. In his days Judah will be saved, and Israel will dwell securely. And this is the name by which he will be called: "The LORD is our righteousness." (Jer. 23:5–6)

You may be thinking, "How do these words comfort us? Aren't they the promise of a better earthly king for the children of Israel?" The New Testament writers understood these words to be specifically about and fulfilled by Jesus alone (see Matt. 2:2; Luke 1:32; 19:38; John 1:49). Ultimately there is only one solution to the many things that break our hearts and complicate our lives: it is the reign of the risen and ascended King Jesus. The righteous Branch has come and is now sitting at the right hand of the Father. His reign guarantees the final defeat of evil and the ushering in of a kingdom of righteousness and peace forever. In the midst of all the bad news that seems to flood into our lives every day, this is very good news. There is a righteous Branch, his will shall be done, and the scourge of evil will end forever.

For further study and encouragement: Luke 4:16–21

———

AUGUST 13

JEREMIAH 26–29

God's plans for his children are never evil. He works
for our welfare, to give us a hope and a future.

Jeremiah 29 not only tells us the story of Israel's history; it reveals who God is and how he works:

> Thus says the LORD: When seventy years are completed for Babylon, I will visit you, and I will fulfill to you my promise and bring you back to this

place. For I know the plans I have for you, declares the LORD, plans for welfare and not for evil, to give you a future and a hope. Then you will call upon me and come and pray to me, and I will hear you. You will seek me and find me, when you seek me with all your heart. I will be found by you, declares the LORD, and I will restore your fortunes and gather you from all the nations and all the places where I have driven you, declares the LORD, and I will bring you back to the place from which I sent you into exile. (Jer. 29:10–14)

To understand this passage properly, we must remember that underlying it is the enormous patience of the Lord. God had been patient with his people as they forsook his commandments and gave their hearts to false gods. With a tender, merciful heart, he sent prophet after prophet to warn them and call them back to worship and service of their Lord. God is patient.

But God's children are taken into captivity in Babylon; this discipline reminds us that God is perfectly holy, and, because he is, he takes sin seriously. Because of his hatred of sin, God disciplines his children. This discipline is not final judgment, but he uses it as an instrument to drive his people to confession and repentance. God's discipline can be hard. After seventy years in captivity, the people of God may have felt forsaken. But they were not forsaken, because God's plan for his children is never evil. It is always for their welfare, to give them a future and a hope.

This passage reminds us of the good news of the gospel. This gospel news is just as present in these Old Testament passages as it is in the New Testament. What is this good news? God's discipline, because of his exhaustible grace, is followed by his *restorative mercy*. Because God's discipline is not a final judgment or an ultimate turning of his back on his chosen children, it is followed by restoration. For his children in the Old Testament, this meant a return from exile in Babylon to the promised land. Restoration reminds us that even the harshest of God's discipline is a tool of his grace.

God will not abandon his children—not because they have earned his loyalty with their obedience, but because he is zealous for the success of his eternal redemptive plan. That plan will end our exile too, and he will welcome us into the final land of promise, forever.

For further study and encouragement: Romans 8:26–30

AUGUST 14

Your hope in this life and the one to come is covenant hope.

Every human being who has ever lived has searched for hope. Hope is what gets us up in the morning and gives us a reason to keep grinding. Hope is where we look for meaning and purpose. Hope tells us that somehow and in some way things will be okay. Hope keeps us going even when things are hard. Your hope is your light in the darkness. Hope always has two parts: an expectation and an object. You long for something, and you look to something or someone to deliver it. For example, you long for love and you search for someone to love you. Sadly, most of our hopes disappoint us, because we place our hope in the wrong person or thing. But we don't give up; we get up off the floor to hope once again, because we have been hardwired for hope. God did this so that our hope-longing would drive us to him.

In all of this life and the one to come, only one kind of hope will not disappoint. It is secure and trustworthy and will always deliver what it has promised. This hope is offered again and again throughout Scripture. It is dependable hope because it doesn't look to a fallen creation to do what fallen creation cannot do. It is reliable because it doesn't look for hope in another person, who by nature has limited wisdom, righteousness, and strength. No, this hope is found in the one who cannot lie but has the power and authority to deliver every single one of his promises, in just the right place and at just the right time. But this hope is even more specific: it is found in the unalterable covenant that God has made with his children. He will never break his covenant promises:

> Behold, the days are coming, declares the Lord, when I will make a new covenant with the house of Israel and the house of Judah, not like the covenant that I made with their fathers on the day when I took them by the hand to bring them out of the land of Egypt, my covenant that they broke, though I was their husband, declares the Lord. For this is the covenant that I will make with the house of Israel after those days, declares the Lord: I will put my law within them, and I will write it on their hearts. And I will be their God, and they shall be my people. And no longer shall each one teach his neighbor and each his brother, saying, "Know the Lord," for they shall all know me, from the least of them to the greatest, declares the Lord. For I will forgive their iniquity, and will remember their sin no more. (Jer. 31:31–34)

We have hope because God has made beautiful and eternal covenant promises that he will not break.

For further study and encouragement: Matthew 26:26–29

———

AUGUST 15

JEREMIAH 32–34

*You can't base your understanding of God and what he is
doing on your own interpretation of your circumstances.
No, it's your knowledge of who God is and what he does that
allows you to understand your circumstances properly.*

As the world watches the travails of the people of God, people will mock us. They will ask, "Where is your God now? Why does he let these horrible things happen? Why does he allow bad things to happen to good people? Can't you see that he's turned his back on you, or don't you see that he simply doesn't exist?" The subtle (or not-so-subtle) mockery of the world is hard enough, but, since God's ways are not our ways and his thoughts are not like our thoughts, even God himself often leaves us confused and wondering. Sometimes we think he doesn't hear us. It doesn't always feel as though he is near. Sometimes it's hard to hold on to the truth that he cares for us. It's tempting, in these moments, to allow ourselves to listen to the voices of those who question not only God's goodness but the very fact of his existence.

As God was disciplining his children for their sin during the time of Jeremiah, it seemed as though he had forsaken them. It was unthinkable that Jerusalem would be devastated and even more unthinkable that the temple would be destroyed. It must have been horrible for families to be ripped apart, forced out of their homes, and taken as captives by enemy forces. Would the children of God end up once again as slaves in a foreign land? Where was God? What happened to the exercise of his power on behalf of his people? Had he turned his back on his covenant promises? Had he abandoned the people whom he had chosen as his own? What would come of his eternal covenantal plan?

In the moments when you are flooded with questions, confusion, and doubt, you are susceptible to listening to those who neither know nor believe in God. Such was the case in Jeremiah's time, so God spoke to his children with words of remembrance and grace:

The word of the LORD came to Jeremiah: "Have you not observed that these people are saying, 'The LORD has rejected the two clans that he chose'? Thus they have despised my people so that they are no longer a nation in their sight. Thus says the LORD: If I have not established my covenant with day and night and the fixed order of heaven and earth, then I will reject the offspring of Jacob and David my servant and will not choose one of his offspring to rule over the offspring of Abraham, Isaac, and Jacob. For I will restore their fortunes and will have mercy on them." (Jer. 33:23–26)

The nations around Israel were saying, "Why don't you give up and quit believing? It's clear that God has rejected you." But God says, "Don't listen to them. My promises to you are as secure as the natural order."

Your faith may not be respected by the culture around you, but don't give in to hopelessness or doubt. God's promises to you are as secure as the earth beneath your feet.

For further study and encouragement: Psalm 14:1–7

———

AUGUST 16

JEREMIAH 35–37

Every hard thing God brings upon his people is designed to be redemptive.

I have written about my physical trials before, but I want to reference them again here. I have had ten surgeries in seven years, and I continue to deal with difficult physical issues. Sometimes, all I am able to pray is, "Lord, help me." It is a daily battle to continue with the wonderful gospel work God has so graciously called me to. It is exhausting and discouraging to be physically unwell. It's hard to make sense of the suffering. I have determined not to let myself get angry with God. I preach to myself that he is perfectly holy and, because he is, that everything he has chosen for me is right and good, even though it does not seem good at street level. I know he hears my cries. I know he is near and active, even when he seems distant and passive.

My situation causes me ask, "Why would a good, holy, wise, and merciful God ever choose for his children to have to endure such hard things?" Either you quit believing that he is good, or you believe that there is a wise and good purpose behind the hard things. The suffering of God's people is a theme of the book of Jeremiah, and I am reminded that there is no unneeded or unprofitable material in God's word. In Jeremiah we read about situations that seem so different from our daily experience, yet this topic touches all of us.

God is bringing unthinkable hardship on his people, and he wants them to know why. The hardship is not the result of vengeful anger. Yes, his children have given themselves to rebellion and idolatry, and, yes, God has warned them that there will be consequences. But he wants them to know ahead of time why he is choosing to lead them through this travail:

> In the fourth year of Jehoiakim the son of Josiah, king of Judah, this word came to Jeremiah from the LORD: "Take a scroll and write on it all the words that I have spoken to you against Israel and Judah and all the nations, from the day I spoke to you, from the days of Josiah until today. It may be that the house of Judah will hear all the disaster that I intend to do to them, so that every one may turn from his evil way, and that I may forgive their iniquity and their sin." (Jer. 36:1–3)

Here is the answer to my question. Hardship, in the hands of the Lord, is a tool of his grace. He doesn't lead his children through difficulty just because he has the power to do so. His intentions are gracious; he desires that we turn to him and find forgiveness in him.

My suffering has produced spiritual fruit that seven easy years would never have produced. Yes, we will suffer, but behind our suffering is a loving God, whose intentions in our lives are filled with grace.

For further study and encouragement: 2 Corinthians 4:16–18

AUGUST 17

JEREMIAH 38–41

*Your Lord is the King of kings. Every human leader
exists and operates under his authority.*

We often forget that there really is a King of kings who sits on the throne of the universe as the ruler of nations. Because we forget that our Lord is the King of kings, we fret too much in the face of the power and corruption of human kings.

Or we look for our hope and security in human leaders, and, because we do, we unite ourselves too closely to them. All human leaders have limited power for a limited time, but this isn't so with our almighty and eternal King. Our King has the power to turn human kings to go wherever he wants them to go, whenever he wants (see Prov. 21:1).

King Nebuchadnezzar was one of the most evil kings in the Old Testament. He took the people of God captive, and then commanded them to worship him. He was self-obsessed, arrogant, and vicious, so much so that God humbled him in a graphic and unforgettable way (see Dan. 4). Yet we find this evil man choosing to do good for the prophet Jeremiah. Remember, Jeremiah was a courageous spokesman for the very faith that Nebuchadnezzar was working to crush in the people of God. Why would the king choose to protect him?

> Nebuchadnezzar king of Babylon gave command concerning Jeremiah through Nebuzaradan, the captain of the guard, saying, "Take him, look after him well, and do him no harm, but deal with him as he tells you." So Nebuzaradan the captain of the guard, Nebushazban the Rab-saris, Nergal-sar-ezer the Rab-mag, and all the chief officers of the king of Babylon sent and took Jeremiah from the court of the guard. They entrusted him to Gedaliah the son of Ahikam, son of Shaphan, that he should take him home. So he lived among the people. (Jer. 39:11–14)

This evil king commanded the captain of his guard not only to do Jeremiah no harm, but also to take care of him. The captain of the guard then called on all the king's chief officers to follow through on the king's order. Why did Nebuchadnezzar choose to be so good to Jeremiah? There is only one answer, and it is found in the very first chapter of the book of Jeremiah. We remember the calling and commissioning of this prophet. God made Jeremiah a promise, knowing that his mission would be difficult and dangerous: "They will fight against you, but they shall not prevail against you, for I am with you, declares the LORD, to deliver you" (Jer. 1:19). God had promised to protect his prophet from harm, and he raised up King Nebuchadnezzar to be his instrument of protection. God worked in the heart of this evil Babylonian, so that he would use his power to protect Jeremiah from harm.

Your Lord is the King of kings, who has power over every earthly king. This means that, ultimately, the will of the King of kings will be done.

For further study and encouragement: 2 Samuel 24:1–25

AUGUST 18

JEREMIAH 42–45

Our Lord hates when we give the worship that
is due him to something in creation.

We have a lot to learn about idolatry. Often when we think of the worship of false gods, we think of Buddhists or Hindus, bowing before something made of wood, metal, or stone. But the sad truth is that many of us who would never bow before a religious idol have idolatry in our lives. An idol functions as a God-replacement in our hearts. Sometimes good things become idols. Things that were once blessings rise in level of importance in our hearts until they control our thoughts, desires, choices, actions, and words. A desire for even a good thing will become a bad thing when it becomes a ruling thing. I have watched seminary students damage their families in pursuit of theological knowledge. Is theology a bad thing? Of course not, but pursuit of it must not take so much control over you that you neglect your wife and children. Someone's love can become a life-shaping idol. Is it wrong to want to be loved? No, but this desire must not be allowed to capture the place in your heart that only God should have.

Here is the point. Anything in creation can function in your heart and life as a God-replacement. Street-level idolatry is subtle and deceptive. And the idol that is most seductive and deceptive is the idol of self. The apostle Paul says in 2 Corinthians 5:15 that Jesus came so that we would no longer live for ourselves.

Because God understands our idol struggles, he recorded and preserved for us his anger with his children's idolatry:

> The word that came to Jeremiah concerning all the Judeans who lived in the land of Egypt, at Migdol, at Tahpanhes, at Memphis, and in the land of Pathros, "Thus says the LORD of hosts, the God of Israel: You have seen all the disaster that I brought upon Jerusalem and upon all the cities of Judah. Behold, this day they are a desolation, and no one dwells in them, because of the evil that they committed, provoking me to anger, in that they went to make offerings and serve other gods that they knew not, neither they, nor you, nor your fathers. Yet I persistently sent to you all my servants the prophets, saying, 'Oh, do not do this abomination that I hate!' But they did not listen or incline their ear, to turn from their evil and make no offerings to other gods." (Jer. 44:1–5)

God's anger is the product of his love. True love is always rightfully jealous. God has chosen us as his own, and he will not share our hearts with other lovers. He reveals his anger and offers us his grace, so that our hearts will be ruled by him alone.

For further study and encouragement: Romans 1:18–25

AUGUST 19

JEREMIAH 46–48

We must never allow ourselves to underestimate the infinite power and authority of God.

I'm persuaded that much of our fear, anxiety, discouragement, and hopelessness is the result of bad theology. At its core, what is the Bible all about? The existence, character, and plan of God. Every other aspect of Scripture flows out of the reality of who God is. A bad or weak theology of God will lead to weakness in other areas of theology, and spiritual weaknesses in daily living. I had this experience again and again in counseling. I would be working with someone who was struggling to trust God, but, as I listened to him describe who he thought God was, I immediately understood why he had trouble trusting him. I would often think, "If I thought that this was who God is, I would have trouble trusting him too."

One common mistake in our functional theology of God is thinking he is too small. The God in our minds lacks the awesome, glorious, and incalculable power and authority that the true God of the Bible has. The God of the Bible created the world out of nothing. The God of the Bible holds his creation together by his power. The God of the Bible commands the forces of nature to do his will. The God of the Bible is sovereign over everything and everyone. The God of the Bible rules the nations, and his will will be done. The God of the Bible reigns in majestic splendor so great that nothing compares to him.

The awesome power and authority of God is on display in the latter part of the book of Jeremiah, as God announces his judgment on the nations that surround his people. This is the Lord, and the nations are answerable to him. No one can question his power or the authority he has to judge whom he will judge. The word of the Lord came to Jeremiah (46:1), and God told him to announce his judgment on Egypt, the Philistines, Moab, Ammon, Edom, Damascus, Kedar and Hazor, Elam, and Babylon. This announcement of his judgment is an awesome testament to God's power. He is the ultimate King over every one of these nations. He has the power to do for them, with them, and against them what-soever he wills, whenever he wills to do it. They have no power to challenge or resist his sovereign will. These announcements are in the Bible so we can know that this is who God is.

He not only rules over these nations; he commands the entire universe. God sits on his throne in infinite power and glory. All the things that scare you or give you anxiety exist under his almighty rule. Because God has this kind of power and authority, nothing that you need is beyond his power to deliver.

May the God of your thoughts not be too small. May the infinite glory of his power and authority overwhelm anything in creation that might paralyze you with fear.

For further study and encouragement: Acts 17:22–31

AUGUST 20

JEREMIAH 49–50

By grace, the restoration that the world desperately needs is on its way.

It is hard to deny the fact that you and I live in a world that desperately needs to be restored. Just look at your media feed, or recall the sad things that have happened in your lifetime. The apostle Paul writes that we live in a world that is groaning, waiting for redemption (Rom. 8:22–23). You groan when you're in pain; you groan when you're tired; you groan when you're disappointed; you groan when things around you seem irreparably broken. Such is the state of the world in which we live. The violence around us takes your breath away. The moral degradation of the culture seems to go on unabated. The witness of the church often seems compromised. Marriages break apart, and parents throw up their hands in frustration at their children. Entertainment media have ceased to be a safe place of escape. Even the physical world around us groans. The world today is not as God created it, and it does not function as God intended.

We sometimes cry out, "God, are you there? Do you see what is happening? Do you hear our cries for help? Have you abandoned what you have made?" We feel weak and powerless, unable to bring about the massive change that is needed. And so we pray and hope. But prayer is not a final act of desperation by people who don't know what else to do. The Bible is punctuated with promises of restoration. These promises should remind you that God hasn't abandoned his creation. They have been recorded and preserved so that you would know that your prayers are not in vain. They assure you that restoration is written into God's unshakable redemptive plan.

We find such a promise in Jeremiah 50. It comes at a time when it looks as though things couldn't get any worse for the children of God. It is a shining light of hope in the darkest of times, sent by a God of love to comfort his children down through the ages:

> Israel is a hunted sheep driven away by lions. First the king of Assyria devoured him, and now at last Nebuchadnezzar king of Babylon has gnawed his bones. Therefore, thus says the LORD of hosts, the God of Israel: Behold, I am bringing punishment on the king of Babylon and his land, as I punished the king of Assyria. I will restore Israel to his pasture, and he shall feed on Carmel and in Bashan, and his desire shall be satisfied on the hills of Ephraim and in Gilead. In those days and in that time, declares the LORD, iniquity shall be sought in Israel, and there shall be none, and sin in Judah, and none shall be found, for I will pardon those whom I leave as a remnant. (Jer. 50:17–20)

God will crush evil and restore and purify his people. Evil will not win. Renewal is on the way. There's reason for hope.

For further study and encouragement: Romans 8:18–25

AUGUST 21

JEREMIAH 51–52

Your Lord has the power to do whatever he has purposed to do.

What is your understanding of the power of God? Do you ever find yourself doubting what he is able to do? Do you ever wonder about his ability to deliver what he has promised? Do you ever question his power or authority over the world he has made? Do you think of him as sitting on his holy throne, reigning with power that not only is beyond our ability to grasp but is without boundaries? How big is your God?

At the end of the book of Jeremiah God announces that he is going to destroy Babylon. This is a big boast. Babylon is the ruling nation of the world. No power on earth is like the power of this nation. Babylon rules with nation-crushing might. It seems as though Babylon can do anything it wants to do. So it is significant that God announces that he is going to raise up instruments to crush mighty Babylon forever. What power must God have to say that he will forever end the mighty reign of Babylon?

God uses the occasion of his judgment of Babylon for self-revelation, not only to the people alive at that time but to us as well. Throughout the Old Testament God shows himself. He doesn't hide in the heavens. He doesn't close himself off from the creatures he has made. As you read through the Old Testament, it becomes clear that God wants to be known. So as God announces his judgment on Babylon, he assures us—lest we doubt or forget—that he has the power to do whatever he chooses to do with whomever he chooses to do it. Who is this one who has pronounced judgment against Babylon?

> It is he who made the earth by his power,
>> who established the world by his wisdom,
> and by his understanding stretched out the heavens.
> When he utters his voice there is a tumult of waters in the heavens,
>> and he makes the mist rise from the ends of the earth.
> He makes lightning for the rain,
>> and he brings forth the wind from his storehouses.
> Every man is stupid and without knowledge;
>> every goldsmith is put to shame by his idols,
> for his images are false,
>> and there is no breath in them.
> They are worthless, a work of delusion;
>> at the time of their punishment they shall perish.
> Not like these is he who is the portion of Jacob,
>> for he is the one who formed all things,
> and Israel is the tribe of his inheritance;
>> the LORD of hosts is his name. (Jer. 51:15–19)

The judgment of Babylon is not difficult for one of such incomparable power. Whether it is the power to judge sin or the power to breathe life into those who are spiritually dead, granting them forgiveness forever, God has the power to do whatever he announces or promises he will do.

Don't let your heart doubt his power. His power, coupled with his grace, is your hope.

For further study and encouragement: Romans 6:15–23

AUGUST 22

Convincing yourself that sin has no consequences
is a dangerous spiritual delusion.

The book of Lamentations begins with great sadness:

> How lonely sits the city
>   that was full of people!
> How like a widow has she become,
>   she who was great among the nations!
> She who was a princess among the provinces
>   has become a slave.
> She weeps bitterly in the night,
>   with tears on her cheeks;
> among all her lovers
>   she has none to comfort her;
> all her friends have dealt treacherously with her;
>   they have become her enemies.
> Judah has gone into exile because of affliction
>   and hard servitude;
> she dwells now among the nations,
>   but finds no resting place;
> her pursuers have all overtaken her
>   in the midst of her distress.
> The roads to Zion mourn,
>   for none come to the festival;
> all her gates are desolate;
>   her priests groan;
> her virgins have been afflicted,
>   and she herself suffers bitterly.
> Her foes have become the head;
>   her enemies prosper,
> because the LORD has afflicted her
>   for the multitude of her transgressions;
> her children have gone away,
>   captives before the foe.
> From the daughter of Zion
>   all her majesty has departed.

Her princes have become like deer
  that find no pasture;
they fled without strength
  before the pursuer. (Lam. 1:1–6)

Why has this sad message from God about the consequences for Israel's sin been preserved for us? What are we to gain from this mournful picture of what is going to happen to the people of God because they have turned their backs on their Lord, rebelled against his commands, and given their hearts to the worship of other gods?

This has been retained for us because we share a spiritual problem with God's people of old. Like them, we are prone to minimize, ignore, or deny the consequences of sin. We tell ourselves that gossip won't hurt our relationships, that lust won't weaken our marriages, that gluttony won't affect our health, that materialism won't lead to debt, that our impatience and anger won't drive away our children. We convince ourselves that grace means that God is tolerant of our sin. So God, because of his fatherlike love, has recorded for us moments when the consequences for sin come to those who have lived as though sin were not so sinful after all.

For us, Lamentations 1 is a call from our heavenly Father to examine ourselves, confess the sin and deceitfulness of our hearts, and turn to him in submission and obedience once again. Lamentations 1 is in your Bible as a tool of God's rescuing, protecting, and keeping grace. The God of mercy calls us back to him so that we do not have to reap the full consequences of our sin.

It is important to remember that God's grace never calls wrong right. Grace reminds us of sin's consequences and then offers us forgiveness and the power to say no.

For further study and encouragement: Psalm 136:1–26

———

AUGUST 23

LAMENTATIONS 3–5

*No matter how stuck you might seem, something in your
life is new every morning: the mercy of the Lord.*

Do you feel stuck? Do you long for change? Does your spiritual life seem stagnant? Does it feel as though your hopes and dreams are in suspended animation? Is your marriage stuck in unhealthy patterns? Are your friendships mired in repeated conflict? Do your children seem stuck? Does your church seem stuck, never becoming the church you wish it would be? Are you trapped in sin patterns that leave you feeling guilty and hopeless? Do you seem stuck in your reading of God's word, never feeling that you walk away with renewed faith and hope? Are your finances stuck in patterns of debt? Are you tempted to give up on change?

In the darkest and saddest moments in the history of the people of God, God gives his children a reason not to give up. It's not because they are wise, capable, or righteous. He does not tell them that they have the power to turn things around. Through his prophet, God communicates the hope for change in just a few words: "His mercies never come to an end; they are new every morning" (Lam. 3:22–23). Here is where hope is found in this "stuck-again" world in which we live. God's mercies never grow old. They are never out of date. They are never inappropriate. They never lack power. They never run out. God's mercies never fail. Each morning the people of God are blessed with mercy from the Lord that is form-fit for the trials, opportunities, pressures, obligations, griefs, and temptations of that day. God's mercies are not sitting dusty in a warehouse. No, like fresh fruit, they are hand-delivered by the Savior every day. Each child gets mercy, but each gets just the kind of mercy he or she needs for that day.

It is also true that the steadfast *love* of the Lord never ceases (Lam. 3:22) and that his *faithfulness* is great (3:23). Therefore, we have reason to hope in the Lord. Your hope is never in vain, because God's mercies are always new. His mercies are always new because his steadfast love never ends. And his steadfast love never ends because God is the ultimate definition of faithfulness. Behind every new and needed mercy is a God of faithful, steadfast, and unceasing love.

The pinnacle of the new mercies of our Lord is the gift of his Son. Jesus lived, died, and rose again so we would have every mercy that we need:

> The steadfast love of the LORD never ceases;
>> his mercies never come to an end;
> they are new every morning;
>> great is your faithfulness.
> "The LORD is my portion," says my soul,
>> "therefore I will hope in him." (Lam. 3:22–24)

Jesus is the new mercy of the Lord, now dwelling with his people with redeeming and restoring power. He is with you, in you, and for you with boundless mercy. He will not leave you stuck. You have reason for hope.

For further study and encouragement: Hebrews 4:14–16

AUGUST 24

EZEKIEL 1–4

God always empowers his people to do what he calls them to do.

There was a time when I took pride in my seemingly endless energy and ability to get a lot done quickly. Then I got sick and experienced weakness I had never known before. My first thought, once I realized that my weakness wasn't going away soon, was, "How will I do what God has called me to do?" I thought I had the greatest gospel influence I had ever known, yet I was weaker than I had ever been. I had to face the truth that God hadn't called me to his work because I was independently strong and capable. No, he had called me because *he* was able and would supply me with what I needed in order to do what he had called me to do. Every command and commission of the Lord is accompanied by his empowering grace. When God sends us, he goes with us. That which he asks us to do, he then enables us to do. God never commissions us to his work and then turns his back and walks away.

It is important to our spiritual health that we confess that we have no natural ability to obey God's holy commands. We have no independent capability to be part of his kingdom work. When God called fearful Gideon to lead his people to defeat the Midianites, he greeted Gideon with these words: "The Lord is with you, O mighty man of valor" (Judg. 6:12). It is clear that Gideon was not naturally brave, but God knew what he would empower Gideon to do.

God called Ezekiel to a difficult ministry as his prophet. Ezekiel had to proclaim a message that God's children did not want to hear. God knew his prophet would face threats and opposition, so, in the early chapters of Ezekiel, we find great encouragement and assurance: "The hand of the Lord was upon him" (1:3); "the Spirit entered into me" (2:2); "the hand of the Lord was upon me" (3:22); "I will open your mouth" (3:27). God assured Ezekiel that he would not be left on his own. He would not be left to the small warehouse of his own resources. God would do through Ezekiel what he had called Ezekiel to do.

Pride in your spiritual life or ministry is moral thievery. When we boast about our spiritual maturity or what we have accomplished in ministry, we steal glory from the one who enables us to be what we have become and to do what we do. We live and minister in a way that is pleasing to our Lord only by the power of his grace.

Like Ezekiel, you don't have to be afraid to take up God's call. You don't have what it takes; but he does, and infinitely more. He will give you what you need when you need it. When he sends his children, he goes with them. When he calls his children, he empowers them. The fearful person and the proud person make the same mistake: each focuses on his own power rather than on the amazing grace of the Lord.

For further study and encouragement: 2 Corinthians 12:1–10

———

AUGUST 25

EZEKIEL 5–8

The severe warnings in Scripture were not just for the people of that time; they are God's tools of protecting grace for us as well.

The apostle Paul declares that all Scripture is profitable (2 Tim. 3:16). This means that there are no useless, unneeded parts of God's word. Everything that God intended to be written down and preserved for us has been recorded because it is spiritually beneficial for us in some way. There are no passages that you should buzz through or skip over. Everything is there because your Lord of wisdom and grace knew that you would benefit from it. It is not up to us to decide what is useful; God has already made that decision for us. So, as you read and study Scripture, you should always be asking questions: How does God intend for me to benefit from this portion of his word? What does it reveal about God, about myself, about the nature of sin, about life in this fallen world, about his grace, about the enemy of my soul, or about what I have in Christ or about my future hope?

So why has this terrifying warning in Ezekiel been recorded and retained for us?

The word of the LORD came to me: "Son of man, set your face toward the mountains of Israel, and prophesy against them, and say, You mountains of Israel, hear the word of the Lord GOD! Thus says the Lord GOD! Thus says the Lord GOD to the mountains and the hills, to the ravines and the valleys: Behold, I, even I, will bring a sword upon you, and I will destroy your high places. Your altars shall become desolate, and your incense altars shall be broken, and I will cast down your slain before your idols. And I will lay the dead bodies of the people of Israel before their idols, and I will scatter your bones around your altars. Wherever you dwell, the cities shall be waste and the high places ruined, so that your altars will be waste and ruined, your idols broken and destroyed, your incense altars cut down, and your works wiped out. And the slain shall fall in your midst, and you shall know that I am the LORD." (Ezek. 6:1–7)

First, this passage reveals the complete and perfect holiness of God. In the perfection of his holiness, he cannot and will not tolerate the sin of his people. Second, it reveals his love. Because he has taken these people as his own and showered them with his love, he will not share them with another. Third, these verses reveal God's grace. Every warning is an invitation to confess our sin and turn from it.

Finally, this passage, which reveals the waywardness and disloyalty of the human heart, is a powerful argument for the person and work of Jesus. Because my heart is capable of this kind of idolatry, I have no hope, in this life or the one to come, apart from the rescuing, forgiving, and delivering grace of Jesus.

For further study and encouragement: 2 Timothy 3:10–17

AUGUST 26

EZEKIEL 9–12

Hope in this life and in the one to come is found in the presence of the Lord, who dwells in and among his people.

Ezekiel 10 is one of the saddest passages in the Old Testament. If this passage doesn't break your heart, then you don't yet understand the nature of God's relationship to his covenant children. Let me provide the background for this account. God had chosen to take the Israelite children as his own. He had delivered them out of Egypt and given them his law. He had provided for them and protected them during their wilderness journey. And he had given them the promised land. All of these amazing acts depict a God who chooses to unleash his power on behalf of his people. They depict the operation of his love and grace.

But God had promised to do something even more amazing for his children. He had promised to dwell with his people (Ex. 29:45). His presence had descended upon and lived among his chosen people. This is so miraculous and mind-blowing that it is almost impossible to grasp. The Creator, Sovereign, King of kings made his presence most known among his children. What set the children of Israel apart from every other nation on earth? Was it their human leaders, their military power, their history, their culture, or their land? No, it was the presence of the Lord. They were unique because God dwelled with them.

But then comes the moment when the presence of God leaves the temple. What could be worse than this? Because of the people's rebellion, sin, and idolatry, God's presence tragically no longer dwelled among his people.

This sad historical moment points to the necessity of the person and work of Jesus. Only through Jesus's righteous life, the acceptable sacrifice of his death, and his victorious resurrection will God again dwell within his people. Those who are in Christ become the true temple where Almighty God dwells. Through his Spirit, God now lives in glory and grace among his people. By grace, we are set apart, not because we are independently worthy or holy but because, by the miraculous working of God's sovereign grace, God has chosen us to be the place where he dwells as Christ pours his Spirit into us. Rest assured that, unlike in the sad moment of Ezekiel 10, his glory will never depart.

For further study and encouragement: 1 Corinthians 6:19–20

―――

AUGUST 27

EZEKIEL 13–15

The most spiritually dangerous kind of idolatry is idolatry of the heart.

Ezekiel 14 provides one of the clearest and most helpful discussions of idolatry in the Old Testament:

> Then certain of the elders of Israel came to me and sat before me. And the word of the LORD came to me: "Son of man, these men have taken their idols into their hearts, and set the stumbling block of their iniquity before their faces. Should I indeed let myself be consulted by them? Therefore speak to them and say to them, Thus says the Lord GOD: Any one of the house of Israel who takes his idols into his heart and sets the stumbling block of his iniquity before his face, and yet comes to the prophet, I the LORD will answer him as he comes with the multitude of his idols, that I may lay hold of the hearts of the house of Israel, who are all estranged from me through their idols." (Ezek. 14:1–5)

We can learn at least five essential truths about idolatry from this passage.

1. *The most significant and spiritually dangerous form of idolatry is idolatry of the heart.* An idol of the heart is anything other than God that you allow to rule your heart. The heart is the control center of your personhood. When something other than God takes control of the thing that controls everything else in your life, you find yourself on a path to destruction.

2. *When an idol controls our hearts, it shapes the way we live.* An idol of the heart exercises inescapable influence over our thoughts, desires, words, and behavior. That's why Ezekiel warns against setting a "stumbling block of his iniquity before [your] face" (14:4). Nothing that rules your heart, other than God, will lead you where God wants you to go.

3. *No matter what we are seeking from God, the thing that he is most concerned about is that which controls our hearts.* These leaders of Israel had questions for the Lord, but God wanted to talk about the things that had replaced his rule in their hearts.

4. *God wants nothing less than the reclamation and rulership of our hearts.* God will not share his rule over the hearts of his children with another. He is jealous for the surrender of our hearts to him and will accept nothing less.

5. *Idolatry of the heart is why the person and work of Jesus are essential.* Jesus came to break our bondage to anything or anyone besides him. Freedom from idolatry is possible only by the power of his rescuing grace.

Anything in creation can function as a God-replacement. What tends to replace God as the functional ruler of your heart? In what ways are you in need of his rescuing, liberating grace? That grace is yours because of the work Jesus has done on your behalf.

For further study and encouragement: Colossians 3:5–11

AUGUST 28

EZEKIEL 16–17

Because of sin's deceitfulness, sin doesn't always look sinful to us.

We are deceived by sin more often than we like to think. Sin often doesn't look sinful to us. The angry man convinces himself that he's not angry; he's just standing strongly for the truth. The envious mom eases her conscience by saying that she just wants what is best for her family. The person addicted to food doesn't think another piece of cake is such a big deal. The man lusting after a woman at the gym tells himself it's not lust; he just appreciates beauty. We are all able to erect self-atoning arguments that make our sin seem not so sinful after all. When we do this, we are fighting against the grace of conviction that God uses to protect us and draw us back to him. It is impossible to minimize your sin without denying God's grace. It is also impossible to deny, ignore, or minimize your sin without giving it more room to grow in your heart and life. Where are you tempted to name your sin as being less than sinful?

Because God loves us, because he knows the destructiveness of sin, and because he is aware that we often don't see sin as sinful, he has filled his word with passages that alert us to the ugliness of sin. Ezekiel 16 is one of those passages:

> When I passed by you again and saw you, behold, you were at the age for love, and I spread the corner of my garment over you and covered your nakedness; I made my vow to you and entered into a covenant with you, declares the Lord God, and you became mine. (Ezek. 16:8)

God says, "When you were unlovable, I loved you, covered your nakedness, made a covenant with you, and took you as my bride." Then God says, "But this is how you responded to my love":

> But you trusted in your beauty and played the whore because of your renown and lavished your whorings on any passerby; your beauty became his. . . . And in all your abominations and your whorings you did not remember the days of your youth, when you were naked and bare, wallowing in your blood. (Ezek. 16:15, 22)

The language is strong, but important. Sin is much more than the breaking of an abstract set of moral laws. Sin is spiritual adultery. Because of the magnitude of his love and grace, God took us, unworthy as we were, as his bride. Sin is offering the love that belongs to God to any passerby that attracts us. Sin is more than breaking a rule; it is a betrayal of a relationship that is ours by grace. How serious is sin? It is an act of spiritual adultery against a God of grace.

Even with all of the outrage of Israel's spiritual adultery, at the end of Ezekiel 16 God promises to atone for the sins of his people. That promise is fulfilled by Jesus on Calvary. We, too, have committed spiritual adultery. So, like God's children of old, our only hope is found in his atoning grace. That grace is ours in Jesus.

For further study and encouragement: Hebrews 12:1–2

AUGUST 29

EZEKIEL 18–20

Although God has a holy hatred of sin, he takes
no pleasure in the death of the wicked.

Ezekiel 18 shows us two things that every human being desperately needs:

> The soul who sins shall die. The son shall not suffer for the iniquity of the father, nor the father suffer for the iniquity of the son. The righteousness of the righteous shall be upon himself, and the wickedness of the wicked shall be upon himself. . . .
> Have I any pleasure in the death of the wicked, declares the Lord God, and not rather that he should turn from his way and live? (Ezek. 18:20, 23)

First, we need to live in a world that is ruled by one who is perfectly holy all of the time and in every way. And, because God is holy, he has a holy hatred of sin and every destructive consequence of it. Because of his hatred of sin, God announces that sin is not okay, that it has consequences. The final consequence of sin is death. We would have no hope of any kind of moral order, any kind of human safety or peace, without God's holy moral rule. His hatred of sin is our hope. His hatred of sin and his meting out the consequences of sin led Jesus to the cross. God's anger with sin is what caused Jesus to take our sin upon himself and bear the penalty for our sin by his death. Jesus took God's holy anger on our behalf.

Second, every human desperately needs our world to be ruled by the one who is the definition of grace. If God were only angry with sin, there would be no hope for us. But his anger with sin is accompanied by his lavish and inexhaustible grace. The one who rules everything has no pleasure in the death of the sinner. What gives him pleasure is when the sinner turns from his sinful ways and lives. This grace, too, drove Jesus to the cross. In Jesus, God provided a way for sinners to be rescued, forgiven, and empowered, so that they might turn from their ways and live.

Without these two things there would be no justice, life would explode into moral chaos, and we would have no hope that what sin has broken could ever be restored.

The righteous life of Jesus, his acceptable death on our behalf, his resurrection, and his ascension allow God to offer us his justifying grace without compromising his holy law, his holy hatred for sin, or the consequences that sin carries. On the cross of Jesus Christ, God's anger with sin and his grace toward the sinner embrace. There we find everything we need to finally be what we were created to be and to live as God designed us to live. Be thankful that God hates sin as you celebrate the grace that grants you his forgiveness.

For further study and encouragement: Ephesians 4:17–24

AUGUST 30

EZEKIEL 21–22

Because wandering away from the Lord is often a process, sometimes it's hard for us to see how far we have fallen from where we once were.

For much of my life, I was a very angry man. Luella, my dear wife, knew I was angry, and my children knew I was angry, but I didn't know I was angry. I was a pastor. I viewed myself not as an angry man but as a man who had given his life to serve the Lord. I was participating in the destruction of my life and ministry, but I did not see or understand it. Luella tried again and again to help me see my anger, but I would tell her what a good guy I was. My anger hadn't exploded overnight. No, it developed over time, until I was no longer the man I had been when I had married Luella and first entered into my ministry calling. I was so blind to how much anger had taken ahold of me that it made me angry every time the subject came up. I had no clue as to how far I had fallen until God opened my eyes in a dramatic moment and provided the rescue I needed from myself and my sin.

I don't think that my experience was unique. I am deeply persuaded that this is how sin works. Sin is deceitful. It is able to hide in the cracks, to work in the darkness, to sneak around the corner, and to whisper in the shadows. Sin doesn't tend to take hold of your heart in one dramatic moment of conquest. It is an enemy that enters your house as a friendly guest, but over an extended time takes control over you and what belongs to you. Sin is a false guide that leads you down a road with promises of a beautiful destination, while actually leading you to your death. Sin is a lamb that turns out to be a lion. Sin presents itself as a lover, while planning to betray you. Sin often does its work so slowly that it lulls you to sleep while you are perched on the edge of a cliff.

The children of Israel progressively wandered away from the Lord. They experienced not one big dramatic moment of moral betrayal, but rather ten thousand steps away from God, away from his commands, and away from the worship that belonged to him alone. They became a very different people from what they once were. It was hard to look at their life, their culture, their leaders, and their worship and think that they were the people of God.

How bad had it gotten? These words say it all: "I sought for a man among them who should build up the wall and stand in the breach before me for the land, that I should not destroy it, but I found none" (Ezek. 22:30). God looked for one righteous man who would fight this progressive cycle of evil, but found none!

May God give us eyes to see where we have wandered away from him.

For further study and encouragement: Hebrews 3:7–19

———

AUGUST 31

EZEKIEL 23–24

It is sad that we not only give ourselves to sin, but also reject God's offer of forgiving and saving grace.

One particular moment in ministry left me stunned. I was counseling a couple whose marriage was in deep trouble. The husband and wife had done a litany of things to weaken their bond of love and to make their home a place of war and not peace. He was selfish, demanding, unkind, impatient, and vengeful. He regularly threw every wrong thing his wife had ever done in her face. She had pleaded with him for years to get help. She had said for years that she would go with him and deal with the wrong things she had done. Finally, only to silence her, he agreed to go to counseling. He had no hunger for change, no willingness to consider how he treated his wife. I was in the room with them not just to point out how sinful they had been but, more importantly, to offer them God's forgiving, transforming, empowering, and delivering grace. I told them that, because of the presence and power of God's grace, I had hope for their marriage, and they should too. I told them stories of how I had watched God, in grace, reach down and completely change the direction of marriages. I talked about the awesome restorative power of God's grace. And I assured them that God's grace was theirs for the asking.

I was in the middle of reminding them again, as we talked about the battles of the past week, that in God's grace they could find everything they needed to love one another as God had designed for them to love as husband and wife.

In the middle of my grace soliloquy, the husband jumped up and said, "I can't do this! I can't come here week after week and act like I want what you have to offer." And with those words, he stormed out of my office, got in his car, and drove away. His wife burst into tears, and I was at the edge of tears. We were grieved not just because he loved his sin, but because he had heard God's offer of grace again and again yet chose to reject the offer.

In a single sad sentence in Ezekiel, as God is announcing judgment on his people, he charges them not just with sin, but with turning their backs on his grace: "On account of your unclean lewdness, because I would have cleansed you and you were not cleansed from your uncleanness . . ." (Ezek. 24:13). God says, "It's not just that you were unclean, but that you have rejected my offer to cleanse you from that uncleanness."

All of us sin, but we have hope because God offers us forgiving and cleansing grace. Yet there is no hope for us if we turn our backs on God's offer of grace. Even in our uncleanness, he looks on us with a tender heart and says, "You come to me, and I will make you clean." May we never turn away from the one place of hope for sinners: God's offer of grace that forgives and restores.

For further study and encouragement: Hebrews 10:19–31

———

SEPTEMBER 1

EZEKIEL 25–27

Life on this side of eternity is one constant glory war.

I saw a change in my friend. He had once been a champion of the gospel. It was the fire in his belly, the passion that constantly motivated him. But now he was different. It hadn't happened all at once, but his ministry had changed. It had been all about his Savior, but now it was all about him. He seemed to have fallen into the lure of his own notoriety. He clearly loved being the center of attention. He liked being surrounded by his fans. He loved hanging around with the "cool kids." He was still in ministry and still doing ministry things, but the glory-focus had radically shifted. Whether he knew it or not, the glory that excited him was not the glory of his Savior. He was obsessed with his own glory, and it would be his undoing.

You and I were hardwired by God for glory. We are attracted to glorious things. That's why we love a great meal, an overtime championship game, a beautiful dress, a dramatic movie, or a multihued sunset. God has packed his world full of glorious things and given us the ability to take in those glories. But every glorious thing God has created points to *his* glorious glory. We were never intended to live for our own glory or some created glory. Our glory orientation should drive us to the Lord, so that his glory would finally satisfy the glory hunger in our hearts.

Sin causes us to search for glory satisfaction outside of our Creator, but God will not share his glory with another. God is jealous for his glory to be the one glory that captures our hearts, and this should shape the way that we live. His holy jealousy for his glory is clearly communicated in a single statement repeated in Ezekiel 25–26: "Then you [or they] will know that I am the LORD" (Ezek. 25:7, 11, 17; 26:6). God is pronouncing judgment on the nations that surround Israel. He exercises his holy justice so that these nations will know that he is the Lord. God exercises his power for his own glory.

Does this bother you? It is wrong to live for your own glory because, as a creature, you belong to the one who made you. You exist by his will and for his purpose. But God is not like you. He reigns in glorious majesty over everything and everyone he has created. His zeal for his own glory is the hope of the universe. It is in living for his glory that we are rescued from our bondage to our own glory, a glory that will never satisfy our hearts.

Only by the power of God's delivering grace are we liberated from our bondage to the glories of creation to find our hope, life, and satisfaction in living for the glory of our Maker. In 2 Corinthians 5:15, the apostle Paul reminds us that we find that grace in the person and work of Jesus. He came so that we would live no longer for ourselves "but for him who for [our] sake died and was raised."

For further study and encouragement: Psalm 50:12–15

SEPTEMBER 2

EZEKIEL 28–30

We find hope not in our ability to cobble together a good life, but rather in the truth that God exercises his power for the good of his people.

Where do you look for your security and hope? Do you look to your ability to put together a good career? To purchase a good house in a good community? To parent children who become successful? To build a satisfying circle of good friends? Do you look for security and hope in the size of your bank account? In your commitment to exercise and live healthy? Where do you look for the "good life"? None of these things are bad to desire or pursue, but they must not be where you look for your deepest security and hope. Despite all your solid intentions and hard work, none of these things are guaranteed to you. You don't have the power or authority to control all the factors involved in achieving your dreams. Take your job or career, for instance. In order for your job to be stable and your career to grow, you need the world economy to be stable, your industry to remain heathy, your workplace to make wise choices, and your boss to respect and trust you. You control none of these things. You can work diligently, but something outside of your control can suddenly shift, and you can find yourself out of a job.

Because of this, our hearts will rest only when they rest in the truth that God graciously and willingly exercises his infinite power for the good of his children. In a long portion of Scripture in which God pronounces his judgment on the nations surrounding his children, he states that he is judging these nations not only because he is holy and just and will crush evil. He says he is judging those nations also because they have made life hard for his children. God is judging the surrounding nations because he loves his children and will unleash his almighty power for their good: "For the house of Israel there shall be no more a brier to prick or a thorn to hurt them among all their neighbors who have treated them with contempt. Then they will know that I am the Lord God" (Ezek. 28:24). The word picture of the brier and the thorn tells God's children that he will remove all the things that the surrounding nations have done to hurt his children. God exercises his judgment not only because he is holy and just, but also because he has a tender heart of love for his children and will do for them what they do not have the power to do for themselves.

It is amazing to think that God constantly exercises his power and his rule for the good of his children. Because he can control what is out of our control, lasting hope and security are found in the exercise of his power rather than in our own power. The "good life" is always found in resting in his loving rule on our behalf.

For further study and encouragement: Proverbs 3:5–6

SEPTEMBER 3

EZEKIEL 31–33

*Your life now and in the world to come is built
on the infinite patience of the Lord.*

I have always loved my children dearly, but I have not always been a patient father. When my children were young, I wanted to protect, guide, instruct, and nurture them. I wanted them to know about God's grace, and I wanted to incarnate that grace in their lives. But I often fell short. I remember being so irritated when the simple act of getting in the car was an act of sibling war-making. We would barely be out of the house before the bickering would begin about who was going to sit where in the car. Then they would pull and yank on one another in an attempt to get the best seat. Before long one of my children would be crying and asking me to do something about the situation. It made me mad that we couldn't get in the car peacefully. I tried assigning seats, but then I would have to listen to my children complain as we drove down the road about how unfair it was that all of them somehow always got the worst seat.

As I think about my struggle to be a patient father, I reflect on the amazing patience of my heavenly Father. I had a hard time dealing with silly little moments of sibling quarreling. But God was patient in the face of the ongoing rebellion and idolatry of his people. I don't mean that he turned his back and acted as though it weren't happening. And he never lowered his holy standards to indulge his children. To ignore the wandering away of his children would have meant that God lacked love for them. But God, without compromising his holy requirements, responded to his wayward children with amazing patience. His patience and his holiness are never in disharmony.

One of the ways we encounter God's patience is in his tender pleas for his children to turn again toward him in worship, submission, and obedience. His judgment waits so that his mercy may do its work. Here is the tender, patient heart of the Lord:

> You, son of man, say to the house of Israel, Thus have you said: "Surely our transgressions and our sins are upon us, and we rot away because of them. How then can we live?" Say to them, As I live, declares the Lord God, I have no pleasure in the death of the wicked, but that the wicked turn from his way and live; turn back, turn back from your evil ways, for why will you die, O house of Israel? (Ezek. 33:10–11)

Because he is perfectly holy all of the time and in every way, God has a holy hatred for sin. So he pleads with his people to turn from sin's road to death and live.

313

Today, in redeeming love, your patient Lord says once again to you, "Turn back from your sin. Why would you choose death over life? Come to me in confession and repentance and live." Your patient Redeemer, in love, pleads for you to turn. Today, will you hear his plea and turn?

For further study and encouragement: 2 Peter 3:8–13

SEPTEMBER 4

EZEKIEL 34–36

It is a good thing that our lives are controlled not by failed human shepherds, but by the good shepherd, who will never fail.

After prophesying against the wicked leaders of Israel, Ezekiel brings God's children promises of a faithful good shepherd:

> Therefore, thus says the Lord GOD to them: Behold, I, I myself will judge between the fat sheep and the lean sheep. Because you push with side and shoulder, and thrust at all the weak with your horns, till you have scattered them abroad, I will rescue my flock; they shall no longer be a prey. And I will judge between sheep and sheep. And I will set up over them one shepherd, my servant David, and he shall feed them: he shall feed them and be their shepherd. And I, the LORD, will be their God, and my servant David shall be prince among them. I am the LORD; I have spoken. (Ezek. 34:20–24)

So often in the middle of Israel's despair, when their trouble has been troubled further by wicked and selfish leaders, God makes promises that, no matter how they are received at the moment by his children, find their full fulfillment only in Jesus. Think of how the Gospel of Matthew begins: "The book of the genealogy of Jesus Christ, the son of David, the son of Abraham" (Matt. 1:1). Jesus is in the royal line of David. All of the promises God made about David's unending kingdom are fulfilled in Jesus. John declares, through the words of Jesus, that Jesus is the promised good shepherd:

> I am the good shepherd. The good shepherd lays down his life for the sheep. He who is a hired hand and not a shepherd, who does not own the sheep,

sees the wolf coming and leaves the sheep and flees, and the wolf snatches them and scatters them. He flees because he is a hired hand and cares nothing for the sheep. I am the good shepherd. I know my own and my own know me, just as the Father knows me and I know the Father; and I lay down my life for the sheep. And I have other sheep that are not of this fold. I must bring them also, and they will listen to my voice. So there will be one flock, one shepherd. For this reason the Father loves me, because I lay down my life that I may take it up again. (John 10:11–17)

Jesus is the full expression of the promise of the good shepherd from David's royal line. Ultimately, what the people of old needed, and what we need as well, was a better human shepherd. Jesus, the God-man, is that better shepherd. Yes, the human shepherds of Israel were derelict in their duties. They loved themselves more than they loved God and his people. Yes, it would have greatly benefited the people of God if they had been led by godly leaders. But, because of the presence and power of sin, what humanity needs is a shepherd who would lay down his life for the redemption of his sheep. Be glad today that Jesus is that shepherd. He laid down his life so that you might have life. You are his sheep and the object of his shepherding care forever.

For further study and encouragement: John 10:11–18

———

SEPTEMBER 5

EZEKIEL 37–39

Jesus is the resurrection and the life. He can make
dry bones live—and that is the best news.

This famous passage in Ezekiel addresses the age-old question, Where do we find hope?

Then he said to me, "Prophesy over these bones, and say to them, O dry bones, hear the word of the LORD. Thus says the Lord GOD to these bones: Behold, I will cause breath to enter you, and you shall live." . . .

So I prophesied as I was commanded. And as I prophesied, there was a sound, and behold, a rattling, and the bones came together, bone to its bone. And I looked, and behold, there were sinews on them, and flesh had come upon them, and skin had covered them. But there was no breath in them. Then he said to me, "Prophesy to the breath; prophesy, son of man, and say to the breath, Thus says the Lord God: Come from the four winds, O breath, and breathe on these slain, that they may live." So I prophesied as he commanded me, and the breath came into them, and they lived and stood on their feet, an exceedingly great army. (Ezek. 37:4–5, 7–10)

When we consider the disastrous history of Israel, a people whom God chose, loved, guided, protected, and provided for, we might ask, Where is hope for these rebellious people to be found? They forsook their Father for other gods. Evil king after evil king led the people astray. God's people lost everything. Jerusalem and the temple were destroyed. And so we ask, Where is hope to be found?

It is clear that hope is not found in human righteousness, because that always falls short of God's holy standard. It is clear that hope is not found in human wisdom, because we are capable of so much foolishness. It is clear that hope cannot be found in human strength, because, in the face of sin and temptation, we can be so weak. Hope is found in only one place: the power of our Lord to bring dry bones together again and breathe life into them. Our God has the power to bring life out of what is dead. It seemed as though God's children were dead and gone—but reigning over Israel was a God who has resurrection power.

That God is your Lord. He has the power to resurrect your dry bones and give you new life. As in the Valley of Dry Bones, resurrection is an event, followed by a process. By grace, when we believe, we are raised to newness of life. Then, through a lifelong process and by means of sanctifying grace, God works to resurrect every area of our lives. Jesus declares himself to be the resurrection and the life, and he is in you and for you.

Where is hope to be found? In the awesome resurrecting power of Jesus, who came so that we might have life, full and eternal.

For further study and encouragement: John 5:25–29

SEPTEMBER 6

EZEKIEL 40–42

We should daily celebrate the gospel's offer of
fresh starts and new beginnings.

The gospel message of fresh starts and new beginnings is our hope after we cross God's moral boundaries and pay the consequences for our disobedience. It is what we wish for when our marriage is in a place we never thought it would be. It is the cry of parents whose children have wandered away from the faith. It is the hope of a pastor whose church seems to be stuck. It is what we hope for when conflict shatters our family. It is what we pray for after we once again give in to temptation. And it is what we hope for when we ask for forgiveness from someone we've wronged. We all have moments when we long for fresh starts and new beginnings. Sometimes the damage seems too great. Sometimes the valley seems so long and so dark that it seems it will never end. Discouragement and hopelessness come over us like a cloud. The enemy whispers in our ears, "Where is your God now?" And we are tempted to give up.

In order to give us hope and to silence the enemy's attacks, God sprinkles his word with encouraging accounts of fresh starts and new beginnings. One of those accounts is in Ezekiel 40–42. Fourteen years after the unthinkable happened—the destruction of Jerusalem and the temple, which stood as the moral and spiritual center of Jerusalem—God gives Ezekiel a vision of the rebuilding of the temple. As long as Jerusalem had still existed, and as long as the temple had stood, God's people had hope. But now the temple is gone and the children of God are in captivity. It looks as though all is lost; God has forsaken his people and Israel is no more. This must be the end.

But fourteen years into this disaster, God comes to Ezekiel with a detailed vision of the rebuilding of his temple. There is a glorious promise embedded in this vision. It is the promise of a fresh start and a new beginning for God's people. They will be granted this fresh start not because they have worked their way back into God's favor, but because God is patient, loving, and full of mercy. He finds pleasure in granting his children forgiveness. He loves to make broken things new again. God is not about to let the rebellion of Israel destroy the redeeming plan that he set in place before the foundations of the world were laid.

The cross of Jesus Christ and the empty tomb stand as symbols to us that God will do what is necessary so that sin and judgment will not be the final chapter for us. In grace he comes to us with forgiveness, he reconciles us to himself, and then he works to make us new again. As you look at broken things in your life, remember that your Lord is the Lord of fresh starts and new beginnings. Because of his grace, what seems irreparably damaged can be restored and live anew.

For further study and encouragement: Luke 19:1–10

———

SEPTEMBER 7

EZEKIEL 43–45

*Nothing is more glorious than the glory of the
Lord dwelling with his people forever.*

We are full of wonder as we read the culmination of Ezekiel's vision for the rebuilding of the temple:

> Then he led me to the gate, the gate facing east. And behold, the glory of the God of Israel was coming from the east. And the sound of his coming was like the sound of many waters, and the earth shone with his glory. And the vision I saw was just like the vision that I had seen when he came to destroy the city, and just like the vision that I had seen by the Chebar canal. And I fell on my face. As the glory of the LORD entered the temple by the gate facing east, the Spirit lifted me up and brought me into the inner court; and behold, the glory of the LORD filled the temple. While the man was standing beside me, I heard one speaking to me out of the temple, and he said to me, "Son of man, this is the place of my throne and the place of the soles of my feet, where I will dwell in the midst of the people of Israel forever." (Ezek. 43:1–7)

This vision is a promise from God that, even though it seems as though things are over for his people, he will grant them a fresh start and a new beginning. But something dramatically important is required. There will be no joy in the rebuilding of the temple if it stands empty, a hollow monument to what once was. The temple is the temple because the glory of the Lord resides there. This is why the old temple was a beacon of hope to God's people. The destruction of the temple meant that God no longer dwelled with his people. Of all the things that Israel suffered in their captivity, nothing was more horrible than that. So this is the crescendo of Ezekiel's vision; God's presence will return, and he will dwell with his people forever.

It is impossible to overstate the importance of the return of God's glory to the temple. Israel was Israel because God, in his glorious glory, resided with his people. Everything they needed was found in the presence of their Lord. His presence gave life, hope, power, security, and a future to his people. He was the focus of their love and the object of their worship. He was there to rule them with power and to guide them with wisdom. Without his presence, they were just another nation in history's catalog of nations.

We should pay attention to the foreverness of this promise of God's presence. It is being fulfilled today for all who believe. By grace, we have become the temple of God. He dwells with us and in us by the Spirit. We are not just a bunch of people trying to make our way in this fallen world. No, we are so much more. We are God's children, the temple where his glory dwells, now and forever. What could be better news?

For further study and encouragement: 1 Corinthians 3:10–17

SEPTEMBER 8

EZEKIEL 46–48

In the presence of the Lord we find life, peace, security, and eternal hope.

I love how the book of Ezekiel ends. If you were the most creative writer ever, you could not write a better ending than this. This is infinitely better than the fairy-tale ending "And they lived happily ever after." This ending not only gets at the core hope for the people of God; it hits even deeper and wider. It gets at why God created humanity in his own image and placed them in the lovely garden of Eden. It reaches to where we are meant to find our identity, purpose, and meaning. It is spoken to the people of old, but rings just as powerfully hopeful for us today. It is expansively glorious, yet practically transformational at the same time.

As the book of Ezekiel ends, we find ourselves at the end of the prophet's extended vision of the rebuilding of the temple and the city, and the distribution of territory to the tribes of Israel. The final word of the vision is the final word of the book of Ezekiel: "And the name of the city from that time on shall be, The LORD Is There" (Ezek. 48:35). There could be no better name for the city of the people of God. This name captures all that God intends to do as he brings them back from captivity, not only restoring them to their land but, more importantly, reconciling them to himself. Here is their identity. They are the people with whom God has chosen to dwell. Here is their hope. No matter what hardships they might face, they will never face them alone. Here is their life. Their Creator, provider, protector, Redeemer, and guide lives forever in their midst. Here is where they find meaning. Everything in their life is infused with new meaning because of the presence, power, and promises of their Lord. Here is where they find their purpose. Everything in their life is meant to be shaped by the worship of the glorious one who has chosen to be there with them.

"The LORD Is There" stands as a forever reminder of who they are by glorious, undeserved grace. God, in all his glory, is what makes this city holy and wonderful. Every place is sanctified if the Lord is there.

Sin separates us from God, just as it separated the children of Israel. Our natural state is to be without hope and without God in the world. So, God sent his Son to live a perfect life, to die an acceptable death, and to rise again, all for us, so that there would no longer be any separation between us and God. What we never could have earned is ours by atoning, justifying grace. God now lives inside of us in the person of the Holy Spirit. We too find our identity, security, life, hope, meaning, and purpose in the Lord. If you were to write a name over the people of God, the church, there would be no better choice than "The Lord Is There." We are what we are and what we'll one day be because "The Lord Is There." He is our identity and eternal hope.

For further study and encouragement: Psalm 73:1–28

SEPTEMBER 9

DANIEL 1–3

*God doesn't always call us to particular tasks because
we are naturally able, but because he is able.*

The book of Daniel focuses on God's sovereign rule over human history and the affairs of the nations. The children of Israel have been taken into captivity by mighty Babylon. It seems unthinkable that, after all of his promises, God would let this happen. It appears that it is over for Israel—but you soon get the sense that it is not. Among the captives are four young men: Daniel, Hananiah, Mishael, and Azariah. They are not just captives; they have been taken to Babylon according to the plan of God, to do his work:

As for these four youths, God gave them learning and skill in all literature and wisdom, and Daniel had understanding in all visions and dreams. At the end of the time, when the king had commanded that they should be brought in, the chief of the eunuchs brought them in before Nebuchadnezzar. And the king spoke with them, and among all of them none was found like Daniel, Hananiah, Mishael, and Azariah. Therefore they stood before the king. And in every matter of wisdom and understanding about which the king inquired of them, he found them ten times better than all the magicians and enchanters that were in all his kingdom. And Daniel was there until the first year of King Cyrus. (Dan. 1:17–21)

Imagine yourself in this situation. How would you have felt if you had been taken out of your homeland, ripped away from your family, stripped of your national and spiritual identity, and placed in a situation where you had no rights or power? What might have run through your mind as you were summoned to stand before the king? These four young men stood before Nebuchadnezzar because of the call of God upon their lives. Because of that call, they were more than lowly captives. They were the servants of the Most High God.

This is one of the most encouraging passages in the Old Testament. God chose these men for important work in Babylon. But he chose them not because of their stellar character, or because of the ease of the location he would call them to, or because of the size of their natural gifts. God called these men to serve him in this foreign land not because they were able, but because he was able. Read the passage again. God "gave them learning and skill in all literature and wisdom . . . ten times better than all the magicians and enchanters that were in all his kingdom" (1:17, 20). When God calls us to a task, he empowers us to do what he has called us to do. Success in his work is never God's endorsement of *our* power, wisdom, and character alone, but instead draws all praise to his.

Do you feel overwhelmed today? When God sends you, he goes with you. When he calls, he empowers.

For further study and encouragement: Acts 1:1–8

SEPTEMBER 10

DANIEL 4–6

We were created to live not for our own glory, but
for the glory of the one who made us.

I don't think I'll ever stop writing about it. I think it is the war of wars. It will either complicate and destroy your life or bless you with lasting peace and satisfaction of heart. It is the thing that attracts and shapes the life of every human being in some way. What am I talking about? *Glory.* God designed us to be oriented toward glory. That's why all of us love glorious, awe-inspiring things. A beautiful sunset over the ocean. A great painting or piece of music. A delicious meal. An exciting sports event. All of us are glory gazers.

God intentionally placed us in a glory-filled world. Every day of your life is a glory display, as you are surrounded by the physical glories that God has created. But every created glory is a sign pointing us to the glory of the Creator of all of this glory. His glory alone has the power to fill and satisfy our hearts. Yet we all, in some way, look to created things to satisfy our hearts—but they never do, because they were not made for that purpose. Your marriage isn't meant to satisfy your glory longing. Neither is your job, bank account, children, or possessions.

The most dangerous God-glory replacement is the glory of self. Nothing is more seductive, attractive, deceptive, or tempting than self-glory. The glory of success, power, acclaim, and control in some way seduces us all. The danger of self-glory is a focus in the book of Daniel, and the human example of that danger is Nebuchadnezzar. This Babylonian king is obsessed with his own power and glory. Even after hearing God's patient and gracious warning, Nebuchadnezzar stands on his balcony overlooking his kingdom and says, "Is not this great Babylon, which I have built by my mighty power as a royal residence and for the glory of my majesty?" (Dan. 4:30). What a clear and outrageous statement of self-glory. While the words are still in the king's mouth, God reduces him to a groveling beast.

Why does the book of Daniel slow down and focus on Nebuchadnezzar's obsession with self-glory? The answer is clear. This story is in the Bible because God loves us. It has been recorded and preserved as a warning for us. But there is more. The story is about more than Nebuchadnezzar; it's about Jesus. He humbled himself and became an obedient servant, even to death, so that we may be liberated from our bondage to ourselves and live in the freedom of a pursuit of a greater glory. The self-exaltation of Nebuchadnezzar cries out for the humiliation of the Son. His humiliation is our liberation.

His death is our doorway to life. In him we find the power we need to fight the seduction of self-glory and to live as those shaped by the heart-satisfying glory of God.

For further study and encouragement: Psalm 115:1–18

———

SEPTEMBER 11

DANIEL 7–9

The entire biblical story marches toward the coming of the Son of Man.

If you were to introduce Jesus to someone who had never heard of him before, what would you say? If you had to summarize who he is and what he has done, what would you write? When you preach the gospel to yourself—and you should—what do you say to yourself about the Jesus who is at the center of that gospel? The central character and eternal hope of the biblical narrative is Jesus. All of the promises of God balance on his shoulders. Everything that we need is supplied in and through him. He is the hope of the Old Testament and the conquering hero of the New Testament. By grace our little stories are embedded in his great victorious narrative. The Bible is the biography of Jesus. It is the revelation of his character, power, wisdom, holiness, and redeeming work. At the center of all the promises of God is the promised Son.

Daniel 7–12 records the apocalyptic visions of Daniel. These visions are meant to assure the people of God at that time, as well as us, that despite persecution and hardship God still reigns, his plan still marches on, and his promises are still trustworthy. At the beginning of Daniel's visions is a vision of the reign of Jesus:

I saw in the night visions,

> and behold, with the clouds of heaven
>> there came one like a son of man,
> and he came to the Ancient of Days
>> and was presented before him.
> And to him was given dominion
>> and glory and a kingdom,
> that all peoples, nations, and languages
>> should serve him;

his dominion is an everlasting dominion,
    which shall not pass away,
and his kingdom one
    that shall not be destroyed. (Dan. 7:13–14)

This amazing scene should make your heart pump, your jaw drop, and your mind fill with awe and wonder. God sits on his holy and royal throne as the sole ruler of the universe he created. The one like a son of man is presented to him. This description of Jesus is a reminder to us that he is fully God and fully man. After Jesus is presented to the Father, God grants him everlasting dominion over all humanity and a kingdom that will never be destroyed. This is a gloriously encouraging and hope-infusing description of the one in whom you have placed your hope.

It is important that we think of Jesus not only as the sacrificial Lamb but also as the risen, ascended, and reigning King. What happens after the resurrection is very important. Jesus ascends on a cloud to be seated at the right hand of the Father to reign forever and ever (Acts 1:9). His reign is not a future promise, but a present reality. We have hope right here, right now because his reign guarantees that he has the power and authority to deliver to us everything that his work on earth purchased for us. His present reign guarantees that he will someday usher in the final kingdom, where we will be blessed with uninterrupted peace and righteousness forever.

Today, celebrate the reign of your Savior and go out and live with courage and hope.

For further study and encouragement: Revelation 1:9–20

SEPTEMBER 12

DANIEL 10–12

At the center of the life of faith is the willingness to wait on the one who accomplishes his will in his time and in his way.

I'm sure you're like me: you don't enjoy waiting. I don't feel blessed when I am waiting in a long grocery line. I don't like it when a highway turns into a parking lot. I don't appreciate that the doctor made an appointment with me for a certain time, but the time has come and gone and I am left waiting. I confess that my struggle with waiting is not just a matter of horizontal situations and relationships. No, my impatience is a spiritual problem. Embedded in my struggle to wait is a frustration with the fact that I am not sovereign, that I do not control all people and situations. I am frustrated with my lack of control, when I should want to celebrate the unshakable and eternal control of the one who sits on the throne of the universe.

I was complaining in traffic many years ago, and my eleven-year-old son asked whether he could say something. I later wished I had said no. But I said, "Sure, you can talk," and he said, "Dad, maybe it's a heart problem and not a traffic problem." It was humbling to have to admit that he was exactly right. He wasn't intending to be disrespectful; he was just repeating to me things I had taught him. Woven into God's call for us to live by faith is a call to patience. Our willingness to wait on God means we really do believe that he exists, that he really is wise, that he is good all of the time and in every way, and that he will ultimately do for us, in us, and around us everything he has promised.

It makes sense then that the book of Daniel, which presents to us God's rule over the history of every people group and every governmental entity, would end with a call to be patient: "Blessed is he who waits and arrives at the 1,335 days. But go your way till the end. And you shall rest and shall stand in your allotted place at the end of the days" (Dan. 12:12–13). When understood in the context of the numerology of Daniel 12, the number 1,335 connotes that the person waiting has been willing to wait longer than expected. He is willing to continue to do what God has called him to do, even though God hasn't acted in the time he expected. The promise in the passage is that, if we are willing to wait, then our promised place and rest will come when the end comes.

Today, God calls us to wait. There are things for which we have longed and prayed that have not yet come. There are promises we have embraced that have not yet been fulfilled. The life of faith is about standing at the intersection of brokenness and longing, not questioning God's presence, power, or goodness, but continuing to trust and obey, assured that he still rules and is marching his world toward the fullness of all he has promised.

Do you struggle to wait? God meets you with empowering grace.

For further study and encouragement: Psalm 27:13–14

SEPTEMBER 13

God's judgment and mercy work together to
accomplish his redemptive plan for his people.

Every time I disciplined my children, I tried to talk to them about God's forgiving and transforming grace. In the midst of what was painful for them, this was something I wanted them to hear, know, and believe. I wanted my sternness in the face of their disobedience to be tempered with mercy. They needed to know I was not turning my back on them. I was not throwing them out of the family. I did not regret that I was their father. And I surely wanted them to know that I was not withdrawing my love. At the same time, I wanted them to know that what they had done was wrong and unacceptable. I wanted them to know that I would never act as though wrong were right.

Your heavenly Father has always responded to his children with a combination of judgment and mercy. Let me clarify. God's judgment of his children in the face of their disobedience and idolatry is not like the sentence of a judge in a criminal court. That judge is not eternally committed to the defendant. In contrast, because of his covenantal commitment to his children, God acts as a Father Judge. Even when he severely disciplines his children, he does not abandon his commitment of everlasting love and mercy. You see this clearly in the first chapter of Hosea. God commands Hosea to give his children specific names. These names are scary, to say the least. The first child is to be named Jezreel, because God is going to "punish the house of Jehu" (Hos. 1:4). The second child, a daughter, is to be named "No Mercy" (Hos. 1:6). The third child is to be named "Not My People" (Hos. 1:9). These names seem to be an announcement that things are over for Israel, that God has had enough and will turn his back on them.

Just when it seems as though all hope is lost, however, we read the first verse of Hosea 2 and encounter these words: "Say to your brothers, 'You are my people,' and to your sisters, 'You have received mercy'" (Hos. 2:1). Do you see the gospel message in these words? Our hope in this life and the life to come is never found in the perfection of our righteousness. On our best days we fall short of God's holy standard and give him cause for judgment. Our hope is only ever in the strength of his unshakable covenant love. It's that love that causes the biblical story to march toward the birth, life, death, and resurrection of Jesus. He had to take our judgment on himself, so that we could be the objects of God's mercy. No matter how stern God's discipline might be, we remain the children of God's mercy forever.

For further study and encouragement: Psalm 103:1–22

SEPTEMBER 14

Nothing is more miraculous and wonderful than the
affection God has for you as one of his children.

It's hard for me to express how much I love each of my children. They are all grown and married, but my love hasn't waned. I get excited when we schedule time to be with them. The love I have for my children now flows over into a special affection for each of their own children. I pray for many people each morning, but my prayers for my children are different. Those prayers are infused with the affection and compassion of a father. Their burdens become my burdens. Their successes cause me to celebrate as though the achievements were my own. Although I know my love for my children is imperfect, I wonder whether it would be possible for me to love them more.

But then I consider the love our heavenly Father has for his children. We should never allow ourselves to forget, question, or devalue the miracle of God's affection for each one of his children. God is not like an idol made of stone, incapable of emotions. Our theology reminds us that, although God the Father is without a body, he is a person. As a person, God has emotions, though his do not change like ours do. We know of God's anger and his love, but maybe we have not thought enough about his fatherly affection that causes him to constantly look at us with tenderhearted compassion. Think about what it means that you have been chosen out of the mass of humanity to be the object of the affection of the one who sits on the throne of the universe in power and glory. This is who you are, this is your identity—not your job, marriage, university, friendships, or ministry. You are a child of the Father and the object of his perfect and eternal affection.

It is striking that this affection is powerfully expressed near the end of Hosea, which is essentially a prophecy of God's judgment:

How can I give you up, O Ephraim?
  How can I hand you over, O Israel?
How can I make you like Admah?
  How can I treat you like Zeboiim?
My heart recoils within me;
  my compassion grows warm and tender.
I will not execute my burning anger;
  I will not again destroy Ephraim;
for I am God and not a man,

the Holy One in your midst,
and I will not come in wrath. (Hos. 11:8–9)

The affectionate love of God bleeds from these words. "How can I give you up? How can I hand you over?" His eternal love means he cannot help but look on his children with compassion. His eternal love means he cannot turn his back on them. He cannot treat them like the destroyed cities of Admah and Zeboiim.

God's affection for his children is seen most clearly in the offering of his Son to pay the penalty for our sin. The Father's affection drove Jesus to the cross. The Father's affection drove Jesus out of the tomb. The Father's affection placed Jesus at his right hand as our intercessor. Our hope is found in the Father's affection.

For further study and encouragement: Romans 5:6–11

———

SEPTEMBER 15

JOEL 1–3

You will never receive a gift sweeter than the gift of God's Spirit.

It was an amazing and miraculous scene. Jesus had ascended on a cloud to the right hand of his Father, and the disciples were all gathered in a room together. All of a sudden, the sound of a powerful wind filled the house, tongues of fire rested on each person gathered there, and each person was filled with the Holy Spirit. Immediately the people began to speak in foreign languages—languages that were understood by the multitudes gathered in Jerusalem. Some onlookers mocked, so Peter stood to address the crowd and to explain what they had experienced:

These people are not drunk, as you suppose, since it is only the third hour of the day. But this is what was uttered through the prophet Joel:

"And in the last days it shall be, God declares,
that I will pour out my Spirit on all flesh,
and your sons and your daughters shall prophesy,
and your young men shall see visions,
and your old men shall dream dreams;

even on my male servants and female servants
    in those days I will pour out my Spirit, and they shall prophesy.
And I will show wonders in the heavens above
    and signs on the earth below,
    blood, and fire, and vapor of smoke;
the sun shall be turned to darkness
    and the moon to blood,
    before the day of the Lord comes, the great and magnificent day.
And it shall come to pass that everyone who calls upon the name of
    the Lord shall be saved." (Acts 2:15–21)

Peter understood that Joel's prophecy of the pouring out of the Spirit was fulfilled that day in Jerusalem. The ascension of Jesus did not mean that God had left his children alone, without his powerful presence. In fact, Jesus had made a promise to his fearful disciples: "I will ask the Father, and he will give you another Helper, to be with you forever" (John 14:16).

The gift of the Spirit is not icing on the cake of redemption, like a sweet but unneeded luxury. No, the presence and work of the Spirit are an essential part of God's saving grace. It is by the work of the Spirit that we are convicted of sin. When we are born again, the Spirit breathes new life into us. The Holy Spirit illumines our hearts and minds so that we can understand the truth revealed in God's word. The Holy Spirit dwells within us, empowering us to do what God has commanded us to do. The unity of the body of Christ is the Spirit's work.

Generations before the birth of Jesus, Joel gave us a glimpse of one of God's most precious gifts: the glorious presence of the Spirit to dwell forever and work tirelessly for his children (Joel 2:28–29). You would not know the Lord, you would not have had the power to believe, and you would not be following him by faith if it were not for this precious gift of the Holy Spirit. Celebrate this gift today.

For further study and encouragement: Ephesians 5:15–21

SEPTEMBER 16

AMOS 1–5

*When a culture turns from God, it always
descends into some kind of moral decay.*

It's not hard to argue that the four most important words in the Bible are the first four: "In the beginning, God" (Gen. 1:1). These words place God where he is meant to be: at the beginning and in the center of all that is. Human beings were designed to live Godward lives. Everything we think, desire, say, and do was meant to bow to his existence, his glory, and his plan. The purpose and direction of every cultural institution were to be shaped by God's presence and will. People were never meant to be at the center. Human will was never meant to be the final decider of what is good, right, or true. Human pleasure was never meant to be the driver of human motivation. Human rationality was never meant to function outside of divine revelation. Human creativity was never meant to express itself outside of the Creator's will. Humans were never designed to have self-sufficient power or autonomy. Everything in a human being's life was meant to exist inside of a recognition of the presence, power, wisdom, and authority of God.

So, when a culture turns its back on God, denies his authority, and follows personal pleasure, good things do not result. In fact, a progressive descent into various kinds of moral decay and corruption always follows. The corruption works its way into every aspect of culture: the family, education, the arts, government and politics, medicine, and all kinds of other cultural structures. Moral decay doesn't happen all at once, but eventually society devolves into moral chaos.

Sadly, you see this progressive moral decay in the people of God in the Old Testament. Though sad to read, this account has been preserved for us as a warning by a God who loves his children dearly. This moral chaos is graphically portrayed for us in the book of Amos:

Thus says the LORD:

> "For three transgressions of Israel,
>   and for four, I will not revoke the punishment,
> because they sell the righteous for silver,
>   and the needy for a pair of sandals—
> those who trample the head of the poor into the dust of the earth
>   and turn aside the way of the afflicted;

a man and his father go in to the same girl,
    so that my holy name is profaned;
they lay themselves down beside every altar
    on garments taken in pledge,
and in the house of their God they drink
    the wine of those who have been fined." (Amos 2:6–8)

Think about what Amos is describing. A sure sign of moral decay is social injustice. Social injustice here is described as justice sold like a commodity while the desperate condition of the poor is denied or ignored. Remember: Amos isn't describing pagan nations. He is describing the people of God.

Decay always happens when God isn't central. Pray for keeping and preserving grace, that God would stay central in everything you desire and do.

For further study and encouragement: Jeremiah 2:4–13

———

SEPTEMBER 17

AMOS 6–9

No one is so far gone that he is beyond the reach
of God's powerful, restoring grace.

The prophecy of Amos, which announces God's judgment on people who have forsaken his ways, perverted his commands, and twisted his justice, ends not with sadness and loss, but with a beautiful picture of the zeal of God's restoring grace:

"In that day I will raise up
    the booth of David that is fallen
and repair its breaches,
    and raise up its ruins
    and rebuild it as in the days of old,
that they may possess the remnant of Edom
    and all the nations who are called by my name,"
    declares the LORD who does this.
"Behold, the days are coming," declares the LORD,
    "when the plowman shall overtake the reaper
    and the treader of grapes him who sows the seed;

the mountains shall drip sweet wine,
    and all the hills shall flow with it.
I will restore the fortunes of my people Israel,
    and they shall rebuild the ruined cities and inhabit them;
they shall plant vineyards and drink their wine,
    and they shall make gardens and eat their fruit.
I will plant them on their land,
    and they shall never again be uprooted
    out of the land that I have given them,"
                        says the LORD your God. (Amos 9:11–15)

God's promise is firm and sure: "I will restore the fortunes of my people Israel." Embedded in this Old Testament promise is hope for humanity. God will not just forgive his people; he will finally and completely restore them. But there is more. He will not just restore his people, but he will restore every single thing that sin has damaged, until everything is made new again. In his restorative promise is the surety that someday the burden of sin, sorrow, and suffering, which the world has carried since the fall of Adam and Eve, will finally be lifted. Peace and righteousness will then reign forever and ever.

The surety of this Old Testament promise of restoration, appearing at the end of a book of judgment, reminds us that no one has been pulled down so far into the pit of iniquity that he or she is beyond the reach of God's restorative grace. No addict, rebellious child, or adulterer is beyond restoration. No troubled marriage is beyond God's restorative power. No thief is beyond restorative grace. No proud person is beyond the humbling power of God's restorative grace. No one is beyond the reach of God's restoration.

If your Lord can restore rebellious Israel, then he can restore you and everything in your life that has been broken, damaged, or destroyed by sin. God's final work for his people is not judgment; it is restoration. He renews what we have no power to renew.

I don't know about you, but God's promise of restoration is one of the things that gets me out of bed in the morning. Although I awake to a world damaged by sin and to my own struggle with it, there is hope. Jesus was sent into this broken-down world as the ultimate restorer. His grace is our hope.

For further study and encouragement: Luke 18:9–14

SEPTEMBER 18

A discernible and dangerous gap often lies between our
formal theology and our functional theology.

If you are familiar with the many stories that God has preserved for you, then you are blessed. It means that God has placed you where you have been exposed to and taught by his word. By his grace, you have heard of his work on behalf of his people again and again, so much so that you know the people and places without having to open up your Bible. Millions of people around the world have never held the Bible in their hands, let alone become so familiar with it that its narrative is embedded in their memory. But there can be a problem with familiarity. Sometimes when we become familiar with something, we get lazy and we quit looking and listening. Luella is an art consultant; she sources and places beautiful pieces of art in her clients' homes and offices. Because of her work, the loft we live in is an art gallery. Wonderful paintings and sculptures are all around us. People who come to our loft are taken aback by all of the art and are often full of questions. But I have a confession to make. I have lived with this art for so long that some days I don't look at it or celebrate the environment that I am blessed to live and work in each day of my life.

The story of the prophet Jonah is one of the most familiar stories in all of Scripture. I was a young boy when I first heard the story of Jonah and the "whale." I have heard that story a thousand times. Because of our familiarity, I am afraid that many of us have quit digging in to this story for gospel insight and wisdom. So here I want to alert you to one thing in the Jonah story that you may have missed.

Jonah says no to God's call to go to Nineveh and preach judgment, and he hops on a boat going in the other direction. God sends a storm, because he is not done with Jonah. The sailors on the boat are searching for a cause for the storm, and they encounter sleeping Jonah. They wake him, cast lots that fall on Jonah, and ask him who he is. He says, "I am a Hebrew, and I fear the LORD, the God of heaven, who made the sea and the dry land" (Jonah 1:9). Jonah makes this formal and cultural confession of belief, which does not depict his functional theology at all. He says he fears the Lord, but he has no problem saying no to God and running away from his call. There seems to be little life-shaping fear of God in this man. His life simply does not depict who he says he is and what he says he believes.

Be warned today. The enemy of your soul will cede you your formal theology if he can control your heart. Pray today for the grace that alone can empower you to live out, at street level, what you say you believe.

For further study and encouragement: Matthew 15:1–20

SEPTEMBER 19

MICAH 1–7

God will not let go of his work of grace until every aspect of sin
has finally been eradicated and the world is forever renewed.

One of the Old Testament's brightest, most glorious visions comes from the prophet Micah:

> It shall come to pass in the latter days
>   that the mountain of the house of the LORD
> shall be established as the highest of the mountains,
>   and it shall be lifted up above the hills;
> and peoples shall flow to it,
>   and many nations shall come, and say:
> "Come, let us go up to the mountain of the LORD,
>   to the house of the God of Jacob,
> that he may teach us his ways
>   and that we may walk in his paths."
> For out of Zion shall go forth the law,
>   and the word of the Lord from Jerusalem.
> He shall judge between many peoples,
>   and shall decide disputes for strong nations far away;
> and they shall beat their swords into plowshares,
>   and their spears into pruning hooks;
> nation shall not lift up sword against nation,
>   neither shall they learn war anymore;
> but they shall sit every man under his vine and under his fig tree,
>   and no one shall make them afraid,
>   for the mouth of the LORD of hosts has spoken.
> For all the peoples walk

each in the name of its god,
  but we will walk in the name of the Lord our God
    forever and ever. (Mic. 4:1–5)

When you come across a glory promise like this one, you should slow down and luxuriate in the beauty of God's unrelenting goodness and the surety of the gorgeous kingdom that awaits you as his child. These kinds of passages are dotted throughout the biblical narrative to give you hope and to motivate you to not let the discouragements of life in this fallen world keep you from continuing to follow your Savior by faith. As you read your Bible, look for these passages where God takes out his brush of grace and paints a picture for us of the glories that are coming for all who have been blessed by his redemptive love.

Clearly, the words of this passage extend beyond the restoration of Israel and describe for us the final restoration of all things and what life will look like for us when the new heavens and new earth are our final address. Passages like this are in the Bible because God loves us. He knows how hard and disheartening life in this broken, groaning world can be. He knows the extent of the evil that is in us and around us. He knows how we struggle with temptation every day. He knows that we grow weary with the daily battle. He knows that there are times when it looks as though his great plan has failed. So, with a tender heart, he reminds us that he is not absent and that his work is not done. He will bring his plan to a final and glorious end. Everything that breaks our hearts and makes life hard will finally and forever end.

Your Savior will return and set up a kingdom of peace and righteousness that will never end.

For further study and encouragement: Revelation 22:1–5

———

SEPTEMBER 20

NAHUM 1–3

*No one can withstand the anger of the Lord; that is why we
are thankful for his forgiving and reconciling grace.*

The little book of Nahum begins with a heart-rattling description of the anger of God. This description has been recorded and preserved as a means of instruction and rescue. Often when people read through the Old Testament and encounter a description of God's anger, they wonder about or even doubt the goodness of the Lord. As you read through Scripture, notice that God does not hide his anger from us. He is not ashamed of his anger, as though it were a mortifying character weakness. It is impossible for God to have character weaknesses of any kind. If God is perfectly holy—and he is—then his anger is not a contradiction of his holiness, but an aspect of it. God could not be perfect in holiness and tolerant of the enormous evil of sin at the same time. Think about a time when you were sinned against, and those around you didn't seem to care. How did you feel? God's unending anger with sin is a constant demonstration to us of just how holy and good he actually is.

God reveals his anger toward sin again and again for good reason. First, God's anger with sin reminds us of how deeply evil and destructive sin is. We need this reminder because sin doesn't always look sinful to us. God's anger with sin is also a call to never minimize or deny it, but to run from it into his arms of grace. God's revelation of his anger with sin is meant to give us hope that there will be final justice, when sin is defeated forever. God's revelation of his anger with sin is also designed to cause us to love the rescuing wisdom of his commands. God's revelation of his anger with sin is meant to cause us to stand in awe of his holiness and to give him the worship that he deserves. But most of all, God's desire to reveal his anger is designed to point us to Jesus. Through Jesus's perfectly righteous life, substitutionary death, and victorious resurrection, God's anger is satisfied and we are no longer under its threat. On the cross of Jesus Christ, God's holy anger against sin and his tender heart of grace met. Jesus had to die because God could never compromise his holiness just to extend grace.

So when you read, "Who can stand before his indignation? Who can endure the heat of his anger?" (Nah. 1:6), know that you are being loved. God is warning you to take sin seriously, to never see it as beautiful, and to never think that on your own you can escape his anger with sin. In these words God lovingly reminds you of how much you need the atoning work of the Lord Jesus Christ. He took your sins on himself. He bore the anger of God in his own body. He endured the Father's rejection. And he did it all so that you may be reconciled to God forever.

For further study and encouragement: Romans 2:1–11

SEPTEMBER 21

Human beings were created for joy; that's why we are always in search of it.

Consider some of Jesus's final words to his disciples: "These things I have spoken to you, that my joy may be in you, and that your joy may be full" (John 15:11). Jesus will soon leave his friends and ascend to his Father, but he wants to leave them with joy. God created human beings for joy. He made us to celebrate the pleasures of knowing, loving, and serving him. He designed us so that we could enjoy the pleasures of the beautiful world he created. He created us for the joy of loving community with one another. There was no sadness or sorrow in the garden of Eden before the fall of Adam and Eve; there was only joy.

Since that tragic moment in the garden, human beings have been in a constant search for joy. We all hunger for it and look for it every day. Some of us hook our joy to our marriages. Some of us look to our children for joy. Some of us think our careers will deliver the joy we seek. Some of us think that assembling a big pile of possessions will give us joy. Some of us think that the height of joy is sexual pleasure. Others of us think that theological knowledge and biblical literacy will give us joy. And others look to ministry success for joy. You should celebrate the gift of all of these things, but they must not be the source of your joy. Each one of these things can disappoint you in some way. When I look to them for joy, my joy is always temporary.

The little book of Habakkuk is about waiting on and trusting in the Lord, even when you are confused by what he is doing, and it ends with one of the clearest statements in all of Scripture about where true, sturdy, and lasting joy is to be found:

Though the fig tree should not blossom,
nor fruit be on the vines,
the produce of the olive fail
and the fields yield no food,
the flock be cut off from the fold
and there be no herd in the stalls,
yet I will rejoice in the LORD;
I will take joy in the God of my salvation.
GOD, the Lord, is my strength;
he makes my feet like the deer's;
he makes me tread on my high places.

To the choirmaster: with stringed instruments. (Hab. 3:17–19)

Pay attention to the word picture here. If you are in an agricultural culture and there is no food to harvest and no cattle in the stalls, you are in dire circumstances. Yet, Habakkuk writes that he would still have reason to rejoice, because God is the source of his joy. The Lord's presence, power, promises, and covenant love give Habakkuk reason for joy no matter what. Vertical joy is the only kind of lasting joy.

Notice the note at the end. Habakkuk's joy poem is actually a lyric, meant to be sung. So, go out and sing for joy; God exists, and, by grace, he is your Father forever.

For further study and encouragement: Psalm 16:1–11

SEPTEMBER 22

ZEPHANIAH–HAGGAI

There will be a day of final judgment, when God will punish evil and right all that has been wronged.

In the busyness of everyday life, it is tempting to live as though life will never change or end. I think many of us live as eternity amnesiacs. We live as though there will never be an end to our days on earth. But when you live with eternity and a final accounting in view, your approach to life radically changes. God is eternal, and we will live on into eternity, but this world and our lives are a march to a final conclusion. There will be a final day of reckoning, when the Lord, in holy and righteous judgment, will mete out his final justice. No one will escape his judgment.

The reality of God's impending judgment is a theme that runs throughout all of the Prophets, but is especially prominent in the book of Zephaniah. The phrase Zephaniah repeatedly uses to speak of this day is "the day of the LORD":

Be silent before the Lord GOD!
  For the day of the LORD is near;
the LORD has prepared a sacrifice
  and consecrated his guests.
And on the day of the LORD's sacrifice—
"I will punish the officials and the king's sons
  and all who array themselves in foreign attire.

On that day I will punish
   everyone who leaps over the threshold,
and those who fill their master's house
   with violence and fraud." (Zeph. 1:7–9)

Think about what this warning means. We live in a moral world ruled by a holy God. This holy one has the power and authority to define for us what is right and what is wrong, what is true and what is false, and what is wise and what is foolish. When you live in a moral world, ruled by a holy God, everything you do has moral meaning to it. What you desire, think, choose, speak, and do matters. You live obediently to God's holy commands, or else you write your own rules and follow the desires of your own heart. What was true for the children of Israel is true for us: we will all face a day when we will give an account for how we have lived.

This means we should take life seriously and live with that final accounting in view. But we also should celebrate that Jesus lived a perfect life on our behalf and paid the penalty for all of our sin, so that in the final day of accounting we can stand before the Lord of lords—even though we have sinned—unafraid of his final condemnation. Jesus took our condemnation, so that, in the final reckoning, our sin will not eternally separate us from God.

So, as you celebrate justifying grace, take life seriously and live joyfully inside of God's wise and holy moral boundaries.

For further study and encouragement: Revelation 21:1–4

———

SEPTEMBER 23

ZECHARIAH 1–7

*In his infinite patience, God holds back his judgment and
gives us room to confess and repent once again.*

When our children were young, I sometimes withheld meting out discipline, giving God room to work confession and repentance in their hearts. I did this because I wanted my parenting to be shaped not only by God's law but also by his grace. I was aware that God's law was a wonderful gift to my children, defining for them the kind of world they had been born into, a world ruled by a perfectly holy God who had the wisdom and authority to tell them how to live.

God's law gave our children moral tracks to run on, a guide for how they were designed to live. But I also was aware of the limits of God's law. I knew that God's law on its own didn't have the power to transform their hearts. I knew that they would never gain acceptance with God by keeping his commands, because they would never keep them perfectly. The law was essential for my kids, but it had no saving power whatsoever.

So, there were many moments when I would come to my children not as a disciplinarian, to mete out some consequence, but as a messenger of mercy, pleading with them to confess and repent. I told them that confession was humbly admitting to the wrong that they had done, that repentance was a change of heart that resulted in a change in how they lived, and that they needed God's empowering grace to do both.

My parenting days come to mind as I read Zechariah. The book of Zechariah is near the very end of the Old Testament. Zechariah writes to the remnant who are now living back in the promised land, calling them to repentance. With tenderhearted mercy, God pleads with this generation not to do what their mothers and fathers did: resist God's warnings, rebel against God's commands, and face his judgment as a result.

Here's how Zechariah begins:

> In the eighth month, in the second year of Darius, the word of the LORD came to the prophet Zechariah, the son of Berechiah, son of Iddo, saying, "The LORD was very angry with your fathers. Therefore say to them, Thus declares the LORD of hosts: Return to me, says the LORD of hosts, and I will return to you, says the LORD of hosts. Do not be like your fathers, to whom the former prophets cried out, 'Thus says the LORD of hosts, Return from your evil ways and from your evil deeds.' But they did not hear or pay attention to me, declares the LORD. Your fathers, where are they? And the prophets, do they live forever? But my words and my statutes, which I commanded my servants the prophets, did they not overtake your fathers? So they repented and said, 'As the LORD of hosts purposed to deal with us for our ways and deeds, so has he dealt with us.'" (Zech. 1:1–6)

I will forever be blown away that our holy God withholds his judgment and, in mercy, stoops to plead with his children to return in repentance to him. And you should be too.

For further study and encouragement: Psalm 32:1–11

The Bible isn't an anthology of stories; it is one unified story.
The Bible isn't a sampling of isolated promises; it is a collection
of promises that all find their fulfillment in Jesus.

When you hold your Bible in your hands to do your daily reading, you should know what you are holding. Your Bible isn't a simple collection of stories with morals for your everyday living. Your Bible isn't a mere collection of wisdom principles to make your life better. Your Bible isn't a systematic theology textbook. Your Bible is the story of God's grand redemptive plan. It is a story with many chapters, but it is one unified story. Maybe the best way to say it is that the Bible is God's grand redemptive story, containing his explanatory and applicatory notes. Your Bible tells the story of how this world was created, how sin entered and damaged the world, how that will get fixed, and what the final end of all things will look like. There is one hero in the Bible. He is the one about whom the Old Testament prophesies, whose life and work the New Testament chronicles, and whose work the Epistles explain. Your Bible is the biography of Jesus.

You should read your Bible with its unity in mind. One of the places where you see this unity clearly is in the book of Zechariah. This book is one of the Old Testament books quoted most by New Testament authors. Under the inspiration of the Holy Spirit, these New Testament writers understood that the many prophecies made to Israel ultimately pointed to and would have their final fulfillment in the coming, the person, and the redeeming work of Jesus. They understood that the partial fulfillment of these passages in Old Testament times was not the end of the story. If, under the guidance of the Holy Spirit, they looked into the Old Testament and saw Jesus, then we should do the same.

One of the most striking and specific passages that finds its ultimate fulfillment in Jesus is in Zechariah 9:

Rejoice greatly, O daughter of Zion!
Shout aloud, O daughter of Jerusalem!
Behold, your king is coming to you;
righteous and having salvation is he,
humble and mounted on a donkey,
on a colt, the foal of a donkey. (Zech. 9:9)

Matthew quotes this passage on the occasion of Jesus's triumphal entry into Jerusalem, where he would be tried for crimes he did not commit, suffer and die for our sins, and rise again to ascend in victory to the right hand of his Father (Matt. 21:5). Jesus is the humble King. He comes not to set up an earthly kingdom, but to suffer and die, so that his kingdom may reign in the hearts of all who believe and so that his final kingdom may one day come. Zechariah writes of more than a promised earthly king. He writes of the King of kings, who is also the Lamb of sacrifice. Here in some of the final words of the Old Testament is gospel hope. We have the assurance that there is one hope in this life and the one to come: Jesus.

For further study and encouragement: Matthew 21:1–11

———

SEPTEMBER 25

MALACHI 1–4

The truth that God does not change is a rock of hope for his children living in an ever-changing world.

We have six grandchildren, and we have a hard time keeping up with them. Just about when we have adjusted to the stage one grandchild is in, she grows out of it and moves on. So it is with everything in our lives. Nothing in life remains the same. Our physical bodies surely don't remain the same. Sickness, accidents, and aging change us. Our marriages don't remain the same. Young married couples become middle-aged couples, who become elderly couples, and the dynamics of the marriage change with each season. The culture around us never stays the same. The culture of the 1970s was radically different from the culture we live in today. We simply can't look horizontally for a rock of unchanging security and hope, because everything changes. Including you.

Yet we all long for a rock to stand on, whether we know it or not. We long for something we can build our lives on that will be a firm foundation. We search for something stable upon which we can build our identity, meaning, rest of heart, and purpose. If you are looking for an unchanging, eternal rock of hope, there is only one place to look: up. In the final book of the Old Testament, Malachi, God calls his children to repent. Repentance is a change of heart that results in a change in the direction of your life. In this call to repent, God says something important about his unchangeability: "I the LORD do not change; therefore you, O children of Jacob, are not consumed. From the days of your fathers you have turned aside from my statutes and have not kept them. Return to me, and I will return to you, says the LORD of hosts" (Mal. 3:6–7).

The words here are very specific and important to understand. First, God reminds his wayward children that the only reason they have not been consumed by the fire of his anger against their sin is that he does not change. He is the same in holiness, faithfulness, and covenantal love. Because he is the same, his promises are trustworthy. But then God says, "Return to me, and I will return to you." It sounds as though God is contradicting himself. The word *return* implies change. Here's what God is saying: "I am the unchanging God, who changes." Even more confused? Let me clarify. God's character remains eternally unchanged. Who he has been, he is and ever will be. But from our perspective his actions and responses toward his children change. We find eternal rest in the fact that God never changes, and constant comfort in the fact that he responds to our prayers for help, our confession of sin, and our commitment to turn. In the face of our repentance, our Lord turns in mercy away from threatening discipline and responds to us with forgiving grace.

It is such a good thing that our Lord is both eternally unchanging and constantly responsive to his children. Because he is, he is our place of eternal rest and right-here, right-now hope.

For further study and encouragement: 2 Corinthians 7:10–12

SEPTEMBER 26

MATTHEW 1–2

In Jesus, God has fulfilled the greatest promise of all:
his promise that a Messiah was coming.

The book of Matthew provides us with one of the most familiar accounts in the Bible of the birth and infancy of Jesus:

Now after Jesus was born in Bethlehem of Judea in the days of Herod the king, behold, wise men from the east came to Jerusalem, saying, "Where is he who has been born king of the Jews? For we saw his star when it rose and have come to worship him." When Herod the king heard this, he was troubled, and all Jerusalem with him; and assembling all the chief priests and scribes of the people, he inquired of them where the Christ was to be born. They told him, "In Bethlehem of Judea, for so it is written by the prophet:

'And you, O Bethlehem, in the land of Judah,
    are by no means least among the rulers of Judah;
for from you shall come a ruler
    who will shepherd my people Israel.'" (Matt. 2:1–6)

Don't let the familiarity of this account cause you to rush over its hope-giving glory. When Herod went to Old Testament scholars to inquire where the promised Messiah was to be born, they had no problem answering. They immediately quoted Micah 5:2. Now, pause and think about this for a moment. It's not just that the Messiah's birth was promised in a general, nonspecific way. The promise of God, made through the prophet Micah many generations before, was specific—down to the exact town in which he would be born. The King of kings wouldn't have a regal birth in a royal palace in Jerusalem, with an adoring court at his cradle. No, the hope of the world would be born in the town of Bethlehem to a mother and father who were far from the royalty of that day.

Every detail of Jesus's birth was part of God's plan before the foundations of the earth were set in place. So the promises and prophecies of his birth were detailed and specific. God is not like a fortune teller, delivering a safe, generic prediction. No, these promises were made by the Lord of heaven and earth, who rules everything, everywhere, all of the time. You see, the promises of God are only as good as the extent of his sovereignty, because he can guarantee the delivery of his promises only in situations over which he has rule. Because he rules everything, everywhere, all of the time, however, his promises are specific and rock-solid.

The specificity of God's promise about where the Messiah would be born is a picture of how infinitely confident God is in his own ability to do whatever he has said he will do, wherever he said he will do it, and whenever he knows the time is right. You can bank on and build your life upon the promises of God. He has the power, willingness, and authority to do everything he has promised to do. It is so good to know today that you can absolutely trust that he will do what he has said he will do.

For further study and encouragement: Micah 5:1–6

SEPTEMBER 27

Jesus is the eternal Son of the Father who came
to give his life as a ransom for many.

I remember the first time we visited Northern Ireland. As we drove on those ribbon roads, I was in awe of the beauty all around me. There really were forty shades of green. White sheep made it look as though God had painted polka dots on the ground. White limestone cliffs dropped down to the sea. The rain seemed to enhance, rather than detract from, the created glories we were trying our best to take in. I thought, "I don't care if it's raining. Sometimes you need to stop, pause your journey for a moment, and take in the beauty." The north coast of Ireland displays a bit of God's glory for his creatures to relish.

The beginning of Matthew presents us with a majestic one-time moment in history that you shouldn't run past in your desire to complete your daily Bible reading. God has recorded and preserved it for you because he wants it to leave you in gratitude and awe. And that awe is meant to capture your heart with such force that it changes the way you think about who you are and how you live your life. This scene, the baptism of Jesus, is in the Bible because God loves you:

> Then Jesus came from Galilee to the Jordan to John, to be baptized by him. John would have prevented him, saying, "I need to be baptized by you, and do you come to me?" But Jesus answered him, "Let it be so now, for thus it is fitting for us to fulfill all righteousness." Then he consented. And when Jesus was baptized, immediately he went up from the water, and behold, the heavens were opened to him, and he saw the Spirit of God descending like a dove and coming to rest on him; and behold, a voice from heaven said, "This is my beloved Son, with whom I am well pleased." (Matt. 3:13–17)

Pay careful attention to the tenderhearted and loving beauty of the voice from heaven: "This is my beloved Son, with whom I am well pleased." With these words you are invited to witness the eternal love relationship between the Father and the Son. Who is Jesus? He is not just a man from Bethlehem; he is the loved and pleasing Son of the Father. But there is something else here. Why would Jesus need to submit to the baptism of repentance? He had no sin. But here Jesus nevertheless humbly and willingly identified with those for whom he had come to suffer and die. In the beginning of his life he identified with them, and at the end of his earthly life he took their sin on his shoulders. Here is your Jesus. He is the Son of the Father and the Lamb of sacrifice. He's the grace of God in the flesh.

For further study and encouragement: John 3:1–21

SEPTEMBER 28

MATTHEW 5–7

*It is vital to understand that the members of your body
will always go where your heart has already gone.*

One particular word in the Bible is so central, so important, and so essential to understanding human nature and the redeeming work of God that it is nearly impossible to understand the central themes of the Bible if you don't understand this word: *heart*. Almost every biblical writer uses this word, and it appears on the pages of your Bible hundreds of times. This word defines why people do the things they do and how change in a person actually takes place. Understanding the word *heart* will open the door to understanding what is wrong with you and what Jesus came to do to fix it.

At some point, everyone asks three questions. Parents ask them. Husbands and wives ask them. Pastors, politicians, and educators ask them. These are the questions of the average person on the street:

1. Why do people do the things they do?
2. How does change take place in a person?
3. How can I be an instrument of change in another person?

If you answer these foundational life questions without talking about the heart, then your answer will never be right.

In Jesus's great Sermon on the Mount, he uses the topic of adultery to teach us the importance and centrality of the heart: "You have heard that it was said, 'You shall not commit adultery.' But I say to you that everyone who looks at a woman with lustful intent has already committed adultery with her in his heart" (Matt. 5:27–28). Jesus alerts us to the fact that adultery is first a sin of the heart before it's ever a sin of the physical members of your body. Why is this true? Because the summary definition of the heart in the Bible is that, as the seat of your thoughts, emotions, desires, and will, the heart is the causal core of your personhood. This means that your body will always go where your heart has already gone. Physical freedom from adultery comes ultimately not from putting moral fences around your behavior, but by putting moral fences around your heart.

People do what they do because of what is in their hearts. Change always goes through the pathway of the heart. Being a tool of change in God's hands always includes addressing heart issues.

So, if my problem is my heart, then it is right to say that my biggest problem in life is *me*. And, since I can't run from my heart and have no independent ability to transform my heart, I need to be rescued. The gospel of the Lord Jesus Christ is the story of how God works through his Son to rescue us from ourselves.

Salvation in Christ Jesus is about the enlivening, recapturing, illumining, transforming, and empowering of our hearts. Lasting heart change happens only through the means of divine grace, and that grace is ours in the person and work of Jesus.

For further study and encouragement: Ezekiel 36:22–32

———

SEPTEMBER 29

MATTHEW 8–10

*It is spiritually dangerous to be more concerned about
the sin of others than you are about your own.*

It happens to husbands and wives. It happens to parents. It happens to adult children. It happens to ministry staffs. It happens to neighbors. It happens in friendships. It happens in the workplace. It happens in every situation where we live and work with others. We focus more on the sin of others than on our own sin. This spiritually dangerous habit is a function of self-righteousness that enables us to argue within ourselves that our sin is not so sinful after all.

Apart from God, no one is more influential in our lives than we are, because no one talks to us more than we do. We are in a constant conversation with ourselves, and what we say to ourselves about ourselves forms how we live and understand the nature of our need for God's grace. Near the end of the Sermon on the Mount, Jesus addresses this, pointedly and graphically:

Judge not, that you be not judged. For with the judgment you pronounce you will be judged, and with the measure you use it will be measured to you. Why do you see the speck that is in your brother's eye, but do not notice the log that is in your own eye? Or how can you say to your brother, "Let me take the speck out of your eye," when there is the log in your own eye? You hypocrite, first take the log out of your own eye, and then you will see clearly to take the speck out of your brother's eye. (Matt. 7:1–5)

Whenever you minimize your own sin, you deny your need for the forgiving, restoring, transforming, and empowering grace of your Savior. The deceit here is that focusing on another's sin makes you feel morally superior and righteous, when in fact you are tolerating glaring and obvious sin in your life. Husbands do this when they focus on the little failures of their wives and not on the enormous anger they have harbored over the years. Friends do this when they focus on the small failures of a friend and not their own long-term patterns of gossip. Parents do this when they obsess over their children's failures and not on their own unkind and unloving patterns of dealing with them.

It is never healthy to be more watchful for the sin of others than you are for your own. The fruit of this is a self-righteous denial of your need for the gospel of God's redeeming grace. We must all remember that Jesus came to rescue us not from our neighbor, but from ourselves.

For further study and encouragement: 2 Samuel 12:1–15

SEPTEMBER 30

MATTHEW 11–12

Are you ever offended by your Lord, or by what
he has called you to stand for or do?

The gospel of Jesus Christ and his moral calling to his children are offensive to the surrounding culture. What the Bible says is right or wrong, true or false, and wise or foolish offends people. The declaration that God exists and is the ruler of everything offends people. Speaking of God as the Creator and owner of all that exists is considered absurd. God's plan for parents, husbands and wives, government, and human sexuality is largely rejected by the culture we live in. The question is, Do your Lord and what he calls you to stand for ever offend you? Do you find it hard or embarrassing to declare your allegiance to him and his moral call? Would you rather please the crowd than your Savior? Do you weaken your moral allegiance to him in order to gain human acceptance? Are you willing to be misunderstood and rejected for his sake?

Consider the following significant moment in Matthew 11:

> When Jesus had finished instructing his twelve disciples, he went on from there to teach and preach in their cities.
>
> Now when John heard in prison about the deeds of the Christ, he sent word by his disciples and said to him, "Are you the one who is to come, or shall we look for another?" And Jesus answered them, "Go and tell John what you hear and see: the blind receive their sight and the lame walk, lepers are cleansed and the deaf hear, and the dead are raised up, and the poor have good news preached to them. And blessed is the one who is not offended by me." (Matt. 11:1–6)

Let me set the scene. As Jesus was going about teaching and preaching, John the Baptist had been thrown in prison. John was confused by this. This was not how he thought the coming of the Messiah would play out. As John the Baptist evidently understood the prophecies of the Messiah, his ministry of preparation would result in blessing, not rejection and imprisonment. So, he said to his disciples, "You better make sure that this guy is the real deal." Jesus's response was, "You know that everything I have done is a direct fulfillment of the prophecies that were made of the coming Messiah." Everything Jesus pointed to in his ministry was a direct fulfillment of the prophecies made by Isaiah. Then he said, speaking to John, "You are blessed if you are not offended by me."

Your life with your Lord may not be the life of comfortable blessing that you thought it would be. You may not have anticipated the mockery you would get at work because of your moral stance. You may not have expected that you'd lose your university job because of your stand on sexuality and gender. You may be tempted to question your Lord. Are you offended by your Savior and his call? There is rescuing and empowering grace for this struggle, and blessing to those who are not offended.

For further study and encouragement: 1 Corinthians 1:18–31

OCTOBER 1

By grace God gives sight to our blind eyes, so that we may
see him and the rescuing wisdom of his truth.

We often take the gift of sight for granted. Without this gift our world is dark and the visual glories that God created are closed off to us. You might recall that Luella and I worked at a school for the blind while I was in seminary. Despite all their amazing skills, the boys we worked with had to navigate life with a huge disability. Imagine never seeing the blooms of spring, the stunning multihued glory of a sunset, the gargantuan size of an elephant, the colorful feathers of a parrot, or a full moon guarding the night. Our boys explained to us that being blind is not like closing your eyes, because, when your eyes are closed, you see darkness. No, they told us that being blind is like trying to look out of the back of your head; you see nothing.

For all the beauty of physical sightedness and the sadness of blindness, there is another vision system that is even more important. Your most essential vision system involves the eyes of your heart. When the eyes of your heart are blind, you don't see the most important things in all of life, and, because you don't, you don't live the way you were created to live. Spiritual blindness is one of the horrible effects of sin. Sin blinds us from seeing God and the wisdom of his truth. Because of the entrance of sin into the world and its blinding power, it is only by grace that we are given spiritual eyes to see and ears to hear.

After explaining to his disciples why he speaks in parables, Jesus says, "Blessed are your eyes, for they see, and your ears, for they hear. For truly, I say to you, many prophets and righteous people longed to see what you see, and did not see it, and to hear what you hear, and did not hear it" (Matt. 13:16–17). He reminds them that they are recipients of the blessing of grace that has opened the eyes and ears of their hearts to see and hear God's truth clearly. Jesus also tells his disciples that grace has empowered them to see and to hear what God's people longed for generations to see and hear, but did not.

If you get up tomorrow morning and are blessed to see the morning sun, may it remind you of the spiritual sight and hearing that you have been gifted by grace. May we never forget the magnitude of the gift we have been given. Every day we live, work, and play among people who are tragically blind and do not know it. But we have been touched by Jesus's healing hands, and we can see and hear. We continue to pray that we might see and hear ever more clearly, so that we might follow our Lord even more closely.

For further study and encouragement: Ephesians 1:15–23

OCTOBER 2

*The transfiguration leaves us with no doubt that Jesus is the
promised Messiah, the one who came with salvation in his hands.*

Matthew invites us into one of the most magnificent scenes in all of the Bible,
the transfiguration of Jesus:

> After six days Jesus took with him Peter and James, and John his brother,
> and led them up a high mountain by themselves. And he was transfigured
> before them, and his face shone like the sun, and his clothes became white
> as light. And behold, there appeared to them Moses and Elijah, talking with
> him. And Peter said to Jesus, "Lord, it is good that we are here. If you wish,
> I will make three tents here, one for you and one for Moses and one for
> Elijah." He was still speaking when, behold, a bright cloud overshadowed
> them, and a voice from the cloud said, "This is my beloved Son, with whom
> I am well pleased; listen to him." When the disciples heard this, they fell on
> their faces and were terrified. But Jesus came and touched them, saying,
> "Rise, and have no fear." And when they lifted up their eyes, they saw no
> one but Jesus only. (Matt. 17:1–8)

For a moment, the eternal divine glory of Jesus is revealed to Peter, James, and
John. Remember, Jesus is fully God and fully man. In this moment, God silences
any doubt these disciples might have as to whether this man born in Bethlehem is, in fact, the promised Son of God. Shining like the sun and clothed in
light, Jesus's deity is on display. This magnificent heart- and life-changing scene
should bring us to our knees in awe, adoration, and worship.

But there is more. On one side of Jesus, Moses appears, and, on the other side
of Jesus, Elijah appears. Why? What do these two Old Testament characters tell
us about Jesus? Moses represents the Old Testament Law, and Elijah represents
the Old Testament Prophets. With their appearance, Jesus is revealed as the
final fulfillment of the requirements of the Law and the one whose person and
work fulfills the prophecies and promises of the Prophets. Jesus really is the
promised Son of God and the promised Son of Man. The biblical narrative had
been marching to the moment when he would come and do for his own what
they could not do for themselves: he would reconcile them to God. And then,
as though this moment of revelation were not glorious enough, God the Father
speaks of his love for his Son (as he did at Jesus's baptism), reminding Peter,
James, and John that they would do well to listen to him.

Upon hearing the voice of God from the cloud, the disciples fall down terrified. Jesus touches them, calming their fear. They look around, and it is only Jesus that they see.

This scene has been preserved for us because God loves us. He knows that we are often troubled by doubt and fear, and he wants us to rest assured that Jesus is worthy of our trust. He is God in the flesh, the one who satisfies God's requirements on our behalf, and the one through whom God's promises are delivered.

For further study and encouragement: 1 Corinthians 15:1–5

OCTOBER 3

MATTHEW 18–19

We should be thankful every day of our lives for the preserving power of God's grace.

What keeps your relationship with God secure? Is it the power of your independent spiritual strength? The breadth of your spiritual wisdom? Perhaps you can rely on the consistency of your righteousness or the gospel-centeredness of your church? Is it the degree of your biblical literacy and theological knowledge? Your daily devotional discipline? Many of these things are good tools in God's hands, but we are kept in a committed, obedient, and worshipful relationship with God by one thing: the keeping power of his grace. The one who sought us, called us, justified us, reconciled us, and now works to sanctify us works within us and outside of us to keep us in his flock forever. We are his now and forever only by the power and protection of his redeeming grace.

Jesus illustrates the nature and activity of his keeping grace:

See that you do not despise one of these little ones. For I tell you that in heaven their angels always see the face of my Father who is in heaven. What do you think? If a man has a hundred sheep, and one of them has gone astray, does he not leave the ninety-nine on the mountains and go in search of the one that went astray? And if he finds it, truly, I say to you, he rejoices over it more than over the ninety-nine that never went astray. So it is not the will of my Father who is in heaven that one of these little ones should perish. (Matt. 18:10–14)

Jesus rebukes his disciples, who see children as a bother and an interruption. Jesus reminds his disciples of his love for these little ones and how much he values them by telling them this parable. One sheep, out of a flock of one hundred, has wandered away. How horrific would it be for that shepherd to say to himself, "Oh well, who cares? I have ninety-nine more." We all know what a good shepherd will do. He will leave the sheep who are safely in his flock and go look for and bring back that one lost sheep. Jesus reminds his disciples that the Father in heaven is unwilling for any of his little ones to perish. We should look at our children with the eyes of Jesus.

It is clear that Jesus's lost-sheep illustration is about more than just valuing children. If you are one of the sheep in God's flock, you have been chosen to be there by his grace. And Jesus, the ultimate good shepherd, is unwilling to let you wander away from him. Jesus works by grace to seek, find, and restore his lost sheep, and that is very good news. Though our strength wanes and our hearts wander, he will keep us to the end.

For further study and encouragement: Psalm 121:1–8

———

OCTOBER 4

MATTHEW 20–21

Jesus, the King of kings who came not to be served but to serve and give his life as a ransom for many, shows us what his kingdom is like.

When we look at politics, entertainment, sports, or industry, it is clear that our culture is obsessed with greatness. The people who are our heroes have lots of power, stacks of money, piles of achievements, tons of human acclaim, warehouses of possessions, multiple houses, and fleets of luxury vehicles. We love to watch videos that take us into their homes or let us see their amazing cars. We view their yachts and mansions with a little bit of longing in our hearts. We like feats of power, and we look up to people who take control. Our heroes are kingdom builders who have accomplished and acquired much, and who have crowds of people around them to serve their purposes. We often watch the coronation of another business leader, entertainment star, sports champion, or national king and silently think, "If only."

But the King of kings is unlike any earthly king. The Lord Creator and sovereign of the universe did not invade the earth he created so that he could set up an earthly kingdom and be served. No, his coming, his life, and his death displayed ultimate humble, self-sacrificing service. What was Jesus's experience on earth? An inauspicious birth and poverty of life. Mocking and rejection. An unjust and violent arrest and trial. Horrific suffering on the cross. Jesus poured out his life—not for his own power and earthly fame, but for the eternal salvation of all who put their trust in him. If this is the way of the King, then why would we think that the call and culture of his kingdom would be any different?

In Matthew 20 we find the mother of the sons of Zebedee asking Jesus to secure a special place of honor for her sons in his kingdom. Here is Jesus's response:

> "You do not know what you are asking. Are you able to drink the cup that I am to drink?" They said to him, "We are able." He said to them, "You will drink my cup, but to sit at my right hand and at my left is not mine to grant, but it is for those for whom it has been prepared by my Father." And when the ten heard it, they were indignant at the two brothers. But Jesus called them to him and said, "You know that the rulers of the Gentiles lord it over them, and their great ones exercise authority over them. It shall not be so among you. But whoever would be great among you must be your servant, and whoever would be first among you must be your slave, even as the Son of Man came not to be served but to serve, and to give his life as a ransom for many." (Matt. 20:22–28)

It is vital to understand that God's kingdom is an upside-down kingdom, where the path to greatness is via humble service. Because of the greatness of Jesus's service, we have hope in this life and the one to come.

For further study and encouragement: Philippians 2:1–8

———

OCTOBER 5

MATTHEW 22–23

God is not satisfied with behavioral reformations alone; he wants to own and rule our hearts.

Several years ago I lost about fifty pounds. I didn't follow some miracle diet that I had found on the internet. I didn't starve myself. The reason so many people yo-yo back and forth between weight gain and weight loss is that they do not address the deeper cause of their weight gain. What I mean is that they address *behavior* only and not the *heart*. So they do well for a while, but eventually they revert to their old bad habits. By God's grace, I became deeply convicted that my excess weight was not just a matter of bad behavior; it was about issues of my heart. I had to confess to gluttony. I enjoyed the pleasures of food more than pleasing my Lord, and I was carrying around with me the physical evidence of my idolatry. My confession was followed by crying out for God's rescuing and empowering grace, and the commitment to change my whole relationship to food. It was very hard, as sacrifice always is, but new, God-honoring habits replaced old sinful habits, and I have maintained my weight since.

Now, I am not a hero, but a sinner in need of God's powerful grace. I have learned that living in the power of that grace begins with confessing that you need it. This is what the New Testament Pharisees never seemed to do. Matthew records Jesus's condemnation of the false spirituality of the Pharisees. Jesus condemns them for their public pride, self-righteousness, legalism, and complete lack of compassionate love. Each of Jesus's condemnations of a particular part of their religiosity begins with the word *woe*. That word signals that you are about to hear a condemnation rather than a commendation. There are seven woes, and the sixth one is a metaphoric way of saying that the Pharisees never deal with their heart issues: "Woe to you, scribes and Pharisees, hypocrites! For you clean the outside of the cup and the plate, but inside they are full of greed and self-indulgence. You blind Pharisee! First clean the inside of the cup and the plate, that the outside also may be clean" (Matt. 23:25–26).

In Jesus's illustration, the outside of the cup is behavior and the inside of the cup is the heart. The Pharisees' religion was all about their "right" behavior, mostly done in public for all to see. But, despite their outward actions, the inside of the cup was still dirty; that is, it was filled with idolatrous greed and self-indulgence. This is not true biblical religion. Then Jesus says something that should get our attention: "First clean the inside of the cup and plate, that the outside also may be clean." You can't do this with your dishes at home, but that is exactly what happens when you deal with sins of the heart. Your behavior will go wherever your heart has already gone. Behavioral reformation without heart transformation never works. As the control center of your personhood, the heart is the target of God's redeeming grace. Today, confess your need for grace that transforms the heart.

For further study and encouragement: Psalm 51:1–12

OCTOBER 6

MATTHEW 24–25

*In a world where few things are permanent, the
word of the Lord endures forever.*

I bought Luella flowers for Easter. We love fresh flowers, and I buy them for her often, but this bouquet was different. At first glance, it looked like any other bouquet, but it was not. These flowers were real, but they lasted for a year. I don't know what the process was, but these delicate flowers defied the laws of decay. You didn't need to water them, but they stayed fresh for months. This is unusual for us, because we are used to the impermanence of fresh flowers. We're used to stretching the life of a bouquet by taking out the dead blossoms and rearranging the rest, watching the bouquet get smaller until there are no live blossoms left.

Usually, flowers are a picture of what happens to just about everything in our lives. We are used to the impermanence of life. Things that seemed as though they would last forever end up wilting and dying. In fact, it is true that everything in this physical world is in the process of dying. In the face of all the impermanence of life, where do we look for stability? Where can we find security, something in life that will not pass away? Our marriage, job, children, friendships, or career can't guarantee that foundational stability. Everyone looks for something permanent to build a life on, but most things fail us in the end.

In Matthew 24, Jesus lays out the signs of the end of the age. He reminds his followers that, although the world might seem permanent, everything in it will one day pass away. Even though we watch things fade and die all around us, the thought that everything will someday be completely gone is counterintuitive to most of us. We often live as though this life will last forever. Jesus warns his followers of the coming end. And in the middle of a list of signs of the end, Jesus says, "Heaven and earth will pass away, but my words will not pass away" (Matt. 24:35). With these words, Jesus answers the question, "What can I build my life on that will never pass away?" Without a shade of doubt, Jesus declares the divine power, authority, and permanence of his words. They will never fail you, they will never prove to be untrue, they will never be out of place, they will never grow old, and they will never pass away. A thousand years into eternity, the words of the Lord will still stand.

Many of us have lost precious things. Many of us have suffered the passing of beloved people. Many of us have faced the disappointment of losing things that we thought would last. Many of us have faced the death of our dreams or the demise of things we had hoped in. But there is a place of rest for your soul and a sure foundation upon which you can build: the word of the Lord. His words last forever.

For further study and encouragement: Isaiah 55:6–11

OCTOBER 7

MATTHEW 26

Jesus is the fulfillment of generations of Passover hope, because he is the Passover Lamb.

Exodus 12 records God's plans for the first Passover:

> It is the LORD's Passover. For I will pass through the land of Egypt that night, and I will strike all the firstborn in the land of Egypt, both man and beast; and on all the gods of Egypt I will execute judgments: I am the LORD. The blood shall be a sign for you, on the houses where you are. And when I see the blood, I will pass over you, and no plague will befall you to destroy you, when I strike the land of Egypt. (Ex. 12:11–13)

God was in the process of delivering his people from slavery in Egypt. He was unleashing his almighty power to redeem his people from the trauma they had suffered over four hundred years. His final act of deliverance would be to strike dead the firstborn of every house in Egypt—except those of Israelites who painted blood on the doorposts. In a sign of redeeming grace, God would pass over those houses, and the children of Israel would live and be delivered out of slavery.

When the disciples gather with Jesus to observe the Passover, they have no expectation that anything will be different from how the Jewish people have celebrated the feast for generations. But that night everything they understand about the Passover changes:

> Now as they were eating, Jesus took bread, and after blessing it broke it and gave it to the disciples, and said, "Take, eat; this is my body." And he took a cup, and when he had given thanks he gave it to them, saying, "Drink of it, all of you, for this is my blood of the covenant, which is poured out

for many for the forgiveness of sins. I tell you I will not drink again of this fruit of the vine until that day when I drink it new with you in my Father's kingdom." (Matt. 26:26–29)

With these words, Jesus tells his disciples that the very first Passover and every Passover since had pointed to him. He wants them to know that there is a deeper form of slavery than the physical slavery that their ancestors had experienced. This slavery is infinitely more tragic and causes infinitely more suffering than the Egyptian slavery. And this slavery is universal; no one escapes it. This deeper slavery is the slavery of every heart of every human being to sin. Jesus wants his disciples to know that every lamb of sacrifice was pointing to him. Jesus is saying, "I am the final Lamb of sacrifice, and by my death I will break the power of sin and purchase forgiveness for all who trust in me."

The bad news all of us have to face is that sin captures us all. It always enslaves and leads to death. The good news is that Jesus is the Passover Lamb who has purchased our freedom and our forgiveness. We do well to put our trust in him.

For further study and encouragement: Exodus 12:1–28

———

OCTOBER 8

MATTHEW 27–28

On our behalf, Jesus took every ounce of the Father's rejection.

Matthew 27 records a terrible and dark moment of suffering for Jesus as he hung on the cross:

Now from the sixth hour there was darkness over all the land until the ninth hour. And about the ninth hour Jesus cried out with a loud voice, saying, "Eli, Eli, lema sabachthani?" that is, "My God, my God, why have you forsaken me?" And some of the bystanders, hearing it, said, "This man is calling Elijah." And one of them at once ran and took a sponge, filled it with sour wine, and put it on a reed and gave it to him to drink. But the others said, "Wait, let us see whether Elijah will come to save him." And Jesus cried out again with a loud voice and yielded up his spirit. (Matt. 27:45–50)

The physical darkness that enveloped the earth for three hours signified how dark that time on the cross truly was. Yes, the scourging of Jesus was horrible, and it is impossible to imagine the pain he experienced when they drove nails through his hands and then hoisted him onto the cross like a cut of beef. None of that physical pain, however, came close to the trauma Jesus went through when he cried, "Eli, Eli, lema sabachthani?" But that horribly dark and painful moment was at the same time a moment of glorious, undeserved grace.

Jesus lived a perfect life as our substitute. In our place, he faced all of the temptations that we face, yet without sin. Then he hung on the cross as our substitute, carrying the heavy load of our sin. He hung there, willingly taking the punishment that we deserved. But as he experienced our rejection, he cried out in emotional and spiritual agony. It seems unthinkable that the Father would ever separate himself from the Son. And the Trinity cannot be separated. But in these words, the man Jesus testified to the fact that, for our redemption, he was separated from the Father: "My God, my God, why have you forsaken me?"

Jesus came to earth knowing his job description. He knew that he was coming as the sacrificial Lamb. He knew there would be a decisive redemptive moment when the Father would not exercise his almighty power to come to his rescue. As a man Jesus would hang between heaven and earth, utterly forsaken and alone, rejected not just by his fellow man, but by his heavenly Father. This was necessary so that what was impossible for us to accomplish on our own would be God's gift to us: sin defeated, forgiveness granted, and reconciliation accomplished.

Jesus's humanity endured the Father's rejection so that the children of his grace never would. He was willing to be left utterly alone, so that we would never be alone. He endured the full extent of the Father's anger, so that his anger would never fall on us again. Celebrate today that, as a child of God, you will never be forsaken. Hanging between heaven and earth, Jesus settled that once and for all. His redeeming love for you will never be broken.

For further study and encouragement: 2 Corinthians 5:16–21

OCTOBER 9

MARK 1–3

Jesus faced and defeated temptation on our behalf, so that
when we face temptation, we can defeat it too.

It is important to understand that the life of Jesus before he went to the cross was as necessary as what he did on the cross. Everything that Jesus did in his earthly life, he did as our substitute. It was essential that he, on our behalf, live a perfectly righteous life all of the time and in every way. It was God's plan that Jesus's righteousness would become our righteousness, so that we could stand unafraid before a holy God. It was also essential that Jesus, the second Adam, face temptation like the first Adam faced—yet, unlike Adam, he did not fail, but resisted temptation and defeated Satan. Jesus fought the battle with temptation and won the victory for us, and so, when we face temptation, we are able to defeat it too. The saving work of Jesus was done not just on the cross, but in his life as he lived as our substitute.

The book of Mark is hard-hitting and fast-paced. Mark's mission is to demonstrate that Jesus of Nazareth is, in fact, the promised Messiah, the Son of God. Mark begins his Gospel with a quick introduction to the substitutionary mission of Jesus. He begins with three essential introductory vignettes: *preparation* (John the Baptist prepares the way for Jesus), *identification* (Jesus identifies with sinners in his baptism), and *temptation* (Jesus defeats Satan in the desert). Each of these things is necessary before Jesus begins his public ministry, but here I want to focus on his temptation: "The Spirit immediately drove him out into the wilderness. And he was in the wilderness forty days, being tempted by Satan. And he was with the wild animals, and the angels were ministering to him" (Mark 1:12–13).

Mark's account of the temptation of Jesus is brief, but the words are important. First, it is vital to notice that it is the Spirit who drives Jesus into the wilderness to be tempted. This isn't an accident. Jesus isn't blindsided. He is driven into the wilderness, because part of God's redeeming plan is for Jesus to engage in a face-to-face battle with Satan and win. The Spirit leads Jesus into this battle for us. The victory is won with us in mind. The timing of this battle is also important. It is accomplished before Jesus begins his public ministry, so that he will enter that ministry having already defeated the enemy.

Notice also that this is not a brief encounter with Satan. No, it is an arduous forty-day battle. God does not abandon Jesus in the wilderness but sends angels to minister to him. All of this is done for us as the children of God. We have the power to resist the devil because the victory of Jesus is our victory, and, because it is, we face an already-defeated foe. Just as God doesn't abandon Jesus, so he won't abandon us, but will deliver the protecting grace we need in times of temptation.

For further study and encouragement: Hebrews 4:14–16

———

OCTOBER 10

MARK 4–5

God's word reveals to us the horrible nature of evil. God includes such moments because he knows evil doesn't always appear to be evil to us.

We have a problem. Evil doesn't always look evil to us. Sin is deceitful. Sometimes, what is evil in God's eyes actually looks good to us. It is scary to think about, but we have the capacity to look at what God says is ugly and see beauty. We can look at what is destructive and see something that will satisfy. For instance, a man goes to the store to pick up an item for his wife, and he lusts after a woman in the produce department. In that moment he doesn't see the horrible selfishness and destructiveness of lust; no, he sees beauty. A woman cheats on her taxes. At that moment she isn't filled with a sense of the ugliness of her thievery, but rather is filled with the excitement of what she can do with her ill-gotten gain. A man eating a third piece of chocolate cake is thinking not about the idolatry of his gluttony, but about the luxury of the taste of chocolate. We are in grave moral danger when evil doesn't look evil to us.

In Mark 5, Jesus heals a man with a demon. This account is surely in Mark's Gospel to support his declaration that Jesus of Nazareth is the Son of God. No one but the Messiah could stand before the legions of demons that possessed and controlled this particular man and command them to depart. In this moment Jesus acts with the unparalleled power of the Almighty. But there is something more that we should notice in Mark's account of this healing:

They came to the other side of the sea, to the country of the Gerasenes. And when Jesus had stepped out of the boat, immediately there met him out of the tombs a man with an unclean spirit. He lived among the tombs. And no one could bind him anymore, not even with a chain, for he had often been bound with shackles and chains, but he wrenched the chains apart, and he broke the shackles in pieces. No one had the strength to subdue him.

Night and day among the tombs and on the mountains he was always crying out and cutting himself with stones. (Mark 5:1–5)

Why does Mark give us such graphic details about the condition of this man? Why doesn't he just say that the man is possessed by many demons and then focus on the miracle of Jesus's delivering him? I am convinced that one reason the detailed description of this man's horrible condition is in the Gospel of Mark is because God loves us. He knows that evil doesn't always look evil to us, so he shows us what it looks like when evil takes complete control of a person. No one would ever read this description and think that evil produces anything good. Your Lord is working here to open your eyes, so you may hate what he hates and understand why he sent his Son to defeat evil for your sake.

For further study and encouragement: Jeremiah 17:5–10

———

OCTOBER 11

MARK 6–7

There is a significant difference between amazement and faith. You can be amazed by God while not actually putting your faith in him.

You should read your Bible with an inquisitive mind. You should ask questions of each passage. Why are these details here? Why did God respond in that way? Why has this passage been preserved for me? What is God telling me about himself and how he works? What does this passage tell me about the nature of sin? How do these words reveal Jesus and his grace? What does it look like to live in light of what is recorded here? Let's ask those questions of Mark 6:

Immediately [Jesus] made his disciples get into the boat and go before him to the other side, to Bethsaida, while he dismissed the crowd. And after he had taken leave of them, he went up on the mountain to pray. And when evening came, the boat was out on the sea, and he was alone on the land. And he saw that they were making headway painfully, for the wind was against them. And about the fourth watch of the night he came to them, walking on the sea. He meant to pass by them, but when they saw him walking on the sea they thought it was a ghost, and cried out, for they all saw him and were terrified. But immediately he spoke to them and said, "Take heart; it is I. Do not be afraid." And he got into the boat with them, and the wind ceased. And they were utterly astounded, for they did not understand about the loaves, but their hearts were hardened. (Mark 6:45–52)

In this passage, Jesus sets up a situation to reveal his messianic glory to his disciples. We can observe much from these verses, but I want to focus on one particular point. Jesus demonstrates that he is Lord Creator, able to do anything with his creation that he wishes—including walking on water. The disciples' response is utter amazement. Now, this is not necessarily a complimentary remark about the disciples. We know this because Mark tells us that the disciples didn't fully understand the identity of Jesus that was revealed by the feeding of the five thousand, and their hearts were hardened. Mark is pointing out that there is a significant difference between amazement and faith. You can be amazed by the biblical story and biblical doctrine, yet not live by faith. You can be amazed by the worship and preaching of your church, yet not live by faith. You can be amazed by the loving community of your small group, yet not live by faith.

Though walking on water was a glorious messianic sign, there was no mature faith in the boat to receive it. As Mark remarks, their hearts were hardened. May God grant us the grace not just to be amazed by him but, by faith, to trust him in a way that gives us rest, even when the storms come.

For further study and encouragement: John 20:24–31

OCTOBER 12

MARK 8–9

*On this side of eternity, nothing is more important
than saying yes to God and no to sin.*

Your marriage is shaped by your commitment to say no. Your parenting is shaped by your willingness to say no. Your friendships are shaped by how often you say no. Your friendships and fellowship in the body of Christ are determined by your discipline in saying no. I am not talking about saying no to your spouse, your kids, or your friends, but rather about how spiritually important it is to say no to yourself. It is important to understand that no one is in greater danger of you than you are, because of the sin that still resides inside of you. That sin makes you susceptible to the myriad temptations that greet you every day. When faced with all of temptation's deception, seduction, and allure, it is important that you say no to the sinful desires that draw you in and make you want to say yes.

You need to understand two things when you are facing temptation. First, in that moment no one can say no for you. Only by God's empowering grace can you turn from temptation's allure and run in the other direction, and no one else can do that for you. Second, you will say no only when you see sin as deeply evil and destructive. Because he knew all of us would struggle with sin and temptation until we were on the other side, God ordained that the following passage be recorded and preserved:

> If your hand causes you to sin, cut it off. It is better for you to enter life crippled than with two hands to go to hell, to the unquenchable fire. And if your foot causes you to sin, cut it off. It is better for you to enter life lame than with two feet to be thrown into hell. And if your eye causes you to sin, tear it out. It is better for you to enter the kingdom of God with one eye than with two eyes to be thrown into hell, where their worm does not die and the fire is not quenched. (Mark 9:43–48)

Does this passage seem extreme to you? The imagery of lopping off your hand, amputating your foot, and gouging out your eye is here because your Savior understands your struggle with sin and temptation. Your commitment to seek the empowering grace you need in order to say yes to God and no to sin is more valuable than your hand, foot, or eye. Of course, God isn't telling you to mutilate your body as a defense against sin, because that wouldn't work. Sin is a battle of the heart and is won or lost there. Jesus's use of hyperbole reminds us that no part of our body is more valuable than resisting sin and temptation.

Remember, however, that, you never fight this battle of resistance alone or in your own power. By grace, the one who defeated Satan is always with you and always fights for you.

For further study and encouragement: Psalm 32:1–11

OCTOBER 13

*It's impossible to trust Jesus as your Savior when
you seek satisfaction in other saviors.*

My friend was a wealthy and successful man. He had come from nowhere and
had singled-handedly built his empire. He had a nose for the next trend and
would beat others to the investment table. But he couldn't stop acquiring things.
Around his estate was a collection of his latest toys. While he was showing me
his latest purchase, I told him that trying to satisfy his heart with the next new
possession wasn't working; that's why he was compelled to keep getting the next
thing. He told me I was probably right and then walked away.

That day I thought of Mark 10. After Jesus told a rich young man to sell
all he had and give to the poor, the man went away sorrowful. This moment
in Christ's ministry was not about money or even about caring for the poor;
it was about what effectively and functionally ruled that man's heart. Jesus
exposed what his heart loved and worshiped most. This man worshiped a
god—it just wasn't the one true God. Despite all his external religiosity, what
really ruled this man's heart was the love of material things, which is why he
walked away sad.

We more fully understand this encounter and why God preserved it for us
when we understand the disciples' reaction and their question: "And they were
exceedingly astonished, and said to him, 'Then who can be saved?'" (Mark
10:26). The disciples' astonishment and their question reveal that they understood something about this encounter that we sometimes don't understand.
We often think of the rich young man as being in a special class of people who
find it hard to trust Jesus because they are rich. But this is not what the disciples
take away from this encounter. Their "Then who can be saved?" question reveals
that they understand that what Jesus has revealed about the young man's heart
is true also of them.

Every unredeemed sinner attaches his identity, hopes and dreams, and meaning and purpose to something other than God. It might not be money. It might
be power, control, fame, physical health, intellectual gifts, and so on. For a while,
these things satisfy our hearts and make us feel as though we don't need a Savior.
But they always leave us empty.

Then who can be saved? This question reminds us that it is impossible to serve
two masters. Your heart can't be ruled by two things. False gods prevent you
from giving yourself fully to the one true God. Every sinner has a worship problem. Only by the power of Jesus's rescuing grace can anyone seek God, abandon

self-sufficiency, confess sin, and submit everything to God. His grace alone has the power to reclaim and transform our hearts. Celebrate this grace today!

For further study and encouragement: Psalm 63:1–11

———

OCTOBER 14

MARK 12–13

What do you live for? What seems best right now?
What does God say will be best in the end?

We all need to read the Bible with inquisitive minds, asking questions of what we're reading. It is possible to read a passage and *technically* understand the words, but move on without understanding why God thought it best to record and preserve that passage for us. Because all Scripture is profitable, there is a divine intention behind every passage we read. There is no superfluous material anywhere in the Bible, not even the following:

> In [Jesus's] teaching he said, "Beware of the scribes, who like to walk around in long robes and like greetings in the marketplaces and have the best seats in the synagogues and the places of honor at feasts, who devour widows' houses and for a pretense make long prayers. They will receive the greater condemnation." (Mark 12:38–40)

You might not think this indictment of the scribes has anything whatsoever to do with you, but it does.

When Jesus says, "Beware of the scribes," he is not just warning his listeners to be careful because the scribes are up to no good. He is also warning his followers (and us) not to act like the scribes. Jesus finds the religiosity of the scribes deeply offensive, and we should too. In his condemnation of them, Jesus combines three things that should get our attention and cause us to do some self-examination: *religious externalism*, *pride*, and *injustice*. These things often go together. Religious externalism concerns public displays of spirituality that do not come from the heart. True biblical religion is always about the capture and transformation of the heart. Pride concerns drawing attention to yourself. Prideful actions are those that are motivated by the worship of self and seek the worship of others. Pride is the enemy of the work of God in the heart. Injustice is a lack of compassion for or activity on behalf of those who are suffering or disadvantaged.

Here's how these things work together. An externally religious person is proud because his religion is about personal accomplishment and not grace. And, because he thinks he has earned his success, he looks down on people who have less than he has, rather than showing them compassion. Externalism produces pride, and pride is the soil in which injustice grows.

Yes, we should be aware of the lifestyle of the scribes. Their public displays are an attractive form of false godliness. They lack a brokenhearted knowledge of sin, fail to celebrate God's grace, and never give grace where grace is needed.

God will not be satisfied with our daily Bible reading, regular church attendance, or episodic moments of ministry if underneath these things are pride of accomplishment and a cold heart toward those in need. God will not be satisfied with external Christianity if he does not own and rule our hearts. May grace cause us to give ourselves to nothing less than a true Christianity of the heart.

For further study and encouragement: Philippians 3:12–21

———

OCTOBER 15

MARK 14

Sometimes God's children are spiritually asleep.

At the end of Mark 13 we find a brief but important command from Jesus:

> Concerning that day or that hour, no one knows, not even the angels in heaven, nor the Son, but only the Father. Be on guard, keep awake. For you do not know when the time will come. It is like a man going on a journey, when he leaves home and puts his servants in charge, each with his work, and commands the doorkeeper to stay awake. Therefore stay awake—for you do not know when the master of the house will come, in the evening, or at midnight, or when the rooster crows, or in the morning—lest he come suddenly and find you asleep. And what I say to you I say to all: Stay awake. (Mark 13:32–37)

Stay awake is good spiritual counsel. Jesus gives this command as part of his teaching on the end times. He says that no one knows when the end will come. Surprisingly, Jesus says that even he doesn't know when that time will be. Of course, in saying this, he is speaking from the vantage point of his humanity.

The command to stay awake concerns living with eternity in view. People who live with eternity in view know that the present is not all they have, and life is not about the pleasures of the moment. The primary goal of life is not acquiring a big pile of stuff. It's not reaching the greatest heights in your career. It's not convincing people to think that you are great. Life is not about big houses, nice cars, great meals, or awesome vacations. Because this fallen world is not your final destination, this life is about preparation. This is God's agenda between the "already" of our conversion and the "not yet" of our homegoing. Everything God brings into your life is a preparation for what is to come. Staying awake is living with a preparation mentality.

Sadly, I think many of us are spiritually asleep. When you are asleep, you are passive and unaware. If you are casual about church attendance, you are probably living asleep. If you rush through your daily devotions, you might be asleep. If you haven't surrounded yourself with loving gospel community, you could be half-asleep. If you don't desire to understand the doctrines of your faith, you are probably living asleep. If you are not participating in the ministries of your church, you might be asleep. If you find it hard to be honest about your faith with friends, family, or coworkers, you're probably sleeping. If you aren't thankful for the blessings of God's grace every day, you're probably a bit asleep.

Jesus's command is a call to an alert, serious, and active faith, one that causes you to make willing sacrifices of time, energy, and money. If you think you've been asleep, don't wallow in guilt. God welcomes your confession and will meet you with his forgiving and transforming grace.

For further study and encouragement: Romans 13:8–14

———

OCTOBER 16

MARK 15–16

*Even when he was tortured and mocked, Jesus
exercised divine power on our behalf.*

This moment in the final days of Jesus might seem, on the surface, to be a moment of defeat:

> The soldiers led him away inside the palace (that is, the governor's headquarters), and they called together the whole battalion. And they clothed

him in a purple cloak, and twisting together a crown of thorns, they put it on him. And they began to salute him, "Hail, King of the Jews!" And they were striking his head with a reed and spitting on him and kneeling down in homage to him. And when they had mocked him, they stripped him of the purple cloak and put his own clothes on him. And they led him out to crucify him. (Mark 15:16–20)

You might read this and think, Where was Jesus's power? Why didn't he do something? Why did he just stand there and take the abuse? Some looked at this moment and concluded that this couldn't be the Son of God, the promised Messiah. Why didn't Jesus call down an army of angels to deal with these blasphemous torturers? How could he let them mock his divine kingship?

But we know that this was far from a moment of weakness. Jesus was not weakly succumbing to humans who hated him and wanted to harm him. No, in this moment Jesus was committed to his eternal redemptive plan; he knew exactly what he was doing. He refused to be diverted. He did not rise to his own defense. He did not let mockery or physical pain cause him to abandon his substitutionary mission. He did not come to earth for his own pleasure, comfort, or acclaim. He could not give in and save himself, because through his suffering he would deliver salvation to multitudes. Jesus's response to this torture did not mock his identity; it *was* his identity (see Isa. 53).

You and I should see through the apparent weakness and be blown away by Jesus's divine power. Rather than a show of defeat and weakness, what we witness here is a display of redemptive victory and strength. Jesus knew that his suffering was part of the plan that his Father had established before the world began. He knew the glory of grace that his suffering would unleash. He stood there with the worshiping multitudes in mind, the redeemed from all times and from every tongue and nation. He endured the torture and mockery for you and me. What appeared to be a defeat was another step in the success of his great redemptive mission. Jesus's power was on display, and his power is our hope.

Now, by grace, that same power is ours as the children of God. We stand in both his power and his victory. In him we have the power to stand true in the face of mockery and suffering. When we are mocked, we do not have to be afraid or retaliate, but we can do what Jesus did. We can commend ourselves into the care of our heavenly Father, knowing that he will vindicate us in the end.

For further study and encouragement: Philippians 2:1–11

OCTOBER 17

*We sing today—and we will sing for all of
eternity—songs of the grace of Jesus.*

God hardwired us to sing. If you pay attention, you realize that we humans sing all the time. We sing spiritual songs, political songs, love songs, protest songs, happy songs, funeral songs, painful songs, and joyful songs. Little children sing nursery rhymes and elderly men hum age-old tunes. Once our five-year-old granddaughter told us, "I made up a song about kitties." We said, "Let's hear it," and off she went, singing the song she had made up on the fly. Composing and singing songs are quintessentially human. Our songs are expressions of the emotions and values of our hearts. Our songs reveal more about us than we might think.

So, when we read and study Scripture, we should slow down and pay attention to the songs along the way. The one who designed us to sing recorded and preserved songs for us. These songs are meant to focus our hearts, instruct us in the ways of the Lord, motivate our joy, and put words to our worship. One of Scripture's most wonderful songs was composed by Mary. An angel had visited her and announced that she would give birth to the promised Messiah. When Mary visited her cousin Elizabeth, Mary sang this song:

> My soul magnifies the Lord,
> and my spirit rejoices in God my Savior,
> for he has looked on the humble estate of his servant.
> For behold, from now on all generations will call me blessed;
> for he who is mighty has done great things for me,
> and holy is his name.
> And his mercy is for those who fear him
> from generation to generation.
> He has shown strength with his arm;
> he has scattered the proud in the thoughts of their hearts;
> he has brought down the mighty from their thrones
> and exalted those of humble estate;
> he has filled the hungry with good things,
> and the rich he has sent away empty.
> He has helped his servant Israel,
> in remembrance of his mercy,
> as he spoke to our fathers,
> to Abraham and to his offspring forever. (Luke 1:46–55)

Notice Mary's humility. She knows she didn't earn the blessing of giving birth to the Messiah. She is but a humble servant, blessed with the favor of the Lord. Then notice how she speaks of her Lord. He is mighty in authority and strength, and at the same time tenderhearted in mercy. He deals with sin, while meeting the needs of his people. He remembers and has been faithful in keeping his covenant promises. Those promises will find their final fulfillment in the life, death, and resurrection of the little one in Mary's womb. Holy is his name.

Mary's gospel song has been preserved for us so that this joyful and Godward expression of her heart would be the song of our hearts as well.

For further study and encouragement: 2 Samuel 6:12–23

OCTOBER 18

LUKE 2–3

Jesus is humanity's great fault line; every person's eternal fate is set by the rejection or acceptance of him. There is no neutral ground.

When Mary and Joseph took young Jesus to the temple, they didn't know that Simeon, a righteous man, would be waiting there for him. The Holy Spirit had told Simeon that he would not die before he saw the Lord's Christ. Simeon took Jesus in his arms. What an amazing scene. Imagine being chosen by God to hold the young Messiah in your arms! As he held Jesus, Simeon spoke these words:

> Lord, now you are letting your servant depart in peace,
>   according to your word;
> for my eyes have seen your salvation
>   that you have prepared in the presence of all peoples,
> a light for revelation to the Gentiles,
>   and for glory to your people Israel. (Luke 2:29–32)

After Simeon spoke his words of blessing, worship, and prophecy, he turned to Mary and said, "Behold, this child is appointed for the fall and rising of many in Israel, and for a sign that is opposed (and a sword will pierce through your own soul also), so that thoughts from many hearts may be revealed" (Luke 2:34–35). These would have been hard and confusing words for the young mother of the Messiah to hear.

Simeon captured the inescapable truth about the identity, person, and work of Jesus. When you are presented with the truth of Christ's birth, God's declaration of who he is, the testimony of his miracles and ministry, and his own self-testimony, you cannot be neutral about Jesus. Spiritually, you either rise or fall with your response to him. It is not enough to say he was a good prophet and teacher. You either say he is the Messiah Savior and bow before him and cry out for his grace, or you reject him and your need for his grace. You either worship him, or you mock him. You either confess your need for him, or you turn in independence away from him. The great line that divides humanity is not political, economic, social, or ethnic. No, the great fault line is Jesus.

When Simeon told Mary that a sword would pierce her soul, he was, of course, speaking of Calvary, when Mary would watch as a sword pierced the side of her Messiah son. What agony awaited this young mother.

The cross of Jesus either is your hope in this life and the one to come, or it represents the death of a man you do not love and do not need. There is no neutrality in the shadow of the cross.

So, today, what will you do with Jesus? Will you bow in worship and gratitude, or will you take life in your own hands and walk away?

For further study and encouragement: John 1:1–13

—

OCTOBER 19

LUKE 4–5

Because Jesus makes his identity and mission clear, we should not question who he is or what he came to do.

The scene we are about to consider occurred early in Jesus's earthly ministry, right after his forty-day temptation in the wilderness.

> And he came to Nazareth, where he had been brought up. And as was his custom, he went to the synagogue on the Sabbath day, and he stood up to read. And the scroll of the prophet Isaiah was given to him. He unrolled the scroll and found the place where it was written,
>
> > "The Spirit of the Lord is upon me,
> > because he has anointed me

> to proclaim good news to the poor.
> He has sent me to proclaim liberty to the captives
>   and recovering of sight to the blind,
>   to set at liberty those who are oppressed,
> to proclaim the year of the Lord's favor."

> And he rolled up the scroll and gave it back to the attendant and sat down. And the eyes of all in the synagogue were fixed on him. And he began to say to them, "Today this Scripture has been fulfilled in your hearing." And all spoke well of him and marveled at the gracious words that were coming from his mouth. (Luke 4:16–22)

There was nothing remarkable about a man's standing up to read from a scroll in the synagogue. People would have seen scenes like this in the synagogue Sabbath after Sabbath. But what happened next was one of the most significant moments in the life and ministry of Jesus—indeed, in all of redemptive history. The people in the synagogue watched Jesus roll up the scroll, hand it back to the synagogue attendant, and sit down. Then they heard him say shocking and unexpected words that no one there ever thought he or she would hear: "Today this Scripture has been fulfilled in your hearing."

At first the crowd seemed to accept his words, but soon they were filled with questions. Wasn't this Joseph's son? Jesus then compared their doubt of his messiahship to their forefathers' rejection of the prophets Elijah and Elisha. At this point the crowd became angry and plotted to kill Jesus by throwing him off a cliff (4:22–30).

This moment in Jesus's life teaches us that it takes grace to be able to recognize, surrender to, worship, and celebrate the Messiah of grace. Apart from the grace that opens the eyes of our hearts, the story of God's coming in the flesh seems like ridiculous religious nonsense. If you have believed, it's because you have been given the grace to believe. Faith is a precious gift from a compassionate heavenly Father. If faith in him has captured your heart and directed your life, do not boast—unless you are boasting in the grace of his coming, suffering, death, and resurrection.

For further study and encouragement: John 6:25–40

OCTOBER 20

If someone were to ask you what trusting God
looks like, what would you say?

It is important to be clear about the nature of true biblical faith. Multiple texts in the Bible define what true faith in God is. Faith is much more than an intellectual assent to the existence of God. Millions of people say that they believe in God, but in no way, shape, or form does this "belief" shape how they live. In fact, many who say they believe that God exists live in a way that actually mocks his holiness, authority, and grace. The way you live is a better indicator of what you truly believe than whatever religious words you might say. Faith is a radical change of heart that leads to a decisive difference in the way you live your life. If you really do believe in the God of the Bible; if you take his self-declaration to be true; if you believe that what he says about you and what you need is true; if you believe in the necessity and historicity of the work of his Son; and if you believe in the moral call of his commands, then every area of your life will reflect this faith.

Luke records a particular *what-faith-looks-like* moment. Jesus turns to his followers and says, "Love your enemies, do good to those who hate you, bless those who curse you, pray for those who abuse you" (Luke 6:27–28). To those listening then as well as to us, this is radically counterintuitive. We understand loving our friends and family, but loving our enemies—even to be willing to pray for them—is another matter. What would motivate us to live in this way? When faced with mistreatment, what has the power to keep us from responding in kind? Jesus answers these questions:

> If you love those who love you, what benefit is that to you? For even sinners love those who love them. And if you do good to those who do good to you, what benefit is that to you? For even sinners do the same. And if you lend to those from whom you expect to receive, what credit is that to you? Even sinners lend to sinners, to get back the same amount. But love your enemies, and do good, and lend, expecting nothing in return, and your reward will be great, and you will be sons of the Most High, for he is kind to the ungrateful and the evil. Be merciful, even as your Father is merciful. (Luke 6:32–36)

Jesus warns us that being kind and loving to people who reciprocate isn't necessarily a sign of true faith, because even unbelievers do that. Only when you're so convinced of God's existence, the wisdom of his commands, and the reliability of his promises can you look evil in the face and not only be unafraid, but respond with the same mercy that God grants people every day. May grace produce the courage and mercy of faith in us.

For further study and encouragement: James 2:14–26

———

OCTOBER 21

LUKE 8–9

There is no competition or tribalism when it comes to the faithful ministry of the gospel.

The disciples have been arguing about who is greatest, so Jesus teaches them that in his kingdom the least among them are the greatest. John responds with a complaint:

> John answered, "Master, we saw someone casting out demons in your name, and we tried to stop him, because he does not follow with us." But Jesus said to him, "Do not stop him, for the one who is not against you is for you." (Luke 9:49–50)

John is upset that someone is exerting divine power in ministry, and that person is not one of the twelve disciples. Now, it is easy for us to be self-righteously critical of the disciples and silently tell ourselves that, if we'd been there, we would have responded differently. But this moment in the life of Jesus and the disciples has been preserved for us because it exposes not only John's heart, but our hearts as well.

If you pay attention to Christian culture, you see too much division, competition, and tribalism. God does not want the different parts of his family to compete with or be threatened by one another. Different parts of God's family should never be jealous of the success of the gospel experienced by other parts of his family. We must remember that our fellow believers, no matter who they are or where they are, are not enemies that we should fear or fight. There is only one enemy: the roaring, devouring lion, Satan. We do well to remember Jesus's words: "The one who is not against you is for you."

We must also remember that ministry fruitfulness is always the result of the operation of divine grace. It is God who chooses whom he will use. He chooses when the winds of the Spirit will blow. He chooses who will hear and respond. He decides when and where his divine power will be displayed. God is the dispenser of his own grace, the giver of ministry gifts, and the one who empowers ministry. He promises each and every one of us that, when he sends us, he goes with us, and that which he calls us to do, he enables us to do. We can rest in his sovereignty, presence, promises, and grace. Because his power is infinite and his grace is inexhaustible, there surely is enough power to go around and enough grace to give.

So we should rejoice when we see gospel ministry producing fruit, even if that fruit is experienced by another part of the family of God. And we should pray that, whenever God's word is read and preached, it would bear fruit—no matter who is doing the reading and preaching. For we know that fruit is a sign that God is once again dispensing his forgiving, transforming, and delivering grace.

For further study and encouragement: Psalm 34:1–3

———

OCTOBER 22

LUKE 10–11

The things that cause you to rejoice reveal what effectively and functionally rules your heart.

My friend was always eager to share stories of what God was doing in his ministry and at his church. Story would follow story so quickly that it was hard to jump in and ask a question. He told his stories with lots of enthusiasm and joy. At first I found this attractive, but then I became concerned. At first it felt good to be around someone who actually enjoyed long-term ministry, with all its peaks and valleys. Initially I found his happiness in ministry attractive, but then I began to see it in another way. His joy seemed to be more about himself than about the Lord who was behind every ministry success. He seemed taken with the fact that God had decided to use *him*. As he told his stories, he always seemed to be the central character. He was always on center stage, with the spotlight trained on him. His accounts were all about how God had used him and his gifts in a particular way with a particular person.

Rejoicing is never morally neutral. Joy in service or ministry is never neutral. Joy in marriage, parenting, friendship, or community is never neutral. Joy can be deceptive. Joy can be idolatrous or rebellious. Joy can be glory thievery, when we take credit for what only God could do and produce. So it is always spiritually beneficial to examine your joy. What sparks the kind of joy that fills your heart? Your joy always reveals what your heart loves.

Jesus talks about joy in Luke 10:

> The seventy-two returned with joy, saying, "Lord, even the demons are subject to us in your name!" And he said to them, "I saw Satan fall like lightning from heaven. Behold, I have given you authority to tread on serpents and scorpions, and over all the power of the enemy, and nothing shall hurt you. Nevertheless, do not rejoice in this, that the spirits are subject to you, but rejoice that your names are written in heaven." (Luke 10:17–20)

Jesus had sent out his followers to minister in his name, and, when they came back, they were excited and filled with joy. They began to tell stories of the power they had been able to exercise against Satan. In the middle of their ministry tales, Jesus said, "Yes, I have blessed you with awesome power and authority, but that is not what you should be rejoicing in. Ministry power should not be the source of your joy." Everyone who has been called into any form of service in God's name needs to hear these words. Be careful how you rejoice over ministry success.

What should be the source of our joy? Jesus is quite clear: "Rejoice that your names are written in heaven." We should never stop celebrating the gift of gifts and the miracle of miracles: that God has chosen us to be the objects of his amazing redeeming grace. The more that saving grace captures your joy, the less you will look for other reasons to rejoice. May redeeming joy satisfy our hearts.

For further study and encouragement: Philippians 4:4–7

OCTOBER 23

LUKE 12–13

Fear of God has the power to defeat all other fears in your life.

I love dramatic moments in Scripture. When I read a dramatic narrative and feel the tension build, I often imagine an orchestra swelling and timpani drums beginning to roll. We find one such drama in 1 Samuel 17. The army of Israel has assembled in the Valley of Elah to battle the Philistine army. Remember, Israel is the people of God. God had promised them that he would unleash his almighty power to defeat the pagan nations and deliver the land he had promised to his people. This is the army of the Most High God, the Lord of hosts. Nothing rivals his power or authority. He can do with the nations whatever he wills.

On the first day of battle, the great giant, Goliath, taunts the Israelite soldiers, and they run back into their tents in fear. This goes on for forty days. What a moral and spiritual scandal! How can God's army live in such fear? Then David shows up. He is not a soldier, but he volunteers to fight Goliath. Why isn't David afraid of this huge warrior? The answer is clear. Fear of God frees him from being afraid of Goliath. David has experienced the power of God. He comes to the valley in the fear of the Lord, so he faces Goliath unafraid and, in God's power, wins the victory.

Are you afraid? Does fear shape your actions, reactions, and responses more than faith does? Does fear cause you to be timid and avoidant? Does fear interrupt your sleep and distract you during the day? If so, read Luke 12:4–7 and take heart:

> I tell you, my friends, do not fear those who kill the body, and after that have nothing more that they can do. But I will warn you whom to fear: fear him who, after he has killed, has authority to cast into hell. Yes, I tell you, fear him! Are not five sparrows sold for two pennies? And not one of them is forgotten before God. Why, even the hairs of your head are all numbered. Fear not; you are of more value than many sparrows.

Notice how this tender passage begins. Jesus addresses his followers as friends. Think about what it means to be chosen as a friend of God. As a friend of the King of kings, what would I possibly fear? If God is my friend, can't I count on him to exercise his power and authority for my good?

As the disciples' friend, Jesus reminds them that he alone holds their eternal destiny in his hands. Then Jesus reminds his followers of the Father's care. He remembers the birds, and are his people not more valuable than birds? Their Father keeps such careful watch over his children that he even keeps an accurate accounting of their hairs.

Remember, only fear of God (an awe that produces a rest of heart) can defeat all other fears.

For further study and encouragement: Proverbs 1:1–7

OCTOBER 24

Are you clear about what it means to be a disciple of the Lord Jesus Christ?

I am continually amazed that everything God ordained to be recorded and pre-served for us has direct application to our identity as children of God, to the life-style he has called us to, and to our daily war with sin and temptation. As you read the Bible, don't allow yourself to skip over a passage simply because it doesn't seem as though it has anything to do with you or the trials you are facing. Know that God is a good and wise Father who knows exactly what we need. He has reached into his vast storehouse of wisdom and knowledge and recorded everything we need to know, understand, and believe, in order to live according to his will.

Luke 14:25–33 is a great example of God's fatherly wisdom:

> Now great crowds accompanied [Jesus], and he turned and said to them, "If anyone comes to me and does not hate his own father and mother and wife and children and brothers and sisters, yes, and even his own life, he cannot be my disciple. Whoever does not bear his own cross and come after me cannot be my disciple. For which of you, desiring to build a tower, does not first sit down and count the cost, whether he has enough to complete it? Otherwise, when he has laid a foundation and is not able to finish, all who see it begin to mock him, saying, 'This man began to build and was not able to finish.' Or what king, going out to encounter another king in war, will not sit down first and deliberate whether he is able with ten thousand to meet him who comes against him with twenty thousand? And if not, while the other is yet a great way off, he sends a delegation and asks for terms of peace. So therefore, any one of you who does not renounce all that he has cannot be my disciple."

Jesus wants the crowd to know that not everyone who has heard the gospel is a true disciple. Some hang around because they are spiritually interested and curious. Others may be hooked because what they've seen and heard has left them in awe and amazement. But that doesn't mean they are disciples of Jesus yet. So Jesus breaks through the confusion and deception and lays out three things that define a true disciple.

1. A disciple of Jesus loves him more than any other person in his life.
2. A disciple is willing to make sacrifices and suffer for the sake of his Lord.
3. A disciple will renounce all other allegiances in order to follow Jesus.

None of these is natural for us. Only by grace can anyone ever choose to forsake everything and follow Jesus. May we be blessed with this grace.

For further study and encouragement: Romans 12:1–2

OCTOBER 25

LUKE 16–18

*God's law and his grace are not in opposition; they
are two aspects of his work in our lives.*

"But it is easier for heaven and earth to pass away than for one dot of the Law to become void" (Luke 16:17). What a clear and bold statement from Jesus. The word *but* at the beginning of the verse tells us that Jesus is correcting a misunderstanding about the law. Jesus came to earth as the ultimate fulfillment of God's law. All of the laws of ceremony and sacrifice would be fulfilled by him as he hung on the cross as the final sacrificial Lamb, fully satisfying God's requirements on our behalf. He is also the final fulfillment of the moral law. As our substitute, he lived a perfectly righteous life all of the time and in every way. He met every moral requirement of the law so that we would be able to stand before God as righteous. Every sinful thought, desire, choice, word, or action of every sinner cries out for the Son of Man to come and live, on sinners' behalf, as they would never be able to live, and to die, on their behalf, so that the curse of the law would finally be removed for all who believe.

But in his ministry, Jesus wanted to make it clear that he did not come to make the law null and void. Contrary to what many Christians think, God's law is a gift of his grace. Think about when the law of God was first given. God gave the children of Israel his law after he redeemed them out of slavery in Egypt. The law was not a means of achieving God's favor; he had already chosen to place his love on this group of people and had already demonstrated his willingness to unleash his almighty power for their welfare. God gave them his law because they had lived as slaves for four hundred years in a pagan land and had no idea how to live in a way that was pleasing in the sight of the one who had provided their freedom. The giving of the law to the children of Israel was a sign of God's love and a tool of his grace.

The law is a tool of grace in our lives as well. God uses his law to reveal and convict us of sin. When we look into the moral mirror of the law, we are to see ourselves as we actually are and to cry out for forgiving and transforming grace. God's law is also a guide for our lives. God's commands reflect his holiness and describe what a holy life looks like. As we submit to God's holy standard, we must cry out for empowering grace to make us holy as he is holy.

God blesses us with his law, but it's important to understand its limits. The law has no power whatsoever to purchase for us acceptance with God, and it has no power on its own to transform our hearts. But we are thankful for God's law as we celebrate his rescuing, forgiving, transforming, and delivering grace.

For further study and encouragement: Romans 10:5–13

———

OCTOBER 26

LUKE 19–20

*God's grace is never too weak to rescue someone
from the powerful hold of sin.*

The following story might be so familiar to us that we forget how scandalous it would have been to its original hearers:

> When Jesus came to the place, he looked up and said to him, "Zacchaeus, hurry and come down, for I must stay at your house today." So he hurried and came down and received him joyfully. And when they saw it, they all grumbled, "He has gone in to be the guest of a man who is a sinner." And Zacchaeus stood and said to the Lord, "Behold, Lord, the half of my goods I give to the poor. And if I have defrauded anyone of anything, I restore it fourfold." And Jesus said to him, "Today salvation has come to this house, since he also is a son of Abraham. For the Son of Man came to seek and to save the lost." (Luke 19:5–10)

Zacchaeus, a rich tax collector who was short in stature, heard that Jesus was coming. Because of the crowd, Zacchaeus climbed up a tree to make sure he could see him. Jesus saw Zacchaeus in the tree and told him to come down because he wanted to stay in his house. The fact that Jesus was willing to stay in this man's house scandalized the self-righteous crowd, who could not believe that Jesus would go into the house of a "sinner." To the crowd, tax collectors were a symbol of the oppression of the Roman government. Men like Zacchaeus would collect an exorbitant tax that broke the economic backs of the Jews. And, like Zacchaeus, many of them would get rich doing so. Tax collectors were viewed as disloyal oppressors, and so they were considered to be sinners beyond redemption.

We aren't told how or when, but we find evidence in the text that Zacchaeus had already been touched by God's grace. First, he was excited about seeing Jesus, and he received him joyfully when Jesus asked to stay at his house. Most tax collectors would have had no time for Jesus, and perhaps would have mocked his claims. Also, Zacchaeus's lifestyle showed signs of transformation. He would gladly give half of his riches to the poor and pay back fourfold the people he had defrauded. Clearly, transforming grace had been operating in Zacchaeus, and Jesus announced to Zacchaeus that salvation was already operating in his life.

It seems as though Jesus spoke his last words here not only to Zacchaeus, but to the grumbling crowd as well: "For the Son of Man came to seek and to save the lost." Of course he would enter the house of this man who seemed so unworthy. This is what Jesus came to do: to seek out lost ones and draw them to himself.

I am convinced that this story is in the Bible to remind us that no one— no matter how seemingly unworthy someone might seem to us—is beyond the reach of the grace of Jesus. Sin levels the playing field. Everyone stands before God unworthy. None of us is more acceptable than anyone else. Grace is why God enters our house and proclaims salvation. God is for sinners; his salvation is for the lost.

For further study and encouragement: 1 Timothy 1:12–17

———

OCTOBER 27

LUKE 21–22

Jesus would not exercise his power to protect himself, and he would not let his disciples defend him, because he came to provide salvation through his suffering and death.

The last week of Jesus's life provides a powerful picture for us of divine, redemptive restraint. The King of kings and Lord of lords, who had legions of angels and infinite power at his disposal, submitted himself to human rejection, betrayal, injustice, and torture till death. Though as the Son of God Jesus had the right to defend himself, he did not exercise his power to do so. He didn't allow his disciples to act for his protection, either. However, as Jesus meekly and willingly submitted to his redemptive calling, he was, in fact, exercising divine power. All of us would have broken at some point. All of us would have been able to bear only so much. All of us would have tried to escape or to fight in our own defense. But in Jesus's last days, there wasn't even a moment of self-preservation. Even when wishing that the cup of suffering would pass by him, he did not seek escape and did not exercise his power to preserve his own life. Jesus never had a moment of self-regarding anger. He exercised divine restraint for the salvation of those who would believe down through the ages. Jesus chose not to defend himself, no matter the cost to himself, because he knew his Father's will and his love for the lost.

In chapter 22, Luke graphically captures this for us:

> "I tell you that this Scripture must be fulfilled in me: 'And he was numbered with the transgressors.' For what is written about me has its fulfillment." . . .
>
> While he was still speaking, there came a crowd, and the man called Judas, one of the twelve, was leading them. He drew near to Jesus to kiss him, but Jesus said to him, "Judas, would you betray the Son of Man with a kiss?" And when those who were around him saw what would follow, they said, "Lord, shall we strike with the sword?" And one of them struck the servant of the high priest and cut off his right ear. But Jesus said, "No more of this!" And he touched his ear and healed him. Then Jesus said to the chief priests and officers of the temple and elders, who had come out against him, "Have you come out as against a robber, with swords and clubs? When I was with you day after day in the temple, you did not lay hands on me. But this is your hour, and the power of darkness." (Luke 22:37, 47–53)

Jesus understood the eternal plan of redemption. He knew the cross was his destiny, and he was willing. On the Mount of Olives, where he had gone to pray, he did not allow his disciples to take up arms in his defense. He submitted to arrest and to all the suffering that followed. This was a display not of Jesus's weakness but of his divine power. He was in control, fulfilling everything that had been planned and promised, all for our salvation.

For further study and encouragement: Romans 3:21–26

OCTOBER 28

LUKE 23–24

Jesus was willing to suffer injustice, mockery, and rejection
so that we might experience eternal acceptance.

My daughter had gone to a roller-skating party with a group of her school friends. She had gotten a ride there but would need a ride home, so we told her to call us when she was ready, and we would pick her up. When she eventually called, she asked us not to come in but to stay in the car in the parking lot, and she would come and find us. We knew what was happening. She didn't want to be seen with us. We knew this was typical teenager stuff, but I would be lying to you if I told you it didn't hurt. It is hurtful when someone you love is embarrassed to be identified with you.

God designed us to be social beings, so we hunger for acceptance. We are made for community with other human beings. We all have hearts that cry out for love. None of us enjoys rejection. None of us feels good about being mocked or being the outsider. Isaiah 53 prophesied that Jesus would be despised and rejected. Being fully human, having feelings and desires like you and I have, means that this was painful for Jesus, as it is for us. But Jesus was willing. He knew what he had come to do, and he was willing to suffer so that sin would be defeated and we would be eternally reconciled to God. Luke 23:18–25 records one of those rejection scenes in the life of Jesus:

> They all cried out together, "Away with this man, and release to us Barabbas"—a man who had been thrown into prison for an insurrection started in the city and for murder. Pilate addressed them once more, desiring to release Jesus, but they kept shouting, "Crucify, crucify him!" A third time he said to them, "Why, what evil has he done? I have found in him no guilt deserving death. I will therefore punish and release him." But they were urgent, demanding with loud cries that he should be crucified. And their voices prevailed. So Pilate decided that their demand should be granted. He released the man who had been thrown into prison for insurrection and murder, for whom they asked, but he delivered Jesus over to their will.

This scene is so heart-wrenching that it is hard to wrap your brain around it. Perfect Jesus, free of guilt of any kind, was in the legal hands of Pilate, who found no wrong in him. But the crowd wanted Pilate to convict Jesus and release the insurrectionist murderer Barabbas. Think about it: the crowd chose a violent criminal rather than the eternally perfect Son of God.

This moment of public rejection was not a failure of God's plan. No, it *was* God's plan, prophesied generations before. It was a necessary step toward the victory of Jesus's substitutionary death on the cross. Jesus was willing to do everything necessary, no matter how painful, to accomplish his mission of redemption. His rejection was a step toward gaining our eternal acceptance. Today, for each of us, that's very good news.

For further study and encouragement: 1 Peter 2:22–25

———

OCTOBER 29

JOHN 1–2

Jesus is the glory of God in the flesh.

Luella and I split our time between Philadelphia and Southern California because we have children and grandchildren on both coasts. When we are on the West Coast, we see gorgeous sunsets. One evening, as we were leaving our son's house, I was stopped in my tracks by a sunset of incredible glory. The beauty painted across the heavens captivated me. I stood silent, enthralled by this natural display. I wanted to capture the moment, so I got out my phone and started taking pictures, but all I got was disappointment. None of my pictures came close to capturing the glory that I was taking in. Soon the sunset glory began to shift and fade, and before long it was gone. For a brief moment, God had poured glory down on us. What we saw that night was a brief, fading reminder of his eternal glory. Reigning over heaven and earth is a God of indescribable glory. He graces us with glimpses of his glory so that we will be in awe of his presence and offer him the worship of our hearts.

We find a glory display in the beginning of the Gospel of John that is infinitely brighter and more beautiful than any sunset. John captures in words a moment in history when God displayed his glory like never before. Words pile upon words as John records God's stunning glory on earth, for human eyes to see:

The Word became flesh and dwelt among us, and we have seen his glory, glory as of the only Son from the Father, full of grace and truth. (John bore witness about him, and cried out, "This was he of whom I said, 'He who comes after me ranks before me, because he was before me.'") For from his fullness we have all received, grace upon grace. For the law was given through Moses; grace and truth came through Jesus Christ. No one has ever seen God; the only God, who is at the Father's side, he has made him known. (John 1:14–18)

God has come to earth in the person of Jesus. Like the presence of God in the Old Testament tabernacle, Jesus pitches his tent with us, so we might see his glory. He is the grace of God in the flesh. He is truth. He is the final fulfillment of all the Old Testament's redemptive promises. Just as the Law of Moses reveals God's character and his righteous requirements, so Jesus reveals to us the magnitude of his mercy. The Son of God has come to earth because God wants to be known by us.

All of history had been marching to this moment. A sin-broken world had been longing for this one to come. Fully man and fully God, Jesus would do what we could never do for ourselves: make a way, in his life and death, for us to be recognized by God. Stop today for a moment and take in the glory.

For further study and encouragement: Exodus 33:12–23

———

OCTOBER 30

JOHN 3–4

God's generosity culminates in the gift of his Son, Jesus.

The Bible records the best generosity story that has ever been penned in human language. God is the great giver of good things, and the biblical narrative records his generosity over and over again. The creation account shows us his generosity as he places Adam and Eve in a beautiful garden where they have everything they need. In generosity, right after the entrance of sin into the world, God promises to fix what sin has broken. God generously makes his covenant with Abraham, through whom all the nations on earth will be blessed. He is generous in delivering his people out of slavery and giving them his law, so that they will thrive. He generously provides manna for them in the wilderness when they aren't able to provide for themselves. He generously provides the promised land so they can grow and thrive as a nation. In generosity, he chooses to dwell with them in the tabernacle; his presence is always with them. In the face of their rebellion, God generously sends prophet after prophet to warn his people and call them back to him.

If you pay attention as you read your Bible, you will see that the generosity of the King of kings is without end. One particular verse captures God's generosity and its final culmination. This verse may be the most famous and well-known of all Bible verses: "For God so loved the world, that he gave his only Son, that whoever believes in him should not perish but have eternal life" (John 3:16).

I am convinced that this passage not only points us to the ultimate gift of gifts, Jesus, but it also summarizes the redemptive story up until this point. We can summarize the redemptive story with these nine words: "For God so loved the world that he gave." The entire biblical story is about a God who gives his creatures what they do not know they need, what they often do not want, and what they could never earn or do for themselves—but which they cannot live without. As we read the Bible, it becomes clear that nothing can keep God from giving. Even in the face of his people's rebellion and idolatry, he continues to give. His generosity is inexhaustible and without limit.

God's generosity reached its crescendo with the gift of Jesus. Every gift he had given pointed to this final gift. In this gift, we get forgiveness, reconciliation, and the transformation of our hearts. In all of God's giving, there is no gift like Jesus.

God is still showering down his generosity on you. He blesses you every day with his presence, promises, power, and grace. He gives to you through his word and his church. Your life—right here, right now, and into the future—rests on God's willingness to keep on giving. It is an amazing grace that we are the objects of such unending generosity.

For further study and encouragement: Matthew 2:1–12

———

OCTOBER 31

JOHN 5–6

*Jesus is manna, the bread of God sent from heaven
and the only bread that can satisfy your heart.*

Your Bible is not simply a collection of stories, but rather one grand story. The diversity of historical situations, locations, and personalities should not deter you from seeing the complete unity of the biblical narrative. This story has one theme: redeeming and reconciling grace. It has one central character: the Lord

Jesus Christ. Scripture's story has one mission: by the power of the person, life, death, and resurrection of Jesus, God will renew everything sin has broken. The entire biblical narrative is God-glorifying, sin-revealing, Jesus-exalting, grace-announcing, and hope-giving. It is the story of stories, the only one worth building your life upon.

We see the wonderful unity of the biblical story in John 6. In this familiar story, Jesus feeds a large multitude with a small lunch of two fish and five loaves. Everyone seems to know this story, but I wonder how many people know what this story is actually about.

The crowd is amazed at this miracle and seeks Jesus out to make him their king. You may think that this is the moment of moments. This is the King of kings; the crowd has it right. But, rather than celebrating their recognition, Jesus hides from the crowd. Why? Perhaps the crowd has gotten something wrong. Here is Jesus's response to the crowd when they catch up with him:

> When they found him on the other side of the sea, they said to him, "Rabbi, when did you come here?" Jesus answered them, "Truly, truly, I say to you, you are seeking me, not because you saw signs, but because you ate your fill of the loaves." (John 6:25–26)

The crowd was excited about Jesus not because they understood what the miracle of the bread revealed about him, but because they had had their bellies filled. But Jesus didn't come to be their buffet king. Now, hear what Jesus says:

> Jesus then said to them, "Truly, truly, I say to you, it was not Moses who gave you the bread from heaven, but my Father gives you the true bread from heaven. For the bread of God is he who comes down from heaven and gives life to the world." They said to him, "Sir, give us this bread always."
>
> Jesus said to them, "I am the bread of life; whoever comes to me shall not hunger, and whoever believes in me shall never thirst." (John 6:32–35)

Jesus is intentionally connecting who he is to the provision of manna in the wilderness (see Num. 11). The entire biblical narrative is about God's providing for his people. Jesus is the manna of God, the bread that takes us from spiritual death to spiritual life. He is the manna that will end your hunger forever. The bread for the crowd is a sign to point them—and us—to how their deeper hunger can be satisfied.

The story of the of the Bible is about hunger and bread. Only Jesus satisfies.

For further study and encouragement: Isaiah 55:1–3

NOVEMBER 1

We should never deny or underestimate the
addicting, enslaving power of sin.

It is dangerous to dabble in sin. We allow ourselves to do what God has forbidden because sin presents itself as good and satisfying—when it is the exact opposite. Part of sin's deception is that it doesn't come with a warning label. It masquerades as beautiful and good, when actually it is ugly and destructive. No matter how sin presents itself, it is never good for us. Sometimes we take a little taste of what is prohibited, thinking we can handle the danger. We enjoy the temporary pleasure of the taste of sin, so we go in for more. What we don't realize is that we have begun to develop a taste for what we never should have consumed. Before long, that momentary rebellion has become a habit. This sinful pleasure is now a regular part of life. Our conscience is guilty, but we brush it off with excuses. We tell ourselves that everything will turn out okay in the end. After a little while, we find that this sinful habit has become an addiction. Now we can't live without the thing we once dabbled in. We tell ourselves we're going to stop, but we don't. We hide our addiction to this evil thing, while denying that we live under its control. We have become a victim of the enslaving power of sin. It is depressing to admit, but we now live under the power of something we cannot control.

The Gospels record for us many of Jesus's wise and loving warnings. One of the most important is found in John 8. We do well to take these words to heart. They are the result of God's keeping and protecting grace:

Jesus said to the Jews who had believed him, "If you abide in my word, you are truly my disciples, and you will know the truth, and the truth will set you free." They answered him, "We are offspring of Abraham and have never been enslaved to anyone. How is it that you say, 'You will become free'?"

Jesus answered them, "Truly, truly, I say to you, everyone who practices sin is a slave to sin. The slave does not remain in the house forever; the son remains forever. So if the Son sets you free, you will be free indeed." (John 8:31–36)

Jesus taught his followers that the truth would set them free, but they were confused. They thought that because they were the offspring of Abraham, they weren't enslaved to anyone or anything. So Jesus spoke a very needed word of warning about the enslaving power of sin. His broad statement includes us all and allows no exceptions: whoever sins is a slave to sin. You cannot sin and escape its slavery.

Sin enslaves each and every one of us, and we have no power on our own to escape its hold. This means we are in need of rescue, and that rescue is found only in the freeing grace of the Son, the Lord Jesus. Praise Jesus today for his liberating grace, and don't allow yourself to dabble in what God has forbidden.

For further study and encouragement: Proverbs 5:22–23

NOVEMBER 2

JOHN 9–10

God leads us through difficult hardships, so that
through us his glory will be on display.

Much has been written about Jesus's restoring a man's sight in John 9. Why did he make mud and put it on the man's eyes? Why did the man then have to go and wash in the pool of Siloam? But I think that the most important part of what John records is the discussion that takes place right before the miracle:

> As he passed by, he saw a man blind from birth. And his disciples asked him, "Rabbi, who sinned, this man or his parents, that he was born blind?" Jesus answered, "It was not that this man sinned, or his parents, but that the works of God might be displayed in him. We must work the works of him who sent me while it is day; night is coming, when no one can work. As long as I am in the world, I am the light of the world." Having said these things, he spit on the ground and made mud with the saliva. Then he anointed the man's eyes with the mud and said to him, "Go, wash in the pool of Siloam" (which means Sent). So he went and washed and came back seeing. (John 9:1–7)

Jesus's disciples assume that this man was born blind as a punishment either for his sin or for his parents'. The disciples don't even question whether the blindness is the result of sin; they are convinced it is. They simply wonder whose sin it was. I am afraid that many of us make the same assumption. We think that when we suffer, we are being punished for some wrong we have done. For a believer, that can never be the case, because every ounce of the penalty for our sin was carried by Jesus on the cross. Our sin-debt has been fully paid.

Jesus speaks to the disciples' assumption about sin and punishment in a way that they never could have anticipated. He says that the man was born blind so that "the works of God might be displayed in him." You may be thinking, "Paul, are you saying that there are situations in which God ordains suffering so that his power and glory will be put on display?" That is exactly what Jesus teaches his disciples. You and I will suffer not just because we live in a fallen world or because we have an enemy who devours and destroys. We also will suffer because of God's zeal for the display of his own glory. He works so that things will be visible in us that are explainable only by his presence and power. He ordains hard things that we do not want to go through so that in us his power will be revealed.

We were not created for our own comfort, pleasure, or glory. We were created to display the presence, power, and glory of the one who made us. God will not leave us alone in our suffering; he will meet us with his power and, through us, publicly display his glory.

For further study and encouragement: 2 Corinthians 12:1–10

—————

NOVEMBER 3

JOHN 11–13

Surrounded by death and grief, Jesus proclaims,
"I am the resurrection and the life."

Everyone who is familiar with the Bible knows the story of the raising of Lazarus. John gives this amazing story a lot of ink in his Gospel, but I want to focus on the conversation between Jesus and Martha after Jesus finally arrives on the scene—four days after Lazarus dies. For many Jews, the fourth day was important because it signified that Lazarus was officially dead:

> Now when Jesus came, he found that Lazarus had already been in the tomb four days. Bethany was near Jerusalem, about two miles off, and many of the Jews had come to Martha and Mary to console them concerning their brother. So when Martha heard that Jesus was coming, she went and met him, but Mary remained seated in the house. Martha said to Jesus, "Lord, if you had been here, my brother would not have died. But even now I know that whatever you ask from God, God will give you." Jesus said to her, "Your brother will rise again." Martha said to him, "I know that he will rise again

in the resurrection on the last day." Jesus said to her, "I am the resurrection and the life. Whoever believes in me, though he die, yet shall he live, and everyone who lives and believes in me shall never die. Do you believe this?" She said to him, "Yes, Lord; I believe that you are the Christ, the Son of God, who is coming into the world." (John 11:17–27)

Martha's first words to Jesus are exactly what you would expect from someone who has witnessed the power of Jesus firsthand: "If you had been here, my brother would not have died." Jesus's response is both clear and radical: "Your brother will rise again." There is no hesitation or equivocation in these words. Martha misunderstands what Jesus is saying. He is making a present declaration, but what she hears is a future promise. Jesus is not talking about the final resurrection; he is talking about what he intends to do to Lazarus *now*. The Son of God knows himself and understands the power that is at his disposal.

What Jesus says next is glorious. He declares his identity, along with a summary of the hope of the gospel. "I am the resurrection and the life." Resurrection power and the giving of eternal life are inextricably connected to Jesus—and to no one else. So it is right for him to say, "I am the resurrection" and "I am the life." But Jesus is not done. He then says, "Whoever believes in me, though he die, yet shall he live."

Here is the gospel of grace. We are all born dead in sin, a condition we cannot escape. By grace, Jesus breathes life into all who believe. And even though believers still physically die, we will rise again and live with him forever. Standing before Lazarus's tomb, Jesus preaches to us his resurrection power.

For further study and encouragement: 1 Corinthians 15:1–28

NOVEMBER 4

JOHN 14–16

The sovereignty of God doesn't crush gospel witness.
It propels it like nothing else can.

One summer my brother turned my biblical world upside down. Tedd began to talk to me about the sovereignty of God; that is, the rule of God over everything and everyone, so that his will will be done, his plan for humanity will be accomplished, and his glory will be eternally known and celebrated. At first I thought this meant that I was nothing more than a mindless robot. It made me mad. I was convinced that my brother couldn't be right. At one point I got so mad at Tedd that I took off my shoe and threw it at him. His response to me was loving, wise, and patient. He gave me a paperback Bible and a yellow highlighter and told me to read through the Bible that summer and highlight all the places where Scripture talked about God's sovereign authority and rule over everything. By the end of the summer, my Bible was yellow almost everywhere, and my view of God and myself had radically changed. Rather than making me passive, the truth of God's sovereignty has propelled my Christianity and given me great rest of heart.

One of the common misunderstandings of the sovereign rule of God is that this doctrine crushes our choices and service. If God has chosen those who will believe in him, then why go out and preach the gospel? The chosen will be saved, no matter what. Right? But this is not what Scripture teaches. Hear and consider carefully Jesus's words in John 15:

> This is my commandment, that you love one another as I have loved you. Greater love has no one than this, that someone lay down his life for his friends. You are my friends if you do what I command you. No longer do I call you servants, for the servant does not know what his master is doing; but I have called you friends, for all that I have heard from my Father I have made known to you. You did not choose me, but I chose you and appointed you that you should go and bear fruit and that your fruit should abide, so that whatever you ask the Father in my name, he may give it to you. These things I command you, so that you will love one another. (John 15:12–17)

John 15 includes some of Jesus's final instructions to his disciples. These verses are a call to action. Jesus calls them to love one another as he has loved them. He reminds them of the friendship they now enjoy with him, which comes only by means of reconciling grace. Jesus reminds his disciples of who they are and what he has called them to do. In giving them these final instructions, Jesus recognizes the importance of their choices and actions. Then he reminds them that they are his—not first because of their choice but because of his—and that he chose them to bear good fruit in character and ministry. God's sovereignty doesn't crush the significance of our belief or our ministry; it motivates them. Because the Lord rules, we know that in choosing to believe him and serve him, we will bear good fruit.

For further study and encouragement: Psalm 67:1–7

NOVEMBER 5

JOHN 17–19

If someone were to ask you how much God loves you, what would you say?

In the middle of talking online with her grandma, our almost three-year-old granddaughter asked to talk to me. When she saw my face on the phone, she smiled wide and began to babble away. I understood about half of what she said. Eventually I told her I needed to get off the phone, but, before I did, I told her that I loved her. With a big grin she said, "I love you too, Grandpa." Those few seconds of life were deeply meaningful to both of us. A young little girl and a not-so-young man both hunger for love, and something happens in our hearts when we hear the words *I love you.*

The hunger to be loved is universal. It unites all human beings, no matter who they are or where they live. This hunger has been wired into our hearts by our Creator. He built us with this hunger, and he pulls us into a loving relationship with him and into loving community with one another. But now our hunger for love also produces fear. Not only do we hunger for love, but we anxiously wonder whether those who say they love us will continue to love us once they get to know us. If we wonder about this in human relationships, how much more do we wonder about this in our relationship with God? How much does God love us? Does his love have limits? Is his love really a faithful, patient, and forever love? Does he ever break his bond of commitment to us? Does God ever regret that he chose to place his love on us? Does his anger with our sin ever get in the way of his love for us?

All of these questions are answered in a few words in the middle of one of Jesus's final recorded prayers. In John 17 Jesus prays for the unity of his followers. He speaks of his love in a way that should bring eternal rest and peace to our hearts: ". . . I in them and you in me, that they may become perfectly one, so that the world may know that you sent me and loved them even as you loved me" (John 17:23). This statement of God's love for us is almost too glorious to fit into our finite human brains. It is so unlike any other experience of love we have ever had that we cannot fully grasp its beauty or extent. The heavenly Father's love for us is the same as his love for his Son, the Lord Jesus. The joy he has in the Son, he has in us. The eternal commitment he has to the Son, he has to us. The unbreakable affection he has for the Son, he has for us. We cannot fully understand God's love for us by simply comparing it to human love. If you want to understand how much God loves you, meditate on his love for his Son. God's love for you is at no greater risk than his love for his Son, and that is the best of news.

For further study and encouragement: Lamentations 3:22–24

NOVEMBER 6

JOHN 20–21

Your Bible is the biography of Jesus. On his shoulders the hope
of humanity rests, both in this life and in the one to come.

I remember my very first Bible. Owning it made me feel so grown-up, and truly part of the spiritual community that I was being raised in. It was a leather-bound, loose-leaf Bible, which allowed you to insert pages for note-taking. As a little boy I was proud of this book, but I had no idea what life-transforming glories it contained. I knew the creation narrative and other well-known Bible stories, but little else. If you had asked me what the Bible was about or why God had given it to us, I'm not sure what I would have answered. What is the central theme of your Bible? What is the unifying cord that holds every part of it together? Why did God go to all the effort over so many years to record and preserve his word for us? How does God intend for us to use our Bibles? Can you describe the Bible in a single sentence? How much do you value Scripture?

Near the end of his Gospel, John recounts the last moments of Jesus's life on earth. He then pauses to tell us why he wrote what he wrote. John's description of his purpose for writing his Gospel is incredibly important—not only for understanding the importance of this Gospel but also for understanding who you are, what you need, and how God will meet that need with his grace. But there is more. John's statement gets at the reason for *every* part of the word of God. It exposes God's central mission for his revelation to us. In fact, John's purpose statement for his Gospel is by far the best way to understand what your Bible is meant to do for you and in you:

> Now Jesus did many other signs in the presence of the disciples, which are not written in this book; but these are written so that you may believe that Jesus is the Christ, the Son of God, and that by believing you may have life in his name. (John 20:30–31)

The first thing you learn about John's Gospel and your Bible is that neither was intended to give you an exhaustive history of the redemptive narrative and its central character, Jesus. What you have in your Bible is selective history, with all of the necessary explanatory notes. The purpose of Scripture is to point you to the one who carries fallen humanity's hope so that you will embrace your need of him, put your trust in him, and receive the greatest gift ever given: *life in his name*. Your Bible was written with a Jesus-elevating, salvation-producing purpose. It is more than history, poetry, and wisdom. The Bible is the biography of Jesus, who is the way, the truth, and the life.

For further study and encouragement: Luke 24:25–27

NOVEMBER 7

ACTS 1–3

It is important to remember that Jesus is not only your Savior; he is also the ascended and reigning King.

The book of Acts records for us the birthing and building up of the church of Jesus Christ. We should pay attention to these beginnings. We should also pay attention to the apostles' first sermons, because they are foundational models of how the gospel is to be proclaimed and explained. These early days are relevant for us because they reveal what God has provided for us in his Son as well as in his church, which will be our spiritual home as we await the final kingdom. One piece of history recorded in Acts is particularly vital to understand:

> When they had come together, they asked him, "Lord, will you at this time restore the kingdom to Israel?" He said to them, "It is not for you to know times or seasons that the Father has fixed by his own authority. But you will receive power when the Holy Spirit has come upon you, and you will be my witnesses in Jerusalem and in all Judea and Samaria, and to the end of the earth." And when he had said these things, as they were looking on, he was lifted up, and a cloud took him out of their sight. And while they were gazing into heaven as he went, behold, two men stood by them in white robes, and said, "Men of Galilee, why do you stand looking into heaven? This Jesus, who was taken up from you into heaven, will come in the same way as you saw him go into heaven." (Acts 1:6–11)

Jesus has assembled his disciples on the Mount of Olives; this will be his final moment on earth with them prior to his return. The question they ask shows that they don't yet fully understand Jesus's mission or their part in it. They are still looking for Jesus to establish a physical kingdom on earth at this time. Jesus doesn't tackle their question, but uses it as an opportunity to tell them of the power they will receive for the work he has chosen them to do. When Jesus finishes speaking, the most amazing thing happens. A cloud of glory envelopes him, takes him out of the disciples' sight, and lifts him up to heaven.

Here's why this is important. You serve a risen Savior who is also an ascended and reigning King. Now sitting at the right hand of the Father, Jesus has managerial rule over God's kingdom. He rules over all things, right now, not only for the sake of his Father's glory but also on behalf of each of his redeemed people. Jesus's righteous reign is a present redemptive reality. His reign guarantees the delivery of everything for which he lived and died. His reign guarantees that nothing will impede God's plan for his children. Jesus's reign guarantees the final defeat of the enemy and the ushering in of his final kingdom of peace and righteousness. His reign is your hope.

For further study and encouragement: Psalm 2:1–12

NOVEMBER 8

ACTS 4–6

No power on earth is greater than the power of God's transforming grace.

The high priest along with the rulers, elders, and scribes demanded that Peter and John explain a healing they had performed in the power of Jesus. Peter boldly spoke before these powerful religious leaders. Read Peter's words, and then consider the man who spoke them:

> "Rulers of the people and elders, if we are being examined today concerning a good deed done to a crippled man, by what means this man has been healed, let it be known to all of you and to all the people of Israel that by the name of Jesus Christ of Nazareth, whom you crucified, whom God raised from the dead—by him this man is standing before you well. This Jesus is the stone that was rejected by you, the builders, which has become the cornerstone. And there is salvation in no one else, for there is no other name under heaven given among men by which we must be saved."
>
> Now when they saw the boldness of Peter and John, and perceived that they were uneducated, common men, they were astonished. And they recognized that they had been with Jesus. (Acts 4:8–13)

Peter was the disciple who consistently did and said the wrong things. It was Peter who pulled out a sword and lopped off the ear of one of the soldiers seeking to arrest Jesus, who immediately confronted Peter and healed the soldier's ear. Peter was the disciple who said he would follow Jesus in his suffering but then after Jesus's arrest denied that he had anything to do with him (see John 18). The man speaking in Acts 4 is a very different Peter. He speaks with gospel clarity and boldness. Not only is he is unafraid of associating himself with Jesus, but he rebukes these leaders for their vile mistreatment of his Savior. Peter confronts them with the fact that the one they crucified is their one and only means of salvation. And he says all of this with clarity and confidence.

Peter stands before these powerful rulers as a living testament to the awesome power of God's transforming grace. Even these coldhearted religious leaders are astonished at Peter's brilliance: "They recognized that they had been with Jesus." There simply is no other explanation for the dramatic change in this man. The power of God's transforming grace in the person of his Son, the Lord Jesus Christ, has transformed this disciple.

That transforming grace is for you too. Jesus accomplished his redeeming work so that you would be rescued from sin's penalty and transformed into his likeness.

For further study and encouragement: 2 Corinthians 5:16–18

NOVEMBER 9

ACTS 7–9

God makes his invisible grace visible by sending people
of grace to give grace to people who need grace.

Political power, career success, public fame, and wealth do not compare to participation in this one mission: being a tool of rescuing, forgiving, empowering, and transforming grace in the life of another person. There is no higher calling in all the world. It is a miracle of God's love that he has adopted me into his family forever. I never could have earned, deserved, or achieved a relationship with the King of kings. But it is equally amazing and mind-blowing that God chose to include me in the most important mission on earth: his work of redemption. Even though you and I have not outgrown our own need for God's grace, he calls us to be his tools of grace in the lives of others. He has given us the honor of visibly representing his grace to others who need that grace. In this way we represent the look of God's face, the tone of his voice, and the touch of his hand. We could receive no higher honor.

This high calling is also a hard calling. People who need God's rescuing grace are often messy, angry, proud, demanding, accusatory, self-righteous, and blind. You cannot be an instrument of God's grace unless you are willing to step into the mess and get your hands dirty. You cannot demand a comfortable life and also be a tool of grace in God's hands. We see this intersection of high calling and hardship in the life of Ananias in Acts 9:10–19. Ananias is a disciple living in Damascus whom God calls to be his messenger of grace in the life of Saul. Ananias is afraid because he knows well the legacy of Saul's evil attacks against the believers in Jerusalem. He has reason to be afraid. And yet, what an honor to be called to be the visible representative of God's grace in the life of the man who, in the history of the church, would be second only to Jesus in fame and influence. God graciously gives Ananias a glimpse of what he will do in and through Saul, and then Ananias departs to meet with Saul.

Are you willing to step into hardship, to be uncomfortable, and to suffer for the sake of being God's tool of grace? The honor of being his representative doesn't come with the promise that it will be easy.

Acts 9:17 tells us that "Ananias departed and entered the house. And laying his hands on [Saul] he said, 'Brother Saul, the Lord Jesus who appeared to you on the road by which you came has sent me so that you may regain your sight and be filled with the Holy Spirit.'" It is beautiful that fearful Ananias addresses Saul as his brother, extending to him God's forgiving, reconciling, and adopting grace. Ananias announces Saul's acceptance into God's family, which is signified by the gift of the indwelling Holy Spirit. There is no greater honor than being an instrument of God's redeeming grace. Are you ready and willing?

For further study and encouragement: 2 Corinthians 4:3–6

———

NOVEMBER 10

ACTS 10–12

There is no ethnic, geographic, social, or economic partiality with God.

It is hard to grasp the glorious scenes that await us in the final kingdom, when we will stand before the Lord's throne. We will be surrounded by people of every tribe, tongue, and nation, from every period of history and every place on the globe. We will stand in perfect unity, all our divisions gone, our differences now unable to separate us. We will all stand unworthy of what we received, because God's grace is the ultimate unifier. We will not think about our differences because our hearts will be consumed with worship and our mouths filled with endless praise. Our eyes will be not on one another, but on the majestic one who sits on the throne. And we will sing songs of his glory and of his faithful delivery of every promise of grace and victory. We will worship with those who came before us and those who came after us, all together grateful to be chosen to be part of this eternal celebration of the conquering King, the Savior, the final Lamb of sacrifice. With hearts at rest, we will know for certain that we are finally home.

One particular moment in Acts points us to this final glory. God chose Peter to extend grace to Cornelius, "a devout man who feared God" (Acts 10:2). God made it clear that, as prophesied in the Old Testament, his redeeming grace flows beyond the believing Jews. Remember: the covenant promise to Abraham was that through him all the nations of the earth would be blessed. Listen to the gospel message that Peter preached to Cornelius's household: "Truly I understand that God shows no partiality, but in every nation anyone who fears him and does what is right is acceptable to him" (Acts 10:34–35). Let these wonderful words ring in your ears and in your heart: "God shows no partiality." May that be true of us as well. If God showed partiality, none of us would be in his family or have a guaranteed place in his final kingdom. May we never let prejudice or partiality of any kind get in the way of our ministry of the gospel of forgiving, accepting, and reconciling grace. No one has a special "in" with the Lord. We are his only by grace and grace alone.

I love what happened in the middle of Peter's gospel sermon: "While Peter was still saying these things, the Holy Spirit fell on all who heard the word. And the believers from among the circumcised who had come with Peter were amazed, because the gift of the Holy Spirit was poured out even on the Gentiles" (Acts 10:44–45). There was no prejudicial pause from the Lord. Before Peter even completed his message, the Spirit fell on his hearers. Jews and Gentiles stand before the Lord equally unworthy of his favor, but accepted by his grace. There is no partiality with our Lord.

For further study and encouragement: Romans 2:1–16

NOVEMBER 11

*The Lord demonstrates again and again that he is
able to bring good things out of bad things.*

You probably wouldn't say that division is a good thing or that our inability to cooperate with one another is a blessing. You likely agree that it is disheartening when believers allow differences to hinder our effectiveness when doing kingdom work. Perhaps division is harming your church. Perhaps you are mourning that your family is unable to live at peace. Maybe you are no longer able to serve alongside a certain person. Perhaps disagreements have separated you from a long-term partner in God's work. Few things are more beautiful than brothers and sisters in the faith living and serving together in unity. But when we are enduring something that is not good, we should not allow ourselves to forget the message of the cross.

The cross looms in redemptive history as a powerful reminder that God can bring eternal good out of something that is very bad. The cross of Jesus Christ was a horrible evil perpetrated against a perfectly innocent man. Tragic injustice allowed life-ending torture. The one who deserved to be worshiped was mocked, reviled, and murdered. Peter says that Jesus was crucified and killed "by the hands of lawless men" (Acts 2:23). But he also says that Jesus was delivered to the cross by "the definite plan and foreknowledge of God" (2:23). It was God's plan that eternal, redeeming good would come out of the evil that was done to Jesus. The cross stands as a reminder that God is able to bring very good things out of very bad things. We cannot allow ourselves to give in to fear and discouragement when we are going through heartbreaking divisions. We must not underestimate what God is able to do in and through these hard moments.

We see this in the ministry of Paul and Barnabas:

> After some days Paul said to Barnabas, "Let us return and visit the brothers in every city where we proclaimed the word of the Lord, and see how they are." Now Barnabas wanted to take with them John called Mark. But Paul thought best not to take with them one who had withdrawn from them in Pamphylia and had not gone with them to the work. And there arose a sharp disagreement, so that they separated from each other. Barnabas took Mark with him and sailed away to Cyprus, but Paul chose Silas and departed, having been commended by the brothers to the grace of the Lord. And he went through Syria and Cilicia, strengthening the churches. (Acts 15:36–41)

We don't know who was right and who was wrong in the disagreement between Paul and Barnabas over John Mark, but we do know what God did with it. Because Paul and Barnabas went in separate directions, the gospel of grace was spread even more widely, welcoming perhaps even more people to trust in God's grace than if these men had worked together.

God brings good things out of bad things, so that no human weakness or failure will ever stop the march of his redeeming grace.

For further study and encouragement: Genesis 50:15–21

NOVEMBER 12

ACTS 16–18

It is important to understand clearly what it means to believe in God.

In Acts 17 Paul, who has been traveling from city to city, stops in Athens to connect with Silas and Timothy. I see this scene over and over in Center City Philadelphia. I'll walk by someone standing on a corner looking at her watch, and I know she's waiting for someone. Or I'll see two people greet one another, and I can tell from the convention tags they're wearing that they're out-of-towners making a connection. Paul, an out-of-towner waiting for his partners, is invited to speak at the Areopagus, the center of the civil and religious life in Athens. Having observed an altar with the inscription "to the unknown god," he proclaims to the Athenians that the God of the Bible is, in fact, the God whom they seek. He then tells his listeners who God is, and in his brief public explanation Paul defines what it means to believe in God:

> The God who made the world and everything in it, being Lord of heaven and earth, does not live in temples made by man, nor is he served by human hands, as though he needed anything, since he himself gives to all mankind life and breath and everything. And he made from one man every nation of mankind to live on all the face of the earth, having determined allotted periods and the boundaries of their dwelling place, that they should seek God, and perhaps feel their way toward him and find him. Yet he is actually not far from each one of us, for
>
> "In him we live and move and have our being";
>
> as even some of your own poets have said,
>
> "For we are indeed his offspring." . . .

The times of ignorance God overlooked, but now he commands all people everywhere to repent, because he has fixed a day on which he will judge the world in righteousness by a man whom he has appointed; and of this he has given assurance to all by raising him from the dead. (Acts 17:24–28, 30–31)

Three inescapable commitments define what it means to acknowledge God's existence and live in light of it. First, you must acknowledge God as *Creator*: "The God who made the world and everything in it . . ." You must also acknowledge him as *Sovereign*: ". . . having determined allotted periods and the boundaries of their dwelling place . . ." And you must acknowledge him as *Savior*: ". . . now he commands all people everywhere to repent, because he has fixed a day on which he will judge the world in righteousness by a man whom he has appointed; and of this he has given assurance to all by raising him from the dead."

Acknowledging God as Creator means acknowledging that he owns you and has a purpose for you and everything in your life. Believing him as Sovereign means resting in his active control of every detail of your life. Trusting him as Savior means repenting of your sin and trusting in his resurrection grace.

Today, may God give us grace to submit continually to the one who is Creator, Sovereign, and Savior.

For further study and encouragement: Philippians 1:18–26

NOVEMBER 13

ACTS 19–21

What do you value most in life? What influences the choices you make?

I'm going to say something that might surprise you. You may value your life too much. What do I mean? You may love what is comfortable and pleasurable too much. Your desire for respect and appreciation might be extreme. You may overvalue achievement and success. You may enjoy material things too much. You may love being right and in control too much. You may overvalue physical attractiveness or strength. Do you value your life too much? If you do, you will resist when the Lord calls you to something hard. If you overvalue your life, you will be tempted to question God's goodness, faithfulness, and love in times of suffering. If you love your life too much, you will tend to choose what you think is best for you rather than what God says is best.

God never promised that he would exercise his infinite power to make your life predictable and comfortable. He never promised you a life free of suffering. He never promised that you would escape mockery, betrayal, or rejection. He never promised that you would be surrounded by lots of human love and respect. In fact, he has promised the opposite.

God makes it clear in his word that, for our good and his glory, he will lead us through the unexpected, the unwanted, and the difficult. In the hands of our Lord, suffering is a workroom of glory and grace. God will take you places you don't really want to go, to produce in you and through you what couldn't be produced in any other way.

The apostle Paul stands as an example for us of what it means not to value your life too much. The following moment in Paul's life has been recorded and preserved for us because God loves us. In faithful, rescuing grace, the Lord speaks to a struggle many of us experience:

> Behold, I am going to Jerusalem, constrained by the Spirit, not knowing what will happen to me there, except that the Holy Spirit testifies to me in every city that imprisonment and afflictions await me. But I do not account my life of any value nor as precious to myself, if only I may finish my course and the ministry that I received from the Lord Jesus, to testify to the gospel of the grace of God. (Acts 20:22–24)

Paul knows that suffering awaits him in Jerusalem, as it has in many of the cities to which God has called him. So why is Paul willing? His reason is clear: "I do not count my life of any value nor as precious to myself." Paul doesn't value his own comfort and ease so much that he would say no to God's calling. Paul values finishing his life well and continuing to testify to the gospel of grace.

Is there something that God is calling you to, but that you are avoiding because you value your life too much?

For further study and encouragement: 2 Corinthians 4:7–18

NOVEMBER 14

ACTS 22–25

*No one—no matter how influential or powerful—
can hinder God's eternal plan.*

I fear many of us are shaped more by fear than by faith, no matter how clear our confessional theology might be. We are haunted by anxiety. We live in the shadow of "if-onlys" or "what-ifs." Many of us live avoidantly or timidly because we are afraid. But the God who is at the center of our theology is awesome in power and authority, and he willingly unleashes both for the sake of his own. Our theology tells us he is always present, always faithful to his promises, and always abundant in mercy. Our theology tells us he is strong when we are weak, wise when we are foolish, and in control when we feel out of control. These truths about God should give us rest and confidence. But in the hallways, bedrooms, family rooms, and vans of everyday life, our lives often seem devoid of God. We worry about the difficulties of this fallen world and things that are out of our control. Meanwhile, God says to us in his word, "I am perfectly good. I am in control. I love you, and my plan of grace for you will never, ever fail."

In Acts 23 God tells Paul's story for us in a way that is intentionally self-revealing. God wants us to know him, and he wants us to know that nothing can stop his sovereign plan. These brief words of reassurance to Paul have been preserved for us, so that in moments when we are not sure of what God is doing, our hearts will rest in the unstoppable surety of God's holy, wise, and gracious plan.

Paul had been hauled before the most powerful religious leaders of his day to explain who he was and what he had been doing. After Paul spoke, this happened: "When the dissension became violent, the tribune, afraid that Paul would be torn to pieces by them, commanded the soldiers to go down and take him away from among them by force and bring him into the barracks" (Acts 23:10). The situation quickly became so violent that Paul had to be whisked away for his own safety. Imagine being in that room—hands sweating, heart pounding, wondering what was going to happen to you next. Paul had a valid reason to be afraid. But the next night, "the Lord stood by him and said, 'Take courage, for as you have testified to the facts about me in Jerusalem, so you must testify also in Rome'" (Acts 23:11). God wants his children to take heart, because he has a plan that cannot be thwarted.

For further study and encouragement: Isaiah 14:24–27

NOVEMBER 15

ACTS 26–28

*God's sovereign rule over all things, all of the time, does not make
our decisions and choices meaningless or inconsequential.*

The book of Acts records the incredible story of the apostle Paul's shipwreck.
But this is much more than just another story about an accident at sea. What
we need to focus on as we read this account is not the drama of the moment,
but the way in which the story is told. This tale is preserved for us to increase
our knowledge of who God is and how he works, as well as our understanding
of our responsibility as his creatures. This theologically rich story instructs us
in God's ongoing work of rescue and transformation:

> When neither sun nor stars appeared for many days, and no small tempest
> lay on us, all hope of our being saved was at last abandoned.
>
> Since they had been without food for a long time, Paul stood up among
> them and said, "Men, you should have listened to me and not have set sail
> from Crete and incurred this injury and loss. Yet now I urge you to take
> heart, for there will be no loss of life among you, but only of the ship. For
> this very night there stood before me an angel of the God to whom I belong
> and whom I worship, and he said, 'Do not be afraid, Paul; you must stand
> before Caesar. And behold, God has granted you all those who sail with
> you.'" (Acts 27:20–24)

Paul and the other people on board were enduring a powerful storm. It had
not relented for days. They were too anxious to eat. It seemed sure that there
would be a great loss of life, but Paul told them otherwise. God had revealed
to him that he had ordained that no one on this ship would be lost. This preordained plan was not just for Paul, but for all of the 276 people on board. After
Paul revealed God's plan to them, we read:

> And as the sailors were seeking to escape from the ship, and had lowered
> the ship's boat into the sea under pretense of laying out anchors from the
> bow, Paul said to the centurion and the soldiers, "Unless these men stay in
> the ship, you cannot be saved." Then the soldiers cut away the ropes of the
> ship's boat and let it go. (Acts 27:30–32)

Now which is true? Were all the lives in the ship preserved because God
had ordained it, or because they chose to do what Paul had advised and to

remain on the ship? The best biblical answer to this question is *both*. God accomplishes his sovereign plan through the means of our valid choices and actions. The Bible says God's sovereignty is a call to both rest of heart and a life of wise and obedient choices. Take heart: God is sovereign. Live wisely: your choices matter.

For further study and encouragement: Psalm 33:1–22

NOVEMBER 16

ROMANS 1–2

*At the heart of sin is a great exchange of love for
the Creator for love of created things.*

Every human being worships. The deepest motivational force in all humans is not experience or emotion; it is worship. Some think of worship as cold, formal ritualism. But the inclination to worship lies at the heart of every human being. It is placed in our hearts by God to drive us into loving and worshipful surrender to him. More than just an *activity* that we give ourselves to, worship is part of our *identity* as humans that none of us can escape. This also means that even the life of the most irreligious person is shaped by worship. So, at the center of sin is misplaced, misdirected worship. Sin originates from and is driven by the worship of something in creation rather than of God. Sin is not just wrong behavior. Sin is the idolatry of the heart that expresses itself by pursuing things that God forbids.

Paul writes in Romans 1 that God designed his world in a way that makes his existence obvious to everyone. He then says:

Although [the ungodly] knew God, they did not honor him as God or give thanks to him, but they became futile in their thinking, and their foolish hearts were darkened. Claiming to be wise, they became fools, and exchanged the glory of the immortal God for images resembling mortal man and birds and animals and creeping things.

Therefore God gave them up in the lusts of their hearts to impurity, to the dishonoring of their bodies among themselves, because they exchanged the truth about God for a lie and worshiped and served the creature rather than the Creator, who is blessed forever! Amen. (Rom. 1:21–25)

At the center of every sin is foolishness and futility. What is this foolishness? It's the exchanging of the heart-satisfying glory of God for some created God-replacement. What is the big lie of sin? It is that we can find human fulfillment by serving the creature rather than the Creator. Behind every evil desire, every evil choice, and every evil word or action is this great moral exchange. Sin is God-denying and creation-deifying.

Paul describes the result of this great exchange:

> Since they did not see fit to acknowledge God, God gave them up to a debased mind to do what ought not to be done. They were filled with all manner of unrighteousness, evil, covetousness, malice. They are full of envy, murder, strife, deceit, maliciousness. They are gossips, slanderers, haters of God, insolent, haughty, boastful, inventors of evil, disobedient to parents, foolish, faithless, heartless, ruthless. Though they know God's righteous decree that those who practice such things deserve to die, they not only do them but give approval to those who practice them. (Rom. 1:28–32)

May God rescue us from us, and by grace enable us to offer the allegiance and worship of our hearts to him alone. Heart-ruling and life-shaping worship of him happens only by the power of his grace. That grace is ours in Jesus.

For further study and encouragement: Exodus 20:1–6

———

NOVEMBER 17

ROMANS 3–4

No mere human has ever achieved acceptance with
God through obedience to his law. No one.

I was raised in a Christian home. I attended Sunday school and youth group every week. My family almost never missed a Sunday morning or evening worship service. We had family devotions every day. I memorized portions of God's word. Even as a little boy, I took notes during the sermon. I was convinced early in life that I was okay with God. I was one of the good guys. I was from a righteous family. Surely God looked down on me and judged that I was good. Because of my Christian performance and my family, I was quite confident of my standing with the Lord . . . until one summer at camp. My counselor read Romans 3 aloud, and verse 20 was the pin that completely deflated my self-righteousness balloon. All of a sudden, the Holy Spirit opened my eyes, and I saw my sin. No longer did I see myself as righteous. I could no longer think that I was okay with God. My righteousness had been devastated by fourteen words, in one verse in one book of the Bible: "By works of the law no human being will be justified in his sight . . ." (Rom. 3:20). I looked into the perfectly accurate mirror of Scripture and found myself wanting.

Romans 3:20 is one of the most humbling passages in the Bible. It crushes human pride. It makes it impossible for us to continue to caress the delusion that we can perform our way into a relationship with God. It lets us know that our best track record of obedience falls woefully short of God's holy requirement. This passage silences our pride in family, in our participation in formal worship, in our biblical literacy, and in daily obedience. If any of these things could justify us, there would have been no need for the righteous life, substitutionary death, and victorious resurrection of Jesus.

There is a second part to this very humbling verse: ". . . since through the law comes knowledge of sin" (Rom. 3:20). Having crushed our hope in our obedience, the apostle Paul then reminds us of one of the most significant functions of the law. God never intended the law to be a means of justification, that is, a way to be made right with him. May we abandon forever the idea that law has the power to justify us before God. This is one of Satan's most horrible lies. If you believe this lie, then you will trust in your righteousness and deny your need for grace. This leads to spiritual death. Paul reminds us that one reason the law was given was to expose our sinfulness to us. Millions of people are in spiritual danger simply because they don't see themselves as sinners. God gave us his laws to convince us that we are suffering from a terminal disease: sin. But God doesn't leave us only with the knowledge of sin. No, he gives us the gift of his Son. Jesus's life, death, and resurrection are the means by which we can know eternal acceptance with God. There simply is no other way.

For further study and encouragement: Galatians 3:1–14

NOVEMBER 18

*If someone were to ask you to explain God's
justifying grace, what would you say?*

It is hard to comprehend the riches that are ours because of the justifying work of Jesus. Paul tells us in Romans 5 what we possess because of Christ's perfectly righteous life, his anger-satisfying death, and his victorious resurrection:

> Since we have been justified by faith, we have peace with God through our Lord Jesus Christ. Through him we have also obtained access by faith into this grace in which we stand, and we rejoice in hope of the glory of God. Not only that, but we rejoice in our sufferings, knowing that suffering produces endurance, and endurance produces character, and character produces hope, and hope does not put us to shame, because God's love has been poured into our hearts through the Holy Spirit who has been given to us. (Rom. 5:1–5)

To be justified by faith means:

1. *We have peace with God.* May we never devalue these words. It is a miracle of grace that we who were born in sin and are still giving in to sin can have peace with God. Born as natural enemies of God, we are now blessed with eternal peace with him—not because of anything we have done but because of what God did for us in Jesus.
2. *We have permanent standing with God.* The peace we have with God isn't temporary. Because of justifying grace, we stand forever at peace with God. He will never turn his back on us. He will never turn against us. He will never unleash his anger on us. Our eternal standing with him is another miracle of grace.
3. *We have eternal hope.* We no longer live without hope in this world. Our hope in God will never fail, disappoint, or shame us. Because of Jesus, we have been liberated from the hopelessness of self-reliance and have been blessed with eternal hope.
4. *We have sturdy joy.* In Christ we are blessed with undefeatable joy. Because our joy is vertical—that is, in God and not in people, possessions, or circumstances—we have reason to be joyful no matter what. Redemptive joy is the strongest, sturdiest joy we could ever have, and it is ours in Jesus.

5. *We have God's love poured into our hearts.* Because of the justifying mercies that are ours in Jesus, we are the objects of God's eternal love. He hasn't sprinkled a few drops of love over us and then walked away. No, God has poured his love into our hearts. No matter how you feel on a given day, your heart is filled to the brim with God's love.
6. *We have the gift of the Holy Spirit.* Our once-dead hearts have been animated by the Holy Spirit. He lives inside of us to convict us of sin, empower us for good works, and open our hearts to understand God's truth.

This is what it means to stand before God as justified. These are the riches of his grace. This is the legacy of Jesus's redeeming work. May we celebrate what is ours in Christ every day of our lives.

For further study and encouragement: Genesis 15:1–6

NOVEMBER 19

ROMANS 7–8

We must never allow ourselves to underestimate
the presence or power of remaining sin.

The apostle Paul gives us an important and accurate description of the presence and power of indwelling sin:

> I do not understand my own actions. For I do not do what I want, but I do the very thing I hate. Now if I do what I do not want, I agree with the law, that it is good. So now it is no longer I who do it, but sin that dwells within me. For I know that nothing good dwells in me, that is, in my flesh. For I have the desire to do what is right, but not the ability to carry it out. For I do not do the good I want, but the evil I do not want is what I keep on doing. Now if I do what I do not want, it is no longer I who do it, but sin that dwells within me.
> So I find it to be a law that when I want to do right, evil lies close at hand. For I delight in the law of God, in my inner being, but I see in my members another law waging war against the law of my mind and making me captive to the law of sin that dwells in my members. Wretched man

411

that I am! Who will deliver me from this body of death? Thanks be to God through Jesus Christ our Lord! So then, I myself serve the law of God with my mind, but with my flesh I serve the law of sin. (Rom. 7:15–25)

This passage describes a believer's struggle with sin, because only a believer would "delight in the law of God." If you can't relate to this passage, then you're probably in some form of denial. Who hasn't been confused by his or her own actions? You determine to do what is right, but then you get into a tempting situation and end up doing all the things you had determined not to do. Your good intentions fall flat. Why do we still struggle to do what is right? Paul's answer is that we struggle because sin still lives inside of us. Yes, we have been justified, but our sin has not yet been totally eradicated.

To help us understand the power of remaining sin, Paul describes sin as a *law*, a *war*, and a *captor*. When he says that sin is a law, he doesn't mean a moral law, such as the Ten Commandments. He's talking about law here as an inescapable force, like gravity. You cannot will yourself free of gravity on earth, no matter how hard you fight its force. And you cannot will yourself free from the power of sin. Paul also says that sin is a war. We fight in this war, and the battleground is our hearts. Finally, he tells us that sin is a captor. It takes us captive to its deception and power, and we have no power to set ourselves free.

These three descriptors powerfully argue for the necessity of the grace of Jesus.

For further study and encouragement: Mark 8:31–38

———

NOVEMBER 20

ROMANS 9–11

As a child of God, you have a reason to give endless praise. What is your daily doxology?

What is a *doxology*? The word is a combination of two Greek words: *doxa*, which means "glory," and *logos*, which means "word." A *doxology* is a hymn or a statement of praise. To pronounce a doxology is literally to give something glory by words. It is inarguable that human beings have a glory orientation. All of us are magnetized by things that we find glorious. For some of us that may be a fantastic meal or a well-written novel. For others it could be an exciting athletic contest or simply a good night's sleep. God has oriented us toward glory to drive us to worship him. Nothing in the universe is more glorious than Almighty God. He is the definition of *glorious*; he has all glory in and of himself and is glorious all of the time and in every way. And his glory is reflected in the glory of the things he has created. Flowers, sunsets, birds, mountains, seas, lions, and mighty storms are glorious because the one who made them is glorious.

Because you are oriented toward glory, you are doxological. You will speak and sing of glory. You will utter words of praise. You will tell of what has captured your awe. With passion and excitement you will share your glory experiences with others, encouraging them to experience those glories as well. You will hunt for glorious things, and, when you find them, doxologies will come out of your mouth. Who or what has captured the doxologies of your heart and mouth? What most often captures your glory attention, your glory excitement, and your glory praise? Who or what owns your daily doxologies? No, I'm not talking about Sunday morning, when Godward doxologies are drawn out of you by those who lead you in worship. I'm talking about your Tuesday and Wednesday doxologies. I'm talking about your doxologies on a beautiful Saturday afternoon. What gets your praise?

After an extensive discussion of God's electing mercies in Romans, the apostle Paul breaks into one of the most beautiful doxologies in all of Scripture:

Oh, the depth of the riches and wisdom and knowledge of God! How unsearchable are his judgments and how inscrutable his ways!

"For who has known the mind of the Lord,
or who has been his counselor?"
"Or who has given a gift to him
that he might be repaid?"

For from him and through him and to him are all things. To him be glory forever. Amen. (Rom. 11:33–36)

It is right to celebrate the gift of glorious created things, but these things must not dominate our daily doxologies. May our daily doxologies be captured by the glory of the Lord and his glorious grace. May all other doxologies give way to the praise of him, because it really is true that "from him and through him and to him are all things."

For further study and encouragement: Psalm 96:1–13

413

NOVEMBER 21

*God calls us to love not just our family and
friends but our enemies as well.*

Perhaps of all God's commands to us, the call to love our enemies is the most unnatural. It is natural for us to love those who love us in return, but sometimes even that is difficult. As sinful people, it is positively unnatural for us to look for ways to be kind and loving to those who have mistreated us. You can almost feel your heart harden with anger when you recall someone's hurtful or harmful actions toward you. You play scenes over and over in your head, getting more upset with every replay. You fantasize about ways to retaliate. You certainly don't think how you might respond to mistreatment with love.

The only thing that can turn what is unnatural for us—loving our enemies—into something more natural is a robust, street-level trust in the Lord. If you really do believe that he is perfectly holy and just; if you really do believe that he cares for his own; and if you really do believe that he will somehow defend your cause, then you can reject responding in kind and instead love as you have been called to love. Loving your enemy is a sure test of the depth and practicality of your faith in the Lord. It is also a stark reminder of how much you need God's empowering grace to desire and to do what is right in the eyes of the Lord, no matter what.

So what does it look like to love your enemy?

> Repay no one evil for evil, but give thought to do what is honorable in the sight of all. If possible, so far as it depends on you, live peaceably with all. Beloved, never avenge yourselves, but leave it to the wrath of God, for it is written, "Vengeance is mine, I will repay, says the Lord." To the contrary, "if your enemy is hungry, feed him; if he is thirsty, give him something to drink; for by so doing you will heap burning coals on his head." Do not be overcome by evil, but overcome evil with good. (Rom. 12:17–21)

Loving your enemy means never repaying evil with evil.
Loving your enemy means determining to live peaceably with everyone.
Loving your enemy means never responding in vengeance.
Loving your enemy means trusting the perfect justice of the Lord.
Loving your enemy means overcoming evil with good.

When it comes to loving our enemies, God calls us to believe that what he asks us to do is always good, that he is always with us and faithful in justice, and that he will meet us in our struggle to love with his empowering grace.

In this fallen world, you will face mistreatment. Will you respond with love? Will you leave vengeance to the Lord? Will you seek to overcome evil with good? Will you rest in God's empowering and transforming grace? His grace is yours for the taking.

For further study and encouragement: Matthew 5:38–48

———

NOVEMBER 22

ROMANS 14–16

The Christian life is not a sprint but an extended journey. Will you endure to the end?

In high school I ran long-distance races for our track team. I remember well the three phases of the race. Standing on the starting line, I was filled with excitement. I felt the rush of adrenaline before the starter's gun went off and the race commenced. Those first few steps were a fog of emotions, adrenaline, and athletic motivation. It felt as though I were being carried along. Later, as part of the final stage of the race, I felt renewed joy at seeing the finish line in the distance. I forgot how tired I was. My arms and legs no longer felt heavy as I ran faster and faster until I crossed that line.

But in every race, the middle phase was always the hardest. The starting-line adrenaline was gone and the finish-line passion was a long way off. In the middle I experienced the monotony of step after step, the growing tiredness of my body, and the mental struggle to just keep going. In a long race, the middle is always the hardest.

The race of faith is not a sprint; it is a life-long journey. And it is not a journey over beautiful, smooth terrain. In our Christian journey, we run through dark valleys and high mountains. We stumble along rocky and twisted roads, and we encounter unexpected obstacles. The initial shot of new-faith adrenaline fades, and the finish line isn't in sight, but we must press on.

This journey requires endurance. The commitment to be faithful, to press forward no matter what, is essential for the life to which God has called you. What has God given you to stimulate endurance? How does he meet you with his grace when you face midrace hardships? At the end of the Bible's longest examination of the gospel—the book of Romans—the apostle Paul answers these questions:

Whatever was written in former days was written for our instruction, that through endurance and through the encouragement of the Scriptures we might have hope. May the God of endurance and encouragement grant you to live in such harmony with one another, in accord with Christ Jesus, that together you may with one voice glorify the God and Father of our Lord Jesus Christ. Therefore welcome one another as Christ has welcomed you, for the glory of God. (Rom. 15:4–7)

Paul wants you to know that in your long journey of faith God hasn't left you without help. He has given you his word, which was written to encourage endurance. He has also given you his people, so that you never need to run the race alone. Endurance is a word project. It is also a community project. Each is meant to meet you, strengthen you, and encourage you when the going in the middle becomes tough.

For further study and encouragement: 1 Corinthians 9:24–27

———

NOVEMBER 23

1 CORINTHIANS 1–4

We should never underestimate the Holy Spirit's ministry of illumination.

The message that has the power to change us is a mystery. It reveals God's eternal plan, exposes the depth of our spiritual need, and shows us how this need is met in Jesus. But it remains in darkness for most of humanity:

Among the mature we do impart wisdom, although it is not a wisdom of this age or of the rulers of this age, who are doomed to pass away. But we impart a secret and hidden wisdom of God, which God decreed before the ages for our glory. None of the rulers of this age understood this, for if they had, they would not have crucified the Lord of glory. But, as it is written,

"What no eye has seen, nor ear heard,
    nor the heart of man imagined,
what God has prepared for those who love him"—

these things God has revealed to us through the Spirit. For the Spirit searches everything, even the depths of God. (1 Cor. 2:6–10)

When you need to see something in the dark, you turn on the lights. The illumining ministry of the Holy Spirit is God's means of turning the gospel lights on for us. As Paul reminds us, the wisdom of the gospel is not a natural body of wisdom. If it were, then everyone would believe it and live in light of it.

Human wisdom never saw in advance exactly what God would do to redeem his fallen world. It never could have imagined the move of the gospel of grace and the amazing gift of the Son. Human wisdom could not have predicted the glorious things that God had prepared for those who love him. We were all born into the same miserable state. The eyes of all of our hearts were closed to the gospel, and all of our minds were closed to its life-giving wisdom. We all sat in darkness, unable to see the one thing that could have given us life right now and on into eternity. We were without hope until God met us in the darkness and, by the presence and power of his Spirit, turned the gospel lights on for us. If you know and love the gospel of Jesus Christ, then you do so because you have been met by the illumining ministry of the Holy Spirit.

There is something else that you need to know and celebrate. This illumining ministry is not an event but a process. Have you ever studied a biblical passage that you have read many times before, but all of a sudden it bursts with new meaning? That happens because the Holy Spirit continually shines his light on his word so that you may understand it more fully and deeply.

In your darkness, you were met by light-giving grace, and the lights haven't gone out. They're still shining, illuminating the best message ever written: the heart-changing, life-giving gospel of Jesus Christ.

For further study and encouragement: John 16:5–15

NOVEMBER 24

1 CORINTHIANS 5–8

The allure of sexual immorality seems to be everywhere in this world. How are we to deal with this temptation?

Paul directly addresses our struggle with sexual purity in 1 Corinthians 6:

"All things are lawful for me," but not all things are helpful. "All things are lawful for me," but I will not be dominated by anything. "Food is meant for the stomach and the stomach for food"—and God will destroy both one and the other. The body is not meant for sexual immorality, but for the Lord, and the Lord for the body. And God raised the Lord and will also raise us up by his power. Do you not know that your bodies are members of Christ? Shall I then take the members of Christ and make them members of a prostitute? Never! Or do you not know that he who is joined to a prostitute becomes one body with her? For, as it is written, "The two will become one flesh." But he who is joined to the Lord becomes one spirit with him. Flee from sexual immorality. Every other sin a person commits is outside the body, but the sexually immoral person sins against his own body. Or do you not know that your body is a temple of the Holy Spirit within you, whom you have from God? You are not your own, for you were bought with a price. So glorify God in your body. (1 Cor. 6:12–20)

Few topics are more relevant for every Christian than sexual temptation. We live in a deeply sexualized culture, where every biblical sexual norm has been rejected. It is nearly impossible to look at your phone or your favorite streaming service without being assaulted by illicit sexuality. What God says is ugly and wrong is pushed at us as being beautiful and right. So this ancient passage is timely.

Paul lays out four principles to guide us in the area of our sexuality. These principles are God's guardrails, designed to keep us on God's path of righteousness and safety.

1. The principle of *mastery.* Paul argues that, even if all things were lawful (they're not), we must still be aware of the addictive nature of sin, and must determine to be mastered by Christ alone.
2. The principle of *eternity.* We must approach everything with eternity in view. This life is not about getting all the pleasure you can but rather about preparing for the glorious pleasures to come.
3. The principle of *unity.* By amazing grace, we are eternally united to Christ. This means that we drag him with us into whatever sexual sin we pursue.
4. The principle of *ownership.* Since we are children of God, the members of our bodies no longer belong to us to use as we will. By grace, we now live under divine ownership.

These principles are gifts of God's grace. With them, he is wrapping his arms around you and drawing you close, so that you might be free from the moral dangers all around you. Thank him for his restraining grace.

For further study and encouragement: Matthew 5:27–30

1 CORINTHIANS 9–11

Everything that has been recorded and preserved in the
Bible has been placed there by our Lord for our good.

When reading the Bible, you might be tempted to skip over things that don't interest you or that seem to have no connection to your life. Perhaps you wonder why you need to read all those laws in Leviticus or the chapters that record the numbering of the tribes of Israel or yet another genealogy. Perhaps you've wondered why you need to know all that Old Testament history. But God's word was recorded, preserved, and delivered to us for his glory and our good. He guided every part of it so that we would know him, ourselves, the depth of our struggle with sin, the solution to sin's disease in the person and work of Jesus, the realities of life in a fallen world, what it means to live as God intended, the assurance of our future hope, and more. Every part of God's word is loaded with loving, redemptive intention.

Consider this passage from 1 Corinthians 10:

These things took place as examples for us, that we might not desire evil as they did. Do not be idolaters as some of them were; as it is written, "The people sat down to eat and drink and rose up to play." We must not indulge in sexual immorality as some of them did, and twenty-three thousand fell in a single day. We must not put Christ to the test, as some of them did and were destroyed by serpents, nor grumble, as some of them did and were destroyed by the Destroyer. Now these things happened to them as an example, but they were written down for our instruction, on whom the end of the ages has come. Therefore let anyone who thinks that he stands take heed lest he fall. (1 Cor. 10:6–12)

The Bible we hold in our hands is physical proof of how much God loves us. In an act of sovereign love, God preserved the history of his people, which serves as an example to us. He did so to protect us from the temptations that captured his people in the Old Testament. All of this has been recorded because the Lord who created you also knows you. He knows the world you live in and the temptations you face, and he uses the history of his people to warn and remind you that true life is found only in him.

Paul ends his discussion of the value of the history of God's word in this way: "Therefore let anyone who thinks that he stands take heed lest he fall." We must not avoid any part of God's word or tell ourselves that we don't need it. We must not think that we know what we need better than God knows. We must humbly accept that we are capable of falling prey to all the sinful things that captured those who came before us, and that we need everything God has given us in his word.

For further study and encouragement: Psalm 1:1–6

———

NOVEMBER 26

1 CORINTHIANS 12–14

Your walk with God is a total-body project.

I was in the hospital because I thought I had a severe urinary infection, but as the days passed, it became clear that something even more serious was wrong inside of me. The urinary issues had permanently damaged my kidneys, and I was in acute renal failure. I later learned that I had lost about 65 percent of my kidney function. I was shocked and confused as to what this meant for my life going forward, but there was more shock to come. When one major organ is damaged, it negatively affects other systems in your body. I didn't just have kidney problems; I had other physical problems because of the kidney problems.

God did not design the systems and members of our body to function independently. Our bodies have a systemic cooperation and interdependency, which means that if one part of the body is damaged, other parts are affected as well. This interdependency means that no organ can function on its own. Every system works well only when it is working in concert with the other systems in the body. The human body is a marvel of divine design. So is the body of Christ:

> The body does not consist of one member but of many. If the foot should say, "Because I am not a hand, I do not belong to the body," that would not make it any less a part of the body. And if the ear should say, "Because I am not an eye, I do not belong to the body," that would not make it any less a part of the body. If the whole body were an eye, where would be the sense of hearing? If the whole body were an ear, where would be the sense of smell? But as it is, God arranged the members in the body, each one of them, as he chose. If all were a single member, where would the body be? As it is, there are many parts, yet one body. (1 Cor. 12:14–20)

Just as God carefully designed the systems of the human body to be interdependent, so he designed the body of Christ—the church—to be an interdependent organism. You have been placed right where God wants you, and you need the gifts and graces of the people whom God has placed around you. There is no such thing as independent, isolated, self-sufficient, Jesus-and-me Christianity. Independent Christianity is a delusion and a rejection of God's loving and wise design. Your walk with God is a total-body project.

Do you see yourself as part of an interdependent organism? Who knows you? Who knows your spiritual weaknesses and struggles? Whom have you invited to speak into your life? Are you submitting to God's design, or are you trying to make it on your own?

For further study and encouragement: Ephesians 4:1–16

———

NOVEMBER 27

1 CORINTHIANS 15–16

Do you ever wonder what Jesus is doing at this very moment?

I will never forget the first time 1 Corinthians 15:20–26 got my attention. I knew that 1 Corinthians 15 was the Bible's premier resurrection chapter. Paul's discussion of the necessity, power, and implications of the resurrection of Jesus Christ is unlike any other discussion in Scripture. You walk away from this chapter convinced that, if Jesus hadn't risen out of the tomb, our faith would be vain and we would be spiritually doomed. First Corinthians 15 digs deep into the riches of Christ's resurrection. But one day, during my devotional reading of this passage, I saw something else. I don't know how I hadn't seen it before, but that day it jumped off the page with comfort and glory. Right in the middle of his discussion of the resurrection, Paul gives us an amazing picture of what Jesus is doing for us *now*. Once you see this, your view of life as a child of God is altered forever:

In fact Christ has been raised from the dead, the firstfruits of those who have fallen asleep. For as by a man came death, by a man has come also the resurrection of the dead. For as in Adam all die, so also in Christ shall all be made alive. But each in his own order: Christ the firstfruits, then at his coming those who belong to Christ. Then comes the end, when he delivers the kingdom to God the Father after destroying every rule and every authority and power. For he must reign until he has put all his enemies under his feet. The last enemy to be destroyed is death. (1 Cor. 15:20–26)

Notice the last few sentences of this passage. Paul explains what is happening between the resurrection of Jesus and the moment when he will deliver the final kingdom to God the Father. What is Jesus doing? He is reigning. Jesus's reign began at his ascension to the right hand of the Father. As the royal, reigning Son, he is destroying every authority, power, and enemy that stands in the way of the final victory of the redeemed. He will not stop exercising his royal power until every last enemy is under his feet, including death. Then he will welcome us into his final kingdom forever.

This means that you are never alone in your spiritual struggles. Your royal King is right now defeating all the enemies that seek to defeat you. He is conquering foes that you do not have the power to conquer. He is putting under his divine feet the things that seem to overpower you,. His reign is not just your future hope; it is your hope right now. Yes, you serve a risen Savior, but it's vital to remember that he is also a conquering King. He is right now harvesting the spoils of the victory of his life, death, and resurrection. That harvest is for you. In the reign of Jesus the King, you have hope for today—and for all time.

For further study and encouragement: Hebrews 1:1–4

———

NOVEMBER 28

2 CORINTHIANS 1–4

Your Lord owns you and everything in your life, even your suffering.

Perhaps you have wondered, as many have, why a good, loving, patient, kind, and gracious God would allow his children to suffer. He surely has the divine power and authority to protect us from hardship and to make our lives comfortable. There is never a moment when his care for us fails. There is never a moment when we slip beyond his gaze. There is never a moment when he turns his back on us. There is no hardship beyond his ability to defeat. There is never a time when his love and grace for us wane. He is always present, always faithful, and always good. Yet, every one of his children suffers somehow and in some way. If you are not suffering now, you will someday; and, if you are not suffering now, there is a good chance you're near someone who is. Why is suffering the universal experience of the children of God?

In the beginning of 2 Corinthians, the apostle Paul gives us one reason why God leads his children through suffering. This is not Scripture's only answer to the question of suffering, but it is an important one:

> Blessed be the God and Father of our Lord Jesus Christ, the Father of mercies and God of all comfort, who comforts us in all our affliction, so that we may be able to comfort those who are in any affliction, with the comfort with which we ourselves are comforted by God. For as we share abundantly in Christ's sufferings, so through Christ we share abundantly in comfort too. If we are afflicted, it is for your comfort and salvation; and if we are comforted, it is for your comfort, which you experience when you patiently endure the same sufferings that we suffer. Our hope for you is unshaken, for we know that as you share in our sufferings, you will also share in our comfort. (2 Cor. 1:3–7)

Paul gives a surprising answer to the question of suffering. He says that we suffer precisely because God is the Father of mercies and the God of all comfort. Does this confuse you? The Father leads us to share in the sufferings of Jesus, who, like us, had to deal with the harsh realities of life in this fallen world. This is how we share in God's comfort. Why is it important for us to share in God's comfort? We are put in the position of needing God's comfort so that we may then be able to comfort those around us who are facing some kind of affliction, suffering, or hardship.

Here's the plan. God makes his invisible comfort visible by sending people who have received his comfort and can give that same comfort to other sufferers. God has a redemptive purpose for your suffering. He leads you into what you never would have planned for yourself so that you may be prepared to be part of his gracious plan in the lives of others. It is true that even your suffering belongs to God. Although unexpected and hard, your suffering has meaning and purpose in the hands of the Lord.

For further study and encouragement: Romans 8:26–38

NOVEMBER 29

2 CORINTHIANS 5–9

Living with eternity in view means living with a tent mentality.

I tell my camping friends that the whole purpose of camping is to make you long for home. You start out enthusiastically, imagining spending time with your family or friends in the great outdoors. You arrive at your campsite, put up the tent, gather firewood, and enjoy your first night. But, about three days in, you find it harder to find firewood, your back hurts from sleeping without your mattress, and your tent doesn't smell so good. You're getting near the end of your supplies, and wondering whether what is left is edible. It's hot and sticky, which makes sleeping difficult, and as you lie down to sleep, you begin to dream of home. You think of the convenience of your stove, the luxury of your mattress, and the comfort of air conditioning. You long for home.

The apostle Paul likens us to tent dwellers:

> We know that if the tent that is our earthly home is destroyed, we have a building from God, a house not made with hands, eternal in the heavens. For in this tent we groan, longing to put on our heavenly dwelling, if indeed by putting it on we may not be found naked. For while we are still in this tent, we groan, being burdened—not that we would be unclothed, but that we would be further clothed, so that what is mortal may be swallowed up by life. He who has prepared us for this very thing is God, who has given us the Spirit as a guarantee. (2 Cor. 5:1–5)

Paul's word picture in this passage is important. Everything in the here and now is temporary. This isn't our final destination. A day is coming when we will be at home with the Lord. So, as the children of God, it's important that we not think of this life with a *destination mentality*. What does this mean? We don't live as though this is all we have, that this is our final destination. Therefore we don't strive to experience all the pleasures and comforts we can get our hands on, and we don't get mad at God when life is uncomfortable. We don't work to build a big pile of earthy possessions, and we don't get mad at God when he chooses to provide only for our daily needs and little more. We don't live for power, acclaim, or control, and we don't question the goodness of God when we have none of these.

Rather, we live with a *tent mentality*. We recognize that this present life is temporary, because an eternal home has been prepared for us. So in every area of our lives we live with eternity in view. We don't allow ourselves to be controlled by the pursuit of money, family, sex, career, material possessions, or any other earthly thing, because, by grace, we are going home.

The Christian life is a temporary time of preparation for the final destination that is guaranteed to all God's children. Do you live with a tent mentality, or do you live as though this were your final home?

For further study and encouragement: Colossians 3:1–4

NOVEMBER 30

2 CORINTHIANS 10–13

Weakness does not hinder God's plan. It is an essential part of it.

I sat in my favorite chair, too weak to move. I hated being that weak. I had never envisioned myself becoming so frail. I am project oriented. I always wake up with an agenda for the day. I have always been strong and productive and able to work quickly. But suddenly all of those abilities were gone. As I sat in that chair day after day, the Holy Spirit worked conviction into my heart. I had to confess that much of what I had thought was faith in Christ wasn't that at all. I had a lot of pride in my own strength and accomplishments. But because he loves me, God did not leave me in that prideful state. Pride is the enemy of grace. Pride drives us away from the Lord, not to him. In those very hard moments of weakness, I began to experience a deeper trust and joy in my Savior. God used my weakness to change me, to rescue me from me, and to wrap his arms of love around me and draw me close. If this was what it took for God to work transformation in my heart, then every moment of weakness was worth it.

We tend to hate weakness because we hate being dependent. We love stories of unusual strength and control because we quietly wish those traits for ourselves. The problem is that God did not create us for independent, self-sufficient living. He created us to be dependent on him and on the human tools he places in our lives. The fact of the matter is that everyone is weak. The humbling truth is that we are all a collection of weaknesses, held together by strong cords of grace and mercy. Because God designed us to be dependent, we know that weakness cannot hinder his great plan for us; rather, weakness and dependence are essential parts of that plan. Note how Paul talks about his weakness:

To keep me from becoming conceited because of the surpassing greatness of the revelations, a thorn was given me in the flesh, a messenger of Satan to harass me, to keep me from becoming conceited. Three times I pleaded with the Lord about this, that it should leave me. But he said to me, "My grace is sufficient for you, for my power is made perfect in weakness." Therefore I will boast all the more gladly of my weaknesses, so that the power of Christ may rest upon me. For the sake of Christ, then, I am content with weaknesses, insults, hardships, persecutions, and calamities. For when I am weak, then I am strong. (2 Cor. 12:7–10)

In the face of his weakness, Paul did what all of us would do: he prayed again and again for it to be removed. God answered Paul's prayer—not by removing his weakness but by meeting him with the grace of divine power. Why? Because weakness was God's tool to deliver Paul from pride and self-reliance. In the hands of the Redeemer, weakness is a workroom for transforming grace. Are you content with weakness, knowing that God uses it to work in you and through you?

For further study and encouragement: Matthew 11:25–30

———

DECEMBER 1

GALATIANS 1–3

Understanding what it means to live by faith is foundational to the Christian life.

"No one is justified before God by the law." These words from Galatians 3:11 challenge our natural thoughts and inclinations. Christianity is not a meritocracy; we don't earn a place in God's family based on our track record of righteousness. Our standing with God does not depend upon our obedience. Keeping the law has no power whatsoever to purchase the most important thing in life: a relationship with God. No one keeps the law perfectly. No one is perfectly righteous all of the time and in every way. This verse devastates all forms of human pride, self-righteousness, and self-sufficiency.

My level of biblical literacy and understanding of theology does not determine my righteousness before God. My faithful participation in a local body of Christ does not secure my good standing with the Lord. Though I am called to be generous and kind, my treatment of others does not, on its own, merit God's favor. My Christian heritage and commitment to ministry do not secure my adoption as God's child. These nine words of Galatians 3:11 crush my pride in achievement and knowledge. They confront my skewed assessment that I am one of the good guys and "those people" are the bad guys. You cannot be self-righteously self-assured and thankful for redeeming grace at the same time. You cannot erect self-atoning arguments that make you look more righteous than you really are and also be thankful for God's rescuing and empowering mercies.

When I am tempted to trust in my own righteousness, the end of Galatians 3:11 sets me straight: "The righteous shall live by faith." These six words must follow the first nine; otherwise we would have no hope. Just as we physically cannot live without oxygen, so we spiritually cannot live without faith. To give your body life and vitality, God provides both oxygen and your capacity to breathe it in. In the same way, God meets us in our sin with divine grace, and he empowers us to take it in by faith. Both grace and faith are gifts from God; he gives us humility, willingness, and belief so that we can breathe into our hearts what he has provided.

These two truths define our standing with God and the nature of the Christian life: "No one is justified before God by the law" and "the righteous shall live by faith." May God give us faithfulness, humility, and steadfastness so that we might live in light of these gospel words that he has recorded and preserved for us. May they shape the way we think about ourselves and how we live. And may they fill us with awe, gratitude, and surrender.

For further study and encouragement: Hebrews 11:1–40

———

DECEMBER 2

GALATIANS 4–6

We should be thankful that the gospel is a message of both reconciliation and restoration.

I have a deep appreciation for the many word pictures we find in Scripture. I love how the biblical writers paint pictures for us of the God who works on our behalf and of the way in which he works. These pictures are meant to inform, confront, and encourage. When you read your Bible, you should never rush past imagery of such things as the sun, wind, trees, water, food, shepherds, judges, fathers, lions, lambs, the temple, houses, bodies, and so on. The imagery in Scripture is loaded with redemptive meaning and is God's way of opening the eyes of our hearts to the great and deep mysteries of the gospel. Restoration is the theme of many of these word pictures. Think of an old, crumbling house. Though it stands broken and neglected, it still has value. You can see glimpses of its original beauty.

God by his grace made me a house for his Spirit. But the house he has entered needs work. It still bears his image, but it has been bent, twisted, and disheveled by sin. So God enters the house with a mission of giving me justifying grace as well as restorative grace. He will not stop tearing down, replacing, and rebuilding until we are fully formed into his image. If you are his child, you are dependent on God's restorative grace—and you are in the middle of its work.

But there is something else we should understand here. God calls us to join him in his mission of human restoration:

> Brothers, if anyone is caught in any transgression, you who are spiritual should restore him in a spirit of gentleness. Keep watch on yourself, lest you too be tempted. Bear one another's burdens, and so fulfill the law of Christ. (Gal. 6:1–2)

Five words in this passage define our restorative calling:

1. *Caught.* This is the condition. The idea is not "Aha, I caught you." Instead, a brother or sister is ensnared in sin. He or she needs to be rescued from that snare.
2. *Restore.* This is the mission. We are not to condemn; we are to be tools of restoration in the hands of the Redeemer. Where and how does change need to take place?
3. *Gentleness.* This is the character of the mission. We come not with wrecking balls but with gentle tools of confrontation and hope.
4. *Watch.* This is the warning. As I join God's restorative mission, I watch myself, so that pride, impatience, and judgment don't get in the way.
5. *Bear.* This is the daily goal. Together we bear with one another in our struggles toward godliness.

God makes his work of restoration visible by sending his restorers to people who need his restorative mercies.

For further study and encouragement: Luke 9:1–6

DECEMBER 3

What do you pray for the most?

Your prayers reveal what your heart truly values. What you want most in life, and the frequency you ask for it, exposes what you think about your meaning and purpose and what is important to you. Your prayers expose where you think life, peace, and satisfaction might be found. Your true hopes and dreams are embedded in your prayers. In prayer, God and idolatry often collide. Prayer can be a battle between what I desire for myself and what God wants for me. Prayer can be an occasion when surrender gives way to demand, when love *for* God gives way to what you would love to get *from* God. Because of this, prayer is a battleground of spiritual warfare.

By God's grace we have the apostle Paul's prayer for the Ephesian Christians, which serves as a model for our prayers:

> For this reason, because I have heard of your faith in the Lord Jesus and your love toward all the saints, I do not cease to give thanks for you, remembering you in my prayers, that the God of our Lord Jesus Christ, the Father of glory, may give you the Spirit of wisdom and of revelation in the knowledge of him, having the eyes of your hearts enlightened, that you may know what is the hope to which he has called you, what are the riches of his glorious inheritance in the saints, and what is the immeasurable greatness of his power toward us who believe, according to the working of his great might that he worked in Christ when he raised him from the dead and seated him at his right hand in the heavenly places, far above all rule and authority and power and dominion, and above every name that is named, not only in this age but also in the one to come. And he put all things under his feet and gave him as head over all things to the church, which is his body, the fullness of him who fills all in all. (Eph. 1:15–23)

After giving thanks for these loved ones, Paul expresses the deep desires of his heart for them. Paul asks that:

- God would give them his Spirit of wisdom and revelation.
- The eyes of their hearts would be enlightened.
- They would understand the hope to which they have been called.
- They would live in light of the rich inheritance that awaits them.

- They would grasp the resurrection power they have been given.
- They would understand the expansive reign of their Savior King.

What are our true daily needs? We need to understand the mysteries of the gospel. We need the Spirit to break through our spiritual blindness. We need to live with hope and with eyes on eternity. We need to understand our power against sin. And we need to rest in our King's reign over everything. May these things be the daily cries of our hearts as we pray.

For further study and encouragement: Psalm 42:1–11

DECEMBER 4

EPHESIANS 4–6

For the sake of your spiritual health and growth, it is important
to remember that your walk with God is a community project.

One of the dark delusions of sin is that you and I are capable of independent living. We see this independence in children, who do not want to be told what to eat, when to go to bed, or how to care for their possessions. But the Bible shows us that God created human beings to be dependent. Adam and Eve were perfect people living in a perfect world, and yet they were deeply dependent on God and one another from the start. An essential element of their perfection was their willingness to live in dependent community. The shalom of that perfection was shattered when they desired to be independent and then acted on that desire. Horrible things happened to them, separating them from God and one another and bringing destruction and dysfunction into the world God had created.

We live in a world that is broken and dysfunctional. And, because sin still lives inside of us, we continue to have delusions of independence. Because God created us to be dependent on him and others, it should be clear that the Christian journey is not about moving from dependence to independence. Rather, we are to leave behind proud self-sufficiency and to embrace willing vertical and horizontal dependence instead. Dependence characterizes the Christian life and the body of Christ. The church is a gathering of people who by grace have been called into both dependent community with God and interdependent community with one another. There is no such thing as isolated, self-sufficient, "just Jesus and me" Christianity. The Christianity of the Bible is deeply and expansively dependent.

So it makes sense that after spending the first half of his letter to the Ephesians defining and explaining the gospel of Jesus Christ, Paul first applies this gospel to our relationships as believers:

> I therefore, a prisoner for the Lord, urge you to walk in a manner worthy of the calling to which you have been called, with all humility and gentleness, with patience, bearing with one another in love, eager to maintain the unity of the Spirit in the bond of peace. There is one body and one Spirit—just as you were called to the one hope that belongs to your call—one Lord, one faith, one baptism, one God and Father of all, who is over all and through all and in all. But grace was given to each one of us according to the measure of Christ's gift. Therefore it says,
>
> > "When he ascended on high he led a host of captives,
> > and he gave gifts to men." (Eph. 4:1–8)

May God grant us the grace to live with one another in humility, gentleness, patience, peace, unity, and interdependence. May this create a context in which his work of grace in and through us may thrive.

For further study and encouragement: 1 Corinthians 12:4–13

DECEMBER 5

PHILIPPIANS 1–4

*Our hope in this life and the one to come rests on
the humiliation and exaltation of the Son.*

It's important to confess that we love being exalted and dislike being humbled. None of us enjoys moments when we are proven to be less than others, and we revel in situations where we are elevated. Acclaim, respect, appreciation, power, control, and position are seductive idols for us all. You and I might walk away hurt if we were at a party where no one noticed us. We are probably devastated when we are mocked and rejected. We hate to be embarrassed or shown to be weak. Being humbled is hard for us.

Philippians 2 makes it clear that Jesus is not like us:

> Have this mind among yourselves, which is yours in Christ Jesus, who, though he was in the form of God, did not count equality with God a thing to be grasped, but emptied himself, by taking the form of a servant, being born in the likeness of men. And being found in human form, he humbled himself by becoming obedient to the point of death, even death on a cross. Therefore God has highly exalted him and bestowed on him the name that is above every name, so that at the name of Jesus every knee should bow, in heaven and on earth and under the earth, and every tongue confess that Jesus Christ is Lord, to the glory of God the Father. (Phil. 2:5–11)

As the apostle Paul calls the Philippian believers to live a life of humility, he encourages them to have the mind of Christ. Jesus, equal with the Father and the Holy Spirit in divine majesty, sovereignty, holiness, and power, willingly humbled himself. Paul assures us that Jesus wasn't humbled, but rather willingly humbled himself. What did his willing humiliation look like?

He emptied himself.
He took on the form of a servant.
He took on human likeness.
He became obedient, even to death on a cross.

Jesus didn't come to earth in a display of divine splendor. From the manger to homelessness, mockery, rejection, and public crucifixion, Jesus's life was a portrait of humility. He came to be not an earthly monarch but a sacrificial Lamb. Our justification and adoption as the children of God rest on the willing humiliation of the Son. We should be his humble and willing children. But, thankfully, our hope rests not on our willingness but on his.

Paul doesn't stop with Jesus's willing humiliation; he also points us to Christ's exaltation. Humble Jesus now sits at the right hand of the Father as the reigning King. The final defeat of sin and death and the delivery of the final kingdom of peace and righteousness rest on the exaltation of the Son. There will be a day when every knee will bow and every tongue will confess that Jesus is, in fact, Lord.

Be thankful today for the willing humiliation and the great exaltation of the Son. Your hope today and for eternity rests on both. The sacrificial Lamb is now a reigning King. Hallelujah!

For further study and encouragement: Isaiah 53:7–12

DECEMBER 6

*There is a war raging for your mind, and you
must be willing to join the battle.*

Human beings, who are all made in the image of God, do not live life based
simply on the *facts* of our lives; we live according to our *personal interpretation* of those facts. We are all thinkers. God has wired into us a desire to make
sense out of who we are and the world we live in. We are meaning makers. We
are interpreters. The sense we make out of life then determines the actions we
take. God has designed our rationality and our conceptual and interpretive
abilities so that we might know him, understand his will for us, and commune
with him.

There is never a moment when you are not thinking, interpreting, and
seeking to make sense of something, someone, yourself, God, or some circumstance. You do what you do because, according to your interpretation of
life, your choice makes sense to you. Because this is how humans function,
we need a standard. We need a grand tool that helps us make sense of life.
I assume you would never lay expensive flooring down in your house without
first submitting yourself to a trustworthy standard of measurement: your
measuring tape. But millions of people live with no higher standard than
their own mind. Nevertheless, God has given us the ultimate interpretive
tool: his word. It is meant to save your life, make you wise, direct your steps
and, most importantly, draw you into an eternal relationship with the Lord
of lords.

But there is a battle being fought for the control of your mind—that is, that
which rules the life-shaping interpretations that you make:

As you received Christ Jesus the Lord, so walk in him, rooted and built up
in him and established in the faith, just as you were taught, abounding in
thanksgiving.

See to it that no one takes you captive by philosophy and empty deceit,
according to human tradition, according to the elemental spirits of the
world, and not according to Christ. (Col. 2:6–8)

As the apostle Paul warns us of the constant battle for our minds, he makes a
devastating appraisal of the philosophy of fallen human culture. He says it's an
"empty deceit." It constantly promises you what it does not have the power to
deliver. Why is this true? Because our culture is the product of the traditions of

fallen human beings, many of whom have not submitted their minds to the one who created everything and is infinite in wisdom. How do we then guard and protect ourselves from having minds that go astray? Here's Paul's answer: we must determine to be rooted and built up in Christ and established in the faith. Social media is not the place to learn how to make sense out of life; your Bible is. And be glad: God fights for your mind even when you don't.

For further study and encouragement: Proverbs 4:20–27

DECEMBER 7

1 THESSALONIANS 1–3

*It's important to understand where the power for
the proclamation of the gospel comes from.*

I am persuaded that, when it comes to gospel ministry, we give too much credit to the work of human thoughts, plans, personalities, gifts, and power. We tend to credit the messenger, or the way that he or she crafted the message, for any fruit that results. Or we look at a successful ministry and want to imitate its strategies, thinking that, if we model those, we will see the same harvest of fruit. Ascribing to weak and failing human beings what God alone can produce never goes anywhere good. It produces a culture of big personality, one of self-assured and controlling leaders who lack the humility to lead and pastor people well.

Does God give gifts and insight to people for the sake of the spread of the gospel and the maturation and protection of his own? Yes, he does, but no human being has the power to produce lasting gospel fruit on one's own, no matter how gifted and dedicated one might be. The apostle Paul gets at this reality at the beginning of 1 Thessalonians:

> We give thanks to God always for all of you, constantly mentioning you in our prayers, remembering before our God and Father your work of faith and labor of love and steadfastness of hope in our Lord Jesus Christ. For we know, brothers loved by God, that he has chosen you, because our gospel came to you not only in word, but also in power and in the Holy Spirit and with full conviction. You know what kind of men we proved to be among you for your sake. (1 Thess. 1:2–5)

The flow of this passage is interesting. Paul first expresses his thanks for the lives of the Thessalonians, their "work of faith," their "labor of love," and their "steadfastness of hope" in the Lord. Then Paul makes it clear that all of this has happened not just because of the words that he preached there. He attributes this wonderful harvest of Christian fruit to two things that we must always remember. First, these people had been chosen by God. God chose us long before the preaching of the gospel caused us to want to choose him. This does not make the proclamation of the gospel unnecessary. No, it makes it essential, because it is the means by which God lays claim to those whom he has chosen.

Second, the power of the Holy Spirit alone convicts us of sin. Human spokespeople have no ability to create this heart transaction. It is the Holy Spirit who illumines, giving us the ability to understand the gospel and our need for it. It is the Holy Spirit who empowers us to believe and to live godly lives. No gospel messenger has the ability to create conviction of sin and trust in the Savior.

We should celebrate the messengers that God raises up. We should want to be one of them. We should quest to proclaim his truth accurately. But remember: the power comes from him.

For further study and encouragement: 1 Corinthians 2:1–5

DECEMBER 8

1 THESSALONIANS 4–5

It is a good and godly thing to mind your own business.

Perhaps now more than ever, we need to heed the apostle Paul's counsel to the believers in Thessalonica:

Now concerning brotherly love you have no need for anyone to write to you, for you yourselves have been taught by God to love one another, for that indeed is what you are doing to all the brothers throughout Macedonia. But we urge you, brothers, to do this more and more, and to aspire to live quietly, and to mind your own affairs, and to work with your hands, as we instructed you, so that you may walk properly before outsiders and be dependent on no one. (1 Thess. 4:9–12)

Having commended them for their love for one another and encouraging them to love more and more, Paul calls these believers to a life that many of us have forsaken. He calls them to three things, which we tend to forget or ignore. Paul tells them to "live quietly," "mind your own affairs," and "work with your hands." I love the deep street-level, heart-protecting, and productive nature of Paul's counsel. Remember, because God has chosen to record and preserve this counsel, it is not just for the Thessalonian believers. It is for us as well.

I want to make one application of Paul's counsel to our current cultural setting. For many of us, social media dictates how we spend our time, and it dominates how we act, react, and respond to others. Social media could be defined as the place where you go *not* to live quietly. The power of social media is that it gives you a voice—and it rewards loud voices. It encourages you to weigh in and to make your presence and opinion known. Social media encourages you to live loudly, and it rewards you if you do.

You do not go to social media to mind your own affairs. No, social media encourages you to mind other people's business. It rewards you for sticking your nose into things that might have nothing to do with you. It tempts you to follow battles and weigh in on controversies, becoming part of the dissatisfied and angry mob. It gives you the false impression that you're a part of something, when in reality your involvement is just a bunch of keyboard clicks. Two things result when we fail to live quietly and to stay out of others' affairs. First, if your attention is dominated by the business of others, then you are not investing time in examining your own heart and life, in confessing what has been revealed, in seeking God's forgiveness, and in surrendering yourself once more to him. This harms your spiritual growth and worship. Second, the time you invest in social media takes you away from developing and using the gifts God has given you, and employing them in the work he has given you.

Godliness is a life of quiet rest in the Lord, of gospel self-attention, and of humble and faithful work. Is your life shaped by Paul's counsel?

For further study and encouragement: Galatians 6:1–5

DECEMBER 9

Because the Christian life is more like a spiritual marathon
than a sprint, we all need the grace to persevere.

Luella and I have been married for more than fifty years. It seems impossible that we have been together for this long. We jokingly told our children on our fiftieth anniversary that we were celebrating about thirty good years of marriage. Marriage is not the romantic amusement park that some make it out to be. A lifelong union between two sinners will not be problem free. Sometimes Luella and I are simply not on the same page. Sin (usually mine) interrupts our peace. At times the busy grind of life makes investing in a relationship hard. Because marriage is an extended journey, perseverance is an important marital character quality.

So it is with our relationship with God. Your spiritual life journey between the "already" and the "not yet" is not simply a series of spiritual high points. There are costs, sacrifices, and hardships along the way. There are times when temptation seems to be everywhere. There are moments when God seems distant. There are seasons when doubt creeps in. Meanwhile, the world around you doesn't encourage your faith. Your love for God is neither understood nor respected by your culture. Yet, you have been blessed with the most important thing in life: a relationship with God. You have been blessed with his constant presence and faithful love. You have been blessed with wisdom that is literally divine. You have been blessed with power for daily living. And you did not have to earn any of these blessings. They are yours because of God's grace. So here's the daily Christian life agenda: perseverance under hardship. Consider how the apostle Paul's words to the Thessalonians can help you on your journey:

> We ought always to give thanks to God for you, brothers beloved by the Lord, because God chose you as the firstfruits to be saved, through sanctification by the Spirit and belief in the truth. To this he called you through our gospel, so that you may obtain the glory of our Lord Jesus Christ. So then, brothers, stand firm and hold to the traditions that you were taught by us, either by our spoken word or by our letter.
>
> Now may our Lord Jesus Christ himself, and God our Father, who loved us and gave us eternal comfort and good hope through grace, comfort your hearts and establish them in every good work and word. (2 Thess. 2:13–17)

Paul captures in two words what it means to persevere as a believer: *stand firm.*

- Stand firm in believing God chose you to be his own.
- Stand firm in your trust in God's sanctifying grace.
- Stand firm in the gospel truths you have been taught.
- Stand firm in resting in God's comforting and enabling grace.

May God bless each and every one of us with gospel stubbornness. May he create in us a spiritual determination not to be moved, no matter what. Though the night of trial may come, may we still be found standing when the morning sun shines.

God is trustworthy. The gospel is true. You have been chosen. Glory awaits. Stand firm.

For further study and encouragement: Romans 5:1–5

DECEMBER 10

1 TIMOTHY 1–3

Nothing can produce beautiful fruit in your life
like the gospel of Jesus Christ can.

I once knew a man who, no matter what the situation or location, always seemed to be ready for a theological fight. He seemed to love debating more than he loved the person he was debating. He seemed to love controversy more than he loved the piece of truth he was defending. He was proud and condescending. When trying to "help" me, he said more disrespectful things to me than any other person in my ministry. He made fun of people whom he thought were his theological inferiors. Because he had a disruptive presence, he was the kind of person you dreaded encountering. His love for truth had not borne good fruit in his life. His gospel expertise had not produced a heart of love. His confident gospel assertions did not help others or praise the Christ of the gospel; they were a means of drawing the light of attention on himself.

At the beginning of his first letter to Timothy, the apostle Paul is very clear about the kind of fruit the gospel of Jesus Christ will and will not produce in a person's life:

As I urged you when I was going to Macedonia, remain at Ephesus so that you may charge certain persons not to teach any different doctrine, nor to devote themselves to myths and endless genealogies, which promote speculations rather than the stewardship from God that is by faith. The aim of our charge is love that issues from a pure heart and a good conscience and a sincere faith. Certain persons, by swerving from these, have wandered away into vain discussion, desiring to be teachers of the law, without understanding either what they are saying or the things about which they make confident assertions. (1 Tim. 1:3–7)

The gospel will not produce vain discussions. It will not produce the pride of being a self-appointed teacher. It will not produce confident assertions about things you don't really understand. It will not produce a lifestyle of endless theological speculation. All of these things are about self-focus, self-elevation, and the pride of knowledge. They are theological forms of attention-getting and glory-seeking. They all masquerade as a love for the truth, but they are propelled by a love for self. Such character qualities and actions are the opposite of what the gospel—and a heart captured by the gospel—will produce.

What is the sure and lasting fruit of a heart and life that are shaped by the transforming grace of the gospel? This question can be answered in one word: *love*. The story of God's redeeming love in Christ Jesus will produce love in those whose hearts have been captured by it. That love is the result of the power of transforming grace. This grace produces a pure heart, a good conscience, and a sincere faith. These are the soil in which the beautiful fruit of love grows. Humble, self-sacrificing, and servant love is not natural for us. This kind of love is only ever produced by the grace of the gospel. May God help us to see that theology without love ceases to be true gospel theology.

For further study and encouragement: John 15:1–11

DECEMBER 11

1 TIMOTHY 4–6

It's important to pay attention to the purity of your theology and to commit to the purity of your life as well.

One of the distinct blessings of my life is that God has chosen me to mentor many young pastors. We meet for two to three hours at a time—not only to talk about ministry strategy, issues of theology, and helps in preaching, but, more importantly, to discuss the condition of our hearts. Because of this, I have a particular affection for this passage in 1 Timothy:

> If you put these things before the brothers, you will be a good servant of Christ Jesus, being trained in the words of the faith and of the good doctrine that you have followed. Have nothing to do with irreverent, silly myths. Rather train yourself for godliness; for while bodily training is of some value, godliness is of value in every way, as it holds promise for the present life and also for the life to come. The saying is trustworthy and deserving of full acceptance. For to this end we toil and strive, because we have our hope set on the living God, who is the Savior of all people, especially of those who believe.
>
> Command and teach these things. Let no one despise you for your youth, but set the believers an example in speech, in conduct, in love, in faith, in purity. Until I come, devote yourself to the public reading of Scripture, to exhortation, to teaching. Do not neglect the gift you have, which was given you by prophecy when the council of elders laid their hands on you. Practice these things, immerse yourself in them, so that all may see your progress. Keep a close watch on yourself and on the teaching. Persist in this, for by so doing you will save both yourself and your hearers. (1 Tim. 4:6–16)

This passage invites us to eavesdrop on the apostle Paul's mentoring of a young pastor, Timothy. I have quoted this lengthy passage because the flow is important.

Paul exhorts Timothy to understand and defend the faith (the gospel), which is at the heart of Timothy's calling and the gifts he has been given. Paul charges him to recognize things that can corrupt the gospel, and to defend himself and those in his care. The gospel needs to be studied, understood, protected, and defended. Paul calls Timothy to read and expound Scripture and to teach the gospel boldly, even though Timothy is young.

We find another theme woven into Paul's counsel. Paul is zealous to remind Timothy that his ministry will be shaped not only by his theological commitment and skill, but also by the godliness of his life: his speech, conduct, love, and purity. We need this counsel too. We are to guard our theology, and we must keep a watch on our lives. Both are necessary for a life of gospel usefulness.

For further study and encouragement: Acts 20:17–35

DECEMBER 12

Every part of Scripture is profitable for you in some way.

I have been deeply blessed by God in many ways. But one particular blessing has influenced me perhaps more than any other. I never could have earned or deserved this. I was born into this blessing, and it has been a central theme throughout all of my life. It has been the central influence over what I have thought, desired, chosen, said, and done. This blessing has rescued, protected, and guided me from my earliest days until now. I can't imagine what my life would have been without it. What is this amazing blessing? From the moment of my first consciousness, the Bible has been in my life. I was raised in a family that was far from perfect, but the Bible was central. Every morning was punctuated by the reading of God's word. My mom was a walking concordance, referencing various Scripture passages throughout the day. Nothing has influenced who I am, what I value, and the choices I've made in life more than the grand narrative of redemption found in Scripture, where Jesus is the central hero and hope.

Perhaps because the word of God has been so present in my life, I've been tempted to take it for granted. Familiarity can cause you no longer to notice and appreciate something you see all the time. But over the years, by God's grace, I had been led to understand the deep, bottomless wonder of the redeeming glory of this book that God so generously placed in my hands. If you have a Bible, if you understand its message, if you love its wisdom, if it has led you to love Jesus, and if it is your moral guide, then you have been deeply and richly blessed by grace.

I love how the apostle Paul captures the transformative glory of Scripture in 2 Timothy 3:16–17: "All Scripture is breathed out by God and profitable for teaching, for reproof, for correction, and for training in righteousness, that the man of God may be complete, equipped for every good work." Notice that Paul's summary of the glory of the gift of Scripture isn't heady or theoretical. This is a street-level description of what God has designed the Bible to be and do in our lives and minds. The Bible *instructs.* The deep mysteries of God and the gospel unfold on its pages. The Bible *reproves.* It lays our hearts bare, exposing how we all have fallen short of God's holy standard. The Bible *corrects.* It introduces us to the person and work of Jesus. By him all that sin has distorted and broken is made new again. The Bible *trains.* It teaches us how to live godly lives in this dark and fallen world.

Paul says that God gave us his word so that between the "already" of our con- version and the "not yet" of our homegoing we will have everything we need for a life of "good work," that is, a life that is pleasing in the eyes of the one who has made us and saved us by his grace. Celebrate the grace of his word.

For further study and encouragement: Psalm 119:97–104

———

DECEMBER 13

TITUS–PHILEMON

It is important to understand the work of God's grace not just in the past or the future, but also right here, right now.

Sadly, many believers have a big hole in the middle of their understanding of the gospel of Jesus Christ. They have a pretty clear understanding of the forgiveness they have received through the substitutionary work of Jesus. They have a fairly clear understanding of their future hope as the children of God. But they are not as clear about the right-here, right-now work of the gospel. Can you identify what God is doing now, in the period between the "already" of Christ's resurrection and ascension and the "not yet" of your final welcome into his final kingdom? Do you see the work of Jesus in the here and now? Why did God plan a long period of time between when he first rescued us by his grace and when he will call us to our eternal home? Wouldn't it be better for us to believe and immediately be taken into glory? Why must we endure a long, hard journey in this fallen world?

The apostle Paul addresses these questions in Titus 2. He wants Titus to know he has a gospel that is rich and full in the present—not just in the past or the future. I call what Paul is addressing with Titus the "nowism" of the gospel. God's grace is working right here and right now as we journey our way through the hardships of life in this fallen, broken, and dysfunctional world. Consider Paul's description of what God is doing right now:

> The grace of God has appeared, bringing salvation for all people, training us to renounce ungodliness and worldly passions, and to live self-controlled, upright, and godly lives in the present age, waiting for our blessed hope, the appearing of the glory of our great God and Savior Jesus Christ, who gave himself for us to redeem us from all lawlessness and to purify for himself a people for his own possession who are zealous for good works. (Titus 2:11–14)

Essentially, Paul reminds Titus that God has blessed us with rescuing, forgiving, and justifying grace, as well as with sanctifying grace. So what is God's agenda for right now? It is radical, personal heart and life transformation. The word that Paul uses for this work of transformation is *training*. That's why God ordained this period we now live in. After coming to Christ, we all desperately need training. We need to be trained to say no to ungodliness and worldly passions. We need to be trained to live godly lives. We need to be trained to wait with hope. We need to be trained to be zealous to do what God says is good. We can be thankful that we have been blessed with powerful transforming grace right here, right now.

For further study and encouragement: Ephesians 2:1–10

———

DECEMBER 14

HEBREWS 1–2

How would you describe Jesus, the one on whom you have hung your hope in this life and the one to come?

No book of the Bible begins as Hebrews does. It's as though the writer of Hebrews invites you into the divine theater and ushers you to a great seat. As the orchestra swells, he pulls back the curtain, and a bright and shining light of glory bursts forth from the stage. He says, "Here is your Savior." This description of Jesus isn't one you should rush through, as though you bumped into him on the street on your way to something more important:

Long ago, at many times and in many ways, God spoke to our fathers by the prophets, but in these last days he has spoken to us by his Son, whom he appointed the heir of all things, through whom also he created the world. He is the radiance of the glory of God and the exact imprint of his nature, and he upholds the universe by the word of his power. After making purification for sins, he sat down at the right hand of the Majesty on high, having become as much superior to angels as the name he has inherited is more excellent than theirs.

For to which of the angels did God ever say,

"You are my Son,
today I have begotten you"? . . .

But of the Son he says,

> "Your throne, O God, is forever and ever,
>   the scepter of uprightness is the scepter of your kingdom.
> You have loved righteousness and hated wickedness;
>   therefore God, your God, has anointed you
>   with the oil of gladness beyond your companions."
>   (Heb. 1:1–5, 8–9)

This portrait of the Savior is majestic and multifaceted, and so it deserves meditation. It is meant not only to deepen and clarify your understanding of the second person of the Trinity, but to change you, that is, to deepen your understanding of who you are as God's child. Sometimes when you come across such glory, it prompts you to stop, be silent, behold, and worship. Hebrews 1 offers us an account of this kind of glory.

So, who is Jesus? He is God's final revelation to us. In him we see the full radiance of God's glory, because he shares God's exact nature. Jesus not only created the world, but he is the one who holds the creation together by his infinite power. Jesus is the only one who has the power to purify us from sin—an amazing act indeed. He is God the Father's beloved Son, who now sits at his right hand. Jesus's throne is forever and ever, and he rules in gladness and righteousness. There is and never will be anyone like him. Jesus is majestic in glory and brimming with redeeming grace. He reigns over his creation for the sake of his own. There is no one more worthy of your hope. There is no one more worthy of your trust. There is no one more deserving of your worship. Today, and all the days that follow, we bow before the majesty of our Savior King and offer our whole hearts and lives to him.

For further study and encouragement: Colossians 1:15–20

DECEMBER 15

HEBREWS 3-6

*Where do you go, where do you hide, and what do you
hold on to when you feel weak, defeated, and alone?*

I felt so defeated. Once again, I had responded in anger—the very thing I had committed myself not to do. I sat on my bed in the dark and felt weak and alone. My son had been disobedient again. I thought he had been looking for ways to challenge me, but that probably wasn't true. I had watched him too closely. I had taken things too personally. I had responded to him too negatively. But that night, I was at the end of my rope and I let him have it. I said things that I should have never said, and, as I did, he crumbled into tears and looked away from me. My anger in that moment was far from righteous. It was not productive. He did not feel helped or loved. There was no wisdom in my words. I had stomped down the hallway and into his room, but I walked afterward back to my room. It was late, I was tired, and, as a parent, I felt utterly defeated. I wanted to be God's tool of grace in the lives of my children, not a wrecking ball of anger.

That night I was powerfully confronted with the truth that there is no area of my life where I can be what I am supposed to be or do what I have been called to do *on my own*. I am a person in desperate need of help. That night I didn't need to be rescued from my son. I needed to be rescued from me. I needed to be delivered from my impatience and anger. I needed something more powerful than the raging emotions that I was unable to control on my own.

Many of us find ourselves in situations where it seems as though there is nowhere to run and nowhere to find help. The writer of Hebrews speaks of these kinds of moments:

> Since then we have a great high priest who has passed through the heavens, Jesus, the Son of God, let us hold fast our confession. For we do not have a high priest who is unable to sympathize with our weaknesses, but one who in every respect has been tempted as we are, yet without sin. Let us then with confidence draw near to the throne of grace, that we may receive mercy and find grace to help in time of need. (Heb. 4:14–16)

I run to this comforting passage again and again. It reminds us that we are never alone, because Jesus our high priest is always with us. Because he took on human weakness and was tempted as we are (but without sin), he understands and sympathizes with our weaknesses. This means he's not disgusted when we struggle, but rather meets us with mercy that is form-fit for each circumstance. So, when we are weak, we can run to him with confidence. He'll give us what we need.

For further study and encouragement: Isaiah 41:1–10

———

DECEMBER 16

HEBREWS 7–10

Do you live as a believer with confidence and a faith that is sure?

I meet many Christian parents, husbands and wives, university students, workers, and church members who lack confidence. They are living a life of unsure faith. Because of this, they are timid when it comes to their faith and lack the ability to live, decide, act, and speak with the confidence that what they have given their lives to is sure, dependable, true, and trustworthy. One man told me he was afraid to share the gospel with others because he was afraid that they might convince him that the good news is not true. Many people claim to be believers, but, when it comes to making decisions, they run to Google or a social media influencer rather than to God's word. Is your life made stable by a confident faith? Do you live with courage because, when it comes to the things of God, you are sure? Or does doubt haunt you? Does fear paralyze you? Are you afraid that what you have given your life to may turn out to be untrue? Where do you run when you are not sure?

The writer of Hebrews gives us the following call to a life of gospel confidence:

Since we have confidence to enter the holy places by the blood of Jesus, by the new and living way that he opened for us through the curtain, that is, through his flesh, and since we have a great priest over the house of God, let us draw near with a true heart in full assurance of faith, with our hearts sprinkled clean from an evil conscience and our bodies washed with pure water. Let us hold fast the confession of our hope without wavering, for he who promised is faithful. And let us consider how to stir up one another to love and good works, not neglecting to meet together, as is the habit of some, but encouraging one another, and all the more as you see the Day drawing near. (Heb. 10:19–25)

What an amazing call to stand up in faith and be sure! Why do we have reason to be sure?

- Because we can enter into God's presence by the blood of Jesus.
- Because we have a great high priest in Jesus.
- Because our hearts and lives are being made clean.
- Because the one who has promised all of this to us is perfectly faithful.

We can hold on to gospel hope without wavering. Resting in the redeeming work and present reign of Jesus should produce in each of us a life of confidence. So with confidence we look for ways to stir up confident lives of love and good works with one another. With confidence we commit ourselves to the body of Christ, to its gatherings and mission. And with confidence we become tools of encouragement in the lives of others.

We have been welcomed into the presence of God, Jesus is our advocate, and we are the objects of his cleansing grace. Therefore, we have reason to live with gospel confidence.

For further study and encouragement: Psalm 23:1–6

DECEMBER 17

HEBREWS 11–13

The Lord's discipline is not punishment for your sin, but loving protection from it.

Every time I disciplined my children, I made sure to tell them how much I loved them. I wanted them to understand that my discipline was not the result of my anger toward them, but rather a sign of my affection for them. They were dear to me, I wanted what was best for them, and I took the protective and guiding part of my job as a parent seriously. That's why those moments of discipline were necessary. So it is with our perfectly holy and loving heavenly Father. If you are the child of his love, then you will experience his discipline, which is the fruit of that love. Notice how the writer of Hebrews talks about our Father's discipline:

Have you forgotten the exhortation that addresses you as sons?

"My son, do not regard lightly the discipline of the Lord,
nor be weary when reproved by him.

447

For the Lord disciplines the one he loves,
and chastises every son whom he receives."

It is for discipline that you have to endure. God is treating you as sons. For what son is there whom his father does not discipline? If you are left without discipline, in which all have participated, then you are illegitimate children and not sons. Besides this, we have had earthly fathers who disciplined us and we respected them. Shall we not much more be subject to the Father of spirits and live? For they disciplined us for a short time as it seemed best to them, but he disciplines us for our good, that we may share his holiness. For the moment all discipline seems painful rather than pleasant, but later it yields the peaceful fruit of righteousness to those who have been trained by it. (Heb. 12:5–11)

This passage begins with an important question: Have you forgotten how encouraging it is that the one who sits on the throne of the universe addresses you as his child? You could experience no greater blessing than knowing that God has chosen you to be his child. Since you are God's *child*, you can expect to be treated as one. You should not take your heavenly Father's discipline lightly or allow yourself to become weary of it, because it is a sure sign of the wonderful reality that you belong to him. What good earthly father fails to discipline his children? If you look back on your childhood and feel thankful for the correction you received from your earthly father, how much more should you be thankful that God loves you enough to discipline you?

After making the connection between fatherly love and discipline, the passage turns to God's reasons for disciplining us. His discipline is never punishment for our sin, because all of our punishment was carried by Jesus. God disciplines us so that we may share in his holiness. His discipline plants seeds of righteousness in our hearts and lives. That's a very good thing.

For further study and encouragement: Proverbs 3:11–12

DECEMBER 18

Are you a doer of God's word?

The Bible is the ultimate mirror; it will always expose you to yourself, helping you to see yourself as you actually are. James writes:

> Be doers of the word, and not hearers only, deceiving yourselves. For if anyone is a hearer of the word and not a doer, he is like a man who looks intently at his natural face in a mirror. For he looks at himself and goes away and at once forgets what he was like. But the one who looks into the perfect law, the law of liberty, and perseveres, being no hearer who forgets but a doer who acts, he will be blessed in his doing. (James 1:22–25)

Imagine that you have just gotten up in the morning and are about to prepare for the day. You stumble your way into the bathroom to take your first look at the damage the night has done. The mirror you look into is accurate; it will not deceive you. You look and see a bit of dried slobber on your cheek next to your mouth; you see that your hair is a tangled mess; and, if you're a man, you see that your beard has made itself known during the night. You don't debate the mirror's accuracy, and you don't think it is being unnecessarily judgmental. No, you immediately pull out your tools of human repair and get to work, getting yourself back into the condition you want to be in before you make your public appearance. When your morning mirror confronts you, you immediately become a doer; you actively respond to what it has told you about your appearance.

What if you were to look into your morning mirror and confront what you actually look like, but then convince yourself that you look okay? You then go about your day, having done nothing about what the mirror has revealed about you. That would take quite a bit of self-deception. Sadly, this is exactly what many of us do with the perfectly accurate and loving confrontation of God's word. The Bible exposes things in us that need to be exposed. It breaks through our blindness and shows us as we actually are. In this way, it calls us to humble confession and a commitment to change. But many of us look into the mirror of Scripture and do nothing about what it has exposed in us. James says that to do so is an act of self-deception. To walk away from God's perfect mirror and do nothing about what it has enabled us to see is spiritual insanity.

It is a beautiful thing that God has blessed us with his word, with its heart- and life-revealing power. By grace it helps us to see what we could never see without it. May God give us the grace never to walk away from his word and do nothing. May we be ready and thankful doers.

For further study and encouragement: Psalm 19:7–14

———

DECEMBER 19

JAMES 3–5

Why do we have such a hard time getting along with one another? Why do we experience so much conflict?

On May 1, 1992, during a press conference in the middle of the Los Angeles riots, Rodney King, who had been a victim of police brutality and who hoped to quiet the anger in the streets, famously asked, "Can we all get along?" It is an age-old question. Why is every marriage marked by conflict at some point? Why does something as simple as getting into the car cause war-making among our children? Why does conflict mar our churches? Why is the workplace often not a place of peace? Why do neighbors argue with each other over seemingly inconsequential things? Why do friendships dissolve into hurt and division? Why is there such a thing as road rage? Why has social media devolved into an angry digital battlefield? Why do we get angry at a long line at the grocery store? Why is conflict one of the great stressors in our lives? We quarrel and fight a lot. These battles then defeat and depress us. They harm people, institutions, and situations that we hold dear. What is the cause of our battles with one another?

James 4 addresses human conflict clearly:

What causes quarrels and what causes fights among you? Is it not this, that your passions are at war within you? You desire and do not have, so you murder. You covet and cannot obtain, so you fight and quarrel. You do not have, because you do not ask. You ask and do not receive, because you ask wrongly, to spend it on your passions. You adulterous people! . . . But he gives more grace. Therefore it says, "God opposes the proud, but gives grace to the humble." Submit yourselves therefore to God. Resist the devil, and he will flee from you. Draw near to God, and he will draw near to you. Cleanse your hands, you sinners, and purify your hearts, you double-minded. Be wretched and mourn and weep. Let your laughter be turned to mourning and your joy to gloom. Humble yourselves before the Lord, and he will exalt you. (James 4:1–4, 6–10)

When it comes to human conflict, James proposes something quite profound. He says that human conflict is rooted in spiritual adultery. What does this mean? When a certain desire replaces God as the ruler of my heart, I can look at you in one of two ways. If you are helping me get what I want, then I love you and am thankful you are in my life. But if you stand in the way of what I want, then I'm angry at you and desire to get you out of my way. James locates the cause of our conflicts not outside of us but rather inside of us, in the desires of our hearts. This means that human conflict must always be solved vertically before it can be solved horizontally. Only when our hearts are ruled by what God wants will we be able to love one another well, even with all our differences and imperfections. And James reminds us that God keeps giving us more grace for exactly this.

For further study and encouragement: Romans 7:7–25

———

DECEMBER 20

1 PETER 1–2

What God wants for you is better than anything you could want for yourself, but it is impossible to achieve it on your own.

Imagine you are in a gym with a forty-foot ceiling, and the owner of the gym tells you that the most wonderful thing you could ever do would be to jump and touch the ceiling. The task seems impossible, but you begin to jump. The more you jump, the weaker your jumps get and the more you are confronted with the fact that the most wonderful thing you could aspire to is utterly, humanly impossible for you. As you stand there exhausted and facing the limits of your humanity, what do you think you would do next?

Because God is perfectly holy in every way and all of the time, it is impossible for him to ask anything of us that isn't for our good. What he wants for us is wonderful in every way. There is no downside to his will. There are no hidden negatives in his plan for us. There is no dark payoff coming. What God calls us to is eternally good in every way. But here's what we have to face: what God calls us to is utterly and completely impossible. It is infinitely more impossible than the impossibility of my gym illustration. We do not have the natural wisdom or power to accomplish what God calls us to. His will for us is the ultimate impossible calling. Are you confused? The apostle Peter alerts us to the five-million-foot ceiling that God calls us to touch:

> Preparing your minds for action, and being sober-minded, set your hope fully on the grace that will be brought to you at the revelation of Jesus Christ. As obedient children, do not be conformed to the passions of your former ignorance, but as he who called you is holy, you also be holy in all your conduct, since it is written, "You shall be holy, for I am holy." (1 Pet. 1:13–16)

This passage confronts us with our inability to be what God has designed us to be and do what he has called us to do. First, I have no ability to escape the sinful passions of my heart on my own. I can run from a situation, location, relationship, or temptation, but I have no ability to run from my own heart. Second, I have no power on my own to be holy as God is holy. How does God demonstrate his holiness? In everything he does. He is always perfectly holy in every way. Here is the core tension of the gospel. I have no ability to do what God calls me to, and God has no willingness to lower his standard. This tension has been resolved in the person and work of Jesus. He was perfectly holy in my place, and by grace he empowers me to grow in his holy likeness. God doesn't curse me because of my inability, but meets me with the forgiving and empowering grace of his Son.

For further study and encouragement: Ephesians 1:3–10

DECEMBER 21

1 PETER 3–5

Are you willing to be misunderstood, mocked, and rejected because you follow the will and ways of the Lord?

I remember my daughter's tearful words: "I don't want to be the only one." We had just told her that she couldn't do what all of her friends were doing. She was afraid of being misunderstood and mocked. She was afraid of looking weird. That night she wished she were part of another family and had other parents. I was not mad at her, because I understood. It's hard to stand quietly for what is right. It's hard not to go with the crowd. God has created us for relationships, so we long to be loved, understood, and accepted. But, as the children of God, we have been called to root our identity and security in something vastly greater than human acceptance. By grace we have been accepted by God. This acceptance into his family should reshape and redefine who we are and how we approach everything in our lives. As God's children, we have been chosen to find joy in pleasing him, no matter how the watching world responds to us.

The recipients of the apostle Peter's first letter were probably not enduring state-sponsored persecution, but they were suffering misunderstanding, mockery, rejection, and mistreatment because of their faith in the Lord Jesus Christ. That is why suffering is a theme in this letter. Although Peter doesn't begin by talking about suffering specifically, he does talk about who believers are in the context of this present fallen world. And this speaks to what their experience will be because of their faith. Peter addresses his readers as "elect exiles" (1 Pet. 1:1). An exile is someone who is from another place. An exile is someone who doesn't belong. An exile is someone who is misunderstood. Exiles are often not welcome. Why are believers misunderstood? Because we are citizens of another kingdom and we serve a greater King. Therefore, what Peter writes later in his letter should not surprise us:

> Beloved, do not be surprised at the fiery trial when it comes upon you to test you, as though something strange were happening to you. But rejoice insofar as you share Christ's sufferings, that you may also rejoice and be glad when his glory is revealed. If you are insulted for the name of Christ, you are blessed, because the Spirit of glory and of God rests upon you. But let none of you suffer as a murderer or a thief or an evildoer or as a meddler. Yet if anyone suffers as a Christian, let him not be ashamed, but let him glorify God in that name. (1 Pet. 4:12–16)

Are you surprised when doors close or relationships end because of your faith? Is the glory of being connected to Jesus so important and satisfying that you feel blessed even in the face of suffering? Are you prepared for the fiery trials that will come? May God give us the grace to believe that there is nothing better than to be "in Christ" and that there is no higher honor than to suffer for his name.

For further study and encouragement: Matthew 5:10–12

DECEMBER 22

In order to commit to consuming the nutrients of God's wisdom every day, you must be convinced of the trustworthiness of his word.

Your Bible is unlike anything else in your life. It is one of God's most amazing and important gifts to you. Everything in your Bible has been recorded and preserved for you by your Creator, Sovereign, Savior Lord. Your Bible has been put together and preserved for you as an irreplaceable tool of God's grace in your life. Through God's word, you can know him and yourself. You can understand the world you live in, see and confess your sin, rest in the grace of Jesus, understand the life to which you have been called, and embrace the eternal hope that is yours as a child of God. You simply cannot be a Christian without being a person of the word. You cannot make proper sense of your life without the interpretive grid of Scripture. You will not be spiritually healthy or live righteously if you aren't being shaped by God's word. The Bible is the soil in which your Christian life is rooted and grows.

Because all of this is true, we have to be persuaded that this essential gift and tool is completely trustworthy. If you stand above Scripture, debating which part is God's word and which part isn't, it will never do the work of grace in your life that it was meant to do. Every part of Scripture is completely trustworthy. In his second letter, Peter makes this clear:

> We did not follow cleverly devised myths when we made known to you the power and coming of our Lord Jesus Christ, but we were eyewitnesses of his majesty.... And we have the prophetic word more fully confirmed, to which you will do well to pay attention as to a lamp shining in a dark place, until the day dawns and the morning star rises in your hearts, knowing this first of all, that no prophecy of Scripture comes from someone's own interpretation. For no prophecy was ever produced by the will of man, but men spoke from God as they were carried along by the Holy Spirit. (2 Pet. 1:16, 19–21)

What is Peter's answer to the question of the trustworthiness of Scripture? He says God did two things. He revealed his majesty to his human instruments, and by the Holy Spirit he guided every interpretation and prophecy they recorded. You can build your life on the content found in your Bible, because it literally is *God's word*. He guided its writing and preserved it as a gift of grace to you.

For further study and encouragement: Isaiah 40:6–8

DECEMBER 23

1 JOHN 1–2

How do you describe your life as a child of God?

I have been driving cars with internal combustion engines for about five decades. I know how to start a car to get the engine running. I know how to put my car in gear and how to make it move forward. I know that, somewhere inside the engine, gas explosions somehow drive the pistons, and somehow that power gets transferred to the wheels of my vehicle. I have just written my way to the end of my knowledge of the internal combustion engine. I'm embarrassed to admit that I know very little about the engines that have been under the hood of all the cars I have owned. If you asked me to provide a detailed description of the structure and functioning of the engine of my car, I could not do it. And when something under the hood breaks, I have no ability to diagnose or fix what is broken. My car knowledge is limited.

I'm afraid that many believers have limited knowledge about the faith they profess. They know that they are the children of God. They know that their sins have been forgiven. They know that they should obey God's commands. They know that they have been given a place in eternity with their Savior. But for many believers that seems to be the extent of their knowledge. They don't know that the gospel they believe should radically reshape everything in their lives. It should be the foundational source of their identity, the lens by which they interpret everything, and the message that shapes how they live. How would you describe your life as a child of God? Consider John's description:

> This is the message we have heard from him and proclaim to you, that God is light, and in him is no darkness at all. If we say we have fellowship with him while we walk in darkness, we lie and do not practice the truth. But if we walk in the light, as he is in the light, we have fellowship with one another, and the blood of Jesus his Son cleanses us from all sin. If we say we have no sin, we deceive ourselves, and the truth is not in us. If we confess our sins, he is faithful and just to forgive us our sins and to cleanse us from all unrighteousness. If we say we have not sinned, we make him a liar, and his word is not in us. (1 John. 1:5–10)

Being a Christian means that you now live in fellowship with God. It means that you are committed to walking in the light, acknowledging and confessing your sin, and embracing God's faithful forgiveness and ongoing cleansing. It means that you share fellowship with others who have been blessed with these graces. *Light, confession, forgiveness, cleansing, fellowship,* and *truth* are words that must mark the life to which we have been called.

For further study and encouragement: Ephesians 5:1–21

———

DECEMBER 24

1 JOHN 3–5

The Christian life is one of love. Do you live a loving life?

I find 1 John 4 to be one of the most humbling and convicting passages in all of Scripture:

> Beloved, let us love one another, for love is from God, and whoever loves has been born of God and knows God. Anyone who does not love does not know God, because God is love. In this the love of God was made manifest among us, that God sent his only Son into the world, so that we might live through him. In this is love, not that we have loved God but that he loved us and sent his Son to be the propitiation for our sins. Beloved, if God so loved us, we also ought to love one another. No one has ever seen God; if we love one another, God abides in us and his love is perfected in us . . .
>
> If anyone says, "I love God," and hates his brother, he is a liar; for he who does not love his brother whom he has seen cannot love God whom he has not seen. And this commandment we have from him: whoever loves God must also love his brother. (1 John 4:7–12, 20–21)

These verses expose the ugliness of my sinful self-focus, with all of its judgment, impatience, and irritation. My root problem isn't horizontal; that is, my main problem is not that I don't love other people enough. No, my problem is that I don't love God enough. And because I don't, I continually try to usurp God and make life all about me. Only when God is in his rightful place in my heart will people be in the appropriate place in my life. Problems of love in marriage, parenting, extended family, friendship, neighborhood, and church cannot be resolved horizontally until they are first fixed vertically. Lack of love for God will always result in lack of love for the people he has placed in my life.

John says that the sure sign you are a born-again child of God is a life of love. Think about this. The sign is not your biblical literacy, theological knowledge, or ministry experience and success. The sure sign that God abides in you, in redeeming power and grace, is that you love those around you. Why is this true? Because love isn't natural for us. Self-focus, self-love, and self-care are natural, but it takes supernatural grace to turn us into people who really do love our neighbors as ourselves.

To make his point crystal clear, John summarizes his call to love by essentially saying, "If you don't love your brothers and sisters, whom you can see, then you don't actually love God, whom you can't see." These are devastating words to read. Open your heart and take them in. They are meant to shock us out of our Christian smugness and drive us to Jesus for his forgiving grace and empowering mercy. May we love one another better because we have come to love our Lord more.

For further study and encouragement: 1 Corinthians 13:1–13

DECEMBER 25

2 JOHN–JUDE

The best defense against the lies that are all around us is to be firmly built up in the truth.

We face two main challenges to the truth of Scripture and its core message of redemption in Jesus Christ. As we would expect, the first challenge comes from the surrounding culture, which has little place for God or his word. When people reject God and his word, they believe lies instead—and then communicate those lies to others. Because we carry devices with us that connect us to billions of voices, the world's influence is more pervasive and dangerous than it has ever been before. Who has your ear? Who shapes your sense of identity? Who interprets life for you? Who defines and explains what is true to you? Who is your final authority?

But there is also a second, more subtle challenge to what the Bible declares to be true. This challenge comes from inside the church. There are those inside the church who obscure the clear message of the gospel. They distort the gospel. Many argue from Scripture, but what they argue for is not what Scripture teaches. These people are even more dangerous than the outsiders who challenge the faith, because these "insiders" claim to be believers who hold the Bible as their authority. And, for a while, they get a listening ear.

The people of God have always had to defend themselves against threats to the truth, from both within and without. The book of Jude speaks about threats to the truth with practical wisdom that we all need to heed:

> You must remember, beloved, the predictions of the apostles of our Lord Jesus Christ. They said to you, "In the last time there will be scoffers, following their own ungodly passions." It is these who cause divisions, worldly people, devoid of the Spirit. But you, beloved, building yourselves up in your most holy faith and praying in the Holy Spirit, keep yourselves in the love of God, waiting for the mercy of our Lord Jesus Christ that leads to eternal life. And have mercy on those who doubt; save others by snatching them out of the fire; to others show mercy with fear, hating even the garment stained by the flesh.
>
> Now to him who is able to keep you from stumbling and to present you blameless before the presence of his glory with great joy, to the only God, our Savior, through Jesus Christ our Lord, be glory, majesty, dominion, and authority, before all time and now and forever. Amen. (Jude 17–25)

How do you defend yourself against lies and distortions of the truth? Take the Bible's warnings seriously. Build yourself up in the truth. Never stop praying for biblical discernment. Keep your eyes on eternity. Remember that standing firm is a community project. Humbly admit that only the Lord can keep you from stumbling. Live for his glory, not your own. May God give us grace to never stop doing all of these things.

For further study and encouragement: Ephesians 6:10–20

———

DECEMBER 26

REVELATION 1–3

You are always assigning some kind of identity to yourself. Who do you think you are?

God designed human beings to think, interpret, and look for meaning and identity. Whether you are a theologian, philosopher, plumber, or chef, you assign yourself some kind of identity. Most people search for identity horizontally. We look for identity in marriage, putting a heavy burden on our spouses that they were not created to carry. Or we look for identity in our children, living through them and asking them to do things for us that they have no ability or desire to do. We look for our identity in a job or career, in our pile of material things, in the size of our bank account, or in our record of successes. None of these things will deliver the rest of heart, the lasting sense of self, or the meaning and purpose that we seek. So, we keep searching.

All of the big identity statements in Scripture root identity not in something you can do, but in something that has been done for you. When I root my identity in the eternal grace and love of God rather than in an ever-changing world, temporary situations, relationships, or achievements, I can live with peace and security of heart, no matter how my circumstances might change. I know that I am an object of divine love, that God will never abandon me, that he looks at me with affection and not with disgust, that he will never turn his back on me but will hold me in his arms eternally. This is how I find rest of heart.

When I think about identity, my mind goes to Revelation 1:4–6:

John to the seven churches that are in Asia:
Grace to you and peace from him who is and who was and who is to come, and from the seven spirits who are before his throne, and from Jesus Christ the faithful witness, the firstborn of the dead, and the ruler of kings on earth.
To him who loves us and has freed us from our sins by his blood and made us a kingdom, priests to his God and Father, to him be glory and dominion forever and ever. Amen.

If you are God's child, then you are blessed to be able to say that this doxology is your identity. You are not your relationships. You are not your possessions. You are not your achievements. You are not your money. You are the son or daughter of the God of glory and grace. Your father is the King of kings. You are a citizen of his kingdom, one of his priests. You have been freed from sin by the shed blood of his Son. The one who has showered you with such love reigns now and forever in glory and dominion.

When you get up in the morning, remind yourself that you are eternally loved, that your Father reigns in power and glory, that sin will never have the final victory over you, and that you have been welcomed into a kingdom that will never end. By grace, your search for identity has ended.

For further study and encouragement: 1 Peter 2:4–12

DECEMBER 27

No story ends more gloriously than the biblical story.

Luella and I were sitting in a room lit only by the huge screen in front of us. The movie we were watching was engaging, dramatic, and surprising. As we sat there, trying to keep up with the twists and turns of the plot, Luella leaned over and whispered in my ear, "I wonder how all of this is going to end." In that moment, she captured one of the most important questions a person will ever ask. How will the grand story of life end? Or, even more personally, how will my life end? What am I living for? Why have I worked so hard for so long? Why have I invested so much time and energy into my relationships? Why have I been so intent on saving so much money? Why have I studied so hard? Why have I had to go through so much hardship and suffering? Where is my life heading?

I have never understood the attraction of atheism. We go through all the effort of work, relationships, physical health, and perseverance through suffering, and then we die and everything just goes black? That's it? Is our existence just an exercise in inescapable futility? How could this ever be a satisfying way of making sense out of life?

Thankfully, the Bible is clear about where the grand march of history is going. Everything in heaven and earth is moving according to God's great preordained plan. The cosmos moves according to his will. And the Bible is clear about where your life is going as a child of God. No, your faith and obedience have not been in vain. No, your endurance in suffering and hardship has not been wasted. No, your steadfastness in your commitment to God and what he says is right has not been meaningless. God has been at work in all that you have experienced to prepare you for your final destination, because by grace your life is moving toward an end more glorious than anything you could imagine. You will look back and say, "All of the effort and hardship was worth it."

The glory of your final destination as a child of God is captured in a hymn of praise, sung before God's throne and captured for us in Revelation 5:

They sang a new song, saying,

> "Worthy are you to take the scroll
> and to open its seals,
> for you were slain, and by your blood you ransomed people for God
> from every tribe and language and people and nation,

and you have made them a kingdom and priests to our God,
and they shall reign on the earth." (Rev. 5:9–10)

Here is where you story is going. You have been ransomed out of the sinful mass of humanity by the blood of Jesus. This means that your story will never end. You will reign with your Lord forever and ever, with everlasting peace and righteousness, in the new heavens and new earth. Now that's a good ending!

For further study and encouragement: 1 Corinthians 15:35–58

———

DECEMBER 28

REVELATION 8–12

*Your hope in this life and the one to come was secured in the
ultimate battle that took place at the birth of Jesus.*

All of history marched toward one decisive event. The entire plan of God, the entire hope of humanity, and the entire work of redemption balanced on this moment. It had been prophesied. It had been promised. The reputation of the Almighty rested on whether it would happen or not. Could the Lord of lords fulfill his promise of the birth of his Son? If the Son would not be born, there could be no righteous life lived in our place, no death to free us from sin's penalty, no victorious resurrection, and no ascension to the Father to reign and intercede on our behalf. There could be no redemption and no hope.

Revelation 12 captures the battle that occurred at this pivotal moment in history:

And a great sign appeared in heaven: a woman clothed with the sun, with the moon under her feet, and on her head a crown of twelve stars. She was pregnant and was crying out in birth pains and the agony of giving birth. And another sign appeared in heaven: behold, a great red dragon, with seven heads and ten horns, and on his heads seven diadems. His tail swept down a third of the stars of heaven and cast them to the earth. And the dragon stood before the woman who was about to give birth, so that when she bore her child he might devour it. She gave birth to a male child, one who is to rule all the nations with a rod of iron, but her child was caught up to God and to his throne, and the woman fled into the wilderness, where she has a place prepared by God, in which she is to be nourished for 1,260 days. (Rev. 12:1–6)

This is a picture of the great spiritual battle that began with the birth of Jesus. Israel is the pregnant woman, Jesus is the male child, and Satan is the great red dragon. Satan and the forces of darkness would have done anything to end the life of the promised Son.

The end of the reign of evil on earth began with the birth of Jesus. Later Satan would be defeated at Christ's temptation, he would be defeated on the cross, and he would be defeated by the empty tomb. Jesus was victorious on our behalf and now reigns in glory. His reign guarantees the end of sin and death and an eternity of peace and righteousness for all who believe. The dragon is defeated. The Son reigns. Hallelujah!

For further study and encouragement: Isaiah 9:1–7

DECEMBER 29

REVELATION 13–16

As a child of God, you will one day stand blameless before the Lamb.

Can you imagine being blameless? Can you imagine being blameless in your marriage? Can you imagine your children knowing you as blameless? Can you imagine blameless friendships? Can you imagine living blamelessly at your university or your job? Can you imagine being blameless in every thought, desire, choice, and action? Most of us have come to accept that we will never be blameless in this life. When we've done something wrong, we are tempted to shift the blame to someone else, because sin still lives inside of us, exercising more power than we wish it did. Even when our intentions are righteous, we often stumble into sin. The sin within us is like spiritual gravity, pulling us down again and again. Yes, by grace we have the power to resist, but the war within still rages.

This is why the following scene is so beautiful and encouraging:

I looked, and behold, on Mount Zion stood the Lamb, and with him 144,000 who had his name and his Father's name written on their foreheads. And I heard a voice from heaven like the roar of many waters and like the sound of loud thunder. The voice I heard was like the sound of harpists playing on their harps, and they were singing a new song before the throne and before the four living creatures and before the elders. No one could learn that song except the 144,000 who had been redeemed from the earth. It is these who have not defiled themselves with women, for they are virgins. It is these who follow the Lamb wherever he goes. These have been redeemed from mankind as firstfruits for God and the Lamb, and in their mouth no lie was found, for they are blameless. (Rev. 14:1–5)

This scene is almost too wonderful to grasp. As prophesied, the Lamb (Jesus) is standing in glory on Mount Zion, but he is not standing alone. There are 144,000 people standing with him, who have his name and the Father's name written on their foreheads. The number 144,000 is not to be understood as a literal number; it symbolizes those who have been redeemed. The names written on their foreheads show to whom they belong. The scene isn't quiet, because the redeemed are singing a song that only those who have been redeemed can sing. Calling these people virgins simply means they are pure. Rescued out of the mass of humanity, they now stand blameless before the victorious Lamb. God has accomplished all he promised through the life, death, resurrection, ascension, and reign of the Lamb. He has finally and completely delivered his children from sin, and they have been gathered with him on Mount Zion to celebrate with songs only redeemed sinners can sing. This is not a scene from a fantasy movie. One day you will join this joyous choir. May this hope fuel your faith as you continue to live in the midst of sin's struggle.

For further study and encouragement: Jude 1:24–25

DECEMBER 30

REVELATION 17–19

The biblical story begins and ends with a meal.

I have to confess that I love food. I love the beauty of a well-dressed plate. I love the smells of something slowly roasting in the oven. I love the sizzle of something frying on the stove. I love the chemistry of food, how heat changes it and how spices enhance flavor. I do the cooking in our family. I love designing and preparing the Thanksgiving and Christmas meals. We have a large market nearby, with about a hundred vendors. Every kind of food you could want is there, along with butchers, fishmongers, and fresh produce. I walk through the market almost every day.

I call it my food museum. I also love how much the biblical writers incorporate food into their narratives, and often use it as a metaphor of the work of God.

It is striking that the grand biblical story is bracketed by two meals. The first meal is the most tragic meal that has ever been eaten. High drama precedes this meal, as Satan tempts Eve and Adam to eat something God has forbidden. As you listen to the serpent's seductive lies, you think, "Don't listen!" And, as they take the forbidden fruit into their hands, you want to scream, "Don't eat; don't eat!" But they do. This first recorded meal is an act of outrageous rebellion against God's authority, warning, and loving provision. When the first bite is taken, the history of the world goes dark. Not only does sin enter the hearts of Adam and Eve, but it spreads its destructive power around the cosmos. This meal is a tragedy, and humanity still suffers its effects today.

But, thankfully, the redemptive story marches toward another meal. This one is not a tragedy, but a victory. It is a meal not of rebellion but of divine love. The beauty and glory of this meal is captured in Revelation 19:

> I heard what seemed to be the voice of a great multitude, like the roar of many waters and like the sound of mighty peals of thunder, crying out,
>
> > "Hallelujah!
> > For the Lord our God
> >   the Almighty reigns.
> > Let us rejoice and exult
> >   and give him the glory,
> > for the marriage of the Lamb has come,
> >   and his Bride has made herself ready;
> > it was granted her to clothe herself
> >   with fine linen, bright and pure"—
>
> for the fine linen is the righteous deeds of the saints. (Rev. 19:6–8)

Open your heart and expand your imagination to take in this scene. This is your guaranteed destiny as a child of God. It is a royal marriage processional. The reigning Lamb takes us as his bride, now pure before him and with him forever. The angel says to John, "Write this: Blessed are those who are invited to the marriage supper of the Lamb" (Rev. 19:9). This is Scripture's final meal. Sin has been defeated. There will be no more rebellious meals. The eternal celebration has begun. The children of God have been forever united to the Lamb. Redemption has been accomplished. God has won!

For further study and encouragement: Isaiah 65:17–25

DECEMBER 31

*A day is coming when everything that sin has
broken will be made new again.*

We've gotten used to living in a broken-down world. The house that humanity has been living in is disheveled, crumbling under the heavy weight of sin. The world of pristine and untainted beauty is no more. Everything has been damaged by sin in some way. And because it has, this world doesn't function as God intended. The Bible says we live in a world that is groaning. Not only do *we* wait and hope for redemption—the physical world does as well. Weeds choke out the flowers, strange gases pollute the air, and toxins poison the waters. Evil intentions corrupt governments, nations war against nations, and entertainment and education celebrate what God has forbidden.

But the brokenness isn't just outside of you. It's also on the inside, and it makes your life hard. Selfish desires and conflict interrupt marital unity. Childish rebellion and parental impatience make family life hard. The workplace is seldom a place of peace or love. Neighbor argues with neighbor over six inches of property. Homelessness and addiction mark our great cities. You and I struggle with envy, anger, lust, greed, and pride. We often fall into worshiping the creation while forgetting the Creator. Suffering, sickness, and sorrow are universal human experiences. We cry out for better, but often wonder if better will ever come.

In the midst of the groaning, we must remember that, by grace, our individual stories have been embedded in the larger story of redemption. The sin that has infected every part of this world and every aspect of our lives does not have the power to stop redemption's holy march. God is at work. The Son is on the throne. Satan is doomed. Sin and death will forever die. Hope and help are on the move. Forever beckons with bright and shining glory. The march of the redeemed is not toward destruction and death. The march of the redeemed is toward endless love and the eternal reign of peace and righteousness.

In the middle of your struggle with life in this fallen world, it is important to remember that you have been included in the greatest movement in the history of the world: redemption. Your life is not an endless stream of hard things. Your life is more than a chronicle of sin and failure. Your life is not just the story of sin and suffering. No, you are part of the company of the redeemed, and your Lord is not content with the way things are. He is going to bring this world to a final end, putting the last enemy under his feet. And he will welcome us into what now seems unimaginable. We will be ushered into that forever kingdom—

the new heavens and the new earth. In an act of tender mercy, God will dry each and every tear and we will weep no more. There will be no cause for fear, dread, anxiety, or shame. Our days will be marked by peace and love. We will experience Revelation's final promise: "And he who was seated on the throne said, 'Behold, I am making all things new'" (Rev. 21:5).

For further study and encouragement: Romans 8:12–25

DAILY READING PLAN

27 2 Kings 20–22
28 2 Kings 23–25
29 1 Chronicles 1–4
30 1 Chronicles 5–9

MAY

1 1 Chronicles 10–11
2 1 Chronicles 12–14
3 1 Chronicles 15–17
4 1 Chronicles 18–21
5 1 Chronicles 22–24
6 1 Chronicles 25–27
7 1 Chronicles 28–29
8 2 Chronicles 1–4
9 2 Chronicles 5–8
10 2 Chronicles 9–12
11 2 Chronicles 13–16
12 2 Chronicles 17–20
13 2 Chronicles 21–24
14 2 Chronicles 25–27
15 2 Chronicles 28–31
16 2 Chronicles 32–34
17 2 Chronicles 35–36
18 Ezra 1–5
19 Ezra 6–10
20 Nehemiah 1–3
21 Nehemiah 4–7
22 Nehemiah 8–11
23 Nehemiah 12–13
24 Esther 1–5
25 Esther 6–10
26 Job 1–3
27 Job 4–7
28 Job 8–10
29 Job 11–13
30 Job 14–16
31 Job 17–20

JUNE

1 Job 21–23
2 Job 24–28
3 Job 29–31
4 Job 32–34
5 Job 35–37
6 Job 38–39
7 Job 40–42
8 Psalms 1–8

9 Psalms 9–16
10 Psalms 17–20
11 Psalms 21–25
12 Psalms 26–31
13 Psalms 32–35
14 Psalms 36–39
15 Psalms 40–45
16 Psalms 46–50
17 Psalms 51–57
18 Psalms 58–65
19 Psalms 66–69
20 Psalms 70–73
21 Psalms 74–77
22 Psalms 78–79
23 Psalms 80–85
24 Psalms 86–89
25 Psalms 90–95
26 Psalms 96–102
27 Psalms 103–105
28 Psalms 106–107
29 Psalms 108–114
30 Psalms 115–118

JULY

1 Psalm 119:1–88
2 Psalm 119:89–176
3 Psalms 120–132
4 Psalms 133–139
5 Psalms 140–145
6 Psalms 146–150
7 Proverbs 1–4
8 Proverbs 5–9
9 Proverbs 10–11
10 Proverbs 12–13
11 Proverbs 14–15
12 Proverbs 16–18
13 Proverbs 19–21
14 Proverbs 22–23
15 Proverbs 24–26
16 Proverbs 27–29
17 Proverbs 30–31
18 Ecclesiastes 1–4
19 Ecclesiastes 5–8
20 Ecclesiastes 9–12
21 Song of Solomon 1–8
22 Isaiah 1–4
23 Isaiah 5–8
24 Isaiah 9–12

25 Isaiah 13–17
26 Isaiah 18–22
27 Isaiah 23–27
28 Isaiah 28–30
29 Isaiah 31–35
30 Isaiah 36–39
31 Isaiah 40–43

AUGUST

1 Isaiah 44–48
2 Isaiah 49–53
3 Isaiah 54–58
4 Isaiah 59–62
5 Isaiah 63–66
6 Jeremiah 1–3
7 Jeremiah 4–6
8 Jeremiah 7–9
9 Jeremiah 10–13
10 Jeremiah 14–17
11 Jeremiah 18–22
12 Jeremiah 23–25
13 Jeremiah 26–29
14 Jeremiah 30–31
15 Jeremiah 32–34
16 Jeremiah 35–37
17 Jeremiah 38–41
18 Jeremiah 42–45
19 Jeremiah 46–48
20 Jeremiah 49–50
21 Jeremiah 51–52
22 Lamentations 1–2
23 Lamentations 3–5
24 Ezekiel 1–4
25 Ezekiel 5–8
26 Ezekiel 9–12
27 Ezekiel 13–15
28 Ezekiel 16–17
29 Ezekiel 18–20
30 Ezekiel 21–22
31 Ezekiel 23–24

SEPTEMBER

1 Ezekiel 25–27
2 Ezekiel 28–30
3 Ezekiel 31–33
4 Ezekiel 34–36
5 Ezekiel 37–39

6	Ezekiel 40–42	15	Mark 14	23	1 Corinthians 1–4
7	Ezekiel 43–45	16	Mark 15–16	24	1 Corinthians 5–8
8	Ezekiel 46–48	17	Luke 1	25	1 Corinthians 9–11
9	Daniel 1–3	18	Luke 2–3	26	1 Corinthians 12–14
10	Daniel 4–6	19	Luke 4–5	27	1 Corinthians 15–16
11	Daniel 7–9	20	Luke 6–7	28	2 Corinthians 1–4
12	Daniel 10–12	21	Luke 8–9	29	2 Corinthians 5–9
13	Hosea 1–7	22	Luke 10–11	30	2 Corinthians 10–13
14	Hosea 8–14	23	Luke 12–13		
15	Joel 1–3	24	Luke 14–15		**DECEMBER**
16	Amos 1–5	25	Luke 16–18	1	Galatians 1–3
17	Amos 6–9	26	Luke 19–20	2	Galatians 4–6
18	Obadiah–Jonah	27	Luke 21–22	3	Ephesians 1–3
19	Micah 1–7	28	Luke 23–24	4	Ephesians 4–6
20	Nahum 1–3	29	John 1–2	5	Philippians 1–4
21	Habakkuk 1–3	30	John 3–4	6	Colossians 1–4
22	Zephaniah–Haggai	31	John 5–6	7	1 Thessalonians 1–3
23	Zechariah 1–7			8	1 Thessalonians 4–5
24	Zechariah 8–14		**NOVEMBER**	9	2 Thessalonians 1–3
25	Malachi 1–4	1	John 7–8	10	1 Timothy 1–3
26	Matthew 1–2	2	John 9–10	11	1 Timothy 4–6
27	Matthew 3–4	3	John 11–13	12	2 Timothy 1–4
28	Matthew 5–7	4	John 14–16	13	Titus–Philemon
29	Matthew 8–10	5	John 17–19	14	Hebrews 1–2
30	Matthew 11–12	6	John 20–21	15	Hebrews 3–6
		7	Acts 1–3	16	Hebrews 7–10
	OCTOBER	8	Acts 4–6	17	Hebrews 11–13
1	Matthew 13–14	9	Acts 7–9	18	James 1–2
2	Matthew 15–17	10	Acts 10–12	19	James 3–5
3	Matthew 18–19	11	Acts 13–15	20	1 Peter 1–2
4	Matthew 20–21	12	Acts 16–18	21	1 Peter 3–5
5	Matthew 22–23	13	Acts 19–21	22	2 Peter 1–3
6	Matthew 24–25	14	Acts 22–25	23	1 John 1–2
7	Matthew 26	15	Acts 26–28	24	1 John 3–5
8	Matthew 27–28	16	Romans 1–2	25	2 John–Jude
9	Mark 1–3	17	Romans 3–4	26	Revelation 1–3
10	Mark 4–5	18	Romans 5–6	27	Revelation 4–7
11	Mark 6–7	19	Romans 7–8	28	Revelation 8–12
12	Mark 8–9	20	Romans 9–11	29	Revelation 13–16
13	Mark 10–11	20	Romans 12–13	30	Revelation 17–19
14	Mark 12–13	22	Romans 14–16	31	Revelation 20–22

SCRIPTURE INDEX

472

PAUL TRIPP MINISTRIES

Paul Tripp Ministries is a not-for-profit organization connecting the transforming power of Jesus Christ to everyday life. Supported by generous donors, they make much of Paul's gospel teaching freely available online, on podcasts, across social media, and in the Paul Tripp app.

PaulTripp.com

 /pdtripp   @paultripp   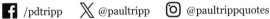 @paultrippquotes

 @pauldavidtripp   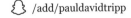 /add/pauldavidtripp    /in/paul-david-tripp/

Also Available from Paul David Tripp

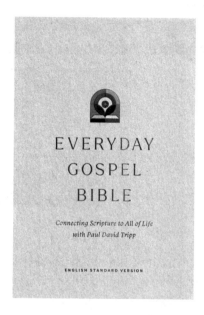

The *ESV Everyday Gospel Bible* includes 365 daily devotions by Paul David Tripp embedded within the full ESV Bible text, plus theologically rich articles, applicational sidebars, and introductions that connect the transforming power of God's Word to everyday life.

For more information, visit
crossway.org or **paultripp.com**.